OF THE
COLISEUM

The Young Bishop

THE MARTYRS

OF THE

COLISEUM

With

HISTORICAL RECORDS OF THE
GREAT AMPHITHEATER OF ANCIENT ROME

by

Father A. J. O'Reilly, D.D.

*"The blood of martyrs is the
seed of Christians."*
—Tertullian

TAN BOOKS AND PUBLISHERS, INC.
ROCKFORD, ILLINOIS 61105

"We recommend to the faithful of our diocese the *History of the Coliseum and Its Martyrs*, written by the Rev. A. J. O'Reilly, Miss. Ap., a priest of our diocese."

✝ John Joseph
Archbishop of Toronto
St. Michael's Palace
April 27, 1874

ISBN: 0-89555-192-6

Library of Congress Catalog Card No.: 82-50595

Printed and bound in the United States of America.

TAN BOOKS AND PUBLISHERS, INC.
P.O. Box 424
Rockford, Illinois 61105

1987

RECOMMENDATION

OF

HIS GRACE THE ARCHBISHOP OF TORONTO.

"WE recommend to the faithful of our diocese the 'HISTORY OF THE COLISEUM AND ITS MARTYRS,' written by the Rev. A. J. O'Reilly, Miss. Ap., a priest of our diocese.

"Nothing conduces more to the appreciation of our faith than the records of its triumphs. We, who are in union with those martyrs, and inheritors of their faith, should, at least in thanksgiving to God for its inestimable boon, labour to extend these triumphs in our own humble way, by our prayers and alms.

"We recommend this work to be read in every family. Besides its intrinsic merit, and the fruit which it has and will produce, we are further consoled to know the proceeds of its sale are to be applied to the Propagation of the Faith.

† "JOHN JOSEPH,
" *Archbishop of Toronto.*

"ST. MICHAEL'S PALACE,
"April 27th, 1874."

THE POPE'S LETTER.

The following has been received from His Holiness PIUS
IX., *through the Secretary of the Propaganda:*

" REV. DOMINE,

" Sanctissimus Dominus Noster mihi in mandatis dedit
Tibi significare se libenter excepisse, una cum tuis
officiosis litteris, volumen cui titulus ' I MARTIRI DEL
COLOSSEO,' a te in lucem editum.
Eo vero gratius hoc tuum opus Sanctitatæ Suæ fuit,
quo magis illud acerbitate et nequitiæ temporum oppor-
tunum visum est. Nam dum religionis hostes ac ethnicæ
licentiæ instauratores gravem injuriam intulerunt sanc-
titati ejus loci triumphali sanguine tot Martyrum conse-
crati, deletis nempe illic venerandis religiosi cultus
monumentis, queis ornabatur, et ipsa precandi potestate
Fidelibus adempta non potest profecto peculiari utilitate
carere tua opera, quæ ad debitam eisdem loci venera-
tionem tuendam spectat, et ad piam memoriam fovendam
gloriosorum certaminum quæ ibidem Christi Martyres
sustinuerunt. Quibus adjiciens Sanctitatem Suam apos-
tolicam benedictionem Tibi benigne impertitam esse
precor Deum ut Tibi fausta quæque largiatur.

"Romæ ex æd. S. Cong. de P. Fide.
" Die 4 Martii, 1874.
" Dom. Tuæ.
" Humillimus addictissimus famulus,
" JOANNES SIMEONI,
" *Secretarius*"
" REV. AUGUSTINO O'REILLY."

(Translation)

"REV. SIR,

"Our most Holy Father has desired me to signify to you that he has been pleased to receive, with the annexed letters of homage, the volume published by you, entitled the 'MARTYRS OF THE COLISEUM.'

"Your work is the more acceptable to his Holiness, as in these days of bitterness and impiety it is the more needed, for whilst the enemies of religion and imitators of pagan outrage have cast deep profanation on the sanctity of that place consecrated with the blood of so many martyrs, removing the very emblems of religious worship by which it was adorned, and even depriving the faithful of the privilege of praying within its hallowed precincts, your work, truly, cannot lack a special utility since it seeks to preserve the due veneration of that holy place, and to cherish the pious memory of the glorious conquests there gained by the Martyrs of Christ. Wherefore His Holiness has been graciously pleased to impart to you the Apostolic Benediction, which we pray God may propitiously extend to you.

"ROME,

"Given at the College of the Propaganda,
"March 4th, 1874.

"Your most humble and devoted servant,
"JOANNES SIMEONI,
"*Secretary.*

"REV. AUGUSTINE O'REILLY."

CONTENTS.

CHAP.   PAGE

I. INTRODUCTION - - - - - - - - - 1

II. THE ORIGIN AND EARLY HISTORY OF THE COLISEUM - 6

III. ITS ENTERTAINMENTS AND SPECTACLES - - - - 13

IV. THE CHRISTIANS - - - - - - - - 25

V. THE FIRST MARTYR - - - - - - - - 29

VI. ST. IGNATIUS - - - - - - - - - 39

VII. THE ROMAN GENERAL - - - - - - - 58

VIII. THE YOUNG BISHOP - - - - - - - - 120

IX. THE SARDINIAN YOUTH - - - - - - - 149

X. ST. ALEXANDER - - - - - - - - 184

XI. THE SENATORS - - - - - - - - - 213

XII. MARINUS - - - - - - - - - - 230

XIII. MARTINA - - - - - - - - - - 239

XIV. THE PERSIAN KINGS - - - - - - - - 251

XV. THE ACTS OF POPE STEPHEN - - - - - - 265

XVI. TWO HUNDRED AND SIXTY SOLDIERS - - - - 287

XVII. ACTS OF ST. PRISCA - - - - - - - - 29

XVIII. CHRYSANTHUS AND DARIA - - - - - - 310

XIX. PERSECUTION OF DIOCLETIAN - - - - - - 335

XX. ACTS OF ST. VITUS AND COMPANIONS - - - - 360

XXI. META SUDANS - - - - - - - - - 374

XXII. THE LAST MARTYR - - - - - - - - 386

XXIII. TELEMACHUS STILL TRIUMPHANT - - - - 398

XXIV. THE COLISEUM IN THE MIDDLE AGES - - - - 411

XXV. OTHER REMARKABLE EVENTS - - - - - - 426

XXVI. THE CONCLUSION - - - - - - - - 442

PREFACE.

THE present work, imperfect as it is, has the recommendation of being the only one on the subject
ever published in the English language. With a
slight modification, this assertion may be extended to
every other European tongue. Some works have been
printed in Italy on the Coliseum, but they treat it as a
pagan monument, or as a work of art. I have not found
any one give more than a couple of pages to its Christian
records. Marangoni's " *Memorie Sacre e Profane dell
Anfiteatro Flavio,*" which is by far the best published,
and from which I have largely drawn in the following
pages, does not give more than some of the names of the
Martyrs of the Coliseum, with references to their Acts.
All admit that the Coliseum was sanctified by the blood
of thousands of martyrs: they mention a few of the
most important, and then pass on as if the world no
longer took an interest in the most sacred and solemn
reminiscences of the Christian past.

Cardinal Wiseman, in his preface to *Fabiola*, wrote
thus: "If the modern Christian wishes really to know
what his forefathers underwent for the Faith during
three centuries of persecution, we would not have him
content himself with visiting the Catacombs, as we have
endeavoured to do, and thus learn what sort of life they
were compelled to live; but we would advise him to

read those imperishable records, the *Acts of the Martyrs* which will show him how they were made to die. We know of no writings so moving, so tender, so consoling, and so ministering of strength to faith and hope, after God's inspired words, as these venerable monuments. And if our reader, so advised, have not leisure to read much upon this subject, we would limit him willingly to even one specimen—the genuine Acts of SS. Perpetua and Felicitas. It is true that they will be best read by the scholar in their plain African Latinity, but we trust that some one will soon give us a worthy English version of these, and some other similar early Christian docu‑ments . . . . . When our minds are sad, or the petty persecution of our times inclines our feeble hearts to murmur, we cannot do better than turn to those golden, because truthful legends, to nerve our courage by the contemplation of what children and women, catechumens and slaves, suffered unmurmuring for Christ."

I need scarcely say how I have taken up, according to my ability, this suggestion of the most eminent of modern writers. I have long loved to prize the deep mine of spiritual riches contained in the *Acts of the Martyrs.* But these valuable records of the past are not in the hands of all. The outlay required to purchase the fifty large folio tomes of the Bollandists, and the erudi‑tion necessary to understand the old Latin and Greek in which they are written, place them above the reach of the great majority of readers. Any translation, therefore, of these memorials of the early Church must be interest‑ing and useful. The virtue, the power, and the extra‑ordinary lives of the first Christians, are in wonderful contrast with those of the Christians of the present day,

Yet Christianity is now as brilliant and powerful as when it was triumphant in the Coliseum. It is the same faith that animates the virtue of the righteous ; it is the same Holy Spirit that guides and preserves the imperish· able Church built upon the rock.

In the following translations I have not always con· fined myself to the literal rendering of the original. I have, on the contrary, endeavoured to avoid the monotony and dryness of verbatim translations. I have taken the ideas given in the Acts, and moulded them into English form, often casting flowers around them, when none such were given in the original. This is particularly the case of the romantic history of Placidus. Where I have met with extraordinary passages in the most authentic Acts, I have quoted the text in the notes, and given the necessary references.

Suddenly called away to the scene of my early labours, I have submitted to the judgment of my superiors in giving the manuscript to the printers in its imperfect state ; and without further thought for its success or failure, I commit the little volume to the indulgence of my readers. If perchance the beautiful and interesting matter I have hastily thrown together should induce some experienced and skilful writer to take up and treat, in a masterly and historical manner, this important part of the early history of Christianity, I shall feel repaid for my humble efforts ; if, moreover, these touching tales of love, these marvels and miracles flowing from the mercy of God, and found in every page of these records, excite in the Christian reader even one sentiment of piety and charity, I shall feel that my labour has not been spent in vain.

PREFACE TO THE SIXTH EDITION.

N the 1st of February, 1874, I was one amongst many, who, through devotion and curiosity, visited the old and venerable ruin of the Coli-seum. It was reported the Italian Government had lent itself to an unmeaning desecration of its arena, so dear in the hallowed memories of the past; the report was true; but though frequently forced in those days of sadness and usurpation to gaze on the traces of persecution and sacrilege, few of those sad scenes caused more indignation than the one before us.

In the centre of the arena a crowd were watching, in silence, some labourers removing the last remnants of the graceful pyramidical steps that supported the indulgenced cross, that, for more than one hundred years had adorned the arena. It was said the cross itself, which we had so often reverently kissed, and had now disappeared, was taken down in the night. Around, some men were destroying the little chapels of the Stations of the Cross, with a diligence and an earnestness not usually seen in Italian workmen: three of the stations had already disappeared; the strokes of the sledge and the axe mingling with fallen masses of masonry were the only sounds that echoed through the vast ruin. Regret and suppressed indignation were strongly expressed on the countenances of the silent crowd. A few pious and courageous souls were visiting, for the last time, the stations that remained. We noticed several Roman ma-trons weep as they beheld the work of demolition, apart from the rest were some French ecclesiastics loudly condemning in excited conversation, the scene that so forcibly reminded of the days of the Iconoclasts. And the reason for all this profanation was officially given :— *These religious memorials were not in keeping with the pagan character of the ruin.*

Truly the Coliseum was once a pagan edifice, but the prayers and the veneration of the generations that have passed in fifteen centuries, the blood of thousands of martyrs, and the dread sacrifice of the Mass itself, offered within its precincts, have rendered it a Christian monu ment. If one martyr only had sanctified its soil with his blood, we would reverence the ruin.

It was the feast of St. Ignatius. On that very morn ing, 1767 years ago, the venerable Patriarch of Antioch was devoured in the arena by the lions. Fancy carried us over the valley of the past ; we heard the shout of the pagan crowd calling for the annihilation of Christianity. We saw the beautiful Martina kneeling like a Seraph amidst the wild animals ; the brave Placidus, the boy Marinus, and the invincible Eleutherus, Potitus, Alexan-der, and Vitus; all the brave band that won their crown in this arena : truly the reminiscences of their combat cast a halo of reverential awe over this battle-field of the Christians' triumph.

The Stations of the Cross which the Goths from Pied-mont were ruthlessly destroying, were erected in memory of events dear to the Roman people. The year 1750 was coming to a close. The Romans had spent it well. There lived amongst them then the great Leonard of Port Mau rice. The vast and magnificent churches of the eternal city were too small to contain the crowds that gathered around this Apostolic follower of St. Francis. He had to leave the churches and preach in the public squares. The Coliseum at length became the great rendezvous, and twenty thousand people would gather around the rude pulpit erected in the amphitheatre. On one occasion the Pope and seventeen cardinals were present. The pious people wished to erect some memorial of those happy hours spent with the eloquent Leonard in the Coliseum. At his suggestion the most befitting memento that could adorn the Calvary of the martyrs, was the Via Crucis. The great ruin was then freed from robbers and outlawed vagrants who were concealed in it at night, when its sombre arches sheltered many a dark treason against human life, and the fugitive perpetrators from crime.

The confraternity of the Lovers of Jesus and Mary, founded by Blessed Leonard, visited every Friday, up to this sad hour, the stations in the arena ; devout pilgrims from every clime under heaven have knelt in tears of de- votion before these touching representations of everything most terrible in the past, which were now being cast down in wanton sacrilege at the feet of a sorrowing crowd.

Besides the love which the Italian Government have for the pagan monument, which induces them to remove the *degrading* emblems of Christianity, the present pro- fanation of the ruin, is also absurdly placed under the auspices of archæological research. This, we fancy, is but a cloak in which they permit us to accuse them of igno- rance rather than infidelity.

They cannot but be ignorant that the arena of the amphitheatre stands at its present level; that in 1810 it was excavated by Fea and Valadier. They found nothing but the supporting walls that allowed subterranean passages for machinery, water conduits, &c. The designs of the amphitheatre of Rome have been the same as those of Capua, Verona, and Pompeii, and the whole ground-plan of the Coliseum may be seen in the Minerva Library, a few hundred yards from the old ruin itself. Yet at the whim of the Goths that rule at the Capitol, the sanctity of the arena, the religious feelings of the people, and the borrowed resources of a bankrupt Government, must be sacrificed to procure new plans of the ground-work of the Coliseum.

Doubtless these excavations will meet the same fate as those of Fea and his supporters amongst the French usurpation. The deep cuttings in the arena became the receptacle of stagnant waters that gave noxious vapours to the winds that swept through the desolate ruin, and by universal desire the arena was restored to its original level.

It is said that the Jews in power in the Italian Government are the desecrators of the Coliseum. Its cross, perhaps, reminds them of the deicide of their fathers; it is the epitomized history of the church, it is the monogram of triumph; in silent eloquence it represents the divine and indestructible faith that triumphed in the Coliseum—a faith persecuted in the past, and persecuted in the present by the miserable offspring of a blinded people who will not learn the lesson read in the history of centuries. It was not archæology, but paganism and infidelity, that have instigated the profanation of this most revered monument of early Rome.

The profanation of the old ruin has had quite another effect to that intended. The Coliseum is now better known ; it is dearer than ever to the Christian, and a cry of indignation has rung through the Catholic press of the world. The lives of its martyrs, the history of its thrilling miracles, are now read in every language in Europe, and sought after in every clime.

" The Martyrs of the Coliseum," is the only work on the subject afloat on the vast sea of literature, and as the demand for it is increasing, we present a revised edition to the American public.

In the pages of this little work will be found sufficient reasons for the protest we make of the desecration of the Coliseum. Our indignation will find an echo in the feelings of many a traveller who, like ourselves, remember the time he stood in rapture in the midst of this stupendous wreck of magnificence ; that echo caught up and repeated by every civilized nation under the sun, has a response far away beyond the stars, where the bright galaxy of the crimson stole seek the vindication of their blood—shed again in the contempt of the pagans of the 19th century.

THE AUTHOR.

TORONTO, ST, MICHAEL'S PALACE,
  Feast of St. Monica, 1874.

THE

MARTYRS OF THE COLISEUM.

CHAPTER I.

INTRODUCTION.

" And thou didst shine, thou rolling moon, upon
All this, and cast a wide and tender light
Which softened down the hoar austerity
Of rugged desolation, and filled up,
As 'twere, anew the gaps of centuries,
Leaving that beautiful which still was so,
And making that which was not, till the place
Became religion, and the heart ran o'er
With silent worship of the great of old,
The dead but sceptred sovereigns, who still rule
Our spirits from their urns."

—*Byron's Manfred.*

IN the year 590, when St. Gregory the Great was
elected to the chair of St. Peter, ambassadors were
sent from the Emperor Justinian in the East to con-
gratulate his Holiness and tender the usual spiritual alle-
giance to the Vicar of Christ. When they were leaving
Rome, they requested the holy Father to give them some
relic to take back to their own country. St. Gregory led
them to the Coliseum. Taking up some of the clay of

the arena, he folded it up in a napkin, and handed it to the ambassadors. They seemed not to appreciate the gift, and respectfully remonstrated. The holy Pope, raising his eyes and his heart towards heaven, with love and kindness beaming in his countenance, said to them, "You know not what you have ; " and taking the napkin in his hand, unfolded it, and showed it to them, stained with blood—the blood of the martyrs who suffered in the Coliseum !*

There is no ruin of the ancient world so interesting as the great amphitheatre at Rome. It stands in stupendous magnificence, in the midst of the seven hills of the old capital of the world, as a monument of everything that was great or terrible in the past. The immensity and majesty of its designs tell the perfection of art, and its reminiscences recall all the horrors of persecution and the triumphs of Christianity. It was the battle-field in which the Church fought for the conversion of the pagan world; the blood of the martyred heroes who fell in the fight still mingles with the clay of the sanctified arena , it was this blood Gregory gave to the ambassadors who wished to have some relics from the city of martyrs.

The storms of seventeen centuries have rolled over the mighty amphitheatre, and left it as gigantic in its ruins as thrilling in its history. Tier rises on tier to the blue vault of heaven ; the wandering eye cannot grasp its immensity ; and although shaken by earthquakes and the lightnings of heaven, and rifled of its travertine by the spoilers of the Middle Ages, it still stands with imperishable grandeur in the midst of the seven hills, "a noble wreck of ruinous perfection."

* The same is recorded of Pius V. See lessons of his feast in the Dominican Breviary.

We remember well our first visit to the ruins of the Coliseum. It was an event of our life. We found in the majestic pile a realisation of the highest flights of fancy. A thousand thoughts rushed to our mind ; the silent majesty that shrouded those immense tottering walls, and their thrilling history, made us stand fixed to the ground in admiration and awe. A momentary glance, a thought filled up the gap of centuries ; the marble seats were again crowded before the mind's eye with thousands of human beings ; the wounded lion—the dying gladiator— the kneeling martyr, appeared in rapid succession on the blood-stained arena ; the deafening shout of the excited populace ; the condemnation of the Christians, and the call for their blood to be given to satiate the thirst of the lions—all formed a picture of the past that sent a thrill to the heart. We stood on the arena that saw Rome's infancy and the Church's glory. The very clay under our feet was holy ! one day it would give up that which, in eternity, would be one of the brightest ornaments of heaven—the blood of the martyrs ! With feelings of awe, veneration and delight, we knelt at the foot of the cross— that cross which was the standard of Christianity, and which now flings its triumphant shadow over the silent arena in which all the power of man had endeavoured to destroy it.

While wrapt in thought, we heard sounds of admiration expressed in several languages from groups of tourists who stood gazing at the mighty ruin. Thousands pour annually into the Eternal City, and justly hasten to the Coliseum as one of the most interesting of the many sights of Rome. Here the trader from beyond the Rocky Mountains stands beside the gold-digger from Australia,

and, as was our case, the missioner on sick-leave from
the Cape of Good Hope could shake hands with an old
school companion from the British Isles. From morning till night the wandering stranger is seen in the arena
of the mighty ruin, and long too after nightfall, when
silence and darkness have lent additional romance. to its
magnificence. When the pale light of the moon swells its
sombre arches into marvellous immensity, the sentimen-
tal tourist stands in the bleak solitude of the gigantic
fabric, and feeds his vivid fancy with shadowy pictures of
castles and towers, and other amphitheatres that spring
from the broken arches and crumbling walls. The
Coliseum, once seen, is never forgotten, whether viewed
under the full blaze of the scorching Italian sun, or under
the magic influence of the pale light of the moon.

Our first hour in the Coliseum was one of regret. The
present contributed more than the past to cast a gloom
over our thoughts. The terrible scenes that passed in
that arena, the wholesale slaughter of innocent victims,
the inhuman shout that consigned the brave gladiator to
his doom, the horrors of its bloodshed, made it well
called by Tertullian *a place without mercy ;** yet the
curse of paganism, that brooded over this temple of
the furies, steeled the hearts of the spectators, and
brought on demoniac infatuation and blindness. This
picture was painful, but another thought gave us sorrow. Thousands that pour into the Coliseum are
strangers to the sacred reminiscences that hang around
its hallowed ruins. That spirit of infidelity which now-
a-days robs literature of every sentiment of religion, will
not permit history to give the most sacred and solemn
part of its records. Irreligious guide-books are in the

* De Spectaculis, cap. xix.

nands of every traveller, books that devote whole pages to the description of the infamous and bloody practices of paganism, but dare not give one paragraph, or even make an allusion, to the sufferings of the martyrs. A description is given of t e pagan monument, but no mention is made of its connection with the first ages of the Church. The educated Christian sees more in the Coliseum than imperishable walls, or sublime designs of architecture, shadowed forth in the gigantic remnants of the mouldering ruin : he sees before him a monument of that alone which was great and noble in the past—the triumph of his faith. He remembers that every niche of that arena has been dyed with the blood of martyrs. He feels that their triumph is his own. After the lapse of seventeen hundred years he is united with them in the unbroken chain of communion, and at the same moment that he is startled with the majesty and magnificence of the ruin, he kneels to kiss the rude cross that is raised within its precincts to commemorate the greatest battle-field of the followers of the Crucified.

It was this thought which suggested this little work. The Coliseum is the largest and most remarkable of the ruins of Ancient Rome; it is more remarkable on account of the martyrs who suffered in it, and the miracles it witnessed. These are but little known. We have employed our leisure hours in putting together a few of the most authentic records. We present them in their rough and unadorned simplicity to the Christian who loves to honour the heroes of the early Church, to the student who loves to pore over the records of the martyrology, and to the tourist who visits the Eternal City, and asks in vain from his guide or from his friends, " Who were THE MARTYRS OF THE COLISEUM ?"

CHAPTER II.

THE memory of the Emperor Augustus was dear to the Roman people. By his great skill and talent, he not only won for himself the sceptre of supreme power, but raised up the Empire itself amongst the nations of the world, and commenced what is generally known as its golden age. His natural virtues stood in agreeable contrast with the debaucheries and vices of his immediate successors. To him is due the honour of having first designed the erection of the amphitheatre. Having embellished the city with baths and temples of surpassing magnificence, he conceived the idea of erecting an immense amphitheatre for the gladiatorial spectacles, which should exceed in dimensions and splendour every other building in the world. Death cut him off before he could carry out his great project. Years rolled on, and seven Emperors, who had neither energy nor talent to carry out the immense design, sat on the throne of Augustus. Yet it was not forgotten, and the cry of the people for the commencement of the amphitheatre was heard by Vespasian; and to this enterprising Emperor is due the erection of this greatest work of antiquity, and now grandest ruin in the world.*

Vespasian was proud and ambitious; he sought to rival the fame of Augustus, and in the second year after his elevation to the throne, he commenced the Coliseum : this was in the year of our Lord 72. He died before it was completed ; and although there were more than thirty thousand persons constantly employed, it took eight years in its erection, and was dedicated by Titus in A.D. 80. The work was not perfectly finished until the reign of Domitian.

This stupendous building was erected on the site of a fish-pond in the gardens of Nero. Standing in the midst of the seven hills, and in the very heart of the ancient city, it not only surpassed in immensity and magnificence the two other marble amphitheatres which Rome possessed, but even outshone the glittering splendours of the golden house of Nero. Both Vespasian and Titus availed themselves of the experience of their travels in the East, for they cast into the designs of the amphitheatre all the boldness and majesty of the Syrian and Egyptian architecture, with the embellishment and refinement of Grecian art. Its immensity, even in its ruins, is surprising, whilst its arches rise in magical proportions over each other, in the Ionic, Doric, and Corinthian orders. Size, beauty and strength have been combined to render it the largest, the most beautiful, and the most durable of ancient monuments. Raised in the air as high as the Palatine and Celian hills, a mountain without and a valley within, it unquestionably surpassed anything

* "Fecit amphitheatrum urbi media uti destinasse compererat Augustus."—*Suet. in Vespas.* ix.

that Greece, or Egypt, or Rome had seen before. Martial, the poet, who saw it spring from its foundation, declares[*] that Rome had no longer anything to envy in the East, since her superb amphitheatre was more wonderful than the pyramids of Memphis or the works of Babylon. Yet the most approved critics define the Coliseum as an oriental edifice dressed in a Grecian costume.

The greatest works of man have generally their origin in destruction. In the history of the world there has scarcely ever been a great building or a nation that did not rise on the ruins of another. The workmen of the Coliseum were the captive Jews that adorned the triumph of Titus; the material was partly taken from the fallen house of Nero. Christians may look on it as a mighty monument, raised to commemorate the fulfilment of prophecy.

The plough has passed over the city and temple of Jerusalem, its proud people have been humbled to the dust and scattered to the four winds of heaven. Seventy thousand of this conquered race were brought to Rome by Titus. Having adorned his triumph, they were divided into three classes; the women and children up to sixteen years of age were sold as slaves for the most miserable prices. Our Blessed Lord was sold for thirty pieces of silver; after the triumph of Titus, you could get thirty Jews for one piece of silver. Some of the men

---

[*] "Barbara pyramidum sileat miracula Memphis:
    Assiduus jacet nec Babylona labor.....
  Aere nec vacuo pendentia Mausolea
    Laudibus immodicis Cares in astra ferant;
  Omnis Cæsareo cedat labor amphitheatro,
    Unum præ cunctis fama loquatur opus."
                              —*Martial Spec.* **l. l.**

were sent to Egypt to work in the marble quarries, but by far the largest number were retained for the works of the Coliseum. The number is variously estimated from thirty thousand to fifty thousand. Thus the walls of that mighty emblem of everything gloomy and horrible were cemented with the tears of a fallen people.

The upper structures of the Coliseum were raised by material taken from the fallen house of the Cæsars on the Palatine. When Vespasian and Titus gave orders for the destruction of the greater part of the house of Nero, they performed an act most pleasing to the Roman people. It was a monument of hateful splendour that rose on the ruins of their burned city ; its riches and its grandeur could but remind them of tyranny and oppression. No sooner was the order given than the populace joined in the work of devastation. Immense boulders of gilded travertine, columns, and capitals, and marble cornices of the most elaborate carving, bonds of iron and gold, and imperishable masses of brickwork, were rudely and indiscriminately hurried away to ornament or fill up the great work of the Coliseum.

The mighty amphitheatre itself will become a ruin, and, after the lapse of centuries, will be stricken by the hand of time, and will, in its own turn, lend the mateterial of its fallen arches to build the mediæval and modern palaces of the Eternal City. The immense quadrilateral palace of the Venetian embassy, the Farnese, the Barberini, and others of lesser note, sprung from the ruins of the Coliseum. Thus it is in the history of man ; the greatest monuments of modern splendour have risen, phœnix-like, from the ruins of the mighty structures that our ancestors vainly imagined imperishable.

We must now take a view of the amphitheatre in its perfect state. Scattered fragments of description have been collected from ancient historians, and the picture is nearly complete. Fancy can fill up many details from the ruins as they now stand.

It has a beautiful elliptic figure, 564 feet in length and 467 in breadth. It was raised on eighty immense arches, and rose in four successive orders of architecture to the height of 140 feet. The whole building covered a space equal to six English acres. The outside was incrusted with marble and decorated with statues. The slopes of the vast concave which formed the inside were filled and surrounded with sixty or eighty rows of seats of marble, covered with cushions, and capable of receiving with ease a hundred thousand spectators.* Sixty-four vomitories (for by that name the doors were very aptly distinguished) poured forth the immense multitudes ; the entrances, the passages, and staircases were contrived with such ex quisite skill, that each person, whether of the senatorian, equestrian, or plebian order, arrived at his destined place without trouble or confusion.

The lowest row of seats next to the arena, now completely covered by earth and debris, assigned to the senators and foreign ambassadors, was called the *podium.* There also on an elevated platform was the Emperor's throne, shaded by a canopy like a pavilion. The place for the manager or editor of the games, as he was called, and the vestal virgins, was beside the Emperor's seat.

* Cardinal Wiseman, in a note in Fabiola, says, it could hold at least a hundred and fifty thousand spectators ; but none of the Italian antiquarians have mentioned more than a hundred thou· sand.

The podium was secured with a breastwork or parapet of gold or gilt bronze against the irruption of the wild beasts. As a further defence, the arena was surrounded with an iron railing and a canal. The equites, or second order of nobles, sat in fourteen rows behind the senators, The rest of the people sat behind on seats called *popularia* rising tier above tier to a gallery with a colonnade in front, running all round the amphitheatre immediately under the awning, and generally occupied by females, soldiers, and attendants.

Nothing was omitted that could in any way be subservient to the convenience and pleasure of the spectators. The immense canopy or awning which at times was stretched over the entire expanse from the outer wall, as a protection from the sun or rain, was one of the wonders of the Coliseum. It requires a stretch of imagination to believe it. When we stand, even now, in the midst of the ruins, and see the vast expanse of the heavens above us, the mind is lost in doubt and conjecture about the possibility of such a marvellous fact. Yet all the historians who have written of the Coliseum mention it as if there was nothing extraordinary about it. Lampridius mentions that the men who were to work this awning were dressed as sailors, and numbered several hundreds.* At a signal given, when there was fear of rain, or the sun was too hot, there would be a simultaneous movement amongst the attendants—the cords would creak, and the mighty sails would roll gradually to the centre, each sail meeting in perfect harmony, and forming together an immense sheet that completely covered

---

* " A militibus classiariis qui vela ducebant in amphitheatro, " &c —*Lamprid. in Commodo.*

the interior. Stranger still the fact that this awning, in the time of Titus, was purple silk, fringed with gold.* The air was continually refreshed by the playing fountains, and an infinity of small tubes dispersed a shower of the most delicious perfumes which descended on the spectators like aromatic dews. The arena, in the centre of which stood the statue of Jupiter, formed the stage, and derived its name from being usually strewed with the finest white sand. Underneath, they had mechanism of the most extraordinary and complicated character, so that the arena could, during the games, assume different forms in quick succession. At one time it would seem to rise out of the earth like the Garden of the Hesperides, and was afterwards broken into the rocks and caverns of Thrace. Subterranean pipes conveyed an inexhaustible supply of water, and what just before appeared a level plain, might suddenly be converted into a wide lake covered with armed vessels to delight the people with nautical entertainments.

" Sous Titus un tissu de soie et d'or avec des broderies s'étend sur le nouvel amphitheatre."—*Gerbet, Esquisse de Rome Chrétienne,* li. 345.

CHAPTER III.

THE ENTERTAINMENTS AND SPECTACLES OF THE COLISEUM.

THE games and amusements which delighted the people of Rome present a spectacle of horror that sends a thrill to the very heart. No entertainment was popular unless accompanied by bloodshed and the loss of life; no mock tragedies would be cheered in this temple of the furies. The amusements of the Coliseum form the darkest page in the records of the past.

During the greater celebrations there was scarcely a day passed in which some hundreds of mangled carcases of men and beasts were not dragged from the arena to the spoliarium or dead-house. The games commenced about ten, and often lasted till dark; during all these hours, victim was falling upon victim; the spectators, more and more intoxicated with each new draught of blood, drunk in by their glistening eyes, yelled for fresh victims and more blood. On more than one occasion it happened that every animal in the vivarium was slain in one day. Eutropius, speaking of Titus, says—"And when he had built the amphitheatre at Rome, he inaugurated the games, and caused five thousand beasts to be slain." (Eutropius, book ix. ch. x.) Gladiators, slaves, and Christians were the principal victims of the games.

Yet there were bright spots in this picture of carnage—there were moments when the universal applause of the populace rung through every portion of the building in approbation of scenes of beauty, innocence, and mechanism that can scarcely be rivalled in modern art. Their great games, which often lasted for entire weeks, were a strange mixture of the comic and the tragic, the jovial and the horrible. A favourite amusement was to witness the acting of trained animals in the circus. The writers of those times tell us of an elephant that was a rope-walker,* of a bear which sat in a chair, dressed as a matron, which was carried around the arena by attendants † Then we have an account of the king of the forest, with gilt claws, and mane bespangled with gold and precious stones, which, as a strange contrast to successive scenes, was made to represent the virtue of clemency, being trained to play with a hare. He would take the frightened little animal in his mouth, put it or his back, and lavish on it a thousand caresses.‡ Then we read of twelve tame elephants, six male and six female, dressed in the togas of men and women, who

---

* " Elephas erectus ad summum theatri fornicem, unde decurrit in fune sessorem gerens."—*Dio. in Neron.*

Also Suetonius in Galba, cap. vi., says—"Galba elephantos funambulos dedit."

† " Vidi ursum mansuetum quæ cultu matronali sella vehebatur." —*Apul. Asin.* lib. xii.

‡ " Leonum
Quos velox leporum timor fatigat.
Dimittunt, repetunt, amantque captos ;
Et securior est in ore præda
Laxos cui dare, perviosque rictus
Gaudent et timidos timere dentes,
Mollem frangere dum pudet rapinam."
—*Martial,* lib. i. Epigram. ov. 14

would sit at table, and eat delicate viands and drink wine from golden cups, and would use with the greatest delicacy and care that extraordinary trunk, with which they can lift a pin from the ground, or tear the forest oak from its roots.*   Others were trained to the Pyrrhic dance, and would spread flowers on the arena. They had a peculiar strong drink to which the elephants were partial ; it inebriated them, and caused them to go through antics and manœuvres that produced incessant roars of laughter from the spectators.

We learn from Martial and others that there was another species of amusement of a grander and more exciting character, but intermingled and tainted with that spirit of cruelty which characterised most of the games of the amphitheatre. As already mentioned, the underground passages served as keeps and caves for the beasts, or might become immense aqueducts to flood the arena, which became a lake for naval entertainments. Ships with armed men were floated, and fought desperately with each other, as if an empire depended on the issue of the battle. On one occasion a large ship was introduced to this artificial lake, full of men and animals, and at a given signal it opened its sides and fell to pieces, casting its living freight into the waters. Then came all the horrors of a shipwreck : the screams from the animals and the piteous cries of the drowning slaves, sounded like music to the Roman ear.

By a combination of mechanical skill the fable of Orpheus was almost realised. The soil of the arena was made to open suddenly in a hundred places, and trees would spring up clothed in the deepest green foliage, and

---

* See Buling de Venation. Circ. cap. xx.

bearing golden apples in imitation of the fabulous trees of the Garden of the Hesperides. Wild animals were let loose into this enchanting forest ; the trees would move to the sound of a flute ; and that nothing might be wanting to the reality of the representation, the unfortu nate slave who had the honour of representing the Orpheus of the spectacle was torn to pieces by a bear.* A failure in any of the mechanism of these shows was considered a slight to the Emperor, and the director was punished with public death. Were it not for this inhuman and barbarous custom, which cramped with fear the greatest genius of the Empire, the Coliseum would have witnessed many great triumphs of mechanical art.

Amongst the spectacles founded on pagan mythology, Martial makes mention in his Epigrams of a parricide who was crucified in the Coliseum ; also of a horrible scene of Dædalus raised in the air with false wings, and then permitted to fall into the arena, where he was devoured by wild animals. On another occasion a slave was obliged to represent Mutius Scævola, and to put his hand into a fire until completely burned. The wretch who had to suffer this awful cruelty had another alternative, for his garments were covered with pitch and tar, and if he wavered or flinched for a moment, he was burned alive.

But by far the most common amusement of the Coliseum were the combats with the beasts and the gladiators. The wild animals were made to fight with each other, then with men ; and lastly, man with his fellow-man. When wild animals were put into the arena to fight with each other, everything that could rouse or excite them

* Martial, Spect. xxi. i.

was studied with the most cruel skill. The colours they hated most were scattered in profusion around them; they were beaten with whips, and their sides were torn with iron hooks; hot plates of iron were fastened to them, and even balls of fire were placed on their backs. Thus the enraged animals would run round the arena; the earth would tremble under the thunder of their agonizing roars, and the inflated chest would seem to burst under the fire of passion that drove them mad. Their eyes sparkled with rage, and tearing up the sand with their claws, they enveloped themselves in a cloud of dust. In their fury they tore each other to pieces.

If, as sometimes happened, an infuriated lioness or tigress should kill the men and animals presented to her, frantic shouts of applause rose from every side of the amphitheatre, and whilst, mistress of the battlefield, she walked over the bodies of her victims, the people called aloud for her liberty, to have her sent back again to her native deserts.

The combats between men and beasts were still more popular. The Emperors themselves used to take part in them, and even women had the hardihood to enter the arena, and combat with the most ferocious animals. There were two classes of people destined for this species of sport—one was armed—they carried weapons according to their choice; the others were poor slaves, captives, or criminals, who were exposed defenceless to the beasts. To this class *the Christians belonged.* They were distinguished from the gladiators by the opprobrious sobriquet of *Bestiaries.*

The combat of gladiators is supposed to have been of Etruscan origin It formed part of the funeral obsequies of great men, according to the pagan belief that the shades or *manes* of the dead were appeased by the shedding of blood. This strange funeral rite was first introduced into Rome at the obsequies of Junius Brutus in the year 490 of the city, and about 260 years before the Christian era. It seems to have been so pleasing to the cruel tastes of the Roman people, as to have soon become a common pastime. The gladiatorial fights were, strictly speaking, the games of the Coliseum, and to these it owes its existence. Such was the rage of the people for these sights, that it is believed that a hundred thousand gladiators fell within its walls. During twelve days Trajan made as many as ten thousand gladiators fight successively; almost all the succeeding Emperors followed his example. The men who fought as gladiators were generally captives taken in war or slaves. At a later period, it became a kind of profession, and freemen and noblemen, maddened by enthusiasm, are said to have entered the lists to fight in deadly combat with the poor captive from Thrace or Gaul. Even women appeared in the arena as Amazons, and fought frantically and bravely amid the unceasing acclamations of the people.

We are told by Herodian and Lampridius that the Emperor Commodus, not content with witnessing the fights of the gladiators, entered the arena himself, almost naked, and armed with a short sword, and would challenge them to combat. Those who contended with him were enjoined not to inflict any wound; but the moment they received a slight wound they fell on their knees before him and, declaring themselves defeated, sued for mercy. Having thus defeated a thousand gladiators, he ordered the head to be taken from the colossal statue of the sun, and his own image placed in its stead; on the base of the monument he put this inscription, " *Mille Gladiato-rum victor* "*—" The conqueror of a thousand gladiators."

After the procession of the gods (with which the games of the amphitheatre, as well as those of the circus, were commenced), the gladiators who were doomed to fight were also led around the arena in procession ; † then they were matched in pairs, and their swords examined by the manager. As a prelude to the battle, and to create the proper pitch of excitement, they fought first with wooden swords; then, upon a signal being given by sound of trumpet, these were laid aside and deadly weapons were substituted. The interest of the assembled thousands was soon carried to the highest pitch of excitement ; from time to time they burst into deafening shouts of applause, or a dread silence reigned throughout the vast amphitheatre, a suspense which only ended in the death of one of the combatants. When a gladiator received a wound, his adversary would cry out, " He has got it"—(*Hoc habet !*) Sometimes the wounded wretch would endeavour to conceal his wound, or pretend it was of no account, and perhaps would fall to the ground in making his last and desperate rush on his adversary. But his fate depended on the pleasure of the people ; if they wished him to be saved, they pressed down their thumbs, and, if to be slain, they turned them up. The latter was more generally the awful verdict of the unfeel-ing mob ; the cry of " *recipe ferrum* " would fall with terrible vehemence on the dying man's ears. This simply

---

* Marangoni, p. 38.

† " Jam ostentata per arenam periturorum corpora mortis suæ pompam auxerant."—*Quintilian Declam.* ix.

meant that he was to submit to his fate bravely and with dignity; that he should show no disgraceful writhings or contortions of pain, that he should have even an art in the awful agonies of death. "The people," says Seneca, "thought themselves insulted when he would not die willingly; and by look, by gesture, and by vehemence of manner, called for his immediate execution."

Lactantius, in the sixth book of his sublime Apology for the true religion, gives an idea of the barbarity of these games in the very words by which he condemns them :— "Whoever takes delight in the sight of blood, although it be that of a criminal justly condemned to death, defiles his conscience. But the pagans have turned the shedding of human blood into a pastime. So totally has humanity receded from men's breasts, that they make their amusement consist in abetting murder and sacrificing human life. Now, I ask, can those be called just and pious who not only permit the slaughter of one who lies prostrate under the drawn sword, supplicating for life, but who demand that he be murdered; who give their cruel and inhuman suffrages for death, not satiated with the wounds and gore of their hapless victim? Nay, when stretched dead before them on the sand, they command the lifeless and bleeding body to be stabbed over and over again, and cut and mangled lest they should be deluded by a sham homicide. They get furious with the combatants who do not quickly despatch each other, and, as if they thirsted for human blood, are impatient of delay. Each company of newcomers, as it pours into the circles, vociferates for fresh victims that they may satiate their eyes."

Thus duels and combats by groups, and mêlées of the

most terrible slaughter passed like whirlwinds under the frenzied gaze of the people. For hours, and even days, the arena of the Coliseum was reeking with the blood of its victims; its sickening vapours would ascend to the pure air of heaven as from an immense cauldron of cruelty and pleasure.

St. Augustine gives us, in the sixth book of his Confessions, a singularly vivid description of the excitement that prevailed among the spectators during these sanguinary struggles.

" It happened," he says, " while his friend Alipius was studying the law at Rome, that he was met one day by some of his fellow-students as they were walking after dinner, who insisted on taking him to the amphitheatre; for it was one of the dismal holidays when Rome took its pleasure in these spectacles of human slaughter.

"As Alipius had an extreme horror of this kind of cruelty, he at first resisted with all his might; but resorting to that sort of violence which is sometimes permitted among friends, they dragged him along, while he repeated, ' You may drag my body along with you, and place me amongst you in the amphitheatre, but you cannot dispose of my mind nor of my eyes, which shall not, most assuredly, take any part in the spectacle. I shall be absent, therefore, although present in body, and thus I shall render myself superior to the violence you practise on me and to the passion by which you are possessed.' But he might as well have been silent ; they drew him along, having a mind, perhaps, to see if he could be as good as his word.

" At length they arrived, and placed themselves as best they could ; and while all the amphitheatre was in transports with these barbarous pleasures, Alipius guarded his heart from taking any part in them, keeping his eyes shut. And would to God," continues St. Augustine, "he had also stopped his ears; for having been struck by a great and universal shout, which was caused among the people by something extraordinary that had occurred in the combat, he was seized with curiosity, and merely wishing to ascertain what it could be—persuaded that, no matter what it was, he would despise it—he opened his eyes, and in so doing inflicted on his own soul a wound more fatal than that which one of the gladiators had just received in his body; it was the occasion of a fall far more dangerous than that of the unfortunate gladiator whose overthrow had occasioned the inhuman shout which had tempted him to open his eyes. Cruelty entered into his heart, the blood which at the same moment was pouring out on the arena, met his eyes, and, very far from turning them away, he kept them riveted to the spot, drinking in long draughts of fury without perceiving it, and allowing himself to be intoxicated with criminal pleasure.

"He was no longer the same Alipius who had been dragged there by force; he was a man of the same stamp as those who made up the crowd of the amphitheatre, and a fit companion for those who brought him there. He looked on, he shouted, mingling his cries with theirs, feverish with excitement, and, like them, totally absorbed in the vicissitudes of the combat. In fine, he departed from the amphitheatre with such a passion for these sights that he could think of nothing else. Not only was he ready to return with those who had been obliged to use force with him in the first instance, but he was more infuriated about the gladiators than they, drawing others with him, and ever ready to lead the way to the amphitheatre." (Book vii. ch. viii.)

So intense was the excitement of the people during these fights, that they seemed to lose all self-control ; from morning till evening, careless of cold or heat, they gazed with mad excitement on the arena, and their minds were agitated with the fluctuating passions of hope and fear, like the ocean tossed by contrary winds. Nor was the demon of discord idle whilst the furies flapped their funereal wings over these bloody scenes. The spectators were divided into several parties. Sharp and bitter discussions concerning the rival merits of the combatants formed an inexhaustible source of broils and disputes ; and sometimes they became so excited, as to pass from criticism and argument to blows, and even to deadly weapons, until the benches of the amphitheatre from end to end became the scene of sanguinary tumult and massacre.

We have an account of one of these terrible scenes in the Circus Maximus, in which upwards of thirty thousand persons were killed or wounded. Something similar happened in the Coliseum on the occasion of a scene of horrible cruelty. One of the Emperors obliged a celebrated gladiator to fight three others in succession. The tyrant Gesler, who made Tell split an apple with his arrow at a hundred paces on his son's head, was not more inhuman. The poor gladiator fought bravely, and slew the first two opponents, but wearied and wounded, fell whilst fighting the third. The excitement of this scene drove the people to madness ; they turned on each other, and terrible bloodshed was the result.

We will conclude this brief notice of the gladiatorial

scenes of the Coliseum by quoting the beautiful and
touching lines of Lord Byron :—

> " I see before me the gladiator lie ;
> He leans upon his hand, his manly brow
> Consents to death, but conquers agony,
> And his drooped head sinks gradually low,
> And through his side the last drops, ebbing **slow,**
> From the red gash fall heavy, one by one,
> Like the first of a thunder-shower ; and now
> The arena swims around him, he is gone,
> Ere ceased the inhuman shout which hailed **the**
>   wretch who won.
>
> He heard it, but he heeded not ; his eyes
> Were with his heart, and that was far **away ;**
> He recked not of the life he lost, nor prize ;
> But where his rude hut by the Danube lay,
> There were his young barbarians all at play,
> There was their Dacian mother—he, their **sire,**
> Butchered to make a Roman holiday.
> **All** this rushed with his blood : shall he expire,
> **And unavenged ?** Arise, ye Goths, and glut your **ire.'**
>   —*Childe Harold.*

CHAPTER IV.

THE CHRISTIANS.

SUCH were the bloody and cruel amusements pre‧ sented from time to time to the Romans. This kind of inhuman sport had a reign of more than a thousand years, and can be traced far back to the remotest antiquity. Long before the dawn of Christianity, and before a stone was laid in the foundations of the mighty Coliseum, the poets made them the subject of their verses, the orators coloured their effusions with descriptions of these sanguinary combats; the frescoes on the walls were scenes of bloodshed, and the dull marble was made to tell their horrors. The two grandest ruins that remain of Ancient Rome are the monuments of its paganism and its cruelty. The magnificence and splendour of the Pantheon and the Coliseum form a terrible contrast with the scenes that passed within them. When we lift the veil which time has flung over the past, and contemplate the Romans in their wealth, their power and magnificence, we cannot but be horrified as well as surprised at those dark and gloomy records of tyranny and cruelty which stain every page of their history. The people who revelled in these scenes of bloodshed were men as we are; then, as now, the heart was capable of noble feelings.

There were in the Coliseum, witnessing its cruel games, senators who could sit with honour in the British Parliament; poets who would return to their homes immediately after the games, and write on scented tablets thrilling accounts of those exciting scenes, with the same hand that had applauded an assassination. There were fathers of families, who would cry out vociferously that the wounded gladiator should be struck again, and his dying frame be hacked and cut to pieces by his triumphant opponent, and in the afternoon would nurse their children with all the tenderness of paternal love. Then there was the tender, loving, sympathising nature of womanhood, blasted by the sight and thirst of blood ; the noble lady and the vestal virgin, clothed in white and crowned with flowers, became furies in the theatre, and turned down the jewelled thumb for the murder of some fallen victim ; yet one felt all the ennobling ties of a wife, a mother, and a friend, and the other pretended to cultivate the Christian virtue of chastity, Alas ! in this we see human nature without Christianity. They were the victims of paganism, that terrible slavery in which the nations of the earth were held captive before the coming of the Liberator of mankind.   We can easily cast a link of union between the impieties and horrid cruelties of the pagan past and the heart-rending and inhuman scenes of those pagan and infidel nations which are yet buried in the darkness of the shadow of death. We can pass in imagination from the carnage and bloodshed of the Coliseum, the merciless massacre of women and children and unarmed captives, whose cries for mercy were the music of a Roman triumph, to the inhuman customs of those nations who expose their infants on the banks of the mountain torrents, destroy their old men, and cast living victims under the wheels of the triumphant car of their idols, or to the bivouac of the wild savages of Dahomey sitting in brutal glee around a blazing fire, consuming their meal of human flesh.

But a new era has dawned upon the earth. In the illumination of that creed which pagan Rome vainly endeavoured to crush in the Coliseum, we read a solution to this terrible enigma of life. They knew nothing of the sublime morality of Him who has said, " By this shall all men know that you are my disciples, if you have love one for another." The dark cloud of primeval guilt hung over the world for four thousand years, and paganism, idolatry, and all their concomitant absurdities were the offspring of that first sin. But when the time decreed by God for the regeneration of man had come, the new state of things did not break on the world like the sunshine bursting from the cloud. It pleased Almighty God that His kingdom should fight its own way and win its own dynasty ; He sent forth His Apostles to the world to overcome it by the invisible arms of faith. They attacked and conquered it. For four centuries the battle raged ; paganism had nothing but its cruelties and its horrors to stem the invisible power of the unarmed Apostles, and the powers of darkness quailed in the presence of the indestructible strength of the followers of Christ. But many a noble victim must fall before the victory is gained, and streams of nobler blood than that of beasts and gladiators must dye the arena of the Coliseum.

Another species of amusement must be added to those already enumerated. About eight hundred years after the building of Rome, there appeared a new race of beings who were to furnish a fresh feast to the cruelty and depravity of the people. They were men who sought no arms to fight, and showed no fear to die. After witnessing the courageous combats of the armed gladiators madly fighting for their lives, the strength and agility of the hunters, the pitiful looks and trembling limbs of the unarmed wretches who were exposed to die without even a chance of self-defence, it was a strange and unusual sight to see men walking into the arena with a fearless step and joyful brow, their eyes raised towards heaven, where they seemed to contemplate brilliant scenes of glory, bravely and intrepidly announcing the religion of the crucified God. These were men who belonged to the detestable sect which had come from Judea; they were the contemners of the gods of the Empire—they were Christians. Not the friendless captives from Thrace or Gaul, nor wretched slaves whose lives were the property of their masters, but some of the noblest families of the state, and some of them members of the imperial household itself. Instead of the brawny and stalwart frame of the hardy gladiator, it is the tender virgin in the bloom of girlhood that is now to face the fury of the lion. Triumphs of another kind will startle the enthusiasm of the crowded seats, and the wildest animals of the forest and the desert will crouch at the feet of the martyrs of Christ.

CHAPTER V.

THE FIRST MARTYR OF THE COLISEUM.

THE ruins of the burnt city were still smoking on the Palatine and Esquiline hills when Nero conceived the idea of satiating the rage of the people by the blood of the Christians. That monster, whose name is associated with everything cruel and impious, was the first Roman Emperor to decree a persecution against the unoffending servants of God. The edicts were issued ; the cry on every side was the extermination of Christianity. The whole pagan world rose in arms against it. No sooner were the terrible decrees promulgated throughout the Empire, than the people seemed possessed with demons, for they rushed with inhuman fury against the innocent and defenceless followers of the Crucified. The frenzied resolve to root out and exterminate the Christians began with Rome and diffused itself through every province and city of the Empire. Members of the same community, and even the same family, became the informers and the executioners of each other. In these pages are recorded two or three instances where fathers have tried in vain, by every species of torture and punishment, to shake the constancy of their tender and innocent children. In every town and village unrestricted license was given to the magistrates to plunder, to imprison, to torture and destroy the Christians ; and these petty officers, in their turn, delegated their power to the most menial and cruel wretches in their pay. The same has happened in our own times in China and Japan.

"It was moreover proclaimed," says a holy martyr quoted by St. Eusebius, "that no one should have any care or pity for us, but that all persons should so think of and behave themselves towards us as if we were no longer men."

These horrors did not cease with the tyrants who commenced them. For three hundred years the powers of hell continued this war against the Church with more or less fury, rising and falling like the swells of the ocean ; at one time pouring down with all the thunder and foam of the billows in the storm, then calm and tranquil as a lake.

The great St. Basil, writing of the persecution of Diocletian, gives a general idea of what were the cruelties and horrors of those terrible times.

"The houses of the Christians were wrecked and laid in ruins, their goods became the prey of rapine, their bodies of the ferocious lictors, who tore them like wild beasts, dragging their matrons by the hair along the streets, callous alike to the claims of pity for the aged or of those still in tender years. The innocent were submitted to torments usually reserved only for the vilest criminals; the dungeons were filled with the inmates of Christian homes which now lay desolate ; and the trackless deserts and the forest caves were crowded with fugitives, whose only crime was the worship of Jesus Christ. In these dark times the son betrayed his father, the father impeached his own offspring, the servant sought his master's property by denouncing him, the brother sought the brother's blood, for none of the claims or ties of humanity seemed any longer to be recognised, so completely had all been blinded as if by a demoniacal possession. Moreover, the house of prayer was profaned by impious hands, the most holy altars were overturned; nor was there any offering of the clean oblation nor of incense; no place was left for the divine mysteries, all was profound tribulation, a sable darkness that shut out all comfort; the sacerdotal colleges were dispersed, no synod or council could meet for fear of the slaughter that raged on every side; but the demons celebrated their orgies and polluted all things by the smoke and gore of their victims."

The Catacombs are lasting memorials of these terrible times; those gloomy caves and dark passages in the bowels of the earth are the most precious archives of the Church, for their rude slabs, with the palm and the crown, tell of nearly a million of martyrs.

The Coliseum is another witness to the triumphs of the past. It sprung up amidst the horrors of persecution; it became the battlefield where innocence and weakness fought with tyranny and guilt. The blood, the miracles, and the victories of the early Church have cast a hallowed reminiscence around this venerable ruin, that makes us approach it with a species of religious awe. Thousands of martyrs are supposed to have shed their blood in its arena, although certain records of all have not come down to us. Amongst these martyrs there were persons of every sex and position of life : there were princes of royal blood, bishops, matrons advanced in age, maidens in the blush of youth and innocence, and children of the most tender years.   Their courage, their meekness, their triumph over pain and death, was the eloquence that planted the cross that now casts its shadow across the desolate arena.   The acts of the heroes of the Coliseum, such as are extant, form one of the most interesting and wonderful pages in the history of the early Church.   They are beautiful, eloquent, and touching, and set in striking contrast the strength, sublimity and magnificence of Christianity with the meanness, the weakness and stupidity of infidelity ; they are incontestible evidences of the divinity of the Church of God.

But who was the first martyr of the Coliseum ?   The answer to this question will involve the answer to another, equally important.   Who was it that designed and built this stupendous masterpiece of architecture ?   What great mind conceived this gigantic fabric, laid out all its proportions in their exquisite order and symmetry, raised arch on arch and tier upon tier, cut and hewed a mountain of travertine into the sublimest work of ancient art ?   Does not all that is said of the splendid amphitheatre redound to the praise of some great man, from whose superior talent and skill it sprung into existence ?   Who was he, that we may raise his effigy on the altar of genius, and offer him the incense of our adulation and praise ?

The architect of the Coliseum needs not the tinsel of human praise ; yet let lovers of art breathe his name with reverence, for he was a Christian and a martyr.

It is a strange fact that for nearly seventeen centuries the architect of the Coliseum was unknown.   Certainly a building of such magnitude, comprising so many details and measurements, must have been the work of a superior mind. Every building of note reflects honour on its architect; the fame of the great builders of the monuments of the past is still bright on the pages of history, although the stupendous works of their genius have long since passed away.

A learned historian of the last century,* writing in the Eternal City and under the shadow of the Coliseum itself, makes these beautiful remarks :—"It is a thing worthy of reflection, that, notwithstanding the magnificence of this work, so excellent in its architecture, so admirable in its construction, and even judged by Martial to be more wonderful than all the wonders of the world, neither he nor any of the writers of the succeeding ages made mention of this great architect."

Martial, as is well known, was a Roman poet, who flourished in the reigns of Vespasian, Titus, and Domitian. He extols with pompous eulogiums the memory of Rabirius, for his skill in erecting a large addition to the palace of the Cæsars during the reign of Domitian. He says this architect raised a palace that reached the skies, and reflected the glory of the stars ; that his genius had penetrated the distant heavens, and drawn from the splendour of the celestial fabrics the magnificence and majesty of his design. "With how much more reason," continues the writer just quoted, "ought he not to immortalize the name and memory of the great architect of the Coliseum—a work far superior to the palace on the Palatine, and built by a man as celebrated, and as well known to Martial himself?"

Martial did not make a mere casual and passing

* Marangoni.

allusion to the Coliseum, he constituted himself its
panegyrist; his best poems are written on the horrors of
the amphitheatre; yet, while he extols with bombastic
praise the merits of the inferior architect who added a
new wing to the golden house, he passes over in silence
the name that should be written in letters of gold in his
stanzas on the Coliseum. Is not this silence of Martial
and of contemporary writers an enigma of history?

Seventeen centuries had passed over the imperishable
walls of this stupendous monument of antiquity; tourists
and strangers poured in from every point of the compass
to gaze with wonder on the ruin, which in its very débris
immortalized an unknown architect. In vain the lovers
of the great past read over the ancient histories and
records to find the name of this man; they pored over
the effaced inscriptions and broken slabs of marble that
still clung to the crumbling walls, hoping to find some
passing encomium in his praise, but eternal oblivion
would have shrouded his name had not an accidental
discovery brought it to light.

During some excavations that were made in the Catacombs of St. Agnes, on the Nomentan way, a rude tomb
was uncovered. It was enclosed by a marble slab bearing the crown and palm, and near it was the phial of
blood, the unmistakable testimony of martyrdom. A
rough inscription declared the praises of GAUDENTIUS,
the architect of the Coliseum.

Here is the explanation of the strange silence of
Martial and his contemporary pagan historians. Gaudentius was a Christian, and a martyr; he belonged to
that sect that was hated and persecuted by all the power
of the Empire; probably he was one of the first victims

whose blood was shed in the arena of the amphitheatre. The Roman Emperor sought not only to annihilate Christianity, but to obliterate it from the memory of man; no public act was permitted in favour of the Christians; it was treason to harbour them, to extol them, or to imagine they were capable of anything great or noble. The sycophant poet, who sought but the smiles of Cæsar, knew the theme that would please; he would not risk his life by expressing sympathy with the persecuted followers of the cross. Thus Gaudentius passed away without a monument; the timid friends who gathered together his sacred remains laid them in a martyr's tomb, in the gloomy crypts of the Catacombs; and in the faint hope that posterity would one day recognise his genius and his talent, they rudely scratched on the marble slab that covered him the verses which declare him to be the architect of the Coliseum.

Nor is it surprising that the remains of Gaudentius, as well as the remains of hundreds of other noble martyrs, were laid silently, and apparently without honour, in the dark recesses of the Catacombs. At a time when all was terror and confusion; when the trembling survivors could only gather the remains of their martyred friends by stealth and in the darkness of the night, there was no opportunity of recording their praises and their triumph in studied epitaphs or imperishable monuments.

There are thousands of saints shining in the bright group clothed in white robes, and "following the Lamb whithersoever he goeth," unknown to the Church militant except in name. Yet in the records of the Catacombs we meet now and then a few short but touching verses to declare the praises of some particular martyr; perhaps the rude composition of some surviving friend, chiselled on the hard stone by a delicate hand and traced under the dim light of an oil lamp. Such are the verses on the tomb of Gaudentius :—

SIC PREMIA SERVAS VESPASIANE DIRE
PREMIATVS ES MORTE GAVDENTI LETARE
CIVITAS VBI GLORIE TVE AVTORI
PROMISIT ISTE DAT KRISTVS OMNIA TIBI
QVI ALIVM PARAVIT THEATRV IN CELO

Here is a panegyric in a few words, but simple and sublime. It declares our hero to be the victim of gross ingratitude, and, although his genius had contributed to the glory of the city, his reward was a cruel death. The Christian who carved his epitaph seemed to console nimself with the glory and appreciation given to his friend in the other world. "Cæsar had promised three great rewards," he seems to say, "but false and ungrateful was the pagan ; He who is the great architect of the heavens, and whose promises fail not, has prepared for thee in reward of thy virtue a place in the everlasting theatre of the celestial city."

At first sight these verses do not seem to possess all the importance we have attributed to them, but a mo- ment's reflection will prove them to be one of the simplest records of the past. There was no other theatre built in the time of Vespasian but the Coliseum ; it was the *glory of the city*, and is still so in its ruins. Vespasian did not persecute the Christians, yet there were martyrs in his reign ; the laws of Nero were unrepealed, and were still enforced with more or less violence in different parts of the Empire. We read of St. Apolinaris, Bishop of Ravenna, in the Roman martyrology under the 23rd of

July, "qui sub Vespasiano Cæsare gloriosum martyrium consummavit." Eusebius, in his History of the Church (book iii., chap 15), as also Baronius (anno 74), assert that Vespasian raised a terrible persecution against the Jews; he put to death all who said they were descendants of David. Now amongst the Gentiles in those times Christians and Jews were considered the same. Dion Cassius says of Domitian that he put to death those "qui in mores Judæorum transierant" (lib. 47), that is, those who became Christians. Superficial readers are inclined to doubt of the inference drawn from this epitaph. A thousand questions may be asked, and many objections raised, but without entering into a tedious and perhaps uninteresting examination of the question, it will be sufficient to state that it is the received opinion of all modern antiquarians that this epitaph can refer only to the architect of the Coliseum. Amongst the authors who assert this opinion as beyond doubt are Arringhi, Nibbi, Rossi, Marangoni, and Mgr. Gerbet, &c.

The slab which contains this inscription may be seen at present in the subterranean church of St. Martina in the Forum. Martina was one of the virgins exposed to the wild beasts in the Coliseum. The underground chapel is a gem of architecture, and is a lasting monument of the genius and munificence of Pietro da Cortona, who designed and built it himself. It is richly ornamented, and possesses many pieces of beautiful and rare marble. Amonst the ornaments which adorn its walls there is not one so interesting as the rude slab of Gaudentius.

Of his life and the manner of his death nothing is known; his history, his martyrdom and his panegyric are all contained in this brief and obscure epitaph. The

Church has emblazoned on her records in brilliant letters the names of those heroes whose talents or whose triumphs were the glory of the early ages, and amongst them may be recognised the architect of the greatest work of antiquity, the Christian and the martyr GAUDENTIUS.

CHAPTER VI.

ST. IGNATIUS.

AFTER the glorious transfiguration of our Blessed Lord on Thabor, He retired with his disciples to Galilee. Having foretold His passion and death, and prepared them for the awful scenes that were to come to pass in a few days, He commenced His last and memorable journey to Jerusalem. His disciples followed Him at a short distance. On the road to Capharnaum they entered into conversation with each other, and disputed among themselves which of them should be the greatest. Their minds were not yet illumined by the light of the Holy Spirit, and they were yet ignorant of the sublime virtues of Christian morality.

But Jesus knew what was passing amongst them. When they arrived at Capharnaum He entered a house and made the disciples sit around Him, and He commenced to teach them those beautiful lessons of humility which are the foundations of all true greatness. With love and kindness beaming in His countenance He asked them : " What did you treat of in the way ? But they held their peace."

A ray of light had penetrated their hearts as the words of Jesus entered their ears, and a blush was the acknow-

ledgment of their pride. Near our Blessed Lord there
stood a beautiful child—a bright-eyed little boy of four
or five years of age, with golden hair falling in ringlets on
his shoulders. He was the type of everything innocent
and beautiful. Jesus called the child towards Him, and
having impressed a kiss on his little forehead, He placed
him before His disciples, and in the sweet tones of His
heavenly voice said to them : "Amen I say to you, unless
you be converted, and become as little children, you
shall not enter the kingdom of heaven. Whosoever
therefore shall humble himself as this little child, he is
the greater in the kingdom of heaven" (Matt. xviii. 3).

That child was Ignatius ! * That infant that was embraced by Jesus Christ, and proposed in its innocence as
a model of everything that was truly great, was in after
years the great Bishop of Antioch, who was devoured by
the wild beasts in the Coliseum.

We know nothing of the early life of St. Ignatius. He
appears on the page of history as the Bishop of Antioch.
St. Peter had first established his see in this city, which
was at that time one of the largest in the Roman Empire, and here ruled the infant Church of Christ for six
years. In the year 44 he came to Rome. In the very
heart and centre of Paganism he erected the indestructible throne of the Papacy, which is to last until the end of
time. St. Evodius succeeded him in the see of Antioch,
and after him came Ignatius. Our Saint was a disciple

* This circumstance, although mentioned by some ancient writers,
has no historical confirmation beyond a constant and pious tradition.
We do not give it as a certainty, but have introduced it as an interesting introduction to the Acts of this great martyr, which are undoubtedly genuine.

of the glorious Apostle himself and of St. John. He had learned from these able masters the sublime science of the love of God, which made him one of the pillars and ornaments of the early Church. After the Apostles themselves, he was one of the most remarkable men in the Church ; his contemporary and the fathers who lived in the three succeeding centuries mention his name with the greatest reverence. St. Polycarp and St. Chrysostom have made him the subject of their most eloquent panegyrics. After a life of more than fifty years in the episcopate of Antioch, the Almighty was pleased to call him to his crown, by a death that should be a glory and a model to the Church. The history of his labours and his virtues is not written, but all the particulars of his death were recorded by eye-witnesses, and distributed through the various churches ; hence his Acts are the most authentic in the history of the past. The original document, written in Greek, is still preserved, and was published by Ruinart in Paris in 1690.

The scene of his martyrdom opens, according to the best authority, in the year of our Lord 107. Trajan held the sceptre of the Cæsars and St. Evaristus sat in the chair of Peter. The storm that attacked the Church during the reign of Domitian was subsiding. Historians tell us that Trajan did not naturally love bloodshed, and had a nobler sentiment of humanity than any Emperor who had preceded him, but he was a coward and a slave to public opinion. He stifled his own feelings to pander to the brutal tastes of the mob ; to gain popularity, and under pretence of devotion to the gods of the Empire, he continued from time to time the horrible scenes of persecution against the unoffending Christians. St. Ignatius was one of his victims.

In the eighth year of his reign Trajan had gained a glorious victory over Decebalus, the king of the Dacians, and annexed all his territory to the Roman Empire. The following year he set out on an expedition against the Parthians and Armenians, the allies of the conquered Dacians. Having arrived at Antioch, he threatened with the severest penalties all who would not sacrifice to the gods. The labours and preaching of the venerable bishop of this city were so crowned with success, that the Church was flourishing, and was no longer a despicable community of a few individuals. The pagans saw the Christians increase around them with an evil eye, and availed themselves of the presence of the Emperor to call for their extermination. " The magnanimous champion of Jesus Christ," says the Acts of the Saint, "fearful lest his Church should become a scene of horrible slaughter, voluntarily gave himself into their hands, that they might satiate their fury on him, but save his flock."

He was immediately brought before the Emperor and accused of being the head and promoter of Christianity in the city. Trajan, assuming a haughty and contemptuous tone, addressed the aged bishop, who stood fearlessly before him, in these words : " Who are you, impious and evil spirit, that dare not only to transgress our orders, but exert yourself to bring others with you to a miserable end ? "

The Saint meekly replied, " Impious and wicked spirits belong to Hell, they have nothing to do with the Christians ; you cannot call me impious and wicked whilst I carry the true God in my heart ; the demons tremble at the very presence of the servants of the God whom we adore. I possess Jesus Christ, who is the universal and celestial Lord, and King of all things, by His grace I can trample on all the power of the infernal spirits."

"And who is he," asked Trajan, "who possesses and carries his God in his heart?"

"Every one who believes in Jesus Christ and serves him faithfully," replied the Saint.

"Do you not believe then that we also carry our immortal gods within us? Do you not see how they favour us with their aid, and what great and glorious victories we have gained over our enemies?"

"You are deceived," replied Ignatius, majestically, "in calling those things that you adore gods; they are accursed spirits, they are the demons of Hell; the true God is only one, and it was He that created the heavens, the earth, and the sea, and everything that exists; and one only is Jesus Christ, the only begotten Son of the most High, and Him I humbly pray to bring me one day to the possession of His everlasting kingdom."

"Who is this Jesus Christ thou hast named? Is it He who was put to death by Pontius Pilate?"

"It is of Him I speak," replied Ignatius; "He who was nailed to the cross, who destroyed my sin and the inventor of sin, and by His death places under the feet of those who devoutly carry Him in their hearts all the power and malice of the demon."

"Do you then carry within you this crucified Jesus?" asked the Emperor, with a sarcastic smile.

"It is so," answered Ignatius; "for He tells us in His holy Scripture, '*I will dwell in them, and walk among them.*'" (2 Cor. vi. 16.)

For a moment Trajan was silent, conflicting thoughts passing through his mind. He was urged by curiosity to hear more of the religion of the Christians, and, struck by the venerable appearance of the servant of Christ, he could have almost sent him back to his people with a slight reprimand , but the demon of pride and infidelity sprang up in his heart, and reminded him that any partiality towards the hated sect would be a sign of weakness, a loss of popularity, and a want of piety to the gods. Further hesitation would betray the false zeal of his hypocritical heart, and standing on his throne he pronounced this sentence against the holy bishop :—

"We command that Ignatius, who says he carries with him the crucified Jesus, be brought in chains to the great city of Rome, and amidst the games of the amphitheatre, as a pleasing spectacle to the Roman people, be made the food of wild beasts."

When Ignatius heard this sentence he threw himself on his knees, and, stretching his arms towards heaven, cried out in an ecstacy of joy : "O Lord, I thank Thee that Thou hast deigned to honour me with the most precious sign of Thy charity, and hast permitted that I should be chained for Thy love as was the Apostle Paul." He remained in the same position, his arms lifted up, his eyes fixed on heaven ; he seemed to catch a glimpse of those ineffable joys he so ardently desired, and which he was soon to enjoy. He was startled from his reverie by the rough grasp of one of the soldiers, who seized his feeble hands, and placed them in the manacles of a criminal ; his crime was, " he carried within him Jesus crucified." He made no resistance ; but full of joy, and praying for his poor flock, he moved away with his guards to

one of the cells of the public prisons, to wait his departure for Rome. A crowd of people had gathered around
the court-yard of the governor's palace, in which the
Emperor resided ; when they saw the venerable bishop
chained and condemned to death, a murmur of pity
broke from every lip ; amongst them there was many a
wet eye and a suppressed sob ; they were Christians who
saw their beloved bishop and father rudely dragged away
to an ignominious death.

St. John Chrysostom considers with much eloquence
and piety why Ignatius was taken to Rome for his execution. The martyrs were generally ordered from the tribunal to the scaffold, and even more frequently became
the victims of the impotent rage of the defeated tyrants,
and were tortured and put to death in the very court of
justice itself. But Trajan was not of a brutal disposition, and would have suspended the persecution against
the Christians, were it not that he feared the indignation
of the people. When he ordered the aged bishop to be
taken to Rome and exposed to the beasts before tens of
thousands of spectators, it was that the whole Empire
might praise his zeal in the service of the gods, and that
the people might be deterred from embracing Christianity
by witnessing the terrible fate of its leaders. But divine
Providence, which can draw good from the evil actions
of men, destined this journey for the edification of the
Church and for the salvation of innumerable souls. The
constancy, the piety and eloquence of the martyr on his
way to death, scattered far and wide the sublime truths
of the divine law ; he poured out from his own heart the
fire of charity which burned within it ; the Christians
were animated to new fervour wherever he went, and

many infidels recognised in the venerable prelate a reflection of the divinity of the gospel he preached, and, abjuring the false gods of paganism, became children of the Church.

During **his journey** to Rome, his happiness and peace of mind were beyond description. Every day his desire for martyrdom increased. He was taken from Antioch to Seleucia, and there embarked for Smyrna. They landed safely after a long and painful voyage, and St. Ignatius endeavoured immediately on landing to have an interview with the holy Bishop St. Polycarp, who was his fellow disciple under the great Apostle St. John. By the exertions of the Christians who accompanied him, who probably bribed his guards, this privilege was given him, and he spent some days with St. Polycarp.

The student of ecclesiastical history will find, perhaps, at first sight, some difficulty in bringing into the same page the remarkable names of John, Ignatius and Polycarp. St. John was the beloved disciple who leaned on the bosom of our Blessed Lord ; St. Ignatius was martyred in 107, and St. Polycarp is generally supposed to have suffered martyrdom towards the end of the year 169. St. Ignatius was bishop before St. Polycarp was born, yet they were both disciples of St. John. These facts are easily reconciled. St. John lived to the age of one hundred and one years. He consecrated Polycarp Bishop of Smyrna about the year 90 of our Lord, before he had the mysterious visions of the Apocalypse in the Isle of Patmos. He dwelt for some years in Asia Minor, and must have been frequently in the city of Antioch whilst Ignatius was its bishop. Moreover, in the first century, those who could consult with the Apostles by

letters, or by interview, on doubts that would arise connected with the discipline or teaching of the Church,
were called disciples of the Apostles. In either of those
cases, then, Ignatius and Polycarp were fellow-disciples of
St. John.

From the abode of St. Polycarp, St. Ignatius wrote
some beautiful and sublime letters, begging the Christians in the different churches, especially at Rome, not to
prevent his martyrdom. Not that the Christians were
accustomed to rescue the martyrs from the hands of the
tyrants by physical force, but Ignatius well knew they
had weapons more powerful than armies set in battle
array ; it was the invisible, the irresistible, the all-powerful weapon of prayer. By this the rage of the tyrants
was baffled, and death itself defied ; and Ignatius besought
them with all the fervour of his heart to let him have
his crown, and pass away now in his old age from a
weary life of trial to the ineffable bliss of the celestial
kingdom. The Christians consented, and the martyr
won his crown.

" I have at length gained from Almighty God," he
writes in his letter to the Romans, " that which I have
so long desired, to come and see you who are the true
servants of God ; and more than this I hope to gain
from His mercy. I come to you chained for the love of
Jesus Christ, and so chained, I hope to arrive soon in
your city to receive your embraces and my long-sighed-
for end. Things have commenced auspiciously, and I
sincerely pray to the Lord to remove every impediment
or delay to the glorious end He seems to have destined
for me ; but alas ! a terrible fear damps my hopes, and
you, my brethren, are the cause of this fear—I fear you"

charity will stand between me and my crown. **If you**
wish to prevent me from receiving the crown of martyrdom, it will be easy for you to do it, but sad and painful
to me will be that kindness which will deprive me of an
opportunity of thus laying down my life, which may never
come again.   In permitting me to go quietly to my end,
you aid me in that which is most dear to me ; but, if, in
your misguided charity, you wish to save me, you will
stand like the most cruel enemies in the very portals of
heaven, and fling me back into the deep and tempestuous
sea of life, to be tossed again on its billows of sorrow.
If you love me with true charity you will allow me to
mount the altar of sacrifice, you yourselves will gather
around and sing hymns of thanksgiving to the Eternal
Father, and to Jesus Christ, that He has brought, from
the East to the West, from Smyrna to Rome, the Bishop
of Antioch, to make him the confessor of His great name,
His victim and His holocaust. Oh ! how happy and
blessed our lot, to die to this world, to live eternally in
God !"

In another portion of his letter he uses these sublime
and touching words :—" Let me be the food of the
beasts ; let me come thus to the possession of God. I
am the wheat of Jesus Christ ; I must therefore be
ground and broken by the teeth of wild beasts, that I
may become His pure and spotless bread. Caress those
animals that will soon be my honoured sepulchre. I desire and pray God that they may not leave anything of
me on the earth, that, when my spirit will have flown to
eternal rest, my body may not be an inconvenience to
any one   Then shall I be a true disciple of Jesus Christ,
when the world can see no more of me. Oh ! pray to

Him that this may be the case, that I may be consumed by the beasts, and be the victim of His love. It is to solicit your aid that I write to you. I do not send you commandments and precepts as St. Peter and St. Paul. They were Apostles, I am but a miserable criminal; they were free, I am a worthless slave; but if I suffer martyrdom I shall be free. Now that I am in chains for Jesus Christ, I recognise the vanity of all worldly things, and have learned to despise them. In the journey I have made from Syria up to this, by land and by sea, by day and by night, I have fought and still fight with ten fierce leopards who press on me from every side; they are the ten soldiers who keep me in chains and are my guard, who even become worse and more cruel from the benefits they receive; but these things are to me lessons of the sublimest character, yet I am not perfect." (See Acta Sincera, Ruinart, vol. i. etc.)

Whilst the letters of St. Ignatius excite the deepest sentiments of devotion in the heart, they bring tears of pity to our eyes. That he suffered much in his long and tedious journey to Rome, there can be no doubt. That journey must have lasted more than six months; his letter from Smyrna is dated the 24th of August, and he was not martyred until the 20th of December. Having arrived in Greece, they crossed overland through Macedonia, and set sail again from Epidamus for Italy. They crossed the Adriatic and came round the southern shores of Italy to the western coast. Passing the city of Pozzuoli, the Saint was very anxious to land there in order to go to Rome by the same road that St. Paul had passed over many years before. But a fair wind sprung up and all sail was made for the port of Ostia. "For a day and

a night," say the Christians who accompanied St. Ignatius
and wrote the acts of his martyrdom, " we had this fa‑
vourable wind.   To us, indeed, it was a source of great
sorrow, because it would oblige us sooner to separate
from the company of this holy man, but to him it caused
greater joy and happiness, as it brought him nearer his
wished-for end."   They arrived at Ostia just before the
termination of the annual games of the kalends of Janu‑
ary.   These games were called *sigillaria*, and were the
most popular and best attended.   The soldiers, wishing
to arrive in Rome before their termination, hurried on
from Ostia without any delay.   Many of the Christians
heard of his arrival, and went to meet him somewhere
near the spot where now stands the superb Church of
St. Paul.   He was hailed with mingled sentiments of joy
and sorrow ; some were delighted to see the venerable
confessor of the Church and receive his last blessing, whilst
others wept aloud that so great a man was to be taken
from them by an ignominious death.   He consoled them
by the joy of his own heart, and begged of them again
not to prevent his sacrifice by their prayers.   Having
arrived near the gates, they all fell on their knees and
received his last solemn benediction.

It was the morning of the 20th of December, A.D. 107.
The sun had already risen high in the heavens, and was
pouring its golden flood of splendour over the city.   The
body of soldiers, and the aged bishop in chains, entered
that gate through which had often rolled the stream of
triumph, and through which had been dragged many a
poor captive from the East, to be slaughtered on the
Capitol as the climax to the glory of barbarian triumph.
Ignatius had longed from his childhood to see the great

metropolis of the Empire, and now it burst on him with dazzling splendour ; it was a forest of temples and tombs and mansions, of snowy whiteness that seemed imperishable. But his eyes were dimmed with tears ; his heart was crushed with sorrow at the awful darkness that brooded over the mighty city ; the splendour and magnificence of its monuments of marble and gold were but the decorations of a mighty tomb. With his arms folded on his breast he prayed that the sun of eternal justice might one day rise over that benighted city ; that the blood of so many martyrs spilt on its soil might fructify into saints, the fruit of that blood which was not shed in vain on Calvary. While Ignatius was rapt in prayer, a short turn in the road brought them in sight of the mighty Coliseum, the gorgeous remnant of the gilded palace of Nero, which crowned the Palatine, and in the distance the lofty temples of the Capitol ; at the same moment they heard the thunder of some thousands of voices, mingled with the roar of lions and wild beasts. Some gladiator had fallen in the amphitheatre, and the brutal populace were cheering the fatal stroke that felled him ; the animals were startled in their dungeons, and the earth seemed to tremble under the horrible chorus of men and beasts. A few moments and Ignatius had arrived under the massive walls of the Coliseum. But let us go before him and take our seat on one of its benches to witness the terrible scenes that are to follow.

We have but cast one glance around the great amphitheatre, and it would take volumes to describe all we see. Immensity and art, beauty and comfort, mingle with the rays of light that bring the first impressions—the motley thousands that fill every available seat, the rainbow of colours, softened by the purple awning, enriched by the brilliant mail of the soldiers, and everything that gold and silver can lend to dazzle the eye. The Emperor's throne is on a raised dais, with crimson canopy, and is gorgeously conspicuous. He himself is away in the hardships of the camp, but his place is filled by the prefect of the city, a worthless wretch, whose god is the will of his master. Around are the editors of the games, the Arval brothers, and the Vestal Virgins, and in the first cycle of the benches all the wealth and grandeur of the city ; the order above them are dressed in beautiful white mantles ; they are the equestrians. Then the immense platform, or gallery of the people, amongst whom are wooden benches for the women, obliged, by law, to be alone and removed at a distance through modesty from the scenes of nakedness and cruelty that pass in the arena. Among the people there were envoys from every country the Roman eagle flew over, and in every variety of colour and costume. There were the hardy race from the icy north, with snow-white features and brown locks, side by side with the swarthy Arab and curly-headed Ethiopian ; there is the inhabitant from the depths of Egypt, who drinks water from the cataracts of the Nile, beside the Sarmatian, who slakes his thirst with the blood of his horses.

> " Quæ tam seposita est, quæ gens tam barbara, Cæsar,
> Ex qua spectator non sit in urbe tua !"—MARTIAL.

The confusion of the voices is like the murmur of the mighty deep. It would seem as if the sovereignty of the people, banished from the Forum, had taken refuge in the amphitheatre, and vindicated with deafening shouts its liberty to insult and abuse. In vain do we imagine ourselves beings of the past, to paint the scenes of the Coliseum in the days of its glory ! We have nothing in the range of our experience to compare to its 100,000 spectators gloating on scenes of bloodshed and murder.

A rumour has passed through them that one of the heads of the Christians has been brought from Syria and condemned by orders of the Emperor to be exposed to the beasts ; a wild frenzy starts from bench to bench, the whole amphitheatre rises and sends forth a universal shout for the Christians to be cast to the lions. The loudest applause of our greatest theatres is but the gentle zephyr of a breeze compared to the yells of fiendish rage with which the Romans called for the extermination of the followers of the crucified Galilean ; like the thunder of the Alpine avalanche echoing through the hills, the mighty wave of human voices roll through the marble palaces and monuments of that city which was, in the grand designs of Providence, to become the very heart and centre of Christianity itself.

Suddenly a dead calm reigns over the living mass, every eye is fixed on the eastern gate ; the soldiers are leading a feeble old man into the arena ; his silvery locks have been whitened with the snows of over a hundred winters ; his gait is firm, his aspect cheerful ; never was a more venerable victim dragged across the sand of that blood-stained arena. He is conducted to the foot of the imperial gallery ; the president having heard of his long journey from the East, and struck with his venerable appearance and age, seemed to feel a sentiment of pity, and addressed him in these words :—" I wonder you are still alive after all the hunger and sufferings you have already endured ; now, at least consent to offer sacrifice to the gods, that you may be delivered from the dreadful death that threatens you, and save us from the sorrow of having to condemn you."

Ignatius, drawing himself up with majesty, and casting a look of scorn on the representative of the Emperor, said :—

" By your bland words you wish to deceive and destroy me. Know that this mortal life has no attraction for me ; I wish to go to Jesus, who is the bread of immortality and the drink of eternal life ; I live entirely for Him, and my soul yearns for Him. I despise all your torments, and I cast at your feet your proffered liberty."

The president, enraged at the bold language of the Saint, said in a haughty tone : " Since this old man is so proud and contemptuous, let him be bound, and let loose two lions to devour him."

Ignatius smiled with joy. Having made an act of thanksgiving in his heart and breathed an ejaculation for strength, he addressed the assembly in these words :— " Romans who witness my death, do not think I am condemned on account of any crime or bad action ; it is permitted that I may come to God, whom I desire with an insatiable desire ; I am His corn, and must be ground under the teeth of the beasts to become for Him a pure and white bread."* Having said this, he fell on his knees and crossed his arms on his breast, and with eyes raised to heaven he waited calmly and resignedly the moment that should set him free from the troubles of

---

* These words were used by him in one of his letters. but according to his Acts they were used a second time by the Saint in the Coliseum itself.

life and send his soul on its flight to eternity. Another moment and the small gates of the subterranean passages are opened and two lions bound into the arena.

A terrible silence reigns through the amphitheatre—they advance—but enough, let the imagination fill up the harrowing details. The martyr is gone to his crown. We can but transcribe the brief touching words of his Acts—" His prayer was heard, the lions left nothing but the harder bones of his body."

Night has crept over the city, and the Coliseum is as silent as a tomb. By the faint light of the moon we see three men stealing cautiously under the shadow of the mighty arches ; they move hurriedly across the arena. Near the centre, and on the side of the Emperor's seat, they go on their knees, and spreading a white napkin, they put into it some sand stained with blood and some bones ; they take them away with them and disappear in the darkness of the night. They are the Christians Carus, Philon and Agathophus, who have accompanied Ignatius from Antioch, and are securing the relics of their beloved bishop.

Near the Coliseum there was a house much venerated and frequented by the Christians. It was the house of Clement, one of the Flavian family, a disciple of St. Peter, and his third successor. Here they bring the relics of the martyr, and according to the custom, they made a temporary altar in one of the most spacious rooms and left the sacred deposit exposed the whole night amidst burning torches. The Christians, many of whom were present at his martyrdom in the amphitheatre, gathered from every side of the city and passed the night in prayer. During the night the Saint appeared to them. " A gentle sleep seemed to steal over us," say the above-named Christians, who wrote his Acts, "and suddenly we saw the holy martyr, who lovingly embraced us; he seemed to be praying for us, and was covered with sweat as if he had just come from a great battle, and then he passed into the glory of the Lord, where he will rest for ever. When we saw this consoling vision our joy was ineffable, and having awakened we spoke over the vision which we all saw, and gave thanks without end to God, the great Giver of all good gifts, who brought to eternal happiness the glorious martyr Ignatius." (Ruinart, vol. i. chap. 10. &c.)

His relics were brought from the house of Clement to Antioch, and were placed in a beautiful shrine outside the Porta Daphnitica; but in the arrangements of Providence they were brought back again to Rome, and laid in precisely the same spot where they were venerated by the Romans the night after his martyrdom. When Antioch fell into the power of the Saracens, under Heraclius, the Christians brought some of their most precious treasures to Rome, and amongst them the relics of St. Ignatius. A few years past, the learned and enterprising prior of the Irish Dominican Convent, now in care of the Church of St. Clement in Rome, was making excavations beneath the more modern church, probably of the twelfth century, and discovered not only the original basilica of the fourth century, but also the relics of St. Ignatius. They were carried in a gorgeous procession from the obscure sepulchre around the arena of the Coliseum, where, seventeen centuries before, he had suffered, and were reposited under the high altar of the Basilica.

There is a tradition, mentioned by Socrates in his

Ecclesiastical History, that it was St. Ignatius who first introduced the custom of alternating the Psalms in choir; —it is said he had a vision in which he saw the angels thus singing the praises of God, and that he introduced it into the Church; but the tradition seems not to have sufficient historic authority.

Although St. Ignatius is the first mentioned in history to have suffered in the Coliseum, yet we have every reason to believe that there were many both before and after his time that were exposed to wild beasts in the same place, of whom no records have reached us. The Coliseum was at the time of his death twenty-seven years in use; the persecution of the Christians was raging with more or less violence during this time, and we have records of Christians having been exposed to the wild beasts in other amphitheatres of the empire. We read of a St. Tecla under Nero, exposed in the amphitheatre of Lycaonia. She is supposed to have been the first female martyr. Accilio Glabrione, who was consul under Domitian (A.D. 93), had to fight with a lion in the amphitheatre of Albano. The servant of God bravely killed the lion, but was afterwards martyred by the tyrant in Rome. Although the authenticated list of those who suffered in the Coliseum of Rome is small, yet we have every reason to presume that thousands were sent to heaven of whom we have no record.* The last and terrible day, which will unveil for man the past and the future, will find among the peerless choirs of martyrs many a triumphant soul who fought in the arena of the Coliseum, whose names we have not been able to honour in the brief sketches of these pages.*

* St. Ignatius is commemorated in the Martyrology on the 1st February.

CHAPTER VII.

THE ROMAN GENERAL.

I.

BEFORE introducing to our reader the extraordinary records that have come down to us regarding the great St. Eustachius and his martyred family, it may be well to contemplate for a moment a grand and consoling feature of triumph which Almighty God vouchsafed to His servants in the days of persecution. Although hundreds of martyrs have gone to heaven from the arena of the Coliseum, yet few have been killed by the wild beasts. This strange fact is a beam of sunshine amid all its horrors of cruelty and bloodshed. He who knew how to change the ferocious nature of those animals which prowl through their native mountains and deserts in search of food, so that they became the protectors and even companions of His hermits and solitaries, made them (instead of being the instruments of the most awful death) the defenders of the chastity of His virgins, and the witnesses of the sanctity of His saints. The great Creator of all things intended the dumb animal to be the servant of man, and, with a few exceptions, He refused to allow it to be the executioner of the innocent.

One of the most consoling pages in the history of these terrible times, is the oft-repeated miracle of Daniel in the lion's den ; not, however, in the silence and darkness of the gloomy cavern into which the youthful prophet was cast, but under the noon-day sun, in the great amphitheatre of the capital of the world, and before 100,000 spectators. Miracles have been destined by God to be the handmaids of truth and the medium of conviction. In the visible interposition of His power in preserving His servants from the fury of the beasts in the Coliseum, He presented to the pagans of Rome an incontestable proof of the divinity of Christianity, and a mercy they knew not how to appreciate. If the old walls of the Coliseum could speak, they would tell us some consoling scenes of the triumph of the martyrs and their wonderful preservation. St. Eusebius, who was eye-witness to some of those terrible scenes, describes with eloquence and feeling how the furious wild beasts were unable to harm the Christians, and would turn on the pagans with destructive rage. " Sometimes," he says, " they rushed on the naked and defenceless champions of Christ, but checked as if by some divine power, they returned to their dens. This happened repeatedly, and excited the wonder of the spectators ; at their demand the first wild beast having been abashed, a second and third were sent against the same martyr, but to no effect.

" You would have been filled with admiration," he continues, " at the steadfast intrepidity of those holy champions, and at the immovable fortitude displayed by persons of the most tender years. You might have seen a youth who had not yet completed his twentieth year, standing motionless in the midst of the arena with his

hands stretched forth in the form of a cross, as he prayed
with fervour to God, and not shrinking from the spot
in which he stood, even when the bears and leopards,
breathing forth rage and death, almost touched his very
flesh with their jaws. Again, you might have seen others
thrown before an enraged bull, which attacked the pagans
who came near him, tossing them with his horns into the
air, and leaving them to be taken away half-dead. But
when with rage and bellowing he rushed upon the martyrs,
he could not approach them, but stamping on the ground
with his feet, tossing his horns to and fro, and breathing
forth rage and madness, by reason of his being irritated
by red-hot goads, the infuriated animal was, in despite of
all, held back by an invisible hand. Other wild animals
having been tried to no purpose, the Christians were at
last put to death by the sword, and their relics, instead
of being interred, were consigned to the surges of the
deep" (Eccles. Hist., book viii).

The scenes described by Eusebius were frequent all
over the Empire. Wherever the name of Christian was
found the persecution raged. It would seem that
Almighty God adopted this means to give His infant
Church publicity and a sign of the stamp of divinity.
Hence in His mercy and goodness He made the persecutions the fruitful harvest of souls. Baronius mentions
(An. 307) that in the persecution of Diocletian, when
the slain were counted by thousands daily, the holy Pope
Marcellus had to appoint twenty-five new parishes in the
city, to baptize and instruct the people who multiplied
beneath the sword. The hideous and execrable character
of the barbarities to which the Christians were subjected,
with a view not only to force them to apostatize, but to

deter others from embracing ,the proscribed belief, had
the very contrary effect. As to the martyrs, persons of
both sexes, and of the tenderest and most infirm age, not
only bore their sufferings with superhuman fortitude, but
hailed them with joy, as tending to the greater glory of
God and the conversion of the pagans. Their very persecutors were forced to applaud the heroism of those whom
they so bitterly hated, and to feel disgusted and afflicted
at the atrocities they were once so vociferous it demanding.

The reverence which the animals shewed the martyrs
is touchingly displayed in a scene we will quote from the
Acts of three martyrs of Tarsus, given in the Annals of
Baronius, under the year 290. They did not suffer in
the Coliseum at Rome, yet their martyrdom took place
in another amphitheatre of the Empire, and the records
of their death serve as a sample of what generally happened in those days of horror. These martyrs, Tharasius,
Probus and Andronicus, had been tortured in a most
cruel manner at Tarsus in Cilicia ; they were conveyed
thence to Mopsueste, and were again submitted to the
most horrible barbarities, and a third time they were
tormented at Anazobus ; so that being covered all over
with wounds, and their bones being broken and wrenched
from their sockets, when the Governor Maximus wished
to have them finally exposed in the amphitheatre to the
wild beasts, it became necessary for the soldiers to press
men from the streets in order carry thither their almost
lifeless bodies.

"When we beheld this," say the three devout Christians who wrote the Acts, and interred the relics of the
martyrs, "we turned away our faces and wept ; but when

their mangled frames were cast down from the men's shoulders on the arena, all the spectators were horrified at the sight, and began to murmur at the president for this order, and many of them rose up and left the theatre, expressing their dislike of this ferocious cruelty ; on which Maximus told his guards, who were near him, to take down the names of all who acted thus, that they might be afterwards brought to an account. He then commanded the wild beasts to be let loose on the martyrs and, when they would not touch them, he ordered the keepers to be scourged. A bear was then let out which had devoured three men that day ; but crouching at the feet of Andronicus, it began gently to lick his wounds, and continued thus mildly to demean itself, notwithstanding that the martyr plucked its hair and tried to irritate the animal. Then the president in a fury, ordered the lancers to run the bear through the body : and Terentianus (the editor of the games) dreading the president's anger, determined to make sure by letting in on the martyrs a lioness which had been sent from Antioch by Herod ; but the lioness, to the terror of the spectators, began bounding to the place where they were reclining ; and when at length she came to the martyrs, as it were kneeling down before Theracius, who dragged and annoyed her, she seemed, by cowering down submissively, to attest her veneration, conducting herself less like a lioness than a lamb. Shouts of admiration burst forth from the whole amphitheatre, overpowering Maximus with confusion ; who screamed to the keepers to infuriate and goad on the lioness. But the beast, with another bound, broke through the palisade back to her den, and the manager, Terentianus, was ordered to proceed, without further interlude, with the gladiators; directing them first to dispatch the martyrs with their swords."

There are on record one or two extraordinary facts where animals refused to touch slaves who were cast to them; but these were exceptional cases of recognition and gratitude—a trait of nobility often found more practised in the brute creation than in reasoning man. Our readers are familiar with the story of Androclus and the Lion.

Seneca also mentions in his 2nd Book, and 9th chap., *De Beneficiis,* that a lion would not touch one of his keepers who was condemned to be exposed to the wild beasts. In the life of St. Sabba, a fact similar to that of Androclus is mentioned, and the grateful lion lived at the monastery with his monks.

These facts, interesting and strange as they may be, were not miracles. There was no more of the supernatural about them than there is in the fidelity of a dog, who would lose his life in defence of even an unkind master. It is only the interposition of the divine power that can stay the enraged animals in their spring upon a defenceless victim, or make them crouch at the feet of persons they could never have seen before, whilst at the same moment the very men who fed them become victims of their rage. These wonders Almighty God worked in behalf of His servants; and the great St. Eustachius, with his family, is another instance of this wonderful preservation.

In the life of this great martyr we have one of the extraordinary sacred romances of the second century, a conversion more wonderful than St. Paul's, a life of trial and affliction like the patriarch Job, and a glorious death by martyrdom, the most terrible in the annals of persecution. No sensational novel of modern days ever detailed the imaginary vicissitudes of life more strange and more interesting than what we have here in reality, and handed down to us with all the authority of history. There are men accustomed to doubt of everything strange in history, and they smile with sarcasm at our credulity in believing some of the most sacred records of the past ; but we will first give an epitome of the extraordinary events of the life of St. Eustachius, and then show that we are recording a scene from the pages of ecclesiastical history, the truth of which there is no reason to doubt.

2.

The Romans were from the very birth of their dynasty a brave and warlike people ; the heroes who led them on to battle and conquest were men of consummate skill and intelligence, and are justly immortalised on the pages of history. In ancient times the art of warfare was rude and undeveloped, and the whole existence of an army depended upon the skill of its general. He had to direct where there was no order, no intelligence, no judgment, save that which flashed from his own superior mind ; he moved the mighty machine of brutal and living force as he willed ; the roughest and wildest spirits were cemented together into the irresistible phalanx by one element alone, it was confidence in their leader ; his skill was more to the army than numbers, position, or courage. Thus it was that Cæsar, one of the greatest warriors of the past, said he feared more the general without an army than an army without a general. Eustachius or Placidus

(by which name he was more generally known) was one
of the great generals of the Roman army at the commencement of the second century.

His influence and name were as great amongst the
soldiers on account of his virtues as for his triumphs and
military skill. He was admired by all for his mildness,
love of justice and charity. He was the father of his
soldiers, and treated them with leniency and justice ; virtues unknown to the barbarian soldier, but loved the
moment their benign influence was felt. He was
generous and charitable to the unfortunate, and although
a pagan, he was eminently chaste. True greatness is incompatible with the indulgence of the brutal propensities of
man. The virtues and exalted position of Placidus
rendered him the most conspicuous man of the time, like
the solitary star shining through the dark masses of cloud
on a stormy night. No wonder he was signalled out by
Providence as the object of special grace and the instrument of great wonders, for Almighty God loves virtue
and order, although practised by an infidel, and He never
fails to reward it in due time.

A soldier offered alms to St. Francis. In recompense
for this act of charity, Almighty God revealed to the Saint
the soldier's approaching death. Francis gave him the
prophetic warning, and prepared him for a happy end.
Perhaps it was charity, some silent act of benevolence in
the life of Placidus that brought down from heaven the
great grace of conversion and made him a vessel of election. This seems even more probable from the words
addressed to him by our Blessed Lord Himself, at the
moment of his call to Christianity.

One day Placidus went out according to his custom to

hunt. He proceeded with some officers of the cavalry division over which he had the command, to the brow of the Sabine hills, and fell in with a troop of beautiful stags. Amongst them there was one larger and more beautiful than the rest, and Placidus immediately pursued it with all the ardour of the chase. In the excitement, which huntsmen alone know, he was soon separated from his companions, and passed over hills and rapid rivers and on the edges of the most terrible precipices. He knew no danger; he was not accustomed to defeat; on he went, over mountains and through valleys, until he came up with his magnificent prize in a wild and lonely ravine, not far from the spot where now stands the picturesque village of Guadagnolo. This was the moment and place in which the providence of God destined to illumine the mind of the great general with the light of Christianity. The stag stood on the ledge of a rock just over him, and between its beautiful and branching horns there was a dazzling light; in the midst of an aureola of splendour he saw an image of the crucifixion. Struck with wonder and amazement, he heard a voice saying to him, "Placidus, why dost thou follow Me? Behold I have taken this form to speak to thee; I am the Christ, whom thou servest without knowing. Thy charity and deeds of benevolence to the poor have stood before Me, and have made Me follow thee with My mercy. The just man, dear to me on account of his works, must not serve devils and false gods, who cannot give life or reward."

Placidus dismounted in terror and confusion. He could not remove his eyes from the beautiful vision that shone more brilliantly than the sun between the horns of the stag, and although he heard he did not understand the voice that spoke to him. At length gaining courage, he cried out in an excited and tremulous tone—

" What voice is this ?   Who speaks ?—reveal Thyself that I may know Thee."

Again the heavenly sounds fell on his ears, and he heard these words :—

" I am Jesus Christ, who created heaven and earth out of nothing, who threw all matter into shape, and made the light spring from the chaos of darkness.   I am He who created the moon and the stars, and caused the day and the night ; who created man from the slime of the earth, and for his redemption appeared in human flesh, was crucified, and rose the third day from the dead.   Go, Placidus, to the city, and seek the chief pastor of the Christians and be baptized."

A ray—the last ray of the brilliant light which had dazzled his eyes, had entered his heart, and he understood all.   He remained for hours on his knees, in his first warm and grateful prayer to the true God.   When he awoke from his deep reverie of adoration and prayer, he found all was dark and silent.   The sun had disappeared behind the mountains, and his faithful and wearied horse and dog slept beside him.   He rose, like the Apostle Paul on the road to Damascus, with the courage of a lion, to proclaim the truth of the Christian religion, and the wonderful mercy of God.   He roused his horse, and returned slowly through the bleak passes of the mountain towards the city.

In the meantime, alarms for the safety of Placidus were increasing at his residence in the city.   He was gifted with a noble and amiable spouse ; their union had

been strengthened by long years of peace. In the simi
lar and moral tendencies of their virtuous souls their
home presented a scene of domestic bliss rarely found in
pagan circles. The unusual absence of the general gave
her immense anxiety; all night she sat up watching for
his well-known tread on the threshold, but the grey
dawn was breaking on the horizon and still no sign of
Placidus.

Starting from the momentary repose of a delusive dream
she found her slave awaiting returning consciousness to
deliver a message.

" Most noble lady, Rufus, who had accompanied the
general this morning to the hunt, has returned and prays
an audience."

" Quick, quick, Sylvia, bring him to my presence."

She sprung from her seat, met the veteran soldier at
the door, and trembling with excitement, she addressed
him :—

" Say Rufus, knowest thou aught of the general ; thou
wert ever a true soldier, and kept by his side in the
darkest hour, how came you separated from him ? Speak,
I fear thy silence."

The veteran leaned on his halbert ; after a moment's
pause, he spoke in a deep, solemn voice.

" Noble lady, I am loath to fan thy misgivings to
darker anticipations of ill, but we fear for the safety of the
general."

" I conjure thee, Rufus, tell me all," she cried frantically, " has his trusty steed fallen and cast him down the
awful precipice, have ravenous wolves fed on his mangled
corpse ? "

" None of these calamities, noble lady, have befallen

our brave commander," interrupted Rufus. "We believe
he has but lost his way in the mountains, and shall be
here before noon. This morning I was by his side when
a large stag started from the copse ; the dogs gave chase,
and our steeds flew over the rugged mountain side. The
stag was the largest ever seen in these hills, and the chase
the fleetest ever run. Our inferior horses soon fell back,
and we saw the glittering helmet of our commander rushing like a ball of fire through the woods ; he was soon
lost from our sight near the ravines of Marino. We
halted under the shade of a figtree, hoping each moment
to see our gallant commander return with the spoils of
his brilliant chase. The hours passed slowly on ; anxiously we listened for the echoes of his horn ; no dog returned with blood-stained mouth to tell of victory ; each
moment of anxiety made the hammer of life beat with a
heavier throb. We searched the mountain side, and
called louder and louder the name of our general ; there
was no response save the mournful echoes that broke the
stillness of the olive groves. Trembling for his safety, I
hurried back to headquarters to ask a detachment of
horse to scour the mountain. Behold, noble lady, how
I am separated from the general. The life stream of my
heart's blood is not dearer than the safety of thy lord—
Rufus shall serve under no other commander but Placidus."

Whilst Rufus was yet speaking a bustle was heard outside, and some excited slaves rushed in, announcing the
general had come. Wearied and covered with dust, he
dismounted. In silence he embraced his wife, and having made a sign for all to leave the room, he addressed
his spouse.

"Stella, I have a strange tale to tell thee. Thou knowest the terrors of war and the crash of empires have ever been my ambition and my joy. Heretofore I feared nothing, and I knew no God but my sword, but since last I sat under the shadow of these ancestral towers and the beams of thy loving smile, a change has come over my dream of ambition. Like the sunrise bursting from a thick bank of clouds, a vision from the invisible world passed before these eyes—a Deity greater than the gods of this Empire manifested Himself to me. Stella, I am a Christian!"

With many tears he described his vision—the miraculous interposition of Divine Providence to call him to the light of faith. That day he arranged his affairs to abandon himself generously to the call of divine grace. Messengers were secured to guide him to the Catacombs, where the Christian Bishop ruled the Church of God. In spite of the remonstrance of his timid spouse, who dreaded the awful consequences involved in the profession of Christianity in these days of terror, he hastened the first hour after nightfall to the crypts on the Salarian Way. Amongst the sublime lessons taught him in his vision on the mountains, was the folly of

"Leaving to the mercies of a moment
The vast concerns of an eternal scene.

It is probable that the terrible persecution of Domitian was but subsiding at this time. The Christians were obliged to seek shelter in the Catacombs from the fury of the storm; and whilst Almighty God permitted that they could not preach the law of grace and redemption publicly to the world, He supplied the ministry by the

interior operations of grace, and gave to His suffering
and banished Apostles the consolation of a more fruitful
harvest. If, as we imagine, the martyrdom of Eustachius did not take place until about sixteen years after
his baptism, the holy Pope Anacletus (according to
Baronius) must have been sitting in the chair of St. Peter.
Trajan was at this time Emperor, and of his character
and reign we have already spoken in the life of St.
Ignatius.

The holy Pope had taken shelter from the storms of
persecution in a crypt in the Catacombs of St. Priscilla on
the Via Salara. God vouchsafed to inform him in a
vision of the conversion of Placidus. He was kneeling
before a rude crucifix placed on the marble slab that covered a martyr's tomb, and constituted the altar of the
dread sacrifice of the mass. A small oil lamp cast a
dim flickering light on the sepulchral slabs ; the silence
of those corridors of the dead was only broken by the
gentle murmur of prayer, or the faint echo of the hammer and axe of the fossores. Suddenly the holy father
saw the walls of the archisolium* fade before his view,
and in their stead a charming scene in the Appenines.
On the ledge of a rock he saw a majestic stag bearing in
his horns, amidst a sun of light, the sacred sign of redemption, and prostrate in prayer lay the Roman General. The vision faded away again, and the holy father,
who understood the mercy God had shown to a noble
soul, remained long wrapt in grateful prayer.

When night had enveloped the city a mysterious party,
thickly veiled and concealed under large cloaks, passed

---

* Archisolium was the niche in which the holy sacrifice of the
mass was celebrated.

through the Salarian Gate. No questions were asked, for the military cloak of Placidus was a guarantee of protection. Two little children of three and five years held with childish fear their mother's garments, and their quick little steps pattered musically on the massive pavement with the solemn strides of their military father. In silence they passed through the stately villas that adorned either side of the road, and soon reached the gentle declivity known to the ancient Christians as the *Clivum Cumeris.* The guide brought them down through the long narrow corridors and introduced them to the presence of the holy pontiff, who rose and embraced Placidus as if he had known and loved him in years gone by.

We can imagine with what joy the holy Pope poured the regenerating waters of baptism on the heads of the Roman general and his family. It was on this occasion he received the name of Eustachius, his wife was called Theopista, and the two children Agapius and Theopiston, all names derived from the Greek, expressing favour with God. The parting words of the venerable Pontiff to the neophyte family were to take up their cross manfully, and bear it, like their crucified Master, to the very utmost of human endurance ; they were called to glorify the Church in the days of its trouble ; the Christian must be tried in the furnace of affliction ; "through many tribulations we must enter the kingdom of heaven." He seemed to speak with a prophetic spirit, for our next chapter will show Placidus proved and found faithful.

3.

God tries those whom He loves. Having chosen Placidus for a vessel of election, he proved him by a series of afflictions, which made the patience of this great servant shine more conspicuously than any other virtue. His biographers have compared him to the great patriarch Job. But that light which had entered his heart had taught him the secret value of trials and afflictions—that they were the choicest favours of Heaven.

He whom he had now taken for his Master and Model was ever in sorrow and affliction ; the disciple is not to be better than the Master. A life of ease, a bed of down, silken garments, and ornaments of jewels and gold, are not the armour which distinguishes the soldiers of a naked and crucified God. When we suffer the slight and passing sorrows of life, we should remember they are tokens of God's predilection and sanctification for our souls.

After his baptism and reception into the Church, Placidus returned to the memorable spot in the Sabine hills where he had beheld the wonderful vision, to give thanks to God.* The Most High was pleased with his prompt and generous response to the call of grace, and vouchsafed to give him again other and consoling visions, and to forewarn him of the trials that were awaiting him.

He had no sooner reached his home after his pilgrimage, than the terrible storm of sorrow broke on him and crushed him to the very earth. The sad tale of his trial would excite pity in the hardest heart. In a few days he lost all his horses and cattle, and every living thing about his house, even his servants and domestics were swept away by a virulent pestilence. The awful gloom that death had spread around, the stench of unburied car-

---

* A little chapel was built on this spot in the fourth century, and rebuilt in after ages. It still stands to commemorate the extraordinary conversion of Placidus.

cases, and the unhealthy state of the corrupted atmosphere, obliged him to leave his home for awhile; but this was a source of new affliction. During his absence thieves had entered his house and removed everything he had; he was reduced to absolute beggary. At this time the whole city was rejoicing and celebrating the triumph of the Roman arms over the Persians. Placidus could not join in these festivities, and, overcome with grief, disappointment and shame, he agreed with his wife to flee to some unknown country, where at least they could bear their sufferings and their poverty without the cruel taunts of proud and unfeeling friends.

They made their way to Ostia, and found a vessel about to start for Egypt. They had no money to pay for a passage; but the captain, who was a cruel and bad man, seeing the youth and beauty of Theopista, the wife of Placidus, felt an impure passion spring up in his heart, and thought, by permitting them on board, he might be able to gratify his wicked desires. But he knew nothing of the beauty, the sublimity, the inviolability of the virtue of chastity in the Christian female; and when he found himself treated with the scorn of indignant virtue at even the whispered suggestion of infidelity, he writhed under his disappointment, and meditated revenge. The devil suggested a plan. Arrived at the shores of Africa, the captain again demanded the fee for the passage, and intimated to Placidus, if it were not paid, he would keep Theopista as a hostage. He was sent on shore with his two helpless little children, and his beautiful and faithful spouse was forcibly detained on board; they immediately set sail for another port.

"Talk not of grief till thou hast seen the tears of warlike men."

Poor Placidus felt the warm tears steal down his cheek as he saw the sails of the little bark filled with a fair wind, and waft from him the greatest treasure he possessed in this world. He saw himself on a barren and inhospitable shore, exiled, poor, and widowed. Did his faithful legions but know of his sad fate, how their trusty swords would flash in vindication of their injured general! Looking on his little ones, robbed of their mother and protector, he drew them near his breaking heart, and pointing, with a trembling finger, to the white speck the little vessel had now made on the blue horizon, he cried out: "Your mother is given to a stranger."* Striking his forehead with his hand, he bent down and wept bitterly. There is no pang in human sorrow so galling as blighted affection, and this is more keenly felt when the object of our love is handed over, not to death, to bloodshed, or want, but to infamy and dishonour. Even the pagan parent would plunge the dagger into the heart of his Virginia rather than let her live in dishonour.

But "better is the patient man than the brave." The man who can bear trials and misfortune is greater than the hero of the battle-field. Remembering his promise to God in the ravine of the Apennines, he instantly checked his grief; and rising up, with an ejaculation like holy Job, and taking his two little children by the hand, he moved towards the interior of the country with a brave and resigned heart. But God had other trials to prove him yet more.

He had not gone far when he came up to a river much

---

* "Væ mihi et vobis quia mater vestra tradita est aliengna marito."—Acts. Bollandists, 20th Sept.

swollen by some late rains; it was fordable, but Placidus saw it would be dangerous to take his two children over together, so he determined to take one first then another. Leaving one on the bank, he entered into the stream with the youngest. He had scarcely reached the opposite bank when the screams of the other child attracted his attention, and looking round, he beheld an enormous lion taking the child in his mouth and carrying it away to devour it. Placidus left the infant in his arms on the bank, and, reckless of fear or danger, plunged once more into the rushing torrent. Grief must be terrible when it can make an unarmed man believe he can chase and fight the king of the forest. He was scarcely out of the stream when his other child was seized by a wolf.* This last afflicting sight paralysed his courage, and he could not move another step. He fell on his knees, and appealed to the great God who he knew had arranged all; with the fervour of his young faith and the natural sorrow of a bereaved father, he prayed for patience that no blasphemy might escape from his lips—that no misgivings might undermine the confidence of his worship He remained for some time in prayer, and felt the balm of heavenly consolation gradually creeping over his troubled soul. Faith alone can break the barriers of time and waft the soul in anticipation to the union that

---

* Portans vero unum infantem super humeras suos reliquit alterum circa ripam et transposuit infantem quem portaverit super terram et ibat ut reportaret et alterum. Cum venisset, autem, in medium fluminis, nimis autem fluvius dilatatus erat intendens vidit et ecce leo rapuit filium ejus et abiit in sylvas. Et desperans de eo, reversus est in patientia, spem habens alterius et cum abiret videt et ecce similiter lupus rapuit alterum filium ejus et abiit et non potuit eum consequi, etc. —Acts, *ib.*

immortality must bring. Placidus committed his family
to God, and knew they were happy; and as for himself,
he determined to bear manfully the few days of trouble
which Providence had yet allotted to him. He arose
once more from his prayer, strengthened and consoled,
more detached from every human consolation, more
united to God. He soon left the vicinity of these sad
and sorrowful scenes, and fled to another part of the
country.

We next find Placidus as a poor labourer in a farm
called Bardyssa. But this is the last part of the dark
night of his trial, the twilight that precedes a glorious
sunrise. Almighty God had now proved His servant by
the severest adversity which can befall a man: in a
whirlwind of affliction he blasted all his temporal comforts, his domestic felicity and paternal affection; and the
neophyte vessel of election was found faithful, and now
comes the sunshine of his crown. Some years had passed
since he lost his wife and children, and he had spent all
that time unknown, in labour, prayer, and solitude,
mounting higher and higher on the ladder of perfection,
and in union with God; but the time of his reward is at
hand, and by one grand stroke of that all-directing Providence which knows no chance, he was restored to all his
former honour and comfort. He was again placed at the
head of the Roman army, and restored to the embraces
of his wife and children, never more to be separated, not
even by death; for they were all brought together to the
endless joys of heaven by the glorious death of martyrdom. Let us follow the course of events that brought
about these great and consoling effects.

4.

The great capital of the Roman Empire is all in commotion. News has been brought from the East that the Persians and other nations had broken over the frontier and were devastating everything before them. Preparations were made for war on every side. Old veterans were brushing up their swords, and armies of young men were pouring in from the provinces. Fresh rumours of the advancing foe gave new impulse to the excitement, and an expedition of more than usual magnitude and importance was speedily equipped. The haughty soul of Trajan, who still sat on the throne of the Cæsars, could not brook for a moment the slightest infringement on the Empire, or the diminution of his own glory ; and he lost no time and spared no expense in striking quickly and heavily on the daring enemy. But to whom will he commit his warlike legions and the very fate of the Empire. There were none but young and inexperienced men around him. He thought of Placidus, the commander of his horse, who had carried the tide of victory, in years gone by, to the farthest limits of the Empire, the great general who was the idol of the army and the terror of every foe. Rumour said he was still alive, but retired from public life. Trajan seized the rumour with all the avidity of a man whose hopes had been blasted and was risking everything on a last chance. He offered immense rewards to any one who would discover the retreat of Placidus, and bring him once more at the head of the iron legions of the Empire. In burning anxiety and doubt he delayed the departure of the expedition from day to day, hoping that some tidings would come of his favourite general.* He was not disappointed. for Placidus was found.

Two veterans, named Antiochus and Achacius, started off towards the Egyptian provinces in search of Placidus. Their wanderings and unceasing inquiries seemed fruitless, when one morning, as they were giving up the search, and were about to return to the sea-shore, they came up to a beautiful and well-kept farm, and a short distance from them they beheld a poor labouring-man at work. They went towards him, and made inquiries if a Roman citizen named Placidus lived in those regions. The two soldiers thought they saw something in the old man which reminded them of their general; the nobility of his appearance and bearing seemed to tell of one who had seen better days; they even thought they saw in his worn features, browned by the sun and wrinkled by grief and care, some traces of the amiable features of Placidus; yet, it could not be; their general an exile, a labourer in this miserable place! What reverse of fortune could have reduced him to this change? how could so great a man be cast from such honour and glory to such obscurity and poverty? But he who stood before them in the tattered garments of a poor labourer had already recognized two of the bravest veterans of his legions.† The memory of the wars and battles and victories of other days flashed across his mind; the very places these two men took in the defeat of the enemy, their bravery by his side in the field of battle, and the

---

* Et misit per unamquamque civitatem et terram quæ erat sub imperio suo et requirerent eum.—*Ib.*

† A longe considerans ex consuetudine incessus eorum ne cognovit eos.—*Ib.*

scars they received in the bloody fight—all rushed on him in a moment, and roused every great and brave feeling of his soul.   He was about to run towards his companions in arms and embrace them, but prudence held him back, and by an act of self-control he suppressed his excited feeling. Drawing himself up majestically with a sigh, which alone told of the struggle that passed within, he asked: "Why seek you Placidus?"* Whilst Antiochus was recounting how the enemies of the Empire had once more declared war in the East, and the Emperor wished to intrust to that general alone the care of the expedition, and had sent the soldiers who served under him to all parts to seek him, Placidus could no longer contain his feelings, and opening the rude garment that covered the scars on his breast, he showed them to the astonished veterans, and told them that he was the general they sought.   Another moment and they were hanging round his neck, and shedding tears of joy.

Rome was once saved by the brave Cincinnatus taken from his plough to defend the threatened city.   Like the great chief of old, Placidus was received with the universal joy of the people—the confidence of the army was restored, and new life appeared in all the troops—battles and triumphs were anticipated and declared before they were fought or won. The Emperor was filled with delight; he embraced his former master of the horse, listened with interest to the history of the vicissitudes of his loss and grief; and, placing around his waist the golden belt of consular command, begged of him to draw

---

* Dic nobis si nosti hic peregrinum aliquem, nomine Placidam, etc. Quapropter eum quæritis, etc.—*Ib.*

his sword once more in the cause of the Empire.* The holy man had already recognized, in the humility and prayer of his heart, the great change that had come over his circumstances so strangely and so suddenly, as the disposition of the loving providence of God, and prepared, even in his old age, to mingle again in the din of arms and fatigues of war. During the days of his trial and resignation in the lonely vineyards of Egypt, the Divine Spirit had revealed to him that a day of restoration to all he had lost in this world would soon dawn on his gloomy path. Here is the first step in the fulfilment of his dream; let us see how God brought about the rest.

Whilst Placidus is casting his rough army into shape, and exercising his soldiers in the terrible science of bloodshed and war, we must retrace our steps for a moment, and take a glance at the poor, wretched Theopista, whom we left in the bark of the tyrant captain who cruelly tore her from her husband and her children.

Doubtless, in the sympathy of his pious heart, the reader has pitied her in her affliction, and hoped that some fortunate circumstance may have saved her. But has Almighty God ever abandoned His servants when the angelical virtue was threatened? Who more powerful before Him than the innocent defenceless female? In the history of the past no virtue has had more visible protection from Heaven than chastity; no vice has caused more terrible vengeance than impurity. The prayer of the virgin for the protection of her innocence not only pierced the clouds, but drew from them the electric bolt that struck the oppressor with judgment. Fear not for the virtuous and faithful Theopista; God is her shield,

---

* Et cingitur ut ante magister militum. —*Ib.*

And who can prevail against the Most High? The means He adopted to protect His servant were silent, consoling, and merciful.* He did not strike the impious captain with a sudden and terrible blow of merited retribution, but he breathed on his heart a sentiment of tenderness and pity that made him blush for his cruelty and impiety towards the young mother. Scarcely had the fair wind wafted the little ship out of sight of Theopista's husband and children, than the sobs which grief was pressing from her breaking heart struck a fibre of pity in the feelings of the pagan captain. At the same moment Almighty God removed the stimulus of the flesh, and made him love and admire in his captive a virtue he never knew before. The virtuous soul is like the fruit-tree in blossom, that gives fragrance to every breeze, and spreads a delicious odour on the atmosphere around. The sublimity of virtue that shone in the fidelity of the Christian matron, the patience and forgiveness of that suffering child of misfortune, so completely won the pagan, that, from being her enemy and oppressor, he became her protector and guardian. He landed Theopista at the next port he touched at, and gave her money and goods to maintain her for some time. She, too, had her share of trial, and fifteen long years of suffering and exile proved her worthy of the joy and crown that were awaiting her.

Everything was ready, and the expedition started for the East. The spirit of joy and bravery which animated the soldiers was the harbinger of the greatest triumphs. They poured in thousands through the eastern gates of the city; and, whilst the morning sun was reflected fr∙·u

* Domini vero gratia obumbravit mulierum, etc.—*Ib.*

their burnished battle-axes and spears, the tombs of their mighty dead, which lined the Appian Way, were made to echo once more with the war-songs of the irresistible legions of the Empire. The octogenarian leader—the Christian Placidus—brought up the rear of the march, and was drawn in a chariot by two beautiful Arab horses.

We need not tarry long over the oft-told tale of Roman triumph. The legions poured like Alpine avalanches into the country of the enemy, crushing in their course everything that was opposed to them. Not only were the rebellious subjects reduced to submission, but the conquering eagle spread its wings over new dominions, and new provinces were added to the boundless territory of the Cæsars.

The meekness and skill of Placidus knew how to turn everything to profit; few of his conquests were purchased with unnecessary bloodshed and carnage. He pardoned freely, and never retributed the resistance of a brave people by the retaliation so terrible in the annals of pagan warfare.

Every army has its heroes. The campaign of Placidus was nearly at an end before its real soldiers were known. Where the conquest was easy all were brave, but a moment of danger and trial came, and the laurels of fame fell to those who won them. The army was surprised in an ambuscade, but was saved by the prompt action of two youths belonging to the Numidian corps. They were two brave young men who had met each other for the first time in the ranks and became friends. They were strolling outside of the camp when the cry "To arms" was heard. They rushed like startled lions to the front and cheered on their companions ; they fought together against fearful odds, but their battle-axes were wielded rapidly and skilfully, and dealt destruction on every side. With a few brave companions they with-stood the progress of the enemy until their own army had come up to the rescue ; such brave and unexpected resistance sent a panic through the enemy, and they fled with terrible massacre ; some thousands were slain, and the army of opposition was so completely destroyed that it never stood in the field of battle again.

The general had seen what had passed, and when the battle was over, he sent for the young heroes who had saved the army, raised them to the rank of captain, and bestowed on them the honour of his intimate friendship.

The army had passed on from triumph to triumph, and we must now open the scene of our tale on a wild plain on the coast of Arabia, where they were encamped before the return to the great capital. There were a few little huts of fishermen on the sea-shore, and here and there, along the banks of a fertile stream, some pretty little houses surrounded by gardens and vineyards. Amongst them there was one more beautiful than the rest, and running on a gentle slope towards the river. It belonged to a poor widow, who lived by the fruits of her little gar-den and the labour of her own hands. Here the old gene-ral, wearied and fatigued from the hardships and priva-tions of the campaign, pitched his tent, and arranged to remain some time before undertaking the fatiguing jour-ney of return. Near him he had the two young captains, whom he had made his confidants, and treated as if they were his adopted children. Doubtless the old man saw in the youth and beauty of the young men what his own

sons would have been if they had been spared to him
Some invisible attraction made him love them tenderly,
and he could not bear them to be absent from his side.
They, too, grew in the deepest friendship with each other;
a similarity of feeling and disposition, a secret love for
virtue, and a certain trait of nobility in every thought and
action, not only knit them together in inseparable bonds
of harmony, but enhanced them in the love and esteem of
all who knew them.

One day, as was their custom, they strolled together
along the banks of the little stream. Everything was
fresh and beautiful around them; the birds sang in the
trees; and the flowers, that grew in great abundance in
the vicinity of the stream, spread a thousand odours on
the gentle breeze that rippled the waters. The young
soldiers sat down under the shade of a fig-tree and entered
into an animated conversation.* The elder was a tall,
handsome young man of about eighteen years, and seemed
about two years older than his companion. He was of a
gentle, silent disposition, and often seemed rapt in
thought as if some cloud hung over him. His younger
companion noticed this to be particularly the case on the
day in question, and during their conversation he would
frequently pause and look abstractedly on the little stream,
which was rapidly rising and swelling up to its banks
from a heavy shower which had fallen in the neighbouring mountains. In that familiarity which their tried
friendship permitted, he affectionately asked his companion the cause of his trouble.

"It is now some time since you and I first met," we can

* Est facto meridie, sedentes exponebant sibi invicens de infantia
sua, etc.--*Ib.*

imagine the young officer to have said, "and **I have all** along thought you had some secrets locked up in **your** heart which it would console and interest me to hear. Do **t**ell me your history, that I may participate in **your** sorrow. You know I am your friend."

The other looking on him with kindness, and **as if** reading his countenance to see if he were in earnest, grasped his hand, and turning his eyes towards **heaven,** gave a sigh ; then drawing his companion nearer **to him,** he said, in an excited manner : "Yes, I will tell **you a** strange story, but you must not betray my secret.   I am a Roman citizen and a Christian."

The young man started up as if a clap of thunder had burst over him, but the other, preventing him from saying a word, and calling him by his name, continued in **a** kind and majestic tone : "Although I enlisted in the Roman army in the same province as yourself, I was not born there.   My father was a Roman general and a man of great esteem.   I remember when I was but five years of age, one day he went to hunt, as was his custom, and did not return until an early hour the next morning.   He came home in an excited state, and said things that made my mother weep.   The following night, when all was dark and still; they took me and my little brother, who was only three years old, to a dark cave in the earth, and after we had passed some winding and gloomy corridors, we entered a little room beautifully lit up.   There was an aged man sitting on a stone chair, and he wore a beautiful stole round his neck.   The walls of the little room were covered with beautiful paintings of men in rich garments of fishes and lambs, and I remember the picture of a man nailed to a cross.   The venerable old man spoke to my

ather and mother for a long time. I do not remember all
he said, but he spoke of the true God whom the pagans
did not know, and all the good things God had done for man
—how He loved him, how He died for him, how He promised him eternal happiness hereafter. My parents were
very much affected, and I remember my father wept
again, as if he had done something wrong. Then the
aged man poured water on our heads, and called us all by
different names ; my name was Agapius. I knew by all
this that I was made a Christian and a child of the great
God he spoke of. After this many prayers were said, and
when leaving that strange place, my father and mother
seemed very much rejoiced.

" Soon after my father suffered the loss of all his property ; his cattle and horses died of a terrible disease ;
even our slaves and servants also died ; and we left the
house and went to a vineyard outside the Nomentan Gate.
While away, my father was robbed of all he had, and was
reduced to poverty. Then one night, taking my brother
and myself and mother, he led us to the sea-shore, and
we got into a ship, and were fifteen days on the rough
sea. When we came to land, my father and my little
brother and myself were sent on shore, but not my
mother, and the little ship went away with her immediately. Oh ! I shall never forget the grief of my poor
father on that occasion."

He buried his face in his hands and wept for some
time, and a tear stole down the cheek of his young companion. Looking up again, he continued his tale amidst
tears and deep sighs.

" Then rising suddenly, he took my little brother in
his arms and me by the hand, and we went into the

country. We came to a river that was running **very** rapidly, and as my father could not take us both over together, he bade me remain on the bank whilst he took my little brother over first, promising to come back for me. But while my father was crossing the stream—oh ! I shall never forget it !—a terrible lion came out of the woods and seized me. A shudder passed over his companion ; he seemed all excitement, and cried out—

"How strange ! But tell me how you were saved." He seemed much agitated ; some words had come to his lips, but he repressed them and listened with motionless anxiety to the remainder of his companion's story.

" Well," continued the young captain, " I screamed for help, but it was too late. The lion caught me in his mouth—I have still the marks of his teeth on my body —and carried me towards the forest. Fortunately there were some shepherds passing by, and when they saw me they set their dogs after the lion. One of the dogs caught hold of me and was pulling me from him, when the lion let me fall and seized the dog, and went away with it. The shepherds carried me to their little house, and a good woman put me to bed and took care of me. I recovered, and grew up in that house; but I never saw my father or my brother since then." Seizing his companion by the arm, and his eyes suffused with tears, he said: " Wonder not, my friend, that I am sad ; this stream, those trees, and this wild plain in which we are encamped, remind me of those terrible scenes of my youth. Can I ever forget that day on which I lost father, mother, brother, all ? " He could say no more, but buried his face in his hands again and wept bitterly.

He remarked, during the recital of his story, that his

young friend was getting more and more excited; and from time to time gave expression to incoherent sentences and ejaculations of surprise. "Strange! It must be! Oh, joy!" was all the young man could say. After a moment's silence, he cried out, with energy and excitement: "Agapius, I believe I am thy brother."*

The other started. "How! speak! say why thou thinkest so—or dost thou trifle with my sorrow?"

The young man replied quickly, and with agitation: "I too lost my parents in my youth. The people who brought me up told me they saved me from a wolf near the stream of Chobar; that I was of a noble Roman family, for I had around my neck this golden ornament."

Whilst he was putting his hand into his breast to look for the ornament, the other sprang to his feet in excitement, and cried out: "Show it! has it got on it the name of *Theophistus* and the *Ides of March?*"—"Yes? here it is." Agapius, recognising the amulet his mother had put round his neck on the morning after their baptism, caught the young man in his arms, and cried out: "My brother, my brother!"

Further explanations placed the fact beyond doubt, and the two brothers remained for hours together, every now and then embracing each other with tears of affection. They told each other all the particulars of their after-lives. Theophistus was saved from the wolf by some ploughmen, who saw the child in its mouth and, rescuing him, brought him up as one of their own children. They were reared some miles apart from each other and did not know it; but God, whose ways are inscrutable, brought them together in the Roman army.

* Per Deum Christianorum, ut audio frater tuus sum ego!

that he might restore them to their lost father and mother, as the reward of their patience and virtue. The joy of the young men was to be increased by another discovery more consoling and more extraordinary. The reader knows it already ; the general is their father.

When the excitement of the first moments of recognition had subsided, they agreed to repair to their general to inform him of the extraordinary discovery they had made. They found the old man in his tent, sitting at a rude table ; his face was covered with his hands, and he seemed rapt in meditation and thought.

The eldest rushed towards him and told him he had strange and joyful glad news to tell him. The old man raised his head ; his eyes were moist, and a cloud of gloom mantled his brow. Looking with a parental smile on the cheerful youth, he said to him—

"Speak, then, my child, for thy joy shall be mine ; the happiness of others makes us forget our own sorrows, thy words will come like sunshine breaking through the gloom of my heart. Alas ! this day has sad reminiscences for me. It is the anniversary of a series of misfortunes which deprived me of my wife and my children."

He paused for a moment, and raising his eyes, dimmed with the filling tears, towards heaven, exclaimed: "But it was the will of Him who reigns above ; He gave, and He took away : blessed be His holy name !"

The young captain was astonished. It was the first time his old general prayed to the true God before him. A thousand thoughts rushed into his mind ; he knew not whether he should first declare that he too was a Christian, or relate the discovery of his brother. He loved the old man as a father, and his softened heart melted once more to see his veteran chief in sorrow. A few hasty explanations sufficed to reveal the truth that he was talking to his own father. Another moment, and the young men were hanging round his neck, and the old chief was pressing his brave sons to his heart. Let the imagination paint the picture that no pen can draw. One moment of joy like this outweighs years of the darkest trial. But the dark and stormy night of Placidus' trial is passing away, and the brilliant sunshine of reward is rising over him—a sunshine which, during the rest of his life, will be clouded but for a moment, to usher in the dazzling brightness of eternal, unchangeable bliss —that moment will be death by martyrdom for the faith of Christ.

5.

Whilst the events we have recorded were taking place, there was a great commotion in the camp. A courier had arrived in great haste. He announced the death of Trajan in Selinonte (a town of Cilicia), and the election of Adrian by the army. This election had been confirmed by the Senate, and the army of Placidus was ordered to return immediately to join in the triumph accorded by universal acclamation to the ashes of the deceased Emperor. The soldiers under Placidus had been nearly two years absent, and were wearied with the fatigues and privations of war. They hailed with delight the news of their return. Deafening shouts that announced the glad tidings had reached the tent of Placidus before the courier could be brought before him. The messenger, foot-sore and covered with dust, handed the general a parchment roll, on which was written—

"It has pleased the gods to raise us to the throne of the Empire.
We decree a triumph for the army of Placidus, and command our
brave general to return forthwith to the Capital.

"ADRIAN."

The general held the parchment for a few moments in
his hands ; he became abstracted ; raising his eyes slowly
towards heaven, he said : "Thou art setting, thou brilliant
sun of my hopes—those grand destinies foreshadowed in
prophetic whispers are fast gliding into realities. Aye !
to Rome !—to triumph !—to martyrdom ! "

He then gave orders to strike the tents and prepare for
general march on the morrow. Dismissing all from his
tent he remained alone to commune with God in gratitude for the felicity of that day. He paced his tent
rapidly ; the vision of his future martyrdom passed before
him. We hear, in fancy, the majestic tones of his fervent soliloquy :—

"Aye ! to triumph !—to step from the golden chariot
to the tomb—to climb the glittering heights of the
Capitol amid the shouts that rend the heavens with
blasphemies against my God—to kindle the fires of impure sacrifice to the demons of idolatry ! Rather shall
Placidus be cast on the burning pile, and be himself the
victim.

"In the dreams of young and misguided ambition I
coveted the honour now within my grasp, but in the
light of the higher destiny that follows, 'tis but a beautiful shadow that floats before the infatuated fancy, like
gilded bubbles on the stream, that break into thin air
when we attempt to seize them.

"My children ! will ye drink of my cup ? Will you
ride in the same chariot, and drink a chalice of earthly

joy till you reach the atrium of the temple of Jupiter ;
then be bound to the same stake ; the flames of our
funeral pyre shall send our freed spirits to the land of
eternal triumph, where the shout of real joy shall ring
out the congratulation of Heaven's choirs for our Christian victory !

" Poor Theopista ! thy noble soul is still wanting to
complete the holocaust ! Art thou pining away in some
villain's home ?

> " ' Perchance you died in youth ; it may be bow'd
> With woes far heavier than the ponderous tomb,
> That weigh'd upon thy gentle dust—a cloud
> Might gather o'er thy beauty, and a gloom
> In thy dark eye, prophetic of the doom
> Heaven gives its favourites—early death.' "

He was interrupted by a servant announcing that the
poor woman who owned the garden on which his tent was
pitched, wished to see him. Placidus was not a proud,
austere man, who left the business of the poor to be
transacted by a cruel and heartless official. He was
accessible to the roughest soldier in his camp, as well as
to the highest of his officers. By a sign of his hand, he
signified assent to have her brought before him.

She seemed advanced in years, and the victim of much
sorrow. Her attenuated frame, and the meanness of her
dress, told of want and poverty ; yet her bearing was
noble. Her eyes were bloodshot, and showed signs
of much weeping ; tears had traced their own channels
down her cheeks ; but her countenance still, in all its
tender expression of care and grief, showed evident traces
of beauty, nobility, and innocence. Having entered the
tent, she fell on her knees before Placidus, and said :—

" Great chief and leader of the armies of Rome ! I beseech thee to commiserate the sorrows of a poor unfortu-nate woman. I am a Roman citizen. Some years ago I was separated from my husband and children, and brought here by force for unlawful purposes; but I pledge my word, before thee and before Heaven, I never lost my fidelity to my husband and my children. I am here an exile, in sorrow and misery. I ask thee, by the love thou bearest to thy own spouse and children, to take me back to Rome—to my friends—to my——"*

She could say no more. In her excitement she sprang to her feet—she clasped her hands—and looking fixedly at Placidus, she recognized her husband. At the moment she appealed to him for the love he bore his spouse, the aged general raised his hand to his forehead to hide the ever ready tell-tale tear of his afflicted heart. In turning his head he exposed a large scar on the back of his ear; the quick eye of the matron recognized the wound her husband received in the Judaic wars, and one steady look at the worn and changed features of Placidus convinced her. She rushed towards him, and with sobs that choked every word :

" Tell me, I beseech thee, art thou Placidus—the mas-ter of the Roman horse—whom the true God spoke to in the mountains of Italy—who was baptized—called Eustachius—lost his wife——"

" Yes ! yes ! " interrupted Placidus. " Knowest thou of her ? Speak !—does she still live ? "

The poor creature made an effort to throw herself into

* Deprecor te Domine ego de terra Romanorum sum et captiva adducta huc, etc., et usque hodie servavit Dominus castitatem meam. —*Ib.*

his arms, but, overcome by emotion, fell to the ground, crying out, "I am Theopista!"*

The weakened frame of Theopista could not bear the shock of the sudden discovery. When motion returned, she was still delirious, and seemed like one who saw a beautiful dream passing before her. At times her reason returned, and she would ask, " Is it true? Does the evil spirit create phantasms to deceive me ? Oh ; how good is God ! "

Another hour, and the little tent of Placidus was the scene of joy seldom felt on this side of the grave. Four widowed and bleeding hearts were healed ; the husband and the spouse, the parents and the children, after years of separation and trial, were thrown together and recognised in the space of a few hours. Almighty God had never abandoned them for a moment from the time He decreed the vicissitudes which were to try them ; finding them faithful, He knew how to reward. The flood of joy which He pours on the faithful hearts of His servants is but as a stray rivulet of the mighty stream of ineffable delight that inundates the souls of the beatified. If Christians would remember that God watches with a special providence over the afflicted—that the troubles and trials of life are often directly sent by Him—how many a pang would lose its sting, how many a bitter loss and disappointment would become, not only supportable, but the source of interior peace ! The troubled soul humbly kneeling before the crucifix is the type of the true Christian. If the strange history of Placidus should fall into the hands of any one in trouble, let him, like that brave

* Et surgens ruit in amplexus, etc.

and generous soul, await the dispositions of Providence without blasphemy, suppressing even a reproachful thought towards God, and every murmur of impatience ; as sure as the hour of trial and affliction is long and dark, so shall the hour of reward come quickly, brilliantly, and unclouded.

Greater joy than the soul can long bear in its earthly tenement is prepared by God for this happy family. Their union here is to last but for a few weeks. When the camp was struck, and the army on the march to Rome Placidus knew, by inspiration, that he was going to the last and most severe struggle which God had in store for him—his triumph in death over self, the world, and the powers of darkness. He gave all his time to prayer and the instruction of his sons in the sublime morality and doctrine of the Christian faith. He asked a favour from God, which was granted—that as He had deigned, in his mercy, to bring him again to the embraces of his family, the happiness of their union might never again be clouded by separation ; that if the testimony of his blood were demanded for the defence of the faith and the glory of the Church, his spouse and children might partake in the same last crowning favour of the Divine mercy.

Whilst the legions are on their march from the East, let us go before them to the great capital, and prepare our readers for scenes that are about to follow. The beautiful and touching history of the noble Roman general is to have a tragic termination—one of the brightest in the pages of the Church, but one of the darkest in the long annals of pagan ingratitude and cruelty.

6.

The weak and superstitious Adrian was sitting on the throne of the Cæsars. He was a man of little ability, but of a low, deceitful and cruel disposition. He was capable of all the horrors which disgraced the reigns of some of his predecessors; but the public opinion was sick of whole-sale bloodshed, and the awful deaths that closed the in famous career of those tyrants made the worthless Adrian tremble, and checked the brutal propensities of his impious heart. He was disposed to put in force the laws of persecution against the Christians, and stain again the great centres of public execution with the blood of hundreds of innocent subjects; but the example of his predecessor seemed to be his guiding star. Under Trajan the Empire was prosperous, and the enemies of the East were conquered, and new provinces were added to its boundaries; yet, in his hypocritical policy of conciliation, men of note among the Christians were publicly executed; their blood was intended to be the pledge of his piety to the demons of public worship. In the first part of his reign, he placed a superstitious confidence in the gods; and the highest exercise of pagan piety was the condem- nation of the contemners of those gods. These of neces- sity were the Christians; but fear, imbecility, and a ridiculous piety seemed to clash in his character, and, like negatives, destroyed each other. The consequence was, that the Christians in his reign enjoyed a tolerable peace.

Yet martyrdoms occasionally took place. St. Symph- orosa suffered under Adrian; and herself and seven children commemorate in ecclesiastical history the com- pletion of his immense villa near Tivoli · the ivy-clad

walls of its surviving ruins are now the favourite stop-
ping-place for excursionists to the ancient Tibur. Amongst
others, we find on the list of martyrs during this reign
the servant-girl of the celebrated Tertullian, named Mary ;
SS. Alexander and Sixtus, Popes ; St. Denis the Areo-
pagite, and many more, of whom not the least remarkable
was the hero of our present notice, and his family. All
agree that the persecution of this time was irregular, and
depended in a great measure on the fickle, impetuous,
and cruel disposition of the Emperor. It was never
during his reign completely extinct, but, like living embers
occasionally burst into a flame, and then died away
again.

Adrian had a great taste for architecture, and the repose which the Empire enjoyed during his reign allowed
him to turn his attention to this favourite pursuit. Some
of the most wonderful ruins of antiquity, which have
withstood the shock of centuries, bear the stamp of his
pride and prodigality. The Tiber, the Danube, the
Rhine, and the Tyne in England still bear on their banks
the mouldering ruins of bridges and tombs, castles and
fortifications, which look down on the mighty rivers that
flow as regularly and majestically as time itself, ever
young in the vitality of nature. Of all the Roman Emperors, the name of Adrian is the most familiar to the
pilgrim who visits the Eternal City. The stranger, after
arriving in Rome, on his way to the Church of St. Peter,
the greatest wonder of modern art, crosses the bridge and
passes under the Castle of St. Angelo ; these are the two
first monuments of antiquity which catch his eye—they
are the works of Adrian. Centuries of war and devastation, and the rains and storms of nearly seventeen hun-

dred winters, have shorn the mighty mausoleum of its ornaments, but its massive, indestructible walls still serve as a fortress, a prison, and a castle, and, like a rock of nature, it looks down on passing generations : for centuries yet to come it will stand on the banks of the Tiber as a landmark by the stream of time !

> "Turn to the mole which Adrian reared on high,
> Imperial mimic of old Egypt's piles,
> Colossal copyist of deformity ;
> Whose travelled phantasy from the far Nile's
> Enormous model doomed the artist's toils
> To build for giants, and for his vain earth,
> His shrunken ashes, raise this dome ! How smiles
> The gazer's eye with philosophic mirth,
> To view the huge design that sprung from such a birth !"
>   —CHILDE HAROLD.

Over the venerable pile now stands the rainbow of the modern covenant—the angel of God sheathing the fiery sword of justice. It was erected to commemorate a vision given to one of the greatest of the Popes—a meet symbol of the most remarkable epoch of Roman history, portraying not only the termination of a momentary scourge, but the close of the bloody days of persecution, and the commencement of the peaceful reign of the Pontificate for the universal benefit of mankind.

At the time we write, the sun of Rome's golden age had passed the meridian, and was in the second or third hour of its decline. Yet the splendour and magnificence of the city was beyond description. The tract of level ground that expanded like an arena from the Capitol, Quirinal, and Pincian Hills to the Tiber, was adorned in its entire extent with theatres, hippodromes, places for various warlike spectacles and games, with temples, surrounded with groves of evergreens, and interwoven one

with the other by shady walks and velvet lawns ; **while**
monuments and trophies of snowy whiteness and of **every**
order lined the river side to the water's edge.   The history of the city's triumphs, written in marble and travertine, from the column of Duilius, down to the magnificent
column which had just been finished in memory of the
deceased Emperor Trajan, presented a scene so fascinating, that Strabo, in his description, says it was almost
impossible to tear one's eyes from beholding it.   But
towering above all, like an alp of marble, rose the mausoleum or tomb of Augustus Cæsar, where the arms **of**
the Julian family and of many Emperors were placed.
When any of them were to be deified or added to the
number of the gods (a ceremony which Adrian performed
for Trajan), his body was carried with great pomp and
ceremony on a couch of gold, and placed on the summit
of a pile of odoriferous wood ; as the flame began to ascend towards the corpse, an eagle, fastened there for the
purpose, was permitted to take wing, that it might be regarded by the applauding thousands as the genius **or**
"mens divinior" of the Emperor soaring aloft to the
skies.   Whilst we smile with the sarcasm of philosophy
and the knowledge of faith, we are struck with the poetry
and skill of the benighted past.

A triumph was accorded to Trajan for his many victories.   He was a warlike man, and went himself at the
head of his legions to the field of battle.   It was on his
way to Armenia he condemned the holy Bishop of Antioch ;
and his choice of Placidus to conduct the legions to the
Syrian frontier was because he was threatened with revolution in the more important territory of Parthia.   He
had, therefore, resolved, in case war was declared, to go

himself in person to subdue the enemies of this part of
the Empire. It happened as he had anticipated, and he
went on the expedition, but he never returned to Rome.
He died during the campaign. Nevertheless, a triumph
was decreed to him; and Adrian, who was one of his
commanding officers, being declared by the soldiers his
successor, wrote to the Senate to intimate that he would
in his own person represent the deceased conqueror.

A triumph was the highest ambition of the Romans;
it was the next thing to divine honour, and outshone in
splendour all other spectacles of the city. According to
the legal usage, no general was entitled to this honour
who had not slain five thousand enemies of the republic
in one battle, and by that victory enlarged its territory.
But whoever had the fortune to have it decreed to him,
advanced with the first dawn from the Vatican fields at
the head ot his companions-in-arms to the triumphal gate.
Here, after a slight repast, he was invested with the triumphal robes; the accustomed rites to the deities sta-
tioned at the gate were performed, and then the procession
moved along the *Via Triumphalis*, the streets, ranged with
altars smoking with incense, being thickly strewn with
flowers.

In the beautiful work of Dr. Miley on "Rome under
Paganism and the Popes," there is a description of the
procession of the triumph. There are items in the for
mality of the ceremony to which we must allude.

"First went musicians of various kinds, singing and
playing triumphal songs; next were led the oxen to be
sacrificed, having their horns gilt, and their heads
adorned with fillets and garlands; then in carriages were
brought the spoils taken from the enemy—statues, pic-

tures, plate, armour, gold and silver and brass, also golden crowns and other gifts sent by the allied and tributary states.   The titles of the vanquished nations were inscribed on wooden frames, on which were borne the images or representations of the conquered countries and cities. The captive leaders and princes followed in chains, with their children, kindred and courtiers ; after these captives came the lictors or executioners (having their hatchets or fasces wreathed with laurel), followed by a great company of musicians and dancers, dressed like satyrs, and crowned with wreaths of gold.   In the midst of them was a clown clothed in female garb, whose business it was with looks and gestures to insult the vanquished.   Next followed a long train of persons carrying perfumes.   Then came the conqueror, dressed in purple and gold, and a crown of laurel on his head, and a branch of laurel in his right hand, and in his left an ivory sceptre with an eagle on the top.   His face was painted with vermilion, in like manner as the statue of Jupiter on festival days, and a golden ball was suspended from his neck, with some amulet in it or magical preservative against envy.   His chariot, in which he stood erect, glittered with gold and was adorned with ivory ; and from the time probably of the Tarquins, certainly of Camillus, was usually drawn by four white horses, and sometimes by elephants or other singular wild animals.   He was attended by his relations, clientage, and a vast concourse of citizens, all in white togas.   His children used to ride in the chariot along with him ; and that he might not be too much elated, a slave, carrying a golden crown sparkling with gems, crouched behind him, frequently whispering in his ear, ' Remember thou art a man.'   His chariot was followed by the con-

suls and senators on foot ; his legati and military tribunes
or staff-officers commonly rode by his side. The victorious army, horse and foot, came last, in martial array,
crowned with laurel, and decorated with the gifts they
had received for their valour, and chanting their own
praises and those of the general, whom they sometimes
assailed with railleries. Shouts of 'Io triumphe' frequently bursting from the warrior ranks, and chorused
by myriads of the Roman people, re-echoed along the
Tiber's banks among the valleys of the seven hills, and
seemed to shake the rock-built Capitol itself.

" Arrived at the Forum, and before his chariot began to
climb the hill of triumphs, through the crowded temples
that rose along its acclivities, the conqueror ordered the
captive kings and chieftains of the vanquished nations to
be led away by the executioners and put to death in the
Gemonium, the horrid dungeon of the Mamertine prison,
which was at the foot of the Capitol to the right.

" On reaching the Temple of Jupiter, it was the usage
for him to wait till informed by the appointed officers
that his sanguinary orders had been complied with ; and
then, having offered incense to Jupiter and other gods
for his successes, he commanded the victims, which were
always white, from the pastures of Clitumnus, to be
sacrificed, and deposited his golden diadem in the lap of
Jove, to whom he also dedicated a great portion of the
spoils."*

The games and rejoicings of a triumph continued for
some weeks. They were celebrated in the circus and
amphitheatre, games which partook more of the character

* Miley, " Rome under Paganism and the Popes," vol. ii, chap. 3

of a scourge than of an amusement, consisting of wholesale immolations of human and animal victims. The
expenditure of the public money on those occasions was
enormous : nothing was spared which ingenuity or skill
could suggest. After the popular excitement had subsided, and the pantomime of adulation had sufficiently
deified the conqueror, some stupendous arch or column
was erected to commemorate through future generations
the merits of the hero, and the triumph of the Roman
arms. Some of these monuments of triumph are still
standing amidst the ruins of Rome, and are undoubtedly
the best records we have of the magnificence of the
ancient city.

Adrian entered Rome in the borrowed glory of the
deceased Emperor; the shouts of triumph resounded
through the city; he deified Trajan from the tomb of
Augustus, and sent the eagle of his spirit to the liberty
of the skies ; he dedicated the superb column erected to
the conqueror, and the arena of the Coliseum was once
more reeking with the blood of gladiators and victims.
During these games more than two hundred lions were
slaughtered, and an immense number of captives and
slaves were put to death.

It was one evening during these celebrations, that
word was brought to the city that the army of Placidus
had arrived, and was already on the Appian Way. A new
impulse was given to the rejoicings, and a new triumph
and procession were prepared for the victorious army.
There is nothing so calculated to excite a people's enthusiasm as the return of its armies from a triumphant
campaign. Those who remember the day on which the
heroes of the Crimea landed on the shores of England

can well picture the veteran armies of Rome entering the capital in triumph. According to custom the Emperor went out to meet the general, and embraced him.* As the evening was far advanced, and the sun was already sinking beneath the blue Mediterranean, the Emperor gave orders that the army should encamp outside the walls for the night, in order to enter the city in triumph next morning. Placidus and his family returned with the Emperor to the Palatine, and were entertained at a sumptuous banquet. He gave the Emperor the history of his campaign, and spoke until a late hour of his battles, his conquests, the bravery of his two sons, and the extraordinary discovery of his wife and family.†

Loud, shrill and cheerful were the trumpet blasts that roused the sleeping army on the following morning. The cup of joy for these poor creatures was full to the brim. They knew of no greater reward for years of hardship and trial, for the scars and wounds which disabled them for life, than the shouts of a brutal and barbarous mob, who hailed them along the road of triumph.

As they poured in through the gates, each of them received a laurel crown, whose freshness and beauty contrasted deeply with the sunburnt features and tattered garments of the veterans. Round their necks and about their persons they carried a profusion of tinsel trinkets, which they took from the conquered people as ornaments for their wives and children. There were waggons drawn by oxen laden with spoils, that made the massive pavements of the Appian Way creak ; armour, gold and

---

* Reverso ergo Eustachio occurrit ei imperator ut mos est **Romani** et victoriæ festivitates celebravit.—*Ib.*

† Prolixius extendit convivium etc.—*Ib*. No. **20.**

brass ornaments, wild animals in cages, and everything that could show the habits and manners of the conquered people.   The general, together with his wife and two sons, was in a gilt chariot, drawn by four white horses, in the rear of his army.   None of the pride and flush of drunken joy that characterised the pagan conqueror was to be seen in the meek countenance of Placidus.   All this rejoicing and gorgeous display was to him and his Christian family the funeral pomp that led them to their tomb.   The king who, on his death-bed, had himself invested with his crown and royal robes to meet death as a monarch, was a picture of Placidus led in triumph to martyrdom—a tale of the emptiness and instability of human greatness, often told in the vicissitudes of history ! He was silent and collected ; not even the deafening peals of applause from crowds of idle spectators, who made his name ring through the palaces and tombs that bend over the streets from the Capena gate to the Forum, induced him to look up with the smile of joyful approbation.   He was well aware that in a few moments his belief in Christianity would be declared, for he could not sacrifice to the gods.

Whilst the procession was moving along, a murmur passed through the crowd.   They asked one another where were the victims ?—where the captive chiefs ? —where the slaves usually dragged at the chariot wheels of the conqueror ?—where the wailing matrons and daughters of the conquered race to sound the mournful music of triumph ? Arrived at the Forum, the procession halted as usual, and the executioners and keepers of the Mamertine prison looked in vain for their victims ; it was the first time in the annals of triumph that their axes had not been steeped in the blood of heroes, whose only crime was that they fought bravely for their homes and their countries. They knew nothing of the sublime morality that can forgive an enemy. Placidus pardoned the moment he had conquered, and instead of dragging helpless victims from their country and family, to be immolated to the demons of Rome, he left his name in the traces of his march in love and benediction.

But now the procession arrived at the entrance to the Temple of Jupiter. The priests were waiting in their robes, and snow-white oxen, with gilded horns and crowns of flowers, were held by the altar. Immense faggots were blazing in the heart of the temple to consume the victims, and fragrant incense was burning in golden vessels. Placidus and his family descended from their chariot and stepped on one side; they refused to enter; they would not sacrifice.

If an earthquake had shaken the temple to its foundations, or a sudden eclipse had darkened the sun, there could not have been given a greater shock or surprise to the assembled thousands. The news ran like fire in a train of powder through the vast crowd. A deep heavy murmur, like the swell of the troubled deep breaking on its boundaries, rose from the multitudes in the Forum. Indignation and fury were the passions that swayed the mob. The demon of paganism reigned in their hearts; pity, justice and liberty were virtues unknown. From shouts of applause with which they hailed Placidus as the conqueror, the glory of the Empire, and the beloved of the martial god, they now hooted him with groans and hisses; and loudly from the gilded temples of the Capitol were echoed the terrible

cries of "Death to the Christians!"—"Away with the
Christians!" But the hour of another and grander
triumph had come for our hero. Let us hurry through
the dark picture of cruelty and ingratitude that closed
his career on this side of the grave, to usher in the
triumph that was to last for ever.

The noble general and his family were brought before
the Emperor. Was Adrian glad to have Placidus brought
before him as a criminal? Doubtless he looked with a
jealous eye on the glory, popularity and real triumph of
one who, a few months before, was his equal as a commander of the army, and his acknowledged superior in
skill and attainments, whilst his own triumph was but a
mockery—the borrowed plumes of a deceased hero,
whose panegyric he reluctantly preached from the chariot
of triumph. Moreover, weak-minded and servile, he must
have rejoiced in an opportunity of pandering to the
depraved taste of a cruel and brutal mob, who were
accustomed to look on all authority as usurpation and
oppression, and who hated Christianity with satanic
virulence. Like Trajan, he determined to prove his
piety towards the gods by the public execution of the
greatest man in the Empire. He received the old chief
in the Temple of Apollo, and, in a prepared speech, pretended what he never felt—sympathy for his folly. When
asked by the haughty Adrian why he would not sacrifice
to the gods, Placidus answered, bravely and fearlessly,
"I am a Christian, and adore only the true God."

"Whence comes this infatuation?" asked the Emperor,
quickly. "Why lose all the glory of the triumph, and
bring thy grey hairs to shame? Dost thou not know
that I have power to put thee to a miserable death?"

Placidus meekly replied : " My body is in your power, but my soul belongs to Him who created it. Never shall I forget the mercy He has shown me in calling me to the knowledge of Himself, and I rejoice to be able to suffer for Him. You may command me to lead your legions against the enemies of the Empire, but never will I offer sacrifice to any other god than the One great and powerful God who created all things, stretched out the heavens in their glory, decked the earth in its beauty, and created man to serve Him ; He alone is worthy of sacrifice ; all other gods are but demons who deceive men."

So also answered his wife and two sons. They bantered the Emperor himself for his folly in worshipping senseless pieces of marble and wood. In vain did Adrian try promises and threats, and all the silly arguments which were used in the defence of paganism. The faithful family were inflexible ; the eloquence of Placidus was simple, but powerful and earnest ; and the palpable defeat of Adrian in his attempt to reason with one gifted with the eloquence promised to those dragged before earthly tribunals, roused his pride and his cruelty, and the desire of revenge. The Coliseum stood but a few paces from them ; the games were going on ; the criminals and slaves of the Empire were the daily victims of its amusements. The condemnation of Placidus would be a stroke of policy to enhance the prosperity of his reign ; it was the fullest gratification of the cruel passions of jealousy and revenge which the demon had stirred up in his heart ; he ordered the Christian general and his family to be exposed to the wild beasts in the amphitheatre.

There is a convent of the Sisters of the Visitation now erected on the spot where this interview took place, and they sing in their office the beautiful and prophetic psalm of David. "*Quare fremuerunt gentes,*" &c.—"Why have the Gentiles raged, and the people devised vain things? The kings of the earth stood up, and the princes met together against the Lord and against His Christ: Let us break their bonds asunder, and let us cast away their yoke from us. He that dwelleth in heaven shall laugh at them, and the Lord shall deride them" (Ps. ii.). How sublime the idea suggested by the matin-song of the poor sisters, gliding over the silent and ivy-clad ruins of the fallen palace of the Cæsars, whence came the direful persecutions of the Church, and all that the powers of darkness, impersonated in the impious Cæsars of Rome, could do to destroy Christianity in its infancy!

It is probable that Placidus and his family passed that night in the dark and fetid prison of the Mamertine. This was a cell cut out of the solid rock at the foot of the Capitol. It consisted of two chambers, one over the other, which could only be entered by apertures in the ceiling (recently a commodious flight of stairs has been erected). The lower and most gloomy of these chambers was destined for persons condemned to death. These prisons have been in existence for nearly three thousand years, and with the *cloacæ,* or great sewers of the city, are the most perfect monuments of the kingly period. In classical literature the prisons are mentioned as the *Gemonium* or Tullian Keep. The historian Sallust, who flourished about fifty years before Christ, speaking of Cataline, writes thus: "In the prison called the Tullian, there is a place about ten feet deep, when you have descended a little to the left. It is surrounded on the sides by walls, and is closed above by a vaulted roof of

....pearance of it, from the filth, the darkness, and ... ., is terrific." Nothing can be imagined more horrible or gloomy than this dungeon in the days of its terrors. The light of the sun had never entered its dark recess, and its stench and filth generated a poison fatal to the human frame. Here Jugurtha was starved to death; here Vercingetorix, a Gaulish leader, was murdered by order of Julius Cæsar; and the companions of Cataline were strangled by order of Cicero. Here the wretched Sejanus, the favourite of Tiberius, met a merited death; and here, too, a Jewish leader, named Joras, was put to death by order of Vespasian. But it is far more remarkable in the annals of the Church for its martyrs and Christian heroes than for its antiquity or political history. It was in this dreary abode that the Apostle St. Peter passed nine months, and converted his gaolers, Processus and Martinianus, and forty-seven others. To this day is shown the column to which the Apostle was bound, and the spring of water that is said by a pious tradition to have miraculously sprung up through the rock that he might baptize those whom he converted. It is a strange fact that the chair or throne of Pius IX. at the Vatican Council was erected over the altar of the martyrs Processus and Martinianus, who, eighteen hundred and six years ago, led to the dark prisons of the Mamertine the first King of the imperishable dynasty of the Papacy. Many holy confessors and martyrs have consecrated these prisons by their prayers, their tears, and their miracles; and there are few spots in Rome so rich in the sacred treasures of the past, more holy, or more attractive, than the Mamertine. It was reserved in a special manner for state-prisoners and persons of distinction, and hence, although the Acts of the Saint do not mention it, we have every reason to presume that Placidus and his family passed the night before their martyrdom in this horrible dungeon. But faith and the consolations of prayer can cast light into the darkest prisons ; no external darkness or material affliction can blight the joy of the faithful soul.*

Next morning, the 20th of September, A.D. 120, the people were hastening in tens of thousands to the Coliseum. They knew what had taken place ; they had heard of the condemnation by the Emperor, and surprise and indignation at the discovery that the general belonged to the hated sect of Christians seemed to be expressed in the frown on their darkened features. Had he been an assassin, or a highway robber, or a political prisoner, who had plotted the ruin of the Empire, pity would have been murmured on every lip, a reprieve would have been called for, and the mob would have saved him ; but deep and bitter must ever be the animosity of the demons who revel in the spirit of error and wage war against the truth. A marvellous and intense hatred of the Catholic Church has ever been the characteristic feature of unbelief, from paganism down to every shade of modern Protestantism ; the intensity of that hostility may be measured in proportion to the total or partial rejection of revelation.

No nation could be sunk more deeply in idolatry, sen- suality and vice than the great Empire whose capital has been considered the Babylon of impiety spoken of in

---

* The author of this work has in preparation the history of the Mamertine prison and its martyrs. It is the oldest monument of ancient Rome and is deeply interesting in its sacred reminiscenses.

the Apocalypse. " Our wrestling," says St. Paul, " is
not against flesh and blood, but against principalities and
powers, against the rulers of the world of this darkness,
against the spirits of wickedness in the high places"
(Eph. vi. 12). It was not in an amphitheatre stained
with the blood of wild beasts and gladiators, and filled
with an excited and unfeeling crowd, that the voice of
pity or reason could be heard ; the impatient clamours
of the multitude denounced the Christians as the enemies
of the gods and men, and the public condemnation of the
Christian general had already rung loudly and repeatedly
through the benches of the Coliseum. The coming of
the Emperor was announced, the buzz of conversation was
hushed, and all eyes were turned towards the entrance
on the side of the Esquiline, which was specially reserved
for the royal cortége. As soon as he entered the amphitheatre, all rose ; the lictors lowered their fasces, and the
senators and vestals bowed profoundly. Shouts of "*great,*"
"*immortal,*" "*divine,*" resounded from every seat. The
crowd of spectators was nothing more than an assembly
of miscreant slaves, who trembled at the beck of their
rulers. Although the spectators of the Coliseum frequently hated the Emperor as an oppressor and a tyrant,
yet, in the wild frenzy of fear, they cried out with lying
tongues that he alone was great and powerful. He carried a sceptre of ivory, surmounted with a golden eagle,
and a slave followed, bearing over his head a crown of
solid gold and precious stones. As soon as he was seated,
the shrill blast of a trumpet called for silence and the
commencement of the games. After the procession of
the unfortunate wretches who were to take part in the
cruel sport of that day's programme and the sham fight

of the gladiators, it was usual to commence with sports of agility and skill, but on this day the order was changed. The crowd called for the condemnation of the Christians, and the Emperor gave the order that Placidus and his family be exposed to the wild beasts.

They were led into the arena in chains. They were silent and rapt in prayer. The editor of the games asked them again to sacrifice to the gods , they refused. The keepers were told to let in some wild beasts to devour them. A death-like stillness reigned around. Every one was struck with their fortitude ; no screams of terror, no trembling, no supplications for mercy, no heart-rending and frantic farewells ; all was calm and tranquil ; they awaited on bended knees with majestic resignation their awful doom. The iron doors of the subterranean keeps grated on their hinges ; two lions and four bears rushed into the arena.

They would not touch the martyrs but gambolled around them ; one of the lions endeavoured to get his head under the foot of Placidus* ; the saint permitted it, and a more beautiful or thrilling sight was never seen in the arena of the Coliseum. The king of the forest voluntarily put himself under the foot of the unarmed old man, and crouched down as if with fear and reverence. " Goad the animals ! " shouted the enraged Emperor to the keepers. " Goad them on ! " " Make them devour ! " rang from every tier, from the senators, the vestals, and the maddened populace of the upper circles ; but the animals turned on their keepers, and drove them from the arena. Other animals were called for, but they only

* Accurrens vero leo et stans prope Beatos et submittens caput, etc.

served to enhance the scene of triumph, and respectfully licked the feet of their intended victims. He who made use of an animal to bring Placidus to the light of faith, and afterwards to be the instruments of his trial and his sorrow, now made them declare His love and protection over His servants.

The indignation and shame of the pagan Emperor was roused to the highest pitch; his impotent rage and natural cruelty broke forth, and to gratify his brutal passion, he commanded the martyrs to be placed in the bronze bull, and to be consumed by a slow fire. This was a horrible instrument of torture and execution used for the persecution of the Christians. It was made in the shape of a bull, and could hold several persons at the same time in its hollow womb; when fire was applied beneath, it became an oven, and it is not difficult to imagine the excruciating torture a slow fire must have caused to its living victims. We find from several authorities that this dreadful instrument of execution was in use both before and long after the time of Adrian, and thus many martyrs were put to death.

In this way Placidus and his family received their crown. Almighty God wished to show it was His will, and not the commands of the Emperor, or the instruments of torture that deprived his servants of life, by performing a great miracle. After three days the bodies of the Saints were taken out in the presence of the Emperor; no trace of fire was to be seen upon them; they exhaled a beautiful odour, and seemed to be lying in a sweet sleep. Their relics were laid on the ground for several days, and the whole city rushed to see the won der.[*] As Almighty God does nothing in vain, many were converted by this miracle, and became fervent Christians. The bodies of the glorious martyrs were stolen by the Christians, and were afterwards buried, together with the brazen bull-in which they suffered, on the spot where their martyrdom took place. A beautiful church sprung up in the very earliest ages of Christianity over the shrine of Eustachius and his family. That divine institution which spreads its maternal wings over every sacred deposit left in her bosom has preserved with scrupulous care the shrines and relics of the heroes of the past. In the very heart of modern Rome there now stands a favourite church, which has been rebuilt and repaired several times during the last fifteen hundred years, and still commemorates the name and preserves the relics of the brave and virtuous Placidus. In the same urn lie the hallowed remains of his faithful spouse and children, awaiting the trumpet call of the angel of the last day.

The Bollandists enter into a long and learned discussion concerning the authenticity of the Acts of Eustachius, which they give in the original Greek version. Although in the above narrative we have endeavoured to avoid the monotony of isolated facts, and have cast around the romantic history of this great Saint an imaginary dress, yet we have substantially adhered to the facts given in the Acts. The obscurity and doubt which the lapse of seventeen centuries, and the extraordinary character of the

[*] Post tres autem dies venit impiissimus imperator in locum et præcepit aperiri æream machinam ut videret quid factum esset de reliquiis Sanctorum, et videntes corpora eorum putaverunt eos adhuc vivere et ejicientes posuerunt eos super terram. —Acts, *Ib.*

facts recorded, must necessarily make us hesitate to declare this strange story an incontestable fact. Yet it
seems to stand the test of the strictest examination.
Some of the oldest and most remarkable martyrologies
mention his extraordinary conversion through a stag,
and his martyrdom in the brazen bull. St. John Damas-
cene quotes the history of Eustachius in a sermon he
preached in A.D. 734. Tradition points out the very
spot in the Apennines where this extraordinary vision
took place. A small chapel was built there in the fourth
century, supposed to have been erected by the order of
Constantine, whose first care, after his conversion and
triumph, was to dedicate and preserve the shrines of the
early Church. A rude mosaic of the fourth century, representing a stag, with a figure between its horns, and
other events in the life of Eustachius, was removed from
this little church, and is still preserved in the Kircherian
Collection. The learned and trustworthy Baronius, after
a close examination of the Acts, can only use these words :
—" Putamus tamen eis multa superaddita esse," An. 120
—(" We think, however, many things have been added to
them"). The authors of the Bollandist, however, seem
to lean to their probability.

It is useless and absurd to ask why Almighty God used
these extraordinary means for the conversion of Placidus.
There are enigmas in the dispensations of the divine favours that can be solved only by the illumined intelligence
of the beatified vision. You may as well ask why St.
Paul was converted on the road to Damascus and not in
the city, and why made a vessel of election before so
many others more deserving ? Why did our Blessed
Lord perform one of His greatest miracles with clay

moistened with spittle ? Why did he make a poor, simple fisherman the head of his Church ? There are things written in the sacred records of revelation more extraordinary than anything in the above narrative. Around us, in every moment of our existence, and in every portion of the Church of God, there are supernatural interpositions of mercy and love—miracles if you wish to call them—that no human intelligence can understand. It is the height of pride, and the first mark of infidelity, to scoff at the works of God because they appear strange.

Who shall set limits to the power or the love of God ? He who has not the humility and simplicity of faith. Although we are not bound under the pain of anathema to accept all that is recorded in the lives of the Saints, yet we are not prepared to say that they are nothing but romances and idle tales. But some of them are, you will add. It may be so, but it is difficult to name them. The moment you come to examine any one of those strange lives that the Church has put under the seal of her recommendation, you are driven back with a storm of proofs and authority that make you ashamed of your doubt. We have tried it, and we speak from experience ; there is no fair and honest student of history who will not acknowledge the same. But there are many ignorant and conceited persons in the world, who look at everything through the coloured glasses of prejudice ; all that is strange, consoling, or terrific in the sacred annals of the past are to them but glimpses from the regions of fancy, and are condemned with the smile of sarcasm ; their faith, their past, and their future, is nought but tinsel, shadow and unreality.*

---

* We can scarcely give the reader a better proof of the authenticity of these Acts than by referring him to the sanction given to them

by the Church ; for in the oldest editions of the Roman Breviary, the lessons for the feast of the 20th of September give this strange tale in an abbreviated form. We will quote the Latin text, that the reader may see the main facts of this tale are perfectly historical :—

" Eustachius, qui et Placidus, genere, opibus et militari gloria inter Romanos insignis, sub Trajano Imperatore magistri militum titulum meruit ; cum vero sese aliquando in venatione exerceret, ac fugientem miræ magnitudinis cervum insequeretur, vidit repente inter consistentis feræ cornua excelsam atque fulgentem Christi Domini e cruce pendentis imaginem, cujus voce ad immortalis vitæ prædum invitatus, una cum uxore Theopista, ac duobus parvulis filiis, Agapito et Theopisto, Christianæ militiæ nomen dedit.

" Mox ad visionis pristinæ locum, sicut ei Dominus præceperat, regressus, illum prænuntiantem audivit quanti sibi deinceps pro ejus gloria perferenda essent. Quo circa incredibiles calamitates mira patientia perpessus, brevi in summam egestatem redactus est. Cumque clam se subducere cogeretur, in itinere conjugem primum, deinde etiam liberos, sibi miserabiliter ereptos ingemuit. Tantis obvolutus ærumnis in regione longinqua vilicum agens longo tempore dilituit ; donec cœlesti voce recreatus ac nova occasione a Trajano conquisitus iterum bello præficitur.

" Illa in expeditione, liberis simul cum uxore insperato receptis, victor Urbem ingenti omnium gratulatione ingreditur. Sed paulo post inanibus diis pro parta victoria sacrificare jussus, constantissime renuit. Cumque variis artibus ad Christi fidem ejurandam frustra tentaretur una cum uxore et liberis leonibus objicitur. Horum mansuetudine concitatus, imperator æreum in taurum subjectis flammis candentem eos immitti jubet, ubi divinis in laudibus consummato martyrio, duodecimo Kalendas Octobris ad sempiternam felicitatem convolarunt. Quorum illæsa corpora religiose a fidelibus sepulta, postmodum ad ecclesiam, eorum nomine erectam, **honorifice translata sunt.**"

CHAPTER VIII.

THE YOUNG BISHOP.

1.

ABOUT twenty years after the martyrdom of Placidus, and in the reign of the same Adrian, we have records of another extraordinary scene in the Coliseum. We have given the title of " young bishop" to our present notice, for our hero was but twenty years of age when he wore the mitre. He was a noble Roman youth of consular rank: he had a saintly mother, who was a convert of the great Apostle St. Paul, and afterwards suffered martyrdom with her son. He was called Eleutherius. Brought up under the care of his pious mother and the holy Pope Anaclete, he made rapid progress in the science of the Saints. So great was his piety and innocence of life, that, at the age of sixteen, he was made a deacon ; at eighteen he was ordained priest, and was consecrated by the hands of the Pope himself for the see of Aquileia (Venice) at the age of twenty.

The preaching and miracles of the youthful Bishop were reaping a fruitful harvest of souls, and his name was carried on the wings of fame to the ears of Adrian. The hypocritical policy of the Emperor was to show his piety to the gods by persecuting the most noted amongst the Christians. Having heard of Eleutherius on his return for the last time from the East, he sent one of his generals named Felix, with two hundred men, to seize the Bishop and bring him to Rome. When Felix arrived with his soldiers, he found Eleutherius in his church, preaching to a great concourse of people. He drew up his soldiers in guard around the church, whilst he and a few of the most trusty entered to seize the Saint. No sooner had Felix entered the church than the grace of God entered his heart. He was struck with the solemnity of the scene. The silence and devotion of the Christians assembled in the temple of the Most High, the heavenly light that shone round the Bishop, the unction and eloquence with which he spoke, made the pagan soldier stand riveted to the ground in awe and reverence. He waited till the ser- mon was over ; but instead of rushing on the defenceless servant of Christ to drag him to martyrdom, he was seen kneeling in the centre of the church, praying to the true God. The people were surprised, and the soldiers looked at each other in amazement. The first to rouse him from his thoughts was the Bishop, who touched him on the shoulder, and said to him : " Rise, Felix ; I know what brought thee hither : it is the will of God that I should go with thee to glorify His name." The general awoke, as if from a beautiful dream, and proclaimed his belief in the God of the Christians.

On the journey to Rome, when they came up to a large river (probably the Po), they halted at a shady place on its banks. Eleutherius, whose heart burned with zeal and love, seized every opportunity of preaching the gos- pel and saving souls. Gathering the little band around him, he spoke at great length of the Christian faith. His fervour and eloquence not only convinced them, but drew tears from many of the rough and benighted soldiers who heard him ; and, when he had ceased speaking, Felix cried out aloud : " I will not eat until I am baptized." The holy Bishop having further instructed him, baptized him and some of the soldiers before they left the banks of the river.

When they arrived in Rome, the Emperor ordered Eleutherius to be brought before him. He was led to one of the halls in the palace on the Palatine, where Adrian had his throne erected. When the martyr stood before him, Adrian was struck with his beauty and modesty ; a peculiar sweetness of countenance, blended with nobility and majesty, forced the pagan persecutors to look on the servant of Christ with a feeling almost amounting to reverential awe. The Emperor was well aware that the father of Eleutherius had thrice borne the consular dignity under his own reign, and he saw in the victim before him every inducement to mercy and compassion that wealth, rank and talent could offer. He addressed him mildly at first, and seemed rather to conciliate and bribe him with the promise of his friendship and a position in the imperial palace ; but finding the noble youth immovable in his profession of Christianity, he gave vent to all the rage that pride and the devil could raise in his soul. The Acts of the martyr give a portion of the conversation that passed at this interview ; it is so beautiful and touching we will translate it.

" The Emperor said : ' How is it that you, such an illustrious man, could give yourself to such a foolish superstition as to believe in a God who was crucified by men ? "

" Eleutherius was silent. Again the Emperor addressed him, and said, ' Answer the question I ask you ; why do you give yourself to the slavery of superstition, and serve a man that is dead, and who died the miserable death of a criminal ? '

" Eleutherius, looking up towards heaven, and making the sign of the cross, said : ' *True liberty* is only to be found in the service of the Creator of heaven and earth.'

" Adrian in a milder tone said : ' Obey my commands, and I will give you a post of honour in my own palace.'

" ' Thy words,' said Eleutherius, ' are poisoned with deceit and bitterness.' " (*Bollandists,* 18th April.)

Adrian was enraged at this answer, and ordered the *copper bed* to be prepared for the servant of God. This was an instrument of torture greatly in use at this period of persecution. It may be better understood by calling it a large gridiron. It consisted of several cross bars of brass or copper, supported by feet about nine inches from the ground; underneath was placed fire to consume the martyrs. It is a strange fact, however, that Almighty God permitted very few martyrs to meet death by this terrible instrument.* Eleutherius will not be its victim.

It was ordained by the laws of Augustus, that the execution of criminals and malefactors should be public, and that a crier should announce to the people the crimes which brought the offender to his miserable end. This law, which was wisely destined to deter others from the perpetration of similar crimes, was in practice in the time

---

* The most illustrious martyr who won his crown in this way was St. Laurence, who suffered in 261, under Valerian. The gridiron on which he suffered, which was made of iron, and not copper, is still preserved in the Church of St. Lorenzo in Lucina, in Rome.

of Adrian. Although it became arbitrary in its application under the rule of some of the tyrants who were permitted to disgrace the throne of Augustus, yet in the case
of Christians it was enforced even beyond the limits of
its requirements. Christianity was the greatest crime
against the state ; a man might be accused of murder,
conspiracy, or robbery, and he would escape with a light
punishment, or be condemned to fight for his life with
the gladiators in the Coliseum ; but it seems to have been
only against Christians that all the horrors of pagan
cruelty were directed.

In consequence of this law, a crier was sent through
the city to announce the sentence pronounced by the
Emperor on the Bishop Eleutherius. An immense crowd
assembled. The Acts say the whole people of Rome
hastened to witness the execution.* The great God
whom they knew not was inviting them to recognize His
power, and serve Him instead of idols. When the fire was
kindled, and was blazing furiously round the copper-bed,
the martyr was stripped and lifted by the rough hands of
the soldiers to his bed of torture. Never did the foot-
sore pilgrim cast his wearied limbs in repose on the mossy
bank with more ease and refreshment, than Eleutherius
did on his bed of fire : the elements of nature are the
creatures of God—they obey when He commands. After
the lapse of an hour, during which he remained chained
to the gridiron, unburnt, and without even a hair of his
head being singed, he was liberated ; seizing the favourable moment, he raised his voice and preached an eloquent
sermon to the Romans whom curiosity had gathered

* "Omnis populus Romanus cucurrit ad hoc spectaculum certa-
minis."—*Bollandists*, 18th Ap.

around. "Romans," cried out the martyr, "listen to me. Great and true is the Omnipotent God. There is no other God than He who was preached to you by the Apostles Peter and Paul, through whom so many cures and miracles were worked amongst you, through whom was defeated the impious Simon Magus, and through whom were broken to pieces the deaf and dumb idols such as your Emperor adores."

Adrian, who was listening, foamed with rage, and ordered another and still more terrible instrument of torture to be prepared for Eleutherius. This was an enormous frying-pan filled with oil and pitch and placed over an immense fire. Whilst the composition in the cauldron was foaming and seething with heat, the Emperor said once more to the holy youth : " Now, at least, take pity on your youth and nobility, and do not any longer incur the anger of the gods, or you will soon be like that burning oil."

Eleutherius laughed at the threat of the Emperor. "I wonder," he said to him, " that you, who know so much, have never heard of the three young men cast into the fiery furnace of Babylon. The flames of the fire rose to forty-seven cubits, in the midst of this fire they sang and rejoiced, for there walked in the midst of them the Son of the God whom I adore, whose unworthy priest I am, who has never abandoned me from my infancy."*

Having said this, he made the sign of the cross, and sprang towards the boiling pan. The moment he placed

* " Cum sis curiosus omnium, miror quomodo non potuisti ad hæc pertingere, quod tres pueri Hebræi missi in caminum flammæ ardentis, cujus altitudo cubitis quadraginta novem elata," &c.—*Acts Bollandists,* 18th April.

his hand on it, the fire was extinguished, and the foam·
ing mass of oil and pitch became cold and solid ; the holy
martyr, turning towards the Emperor, said: " Now where
are your threats ?   Your fire, your gridiron and your frying-pan have become like a bed of roses to me, and have
no power to hurt me.   O Adrian ! thine eyes are darkened with incredulity, so that thou dost not see the things
of God ; recognise thy folly, do penance for thy misdeeds,
and weep over thy misfortune that thou hast not hitherto
known the only great and true Ruler of heaven and earth
and all things."

Adrian was not converted by this extraordinary miracle;
although it is certain he relaxed the rigour of his persecution against the Christians after the death of Eleuthe·
rius.   He must have been astounded at what he saw ;
the extraordinary miracles which were worked by almost
every Christian who was brought before him, the ineffi-
cacy of the most dreadful torments he could devise, and
the attractive sweetness of innocence and virtue which
shines even in the external deportment of a true Chris·
tian must have opened his eyes and raised a doubt in
his mind respecting the truth of paganism.   Hence it is
reported of him by some historians, that shortly before
his death he had resolved to erect a temple to the God
of the Christians.

When Eleutherius had worked the extraordinary miracle
just mentioned, and addressed him in the sublime and
fearless language of reproof for his folly, Adrian was not
able to speak for confusion, and bit his lip with rage.
There stood near one of the sycophants of the palace,
who was the Prefect of the city ; seeing the perplexity
and defeat of the Emperor, he said : "Great Emperor !

the whole world, from east to west, is under your control, and every one trembles at your word except this insolent young man. Let your Majesty order him to be taken to prison ; I will prepare an instrument in which you will see he will not insult you much longer. To-morrow you will see your triumph in my amphitheatre before the whole Roman people."*

These words brought relief to the baffled Emperor, and he immediately gave orders that Eleutherius should be handed over to the Prefect, Corribonus, to be treated according to his wish ; but the servant of God heard what was said, and, filled with a divine inspiration, cried out, in the hearing of the Emperor, as the soldiers were leading him away: "Yes, Corribonus, to-morrow you will witness my triumph, which will be the triumph of my Lord Jesus Christ."

Corribonus undertook to defeat the power of the Most High. He knew nothing of the great Being against whom he was contending. A few hours will show him that mercy is even greater than the attribute of power in the God of the Christians ; for that mercy threw its mantle around him, through the prayers of his victim, from a persecutor he became a vessel of election. He little thought the last words of the holy Bishop were a prophecy, in which he himself was to take part, and that before the sun should set on the morrow he would be singing the eternal praises of the great and merciful God of the Christians in the bright kingdom of real triumph and bliss.

The scenes that follow are extremely interesting; we

* "The Prefect of the city was specially in charge of the Coliseum and the games."

have come to one of the most extraordinary sights the old walls of the Coliseum have ever witnessed.

2.

Corribonus left nothing undone to insure the success of his undertaking. As the public games were not going on at this time, criers were sent through the city to announce a special entertainment for the morrow. The fame of the invulnerable Christian had spread far and wide ; the grief of the baffled Emperor, and the promise of Corribonus to prepare a new and terrible machine that was sure to destroy the Christians, roused the interest of the people, and on the following morning they flocked in thousands to the Coliseum. This was arranged by the providence of God, that not only the Romans, but the world and future ages, might recognise His power and glorify His name. Corribonus spent some time in devising an instrument of torture. The Emperor and the people expected something terrible—a machine that would cut its victims into a thousand pieces, and scatter them in the air, or a fire that no art could extinguish—a death, in fine, the most terrible ever witnessed in the arena of the amphitheatre. But the issue of his labours was an instrument that expressed indeed brutality and ignorance, but no novelty or art. We are tempted to smile when we read of the machine he invented to baffle the power of the Most High. It was nothing more than an immense boiler with a lid ; in it was to be placed oil, pitch, resin, and some nauseous poisonous ingredients ; and then, when a terrible fire had heated the mixture to scalding temperature, the martyr was to be thrown in, and thus consumed, as he thought, in a moment.

The sun is already high in the heavens, and the deafening shouts from the Coliseum tell us the benches are filled with the impatient mob. The immense cauldron is placed in the middle of the arena, and the burning faggots are blazing around it; the air is impregnated with the fumes of the heterogeneous mass, and the thick dark smoke of the fetid composition rises slowly to a cloudless sky. Two or three men, half-naked, and of dark, fiendish looks, are supplying the fire with faggots, and at intervals stirring up the seething and crackling contents of the boiler. The picture was like the vision often given to the saints of the horrors of hell. Around, the demons were calling aloud for the death of the Christians ; there was fire, torment, and hatred of God ; what more is there in hell save its eternal curse !

The Emperor and Prefect arrived, and some games of gladiators and bestiaries were witnessed with the usual excitement and delight. But the great attraction of that day's amusement was the smoking cauldron in the arena. After each contest between the gladiators and the beasts, loud shrill voices would ring from the upper benches calling for the Christian. The Emperor and Prefect cheerfully yielded to the importunities of the people ; and "at the third hour," say the Acts, Eleutherius was brought into the arena. He looked young, beautiful, and cheerful, as he moved, with heavy chains on his hands and feet, towards the tribunal of the Emperor and Prefect. When he was brought under the throne of the Emperor, Corribonus commanded silence with his hand and spoke thus aloud :—

"All nations obey the power of our great Emperor—you alone, young man, despise his wishes; wherefore either obey his orders and worship the gods and goddesses whom he adores, or by Jupiter you will be cast into the boiling cauldron."

Those latter words he pronounced with great emphasis, and pointed towards the dreadful cauldron. He had calculated on a certain victory over the martyr, and thought he had only to use the threats with which he was accustomed to terrify his cowardly slaves. Eleutherius, without showing any signs of fear or trouble, quietly answered the Prefect in this manner :—"Corribonus, listen to me ; you have your king who made you Prefect ; I have my King who made me Bishop. Now, one of these two must conquer, and he who is the conqueror should be adored by you and me. If your cauldron overcome my faith, then I must serve your king ; but if your cauldron be overcome by my King, you must adore the Lord Jesus Christ."

Then the lictors seized him and tore off his garments. Whilst they were leading him towards the boiler, he prayed thus aloud: "O Lord Jesus Christ, Thou art the joy and light of all souls who believe in Thee ! Thou knowest that all sufferings are pleasing to me on account of Thy name ; but to show that the very elements resist those who oppose Thee, do not permit me, Thy servant, to be consumed in this cauldron."

He was flung into the burning mass, and the great lid was drawn over.

All was as silent as death in the amphitheatre. The people bent forward in breathless suspense ; they expected something extraordinary. Another minute passed in silence—the fire still raged and the cauldron was not dashed to pieces; the martyr must be dead. The Emperor smiled, and Corribonus rubbed his hands in complacent glee at his imagined triumph. After a few minutes of suspense, the Emperor ordered the lid to be removed to see if anything remained of the martyr. But all honour and glory to the eternal God! He laughs at His enemies, and sets their machinations at naught. Eleutherius was unhurt—not a hair was touched—not a fibre in his body was contracted—not a movement in his features showed a sensation of pain; but calm, beautiful and collected, he seemed rather to be going through his daily devotions in his own little episcopal chapel, than floating in a terrible cauldron of burning oil before tens of thousands of the Roman populace. When he stood erect in the arena, a murmur of surprise ran through the amphitheatre. Adrian was fixed to the ground in wonder; he looked at Corribonus with anger flashing in his eyes. But at that moment the grace of God entered the heart of Corribonus, and rushing towards the Emperor, he addressed him with vehemence: "O great Emperor! let us believe in the God who protects His servants in this manner. This youth is indeed a priest of the true God. If one of our priests of Jupiter, of Juno, or Hercules were cast into this cauldron, would their gods save them thus?"

The words of the Prefect fell like a thunderclap on the ears of Adrian. Unconverted in his superstition, and hardened in his impiety, the sudden change which grace had wrought in the heart of Corribonus roused his indignation to the highest pitch.

"What!" he cried out, after a moment's pause; "is

it you, Corribonus, that dare speak thus ? Has the mother of this wretch bribed you to betray me ? I have made you Prefect ; I have given you gold and silver ; and now you turn against me to take part with this hated Christian ! Seize him, lictors, and let the caitiff's blood mingle with the burning oil of the cauldron."

" Hear me for a moment, great Emperor ! " cried out Corribonus. " The honours and favours you have conferred on me have been short-lived and temporal. Whilst I was in error I could not see the truth which now shines resplendent before me. If you wish to scoff at the great God of the Christians, and remain a victim of the follies of your impiety, look you to it. I, from this moment, believe Christ to be the true God. I deny your idols to be gods, and I believe in Him, alone great and powerful, whom Eleutherius preaches."

Adrian stamped the ground with passion, and made a sign to the lictors to lead him at once to the arena to be executed.

When the lictors had taken him to the arena, he flung himself on his knees before Eleutherius, and thus addressed him : " Man of God ! pray for me, I beseech thee, to that God whom to-day I have confessed to be alone great ; give me that saving sign thou didst give Felix the general, that I may brave the torments of the Emperor."

Eleutherius shed tears of joy. He thanked God in his heart for the conversion of Corribonus, and prayed to the Almighty to strengthen him to sustain the torments he was about to suffer. The Prefect was cast into the very instrument that he had prepared to destroy Eleutherius ; the lid was closed over him, and he was left in the terrible instrument for several minutes. When the cauldron was uncovered, he was still alive, unhurt, and without pain ; he was singing the praises of the true God, whose power and divinity he no longer doubted ; and, although ten minutes had not passed since he was a pagan, yet his faith was as immovable as a mountain. The Emperor, seeing that he too escaped the destructive power of the burning cauldron, ordered the gladiators to dispatch him in the sight of all the people.* The noble Prefect fell in the arena of the Coliseum under the eyes and bless- ing of Eleutherius. His prompt and generous response to the calls of grace merited for him the peerless crown of martyrdom. The great sacrifice was momentary, yet worth a thousand years of penance. Wealth, friends, family were abandoned without a murmur or a farewell, and torments and death cheerfully accepted. What faith —what confidence—what love is expressed in the neo- phyte's declaration of Christianity ! Happy the exchange he made ! Would that we, born in the faith and grown old in it, could come near him in the brilliant mansions of everlasting joy !

3.

When we contemplate the wonderful works of God, how must not our mind expand and our heart warm and be elevated ! Some have said that our reason alone can comprehend everything within the confines of the vast creation, and account for all that is not beyond the sky ; but foolish and absurd the man that does not recognise the all-present influence of the great God. There are

---

* " Videns autem imperator quod etiam Corribon vinceret, jussit eum in conspectu omnium decollari."—*Acts.*

mysteries and wonders in nature and grace at every moment passing around us that no human intellect can perceive or explain. Strange it is that men who are ready to acknowledge the power and wonders of God in the material creation, deny Him the glory He demands for similar works in the spiritual order. There are many in every position of life, amongst Christians and unbelievers, amongst the educated, the rich and the poor, who are unconsciously prejudiced against God in the manifestation of His power through men. He may cause wonders in the revolving orbits of the heavens; the brute animals, and the very stones of inanimate nature, may become the instruments of the most marvellous effects; but the moment the ordinary laws of nature are suspended in favour of our fellow-creatures—in favour of the rational being, the highest of the works of God— then there is doubt, misgiving, some unaccountable reluctance to believe. The most manifest interpositions of the divine power are explained away by chance, by hallucination, by skill; and where ocular testimony does not prove, the fact is immediately denied. This is the case with all the strange things that are recorded in the history of the past. When we read of a miracle in the lives of the saints we are prepared immediately to doubt; perhaps the records that surprise us are but inventions to amuse us. Thus some of the most consoling and beautiful traits of the paternal providence of God for His suffering creatures are cast to the winds as incredible as the myths of paganism. Is there not some taint of the corrupt spirit of the world and the devil in the proud feeling of contempt and incredulity with which we treat the works of God?

Not everything that is said in history is true, nor yet is everything false. But there are sacred and touching records of the trials and triumphs of the martyrs preserved in the archives of the Church, and transmitted to us with her seal and authority; they record wonders indeed, but neither impossible nor strange if we consider the exigencies of the terrible days of persecution. It would be rash, unfilial, and disrespectful for the children of the Church to fling away the Acts of her martyrs as idle stories simply because they are strange. Why set limits to the power or the goodness of God?

We return, then, with love and respect to the wonderful Acts of St. Eleutherius. We have still more marvellous and thrilling miracles to record. The Coliseum is to be again the theatre and the witness of startling events in the extraordinary career of this holy martyr. We can scarcely say whether we are more struck with the persistent cruelty of the blinded Emperor or the untiring patience of God in working wonder after wonder through the youthful and saintly Bishop.

After the death of Corribenus, Eleutherius was sent to prison. Adrian tore his purple robe in anger, and retired to his imperial saloons to give vent to this impotent rage. He summoned his courtiers, and offered a great reward to any of them who would suggest how he could get rid of the troublesome Christian. The plans suggested were numerous and cruel, but Adrian selected one which would cause less excitement among the people and which seemed to render death inevitable. It was to leave him shut up in a loathsome prison, deprived of food and light, until the exhausted frame could no longer perform the vital functions. He commanded the prison doors to be locked, and the keys to be brought to his own palace, making sure that no bribery or treason would rob him of his victim. But stone walls and prison bars cannot keep out the Spirit of God.

His prison was a dark, subterranean cell below the level of the city. The only light or air that could come into it was through a small hole about the size of a brick in one of the angles of the roof. The accumulation of dirt, the fetid air, and the horrid darkness make the imagination recoil from the contemplation of the terrible lot of being condemned to pass days and nights and weeks in prisons such as served for the cruelty and justice of pagan Rome. History teems with harrowing scenes of madness, despair and death which terminated the career of the victims of these dreary dungeons: Some ate the flesh of their own arms in hunger, others dashed out their brains in madness against the rocky walls of the prison, or strangled themselves in despair, whilst their unburied and corrupting bodies were left to intensify the horrors of the dungeon for the next victim of imperial displeasure. But these gloomy cells were homes of peace and light to the servants of God. Solitude, darkness and confinement were sources of supernatural joy that ravished their souls to pure delights, which are the foretaste of the bliss of heaven.

When the heavy iron doors of the prison were closed on Eleutherius, his soul was filled with celestial joy. The Spirit of God not only went down with him into the pit, but sent him food every day. Each morning of his confinement, a beautiful little dove would come through the narrow crevice that served for light and air, and drop

some delicate refreshment at the feet of the martyr.[*]
When fifteen days had passed—days that were happy and
cheerful to the servant of Christ—the Emperor sent
down the keys of the prison to see if death had rid him
of Eleutherius. When it was reported to Adrian that he
was still alive, and seemed happy and contented with his
vile prison, the Emperor was once more seized with rage
and passion. He had Eleutherius brought before him.
He expected to find the holy youth worn away to a
skeleton, and humbled and terrified like the wretched
pagan victims who had been flung into those prisons but
for a few hours. What must have been his surprise to
find Eleutherius more comely and beautiful than ever—
" in flore primæ juventutis velut angelus fulgens " [†]—still
immovable in his resolve to worship Christ alone, fearlessly confronting the tyrant, and reproving him for his
impiety.

Adrian now ordered the martyr to be tied to a wild
horse, that he might be dragged over the massive pavements of the Roman roads, and thus be bruised and
broken to pieces. The sentence was executed; but the
moment the horse was let free, an angel loosened the
bonds of Eleutherius and, lifting him up, placed him on
the back of the horse.[‡] Away the animal flew across the
Campagna, bearing its precious burden on its back, and
never stopping until it had reached the summit of one of
the highest and bleakest mountains of the Sabine range

---

[*] " Cumque esset B. Eleutherius in custodia multis diebus cibum
non accipiens, columba ei cibum portabat ad satietatem, &c.—*Acts*,
par. 13,

[†] In the flower of early youth shining like an angel.

[‡] " Eadem autum hora angelus Domini suscipiens B. Eleutherium
solvit eum et fecit eum sedere super equum."—*Acts*, par. 13.

of the Apennines. The liberty of the mountain side, **the**
beautiful fresh breeze that bore around him the odours of
a thousand flowers, and the exquisite view of the green
valleys, formed a great contrast with the horrors of the
prison he had just left.

Whilst he was pouring forth the acknowledgments of
his grateful heart to th. true God, the wild animals
gathered round him, as if to express their welcome to the
holy man who was sent to live amongst them.   Eleutherius spent some weeks in happy solitude on the mountain, feeding on roots and fruits, and singing the praises
of God.   He longed to come to the everlasting gardens of heaven, which he saw faintly reflected in the
beautiful world around him; but Almighty God has
still some greater triumphs and trials for his faithful
servant.

One day some hunters from Rome were passing over
the Sabine hills in search of game.   They saw at some
distance a man kneeling in the midst of wild animals;
they hurried back to the city to tell of the strange sight;
and from the description they gave, the people knew **it**
was the immortal Eleutherius, who had escaped once
more from the dreadful fate destined for him by the cruel
Emperor.   If a thunderbolt had split the earth in two,
and placed Adrian on the brink of the yawning gulf, he
could not have been more startled than when he heard
that his victim was still alive.   He ordered a commander
of the army and a thousand men to march at once to the
mountains to seize Eleutherius.

When the soldiers arrived at the spot pointed out by the
hunters, they found the Saint surrounded by an immense
troop of wild animals, which seemed to form a body-

guard around him, and defying the soldiers to come near
The Roman soldiers were brave, and fought desperately
in battle against their fellow-men, but there was something supernatural in the scene before them that unnerved
them and made them cowards. After much exhortation
and intimidation from their general, some of them advanced forward to seize the Saint, but they would have
been instantly torn to pieces by the wolves had not Eleutherius ordered them in a loud voice to desist. The animals obeyed him instantly, and came crouching at his feet
as if afraid of chastisement. He then ordered them to
retire to their home in the mountains, and thanked them
in the name of their common God for the services they
had rendered him. The troop of wild beasts moved away,
and left Eleutherius alone with the soldiers.* These he
gathered around him, and addressed in beautiful and
powerful language. He called on them to recognise the
power of the true God, whom the very beasts of the desert
obeyed. He showed them their folly in adoring a piece
of carved marble or painted wood, and how He who
reigns above can alone give eternal life and happiness.
Before the sun set on that auspicious day, six hundred
and eight sturdy warriors from the Roman garrison were
regenerated in the waters of baptism. Amongst the converted there were some captains of noble families and
favourites of the Emperor. They offered to let Eleutherius remain free, and to return to Rome without him, but
the holy Bishop knew they would only bring the indigna-

---

* " Adjuro vos per nomen Christi Domini ut nullum ex his con-
tingatis sed unaquæque vestrum ascendat ad locum suum ; ad cujus
vocem omnes feræ cum omni mansuetudine abscesserunt." - Par.
14, &c.

tion of Adrian on themselves, and that thus their families would have to suffer a persecution their young faith might not be able to endure ; moreover he was longing to receive the crown of martyrdom, which he knew by inspiration was to come in the end ; he therefore cheerfully accompanied them, to appear once more before the hardhearted and cruel Emperor.

The excitement in the city when Eleutherius was brought back again was beyond description.   Not one of the extraordinary scenes we have just described was private ; they took place before thousands of the populace ; they were discussed and talked over in every triclinium ; and the loungers of the Forum were in constant conversation about the wonderful Christian.   The cause of the Emperor became their own.   There were many amongst the people more wicked and cruel than Adrian, and who vied with him in their hatred of Christianity.   It was not sympathy, but curiosity and indignation, that made them flock round the martyr of Jesus Christ.   Adrian knew well what were the feelings of the mob, and wished to pander to them, and hence felt himself obliged to condemn Eleutherius once more to a public execution ; yet he felt himself subdued ; his mind was changed towards the Christians ; and although the holy and youthful Bishop of Aquileia suffered under him, he was his last victim.   The order is issued ; the people are to assemble again in the Coliseum to witness the execution of Eleutherius.   The events that passed in the amphitheatre on this occasion were strange and terrible, and form a grand tragic finale to the wonder of this marvellous history.

4.

The morning of the 18th of April, A.D. 138, must ever be memorable in the annals of the great city, not only for the passion of one of the greatest of the martyrs, but for the death of thousands of people who came to an untimely end on this day within the walls of the Coliseum. The demons were let loose for an hour in the amphitheatre, and they left the indelible stain of their presence in the records of blasphemy, cruelty and bloodshed. Doubtless the evil spirits were more annoyed than the pagan Emperor at the constancy of Eleutherius. His miracles and prayers were daily swelling the ranks of Christianity, and thousands were beginning to fear the name of the true God. The tortures and public executions which were intended as intimidations to the people were the fruitful source of conversions. They gave them ocular evidence of the divinity of Christianity—the power and sublimity of its faith, which raised men above passion and fear and enabled them to smile with the independence of martyrdom on the most terrible of all the catastrophes know to the pagan—the separation of the soul from the body. The blood of the martyrs fructified the soil of the Church, and for one that fell, thousands were gained.

On the day that Eleutherius fell under the sword of the executioner in the arena of the Coliseum, different emotions animated the crowd which witnessed the terrible scene. Some were excited by curiosity at the extraordinary miracles which were worked in behalf of the holy youth, whilst others raged like the furies of hell for the blood of the Christians. There were Christians, too, amongst them, glad and proud of their champion, who conferred so much honour on the Church and gave so much glory to God. Doubtless there were mixed up in the motley crowd some of the poor soldiers whom Eleutherius had baptized a few days before at the foot of the Sabine hills. How the tears of grateful sympathy must have trickled down the sun-burnt cheek of the hardy warrior as he saw the angelic youth roughly treated by the menials of the Emperor. Christianity softens the heart the moment it enters; it changes the brutal tendencies of the most ferocious nature into mildness, simplicity and love: the pagan who yesterday could bend with delight over scenes of bloodshed and cruelty, to-day turns away in horror and disgust.

The sun is now high in the heavens, and pouring its meridian rays in burning splendour over the city. The people are hurrying in crowds from every side to their favourite amphitheatre. Most of them were present a few days before when Eleutherius was cast into the cauldron of Corribonus, and hoped to see some similar scenes of excitement and wonder on the present occasion. They will not be disappointed.

The Emperor arrives with all his court. He looks sad and anxious. Old age and much travelling have told on his robust frame; he enters feebly and heavily to his crimson couch under the royal dais. He justly fears a repetition of his former defeats in contending with the angel of God, whom his own cruel heart and the voice of the mob bring once more into the arena.

Elevated by pride to absurd ideas of power, and too weak-minded to brook disappointment, he would have given half the Empire to get rid of Eleutherius.

Hark the trumpets have sounded—the games are commenced. A few gladiators pass in procession round the arena and salute the Emperor with the usual words —" Hail, Cæsar! Those who are going to die salute thee."* Some lions and tigers are exhibited, and allowed to frisk about for a few moments. The poor captive brutes appreciated the light and pure air of heaven when set free from the dark and fetid keeps of the Coliseum. Then the trumpet was sounded again, and the gladiators fought—some blood was shed—a captive from Thrace has fallen ;

> " And through his side the last drops, ebbing slow
> From the red gash, fall heavy, one by one,
> Like the first of a thunder-shower ; and now
> The arena swims around him—he is gone
> Ere ceased the inhuman shout which hailed the wretch who won."

Loud and shrill was the call of the excited spectators for the execution of Eleutherius. The order was given, and behold the holy youth is brought in in chains! His lovely, angelic features shone more beautifully than ever. He looked cheerfully round the crowded benches. Terrific yells were succeeded by breathless silence as he moved with a firm step towards the centre. A crier went before him, announcing, in a loud voice, "This is Eleutherius, the Christian." A messenger is sent from the Emperor to know whether he will sacrifice to the god Jupiter ; but a severe, cutting answer about the demons that represented Jupiter proved the martyr was as fearless and invincible as ever. Adrian ordered some wild beasts to be let out on him to devour him.

One of the subterranean passages was opened, and a

---

* " Ave Cæsar morituri te salutant."

hyena was sent into the arena. The animal seemed frightened and ran quickly from side to side; coming gently towards the spot where Eleutherius was kneeling, it lay down, seeming to be afraid to approach the servant of God. Then the keeper, who knew the indignation and disappointment of the Emperor, let loose a hungry lion, whose terrific roars terrified the people. The king of the forest rushed towards Eleutherius, not to tear his tender flesh with his horrid claws, but to reverence him and caress him. The noble animal crouched before the martyr, and wept like a human being. "When the lion was set loose," say the Acts, "he ran to the blessed Eleutherius and wept like a father who had not seen his son after a long separation, before the whole people, and licked his hands and his feet.*

A thrilling scene followed. Some people cried out that he was a magician, but the lightning of heaven struck them, and they were killed in their seats. Others called for his liberty; whilst more, in the enthusiasm of the moment, cried out : " Great is the God of the Christians !" The evil spirit had entered into the worst of the pagans, and, in maddened frenzy, they fell on those who cried out that the God of the Christians was great, and murdered them. They were attacked in turn by the friends of their victims, and a horrid scene of bloodshed ensued. The whole amphitheatre was in commotion, and nothing was heard but the shouts of the infuriated populace, who were tearing each other to pieces, mingled with the screams of terrified women and the groans of the dying. The Emperor had

* " Dimissus autem leo cucurrit ad B. Eleutherium et, tanquam pater filium post multum tempus videns, ita coram omnibus flebat in conspectu ejus, et manus ejus et pedes ejus lingebat."—No. 16.

the trumpet-blast sounded shrill and clear to command attention, but to no effect; the carnage went on, and blood was already flowing from tier to tier. The Emperor at length ordered the soldiers to clear the upper benches; with much difficulty, and even loss of men, they succeeded in quelling the fatal quarrel.

Eleutherius was all this time on his knees in the arena. Many of the people had leaped over the safeguards of the amphitheatre, and had gathered round him for protection. The wild animals dare not touch them. But the holy martyr prayed to the great God to remove him from such revolting and dreadful scenes. His prayer was heard. Almighty God revealed to him by an interior voice that He would allow him to be martyred by the sword. In a rapture of joy he told some of the persons who had gathered round him, that if the Emperor would command him to be put to death by the sword, he would succeed. The message was taken immediately to Adrian, who, in a paroxysm of rage, cried out: " Let him die then by the sword ; he is the cause of all this tumult ! " The trumpets were once more sounded, and, in the midst of confusion and terror, all became silent as the grave ; the spectators bent forward with breathless anxiety to see if the lictor would succeed. He wields the mighty axe— it falls—Eleutherius is no more ! His blood flows on the arena—the earth shook, and thunder was heard in a cloudless sky. A loud voice rang through the vault of heaven, calling Eleutherius to eternal bliss.

Yet he was not the last victim of that terrible day. There was another mother of the Machabees in the crowd of spectators—it was the mother of Eleutherius. She had watched with the joy of a true Christian mother all the scenes that her brave son had passed through ; **and** when she saw him at length passing triumphantly to his crown, her heart was bursting within her with the natural feelings of maternal sympathy and religious joy ; she almost forgot she was in the Coliseum, and in the midst of a pagan crowd, and rushing frantically to the arena, she threw herself on the bleeding corpse of her son. A murmur of surprise and pity roused the attention of the Emperor, who had not yet left the Coliseum. He sent **to** know who she was, and why she came **to** embrace the body of the martyr. When it was reported that she was his mother, and a Christian, who wished to die with her son, the cruel and enraged Emperor ordered her to be executed. The same axe that brought the crown of martyrdom to the son drank the blood of the mother. She was executed while embracing the dead body of Eleutherius, and their virtuous souls were united in the blissful world where separation shall be no more.

During the night their bodies were stolen by some Christians, and buried in a private vineyard outside the Porta Salara ; they were kept there for some days, and then taken to the city of Rieti, where a magnificent church was erected in their honour in the reign of Constantine. Innumerable miracles were performed by these sacred relics. The holy Bishop Eleutherius was more formidable **to** the devils after death than before ; and, during the lapse of seventeen centuries, the poor people who had first the honour of his remains amongst them, never lost their devotion nor called on him in vain. The relics **of** the holy Bishop were subsequently removed to Rome, **to** be distributed amongst several churches that were constantly applying for relics. The principal part of the

body of St. Anthsia, his mother, is preserved in the beautiful little church of St. Andrew on the Quirinal.

The marvellous history of this Saint was written by
two brothers, who were eye-witnesses to most of its extraordinary facts. They conclude their report in these
words :—" These things we, the brothers Eulogius and
Theodulus, who have been ordained for that purpose,
have written ; and being ever assisted by his holy admonitions, we have persevered with him, and we have made
mention of those things which our eyes have seen or our
ears have heard," &c.*

These Acts, which we have quoted from the Bollandists
are preserved in the archives of their church at Rieti.
They were also written in Greek by another eye-witness,
with slight alterations ; and by Metaphrastes, whose version
is given by Surius under the 18th of April. Baronius, in
his Martyrology, mentions the principal facts of his history, and in his notes refers to numerous authors who are
our best authorities for the records of the early Church.

We cannot conclude without saying a word about the
Emperor Adrian. He left the Coliseum on that terrible
morning silent and unwell. Even his hardened soul was
softened, but not converted ; he had learned a lesson
which deterred him from interfering again with the Christians. But, like all the persecutors, he came at length to
his hour of retribution. It was while in the amphitheatre
seeking the destruction of the servants of Christ, that his
frame contracted a loathsome disease, from which he
never recovered ; and so miserable and wretched did he

---

* " Hæc nos duo fratres, Eulogius et Theodulus, scripsimus qui ab
eo ordinati sumus et hortationibus ejus adjuti semper cum ipso per-
severavimus : et ea quæ viderunt oculi nostri et audierunt aures
nostræ nota fecimus," &c.

become, that in the end he died of voluntary starvation.
He lingered for a year in the most frightful pain ; he gave
himself to greater superstition than ever, in the blind
hope that his idols could restore him.   The harpies of
imposture gathered round him, and extorted immense
sums of money under pretence of skill or magic ; but his
malady increased, and his impious spirit was seized with
the horrors of despair and remorse.   The hand that wrote
the terrible judgment in the hall of Balthassar had already
weighed the persecutor of the Church, and the terrible
sentence was written before him, so dreadful in its very
anticipation that he thought to avoid it by death.   He
tried to induce some one to kill him, but was unsuccessful
in the attempt.   At length, filled with remorse and despair, he refused to take any nourishment, and died on the
6th of the Ides of July, in the year of our Lord 140 (according to Baronius).   His death took place at Baja, and
his body was afterwards removed by Antoninus Pius to the
immense mausoleum which he raised on the banks of the
Tiber.   That mausoleum still stands in massive splendour
like an imperishable ruin, reminding the Christian pilgrim
to the Eternal City of the triumph of many martyrs, and
the blindness of the persecutors of the Church.   One cannot but contrast the happy lot of Placidus, and Eleutherius, and the noble souls who were crowned with these
heroes, with the awful ruin and eternal death of their
persecutors.   May those souls which are now crowned
and happy pray for us, to enable us to resist the tyrant
passions which persecute us, so that, if we have not the
happiness of shedding our blood for Christ, we may at
least arrive at the martyrdom of self-love, and join them
one day in the praises of the same God whom we serve
and love ?

CHAPTER IX.

THE SARDINIAN YOUTH.

I.

ADRIAN had been declared a god. Notwithstand
ing the passions that made him contemptible,
and the cruelty that made him hated, he was
deified. The soldiers, the people, and the provinces, that
were greatly benefited by his visits and his generosity,
called for his elevation to divine honours. The Senate,
which was still the most intelligent body in the Empire,
writhed under his tyranny. On his death-bed he had
condemned four of them to be executed. Yet the weak,
degraded Senate consented, and a temple was raised and
sacrifices offered in his honour. The absurdity of these
acts would raise a smile, were it not that they involved a
terrible blasphemy against the true God, and make us
blush for the stupendous degradation of the human race.
It became fashionable in those days to make gods of the
Emperors. Whilst the burning carcass was being consumed on the funeral pile, the surviving family would pay
some vile wretch to swear he saw the divine spirit as-
cending to the skies. "Wherefore," cries out the great
St. Justin in his Apology for the Christians, "do you
condescend to consecrate to immortality the Emperors

who die amongst you, producing some one who assever-
ates that he saw the burning Cæsar ascend to heaven from
the funeral pile ?" *

A few years after the death of Adrian, one of the con-
cubines of Antoninus was declared a goddess ; and Antoninus himself, after his death, was worshipped under
the guise of a bronze statue erected in a magnificent
Temple in the Forum.   One of the most imposing ruins
of the old Forum is the splendid marble portico of this
temple, still bearing on its ruined entablature the mark
of the gilt letters, "Divo Antinino et Divæ Faustinæ."'
What wonder is it that the Emperor Commodus, a few
years later, should be impatient for the honours that
awaited him after death, and declared himself a god
whilst still living, and had sacrifice offered to him as the
son of Jupiter in the full assembly of the Senate ?   Like
the storm-cloud that clings to the mountain, the terrible
sin of idolatry hung for centuries over pagan Rome, and
seemed to wrap the ill-fated city in a dark mantle of
impenetrable gloom : she was the lady clothed in scarlet,
seated on the seven hills, the Babylon of the Apocalypse. †

Pagan historians, and even some Christians, tell us
that one of the best acts of Adrian was the election of
Antoninus to succeed him in the Empire.   His virtues,
for a pagan, were remarkable, and his blind fanaticism in
the worship of the gods procured for him the title of

---

* " Porro cur morientes apud vos imperatores semper immortali-
tati consecrare dignamini, producentes quempiam qui jurejurando
confirmet vidisse se e rogo ascendere in cœlum ardentem Cæsarem ?"

† " C'est une tradition constante de tous les siecles que le Babylone
de Saint Jean c'est l'ancienne Rome." *Bossuet, Pref. sur l'Apocal.*, vii·

Pius. His adopted son Marcus Aurelius, who afterwards succeeded him in the command of the Empire, gives him the highest character it is possible to express in words.*

But notwithstanding the fulsome praise that is lavished on Antoninus, he stands before us as a persecutor of the Church of God. There are stains of cruelty and injustice on his character which cannot be effaced by his natural virtues. When we read of the sufferings of the Chris·tians, tortured with inhuman cruelty, and their blood shed in the Coliseum, and at the Petra Scelerata, we cannot reconcile the horrors of a violent persecution with the character of meekness and justice given him by his pagan successor. There have been found records on the marble slabs of the Catacombs, that form a sad contrast with the encomiums bestowed upon him. Read the following touching inscription rudely carved on the tomb of a martyred child:—" Alexander is not dead, but lives beyond the stars ! His body lies in this tomb. He suffered under Antoninus Emperor, who changed from indulgence to hatred ; for while he was kneeling (Alexander) about to offer the sacrifice (of prayer) to the true God, he was led to death. Oh, unhappy times ! in which, even at our prayers and at mass, we are not safe. What more miserable than life, but what more miserable still that in death we cannot be buried by our parents and friends. But Alexander now shines in heaven. He lived a short time, who lived four years and ten months."†

---

* These reflections of Marcus Aurelius are classed amongst the philosophical works of the past. They are beautifully written, and have a great deal of merit. They may be found in nearly all the great libraries.

† " Alexander mortus non est sed vivit super asstra et corpus in hoc tumulo quiescit vitam explevit. cum antonine

If Antoninus relaxed the rigour of persecution in the latter years of his reign, it was due to the eloquence of St. Justin. With apostolic courage and zeal, he reproved the Emperor, the Senate, and the people for their injustice in shedding the blood of unoffending Christians. He contrasted the innocence, virtue and sanctity of the Christian life with the excesses of paganism, the absurdity and folly of idolatry, and the plurality of gods; he proclaimed the evidences of the divinity of the Christian faith brighter than the sun that shone over them, and warned them of the terrible account they would have to render, whether they wished it or not, to the one great and necessarily supreme Being whom they pretended to ignore, or openly despised in the persecution of His servants. Antoninus was not uninfluenced by noble sentiments, and the eloquence and skilful reasoning of Justin produced a favourable effect upon his mind; the sword of persecution was put back in its scabbard, to await the next tyrant that should wield the sceptre of the Cæsars.

Many celebrated Christians fell victims to the persecution of Antoninus. The Acts of St. Felicitas tell a touching tale of cruelty which shows the virulence of the persecution. Two other scenes are accurately

IMP. QUI MULTUM BENEFITII ANTEVENIRE PREVIDERET PRO GRATIA ODIUM REDDIT GENUA ENIM FLETENS VERO DEO SACRIFICIA TURUS AD SUPPLICIA DUCITUR O TEMPORA INFAUSTA QUIBUS INTER SACRA ET VOTA NE IN CAVERNIS QUIDEM SALVARI POSSIMUS QUID MISERIUS VITA SED QUID MISERIUS IN MORTE CUM AB AMICIS ET PARENTIBUS SEPILIRI NEQUE ANT. TANDEM IN CŒLO CORUSCAT PARUM VIXIT QUI VIXIT IV. X. TEMP." — *Aringhi, Roma Subter.*, tom. I. lib. iii. cap. 22.

The original of this inscription would be a perfect enigma to the inexperienced eye. We have preserved some of the inaccuracies of the rude original to show the intelligent reader how difficult it is to decipher some of the inscriptions of the Catacombs.

described in the Acts of the martyrs. One, a young lad from Sardinia, named Potitus ; and the other a Bishop, named Alexander, whose diocese is not known. The story of Potitus is replete with wonders : it has all the romance of the strange lives we have already recorded, and is, like them, based on the certainty of historical truth, from the unquestionable character ot its records. The beautiful, the simple and natural, twined here and there with the marvellous, render it one of the most interesting of the traditions that hang round the venerable walls of the Coliseum.

2.

The Acts do not mention what was the age of Potitus when dragged before the tribunals to glorify God in the profession of his faith. From the words used we infer that he must have been very young. In one place he is called an infant, in another a little boy, and more frequently a boy. But, from the custom of those times, a person might be called a boy up to his twentieth year, and an infant to ten or twelve. Thus we venture to say that Potitus was not more than twelve or thirteen when the scenes in his extraordinary career commenced.* His father was a pagan, named Hylas. He was opposed to Christianity, and persecuted his son on account of his religious principles. How the son came to the knowledge of the Christian faith is not mentioned ; but the Acts, as we quote them from the Bollandists, commence this interesting record with a touching scene between the pagan father and the Christian child.

* We have since found in a MS. in Naples that his age was thirteen.

Hylas used entreaties and threats to change the determination of the young Potitus to remain a Christian.
He tried in vain. The boy's mind was illumined by a
celestial light, and the knowledge and perception of sacred
truth raised him far above the stupidities of paganism.
The father, finding him inexorable, was angry, and locked
him up in one of the rooms of his house, telling him he
would not give him meat or drink until he consented to
abandon Christianity.

"Let us see if your God will help you now," muttered
the angry father, as he drew the key from the door. He
left Potitus locked up all night; but in the morning his
excited feelings had subsided, and the father's love,
which survives every passion, brought him again to the
room where his son was confined. He found Potitus
cheerful and merry; love, surprise and curiosity rushed
through his mind and urged a thousand questions. Assuming a tone of conciliation and affection, he entered
into the following conversation with his son.*

"O my son! I beseech thee, sacrifice to the gods. The
Emperor Antoninus has issued orders that every one that
will not sacrifice is to be put to the torture and exposed
to the wild beasts. How I regret that you are my only
child, and you so foolish!"

"But, father, what gods am I to sacrifice to? What
are their names?"

"You do not know my child, of Jupiter, Arpha,† and
Minerva?"

---

* We give the conversation from the original, with some slight
alterations to meet the idioms of our language.

† *Arpha* is a name seldom met in pagan mythology. We must
remember there were private gods as well as public. In each patrician's house there was a chamber called the *lararium*, in which were

"Well, indeed, I never heard that God was called Jupiter, or Arpha, or Minerva. How could He have all
these names? O father! if you only knew how powerful is the God of the Christians, who delivered Himself
for us and saved us, you too would believe in Him. Do
you not know, father, that a great prophet said, 'All the
gods of the Gentiles are demons!' 'It was the Lord made
the heavens,' not Jupiter, nor Arpha nor Minerva."

" Where did you learn these things," asked Hylas,
quickly and interrupting him.

" Ah! father," replied Potitus mildly, " He whom I
serve speaks through me ; for He has said in His holy
gospel, ' Do not think how or what you will say, for it
will be given to you in that hour what to say.' "

" But, my child, do you not fear the punishments that
are threatened to be inflicted on Christians? If you are
brought before Antoninus, what will become of you?
Those strange doctrines of yours will cause your flesh to
be torn to pieces by hooks, and you will be eaten up by
the lions."

Potitus smiled. A beam of heavenly joy lit up his
beautiful countenance ; drawing nearer to his father, he
placed his hand on the old man's shoulder, and, looking
affectionately at him, said, with much fervour and feeling—

" Father, you can never frighten me with these things.
You must know we can do all things in Him who
strengthens us. Did you ever hear that David alone
killed Goliah with a stone, and cutting off his head with
his sword showed it to all the people of Israel? His

placed the idols of the family, called *penates.* They consisted of
statues of every size and shape, and were numbered by several hundreds.

armour and strength was the name of the Lord. **Yes,** father," he continued, after a momentary pause, " in the name of the Father, and of the Son, and of the Holy Ghost, **I** am prepared to suffer everything for Jesus Christ."

Potitus made the sign of the cross, and folding his little hands together he became wrapt in prayer. The father watched him in breathless silence. He heard his son speak, with a feeling of awe he could not account for. The courage, the piety, and eloquence of the saintly boy had already won his heart, and the supernatural influence of grace which Potitus drew down from heaven completed the work of his conversion. The holy youth, raising his head, made one more appeal ; his words were accompanied by the more powerful eloquence of tears, and with all the feeling of his loving heart, he said to his father—

" O father ! believe in our Lord Jesus Christ, and you will be saved. Those gods you serve have no existence, they cannot save you. I will tell you what they are, father ! They are spirits that burn in a dreadful fire which they cannot extinguish. How can you be so mad as to worship a piece of coloured wood, or a statue of marble that cannot stir ? If it fall it is broken and cannot lift itself up. It is as lifeless as the clay we tread on, as silent as stones at the bottom of the stream ; the venomous reptiles that creep on the face of the earth have more power than your idols, for they can take your life away. O father ! how can these senseless things have power against the great God who created everything, who stretched out the heavens in all their glory, and dressed our earth in all its beauty, who alone is powerful, and puts His foot on the head of the dragon and the lion ? "

Another moment and Potitus was locked in the arms ɐf his converted fathe1. Their tears flowed in one stream to the ground—the tears of innocence and repentance.

After the conversion of his father, Potitus was admonished by an interior call to retire to solitude to prepare for trials which Almighty God had in store for him. He immediately obeyed and secretly left his father's house, and repaired to the mountains of Epirus. Here he was favoured with many visions, and was tempted by the devil. Almighty God sent an angel to inform him that he was to suffer martyrdom for the faith, and how and where he was to suffer. The angel instructed him how he was to preserve himself from the contamination of any vice—how he was to fight with the devil and overcome his snares and delusions ; an advice poor Potitus had very soon to put into practice, for before he left the mountain he suffered severe temptations and delusions from the wicked spirits.

On one occasion the demon appeared to him in the shape of our Blessed Lord. He seemed so beautiful and venerable that the holy youth thought for a moment it might be so ; but his humility came to his aid, and he feared all was not right, for the great Lord would not come to an unworthy wretch as he thought himself.

"My dear Potitus," said the lying spirit, "why do you trouble your mind so much with these austerities ? You can go back now to your father's house and eat and drink ; I have been greatly moved by your tears, and I have come to console you." Wondering, doubting, and surprised, Potitus could only say: "I am a servant of Jesus Christ." Then the devil, with all that impudence for which he is remarkable, said: "But I am Christ."

"Then," said Potitus, "come let us pray together."
At the same moment he remarked that one of his feet
was of a peculiar shape, and did not touch the ground,
and he remembered what the angel had said to him.
Horrified at seeing the vision was really the devil, he
prayed to God for strength.   Immediately the devil
changed his appearance, and became of gigantic stature,
with a horrible head.*   Potitus took courage, and breathing on the monster, said : " Begone, Satan, for it is written the Lord thy God shalt thou adore, and Him only shalt
thou serve."   Then the devil changed his shape ; he became like an enormous bull bellowing like thunder, and
tried to frighten the holy youth.   But when he made
the sign of the cross the demon seemed to writhe in
great pain, and cried out : " O Potitus ! send me away ;
why torture me with that sign ? oh, how I burn ! "
"Swear to me, by the sign by which I have bound you,
you will never henceforward annoy any Christian."

The devil consented, and immediately he was set free
he cried out: " I will go and show my strength amongst
the pagans.   I have got possession of the daughter of
Antoninus, and now I will go into the heart of the Emperor, and Gelasius the President, and I will make them
kill you with the most dreadful torments ; I will persecute you to death."

"Away, wicked impostor," cried Potitus ; "you can
do nothing but what our Lord Jesus permits.   I fear
not your machinations, but I will go and conquer you in
the name of the Lord."   The devil left, blaspheming God.

When Potitus had spent some time in the solitude of
the mountain preparing himself by prayer and austerity

---

* " Magis crevit cubitis quindecim," say the Acts.

for the mission he was destined for by God, he left his retreat and came to the city of Valeria, at that time the principal city of Sardinia. He knew no one in the great city, and wearied, and hungry, he sat down in the Forum. The people passed without minding him. They were all engaged in their different avocations of life. His eye was caught with the splendour of the beautiful buildings around him. There were columns, and temples, and porticoes of massive and rare marbles; but he drew sweet reflections from the varied scene; each new beauty or perfection of art which he beheld was an additional source of thanksgiving to the goodness of the great Creator who gave man such power over dull nature. Yet Potitus saw a terrible cloud hang over that scene of magnificence and art. He looked in vain for the cross that raised the people's hopes on high to a better world; he did not see the sacred sign of redemption dazzling in the light of the sun from the highest pinnacles of the temples; the smoke of the impure sacrifice which was the abomination of desolation curled in the murky atmosphere, with demons dancing on its wavy circles. Vice and immorality of every description raged around, and the angelic youth felt a shudder run through him as he recollected he was the only servant of the true God in that vast city. Like the diamond, that sparkles with more brilliancy beside a duller stone, his peerless soul was the brighter in the midst of the impiety that surrounded him, and his prayer more powerful before God. Little did the crowds that were passing around think the poor boy they saw resting on the cold stone bench was in a few hours to be the apostle of the Most High to bring them to the knowledge of eternal salvation. The instruments of the greatest designs of God are the humble and lowly things of life.

Whilst our young Saint was musing to himself, and thinking how he could best overthrow the power of darkness that hung like a mist over that benighted people, two old men advanced in earnest conversation, and sat on the same bench that he occupied. He heard the conversation. Almighty God intended he should.

" Sad affair for our president ! " said the taller and more venerable of the two, as he drew his broad laticlave across his shoulders.

" How is that ? " quoth the other ; " have the gods not been propitious to our noble Agathonis ? "

" Thou alone, then, hast not heard how an evil blast swept over his house, and struck Quiriaca, his spouse, with a loathsome disease. See yonder smoke that is rising from the temple of the immortal Jupiter ! It is from the sacrifice of three oxen that Agathonis has been offering to propitiate the angry gods ; but her terrible disease is increasing, and baffles the skill of our best physicians. When I passed yesterday afternoon, sounds of grief were rolling through the marble halls of the palace, and slaves were preparing a funeral pile in the courtyard."

" Let us go to the house of our afflicted chief," said the other, rising, " and see if the sacrifice that greeted the rising sun has not cheated grim death of its victim." So saying, the two senators moved towards the house of Agathonis.

Potitus heard in the conversation of the old men the call of God to proclaim His glory. The powerful name of Jesus would cure this sick woman, and many would believe. He had scarcely a moment's hesitation in determining how to act; he immediately rose and followed the old men at a distance. After passing through one or two of the principal streets, they came up to a mansion of princely magnificence; stairs of marble, ornamented with statues of gold and precious stones, led to a stately portico surrounded by a snow-white cornice carved like lace, and fresh flowers gave their sweet perfumes to the air from priceless Etruscan vases. The senators entered with the liberty of friends. Potitus, who followed close behind, felt he dare not even soil the polished marble with his plebeian tread—there is no admission for the poor into the palaces of the great. He sat down on the steps, and covering his face with his hands, prayed that God would manifest His will, and hasten the dawn of mercy on this hopeless people.

Whilst he was wrapt in prayer and holy thoughts, a sharp, shrill voice from the top of the stairs roused him from his reverie.

" Hallo! young man, what are you doing there ? No beggars are allowed to sit on those steps."

Potitus looked up and saw a eunuch dressed in livery, a proud, haughty youth, of a thin, effeminate form. He mildly replied: "Will you give me a drink of water ? "

What more valueless than a few drops of water ? Yet, when given in the name of Him who loves charity above all other virtues, they may purchase heaven.

" It is strange," said the eunuch, " that you come here to look for water; there are fountains of the purest mountain springs on every side of you; I suspect you have some other object in view, but I will watch you."

" Yes," interrupted Potitus, " you are right; I desired

water, and not water alone, but also your faith in our **Lord**
Jesus Christ, that there may be peace and blessing of God
in this house."

The eunuch, wondering at what Potitus said, asked :
" Who are you ?   I don't remember to have seen you in
this city before ; what's your name ? "

" I am a servant of the Lord Jesus Christ, who is the
Redeemer of mankind, who can heal the leper and the
paralytic, give sight to the blind, and raise the dead to
life."

The eunuch listened with attention, knowing that his
mistress was afflicted with a mortal leprosy, and quickly
asked the strange youth if he could cure leprosy ?

" Yes ! " answered Potitus ; " my Lord would do it
through me ; for he has said in His Gospel, 'Amen ! I
say to you if you have faith as a grain of mustard-seed,
you shall say to this mountain, remove from hence hither,
and it shall remove ; and nothing shall be impossible to
you ' "   (Matt. xvii. 19).

" Then you can really cure my mistress ? " asked the
eunuch, impatiently.

" Yes, if she believe I will cure her."

" She will make you lord of all her wealth."

" Ah ! friend, I don't desire silver or gold, or riches of
any kind.   I sigh only to unite her soul to Jesus in the
light and knowledge of faith."

These last words were not heard by the eunuch ; he had
fled inside the mansion, and rushing into his mistress'
room with that liberty which eunuchs enjoyed, recounted
in breathless haste to the sick matron how a strange
youth was sitting on the steps of the house who could cure
leprosy.   He was ordered immediately to be admitted to

h.. presence. The youth was brought through splendid halls, ornamented with naked statues and figures which made him close his eyes with holy shame. When he had entered into the room where Quiriaca was lying in her loathsome disease, he said: "The peace of our Lord Jesus Christ be with all here."

The sick lady lay on a crimson couch, attended by two or three slaves, holding fresh flowers in their hands, and waving beautiful fans to cause a cooling current of air. The room was hung with rich tapestry, representing scenes from mythology. A beautiful lamp stood in the middle of the room, on a marble pedestal of exquisite carving ; near the couch there was a table of odoriferous cedar-wood, supporting a casket of jewels, a mirror, and a stiletto to punish the slaves, all of which were ever within reach of the patrician dames of the first centuries. Quiriaca seemed advanced in years, but was frightfully disfigured by her disease ; the extremities of her hands and feet had already fallen off, and she was becoming an object of disgust to every one forced to serve her. Her internal agony of spirit was still worse than her corporeal sufferings. Her pride and vanity were stung to the quick ; she saw herself shunned by the other matrons of the city, banished from the tricliniums, and doomed to drag on her miserable existence in involuntary solitude and shame. When she heard that a strange boy had come who could cure her, she raised herself with intense joy ; hope, that had so long been a stranger to her breaking heart, returned to console her, and the moment the door was opened to usher in Potitus, she cried out with animation : "O young man ! cure me, cure me !"

She was struck with the beauty and modesty of the

youth ; a heavenly sweetness beamed on his countenance, and his eyes were cast on the ground. Gently raising his head, and looking towards the matron, he said : " You must first believe, and then you and your whole house shall see the good work."

" Oh ! I believe, I believe !" she cried frantically ; "there is no other God but yours—do cure me."

Potitus knelt. All were silent. A number of slaves and attendants had now gathered into the room, for the eunuch had run to tell them that his mistress was going to be çured. After a few moments' pause, Potitus stretched out his arms, and turning his eyes towards heaven, prayed thus aloud—

" O Lord Jesus Christ, King of angels and Redeemer of souls ! Thou hast said to Thy disciples, ' Make clean the leper, and raise the dead.' Grant to me, Thy servant, that Thy grace may descend on this woman, that this people may see Thou art God, and there is no other God but Thee."

He had scarcely finished his prayer, when a light flashed on the body of Quiriaca—she was cured. All her deformities disappeared ; she sprung from her couch, seized the mirror ; her skin became fairer than the purest Carrara marble, tinted with the blush of the rose. The attendants gathered round in wonder, and their exclamations of joy and surprise filled the chamber with a confusion of sounds. Quiriaca could not contain herself ; messengers were despatched through the city to seek her husband—to call friends—to announce the joyful news. A few moments and the house, the portico, and the street were filled with people, and the miracle was told and retold by a thousand tongues. The Acts say the issue of thi. miracle was the conversion of half the city (media civii atis).

Potitus remained some time to complete the great work God had commenced. But finding too much honour and praise were lavished on him, he stole away once more to his favourite retreat on the hills. Almighty God wished him to prepare for other and greater wonders. Before leaving the city, he sent some of the most trustworthy of his converts to Rome, to announce to the holy Pope, Anicetus, the blessings God had conferred on the city of Valeria. A bishop and some zealous priests were sent to tend the flock ; through their exertions the whole country round embraced the faith, which they never lost. The city of Valeria, however, has long since passed away ; the beautiful but ill-kept city of Cagliari stands near its ruins.

3.

Whilst the events we have just recorded were passing in Sardinia, there was a strange scene of confusion and grief in the palace of the Cæsars at Rome. The only daughter of the Emperor Antoninus, a young girl in the bloom of childhood, bearing the sweet name of Agnes, was possessed by the devil. We dare not investigate the laws that guide these terrible judgments of God : they are wrapt in impenetrable mystery. The child Agnes may have been too young to be steeped in moral guilt ; her greatest crime may have been a love of dress, or a momentary act of disobedience. Around her were parricides, murderers, adulterers, and wretches of the deepest depravity that can load the conscience of man ; yet the lightning of the thunder-cloud that blasts the lily may leave untouched the blasphemer. Say not, 'Tis chance—there is no such thing as chance with God ; 'tis the mysterious embrace of mercy, justice and judgment ! The Divine Spirit strikes with one hand and saves with the other. These awful visitations, so terrible in themselves, have been invariably the commencement of the richest spiritual blessings. Such was the case with the daughter of Antoninus.

The evil spirit so tortured her that she became an object of terror to all the household. She made the marble halls ring with the most terrific screams. At table she was raised as if by some invisible hand by the hair, and let fall with such violence that all wondered that the bones of her delicate frame were not broken. One moment calm and tranquil as of yore, and then a maniac—a fury rushing with deadly violence on her attendants, and dashing to pieces every ornament within her reach. The imperial palace was filled with grief ; the royal physicians were baffled, and knew neither the disease nor the remedies. In vain the *pious* Emperor offered the daily sacrifice in the temple ; in vain he led to the altar of Jupiter victim after victim—oxen with gilt horns, and decorated with garlands of flowers ; the devil laughed through the lips of Agnes, and gloried in the sacrifices offered to himself. At length the Almighty obliged him to tell the Emperor that he would not leave the body of his daughter until the holy youth Potitus would come, giving directions where he could be found, and what he was doing at that moment. Antoninus believing this to be a response from his gods, ordered Gelasius, the president of the city, to go with fifty men to seize Potitus, and bring him to Rome.

A few weeks have passed, and Potitus is standing before the Emperor. Curiosity made him anxious to see the man who alone could drive the evil spirit from his daughter; he expected to see some hoary magician from the sands of Egypt, or some weird gipsy from the banks of the Nile, or some high priest from the provinces who was a favourite with the gods. He was surprised to see before him a poor, ill-clad youth of thirteen or fourteen years of age; yet there shone in his countenance a beauty and a sweetness which made the Emperor and all look on him with wondering delight. After a moment's silence, he asked him : " Who and what are you ? "

Potitus mildly replied : " I am a Chistian ! "

" What ! a Christian ? " exclaimed the Emperor, as if he heard something terrible. " Have you not heard the orders of the Prince, that all who belong to that hated sect must die ? "

" I desire to die," was the meek reply of Potitus.

Antoninus would have given expression to his animosity against the Christians ; but the thought of his suffering child made him conceal and postpone the resolution he had already formed to make the innocent youth before him sacrifice or die. He dissembled the tone of his address, and by bland insinuations of flattery and reward, he thought to gain from the young Christian first the cure of his daughter, and then the gratification of that spirit of cruelty and fanaticism which has been sarcastically called piety towards the gods.

" I have heard of your great name," said the deceitful Emperor. " Can you cure my child ? If you can, I will enrich you with boundless wealth."

" Why don't your gods cure her ? " asked Potitus.

" How dare you speak so contemptuously to me ? "

A troublesome question to a Roman Emperor, reminding him of his weakness, superstition, and pride, was
downright contempt.

" Well," said Potitus ; " if I cure your daughter, will
you believe in the God I believe in ? "

After a few moments' hesitation, he said : " I will."

It was a false promise he did not intend to keep ; but
God, who readeth the secrets of hearts, sent a light into
the soul of Potitus and permitted him to see the hypocrisy
of the impious Emperor, and the judgment already prepared for him as abandoned by God. Looking sternly at
Antoninus, the noble youth spoke with majesty and force:
" False Emperor ! thou art weighed in the balance and
found wanting ; thy heart is hardened and unconverted ;
but that those who stand around may believe in the Lord
Jesus Christ, I will free thy daughter from the spirit
which torments her—let her be brought in."

The young girl was led in, supported by some attendants. She was worn away to a skeleton ; her eyes were
bloodshot and wild ; the fresh bloom of youth had left
her cheek ; she was so weak she could hardly stand, yet
the attendants could scarcely force her into the presence
of the holy youth. She trembled from head to foot, and
the moment she came in sight of him, she screamed, with
terror in her voice, " It is Potitus ! "

He commanded her to be still. He prayed for a moment, and then said aloud : " Impious spirit, I command
thee, in the name of our Lord Jesus Christ, to leave this
girl, who is one of God's creatures."

The devil, answering, said : " If you drive me hence, I
will persecute you to death."

But Potitus, not seeming to notice him, advanced and breathed on her, and immediately she was thrown to the ground with a great shock ; the palace was shaken to its foundations, and the Emperor and all the bystanders saw a horrid figure, like a dragon, going out through the window, leaving in the room an insupportable stench of fire and brimstone. Agnes lay on the ground as if dead; but Potitus came towards her, and took her cold thin hand in his, and lifted her on her feet. She was immediately restored to her senses ; her whole appearance was changed, as if she had been only wearing a mask ; her sunken cheeks became full and rosy ; her beautiful blue eyes sparkled once more with innocence and beauty ; her hair, too, that hung in careless knots in confusion about her, became brilliant and glossy, and fell in charming ringlets on her snowy breast. The touch of the Christian youth changed the emaciated and persecuted little Agnes to a child as bright and as cheerful as Eve when she first trod on the flowers of Eden ! The demons will never again have power over this beautiful child. She is now made for heaven. Potitus himself poured the waters of baptism on her head before tens of thousands of the Roman people in the arena of the Coliseum ; but strange events were first to happen.

Antoninus was not converted. After embracing his Agnes, and convincing himself that the blooming girl before him was really his child, he cried out : " This boy is a magician : I thank the gods for having cured my daughter." Potitus, who trembled at the blasphemy of the Emperor, said immediately : " Woe to thee, foolish prince ! thou hast seen the wonders of God, yet thou wilt not believe. It was not the gods that cured thy daughter but my Lord Jesus Christ."

"Do you yet persist in this silly and proud language I Do you not know that I am the Emperor, and can force you to sacrifice, or have you cut to pieces by slow torture, or devoured by wild beasts in the amphitheatre ?"

"I don't fear thee, nor thy cruel threats. My Lord can preserve me."

"It grieves me to see your folly, for you enrage me to punish you."

"Ah ! Antoninus, grieve rather over thyself, for thou are preparing for thyself a terrible hell, where thou wilt burn with thy father, the devil, who has hardened thy heart."

This was enough to rouse the concealed indignation of the Emperor ; and rising from his seat in a fit of passion he ordered two lictors to seize the youth and flog him. Notwithstanding the murmurs of pity that broke from every one in the room, and the beseeching tears of the beautiful Agnes, Potitus was stripped, and beaten with heavy sticks nearly to death. The only expression that escaped his lips was : " Thanks be to God." Although his tender flesh was torn and discoloured, yet Almighty God took away all pain, and the heavy clubs fell like straws on his back and shoulders.* After they had beaten him thus for some time, the Emperor ordered them to stop, that he might ask the holy youth to sacrifice to the gods.

"To what gods ?" asked Potitus.

"Do you then not know Jupiter, and Minerva, and Apollo ?"——

"Let us see what sort of gods they are, that we may sacrifice to them," said Potitus.

---

* " Et nullum dolorem cædentium sentio."—*Acts.*

The Emperor was filled with joy at this reply. He immediately ordered the youth to be clothed, and led to the temple of Apollo, supposing he had conquered the faith of Potitus, and induced him to apostatize. A great crowd followed them to the temple; the cure of the Emperor's daughter by the strange youth had already passed through the city. Some came to see the girl that was cured, and others were filled with curiosity about Potitus Amongst the crowd, which the Acts say amounted to about ten thousand,* there were many Christians who came to pray that God would give strength to His servant to glorify His name. When they had come up to the splendid temple of Apollo on the Palatine, a passage was made in the crowd for the Emperor and his attendants, and then came Potitus between two lictors. His eyes were cast on the ground—he looked at no one, but seemed wrapt in thought. That thought was prayer. Arrived at the foot of the statue, he knelt and folded his hands on his breast. Whilst a terrible silence reigned in the crowd, they suddenly saw the statue move towards them, and then, with a tremendous crash, fall to the ground. It was broken into a thousand pieces, so small that they looked more like dust than fragments of the colossal god. Potitus, who had destroyed the idol, without stirring hand or foot, by breathing a prayer in his soul, sprung cheerfully to his feet, and turning towards the Emperor before all the people, said : " Are these your gods, Antoninus ?"

"Boy! you have deceived me," cried the angry Emperor; " by your magic you have overthrown the god."

* " **Erat** enim turba hominum quasi decem millia."—*Acts.*

"But if he were a god," said Potitus, sarcastically "Could he not defend himself?"

Confused, defeated, and still hardened, the Emperor ordered him to be taken to prison until some terrible instrument of death should be prepared for him. He told the guards to put one hundred and twenty pounds weight of iron round his neck for fear he might escape. But Almighty God sent an angel to console him in his prison, who touched the heavy weights of iron, and they melted like wax. The guards saw his cell lit up with the most beautiful light, and heard the sweetest music until daybreak in the morning.

Antoninus had determined to expose his victim to the wild beasts in the Coliseum, but first to gratify his revenge by putting him to the torture. He sent criers through the city, and ordered the people to meet him in the amphitheatre on the following day. It would seem that the providence of God gave strength to the voice of the herald, that the entire people, and not a few only, should be witness of His power, and the divinity of His Church proved in the humble youth He had chosen to represent Him. The following day the amphitheatre was filled with all classes, from the senators down to the soldiers and people.* The Emperor and all his court were present. By his side was a beautiful little girl dressed in white—all eyes were fixed on her. A loud and deafening shout of congratulation greeted her as she entered. She thanked them, and moved her little hands in recognition of the public sympathy ; the girl was Agnes. She is not aware of the part she is to take in the spectacle

---

* "Et impletum est amphitheatrum populo."—*Acts.*

that is coming. From the moment she was delivered from her tormentor, she longed to become a Christian. She felt such sincere gratitude towards the youth who liberated her, that she could have done anything he wished. The waters of baptism had not yet purified her soul, and every throb of her heart beat in real human love for him ; her wealth, her affections, herself, were all for him, if he would but deign to accept them. She was, moreover, convinced of the truth of Christianity. Besides the miracle performed in her favour, she was present when the statue of Apollo crumbled to pieces at the prayer of Potitus, and she immediately asked her stern father to allow her to worship the God of the Christians. He rebuked her with severity, and threatened to burn her alive if she dared to invoke the name of the true God. The brave child had already resolved to leave the palace of her father, and live with the Christians in the caves of the earth ; but this will not be demanded of her. God has taken her in hands : a few minutes more and she will be a Christian.

The scene that passed in the Coliseum is one of the strangest we have to record. The amphitheatre was filled. Not all applauded the cruel policy of the Emperor ; there were thousands present who disapproved of the cruelty and fanaticism which condemned the innocent youth to be devoured by the wild beasts. The cries, the hootings, and hisses,* which were poured from every bench on the hypocritical Emperor proved that his false piety to the gods had carried him too far.

---

* It is a strange fact that *hissing* was used in the Coliseum as a sign of displeasure. It is not generally so in the Italian theatres at present.

The trumpet sounds, and Potitus is led into the arena. Half-stripped, chained, and surrounded by the lictors, he is brought before the Emperor. His arms are folded in the form of a cross on his breast; he is wrapt in prayer; he looks more beautiful than ever. What means the deep murmur that rolls like the break of the ocean billow through the vast amphitheatre? What mean those expressions of sympathy and pity so unusual in that temple of the Furies—the theatre of immolation and bloodshed? Antoninus understands it well, but piety to his gods urges him on, and steels his heart against mercy. Potitus must die.

When silence was restored, Antoninus said, "Well, young man, do you see where you are?"

"Yes," answered Potitus, "I am on God's earth."

"Hah! you are in my hands now, and I should like to see the God that will take you out of them."

Potitus smiled sarcastically, and quietly said, "Simpleton that you are, Antoninus! a dog is better than you for it knows more."*

The Emperor ordered him to be stretched on the rack, and fiery torches to be applied to his sides.

The holy youth was stretched at full length on a wooden frame. Ropes were fastened to his hands and feet, and joined underneath to a windlass wheel. By every turn of this wheel the body of the person is drawn several inches beyond its natural length, and when the pressure is too severe, the bones start from their sockets, the flesh breaks, and the most excruciating torture, and even death, ensue. Then, to add to the dreadful pain, lighted flam-

* "Melior est canis quam tu eo quia plus sapit."—*Acts.*

beaux are applied to the sides, so that the tender coating that covers the ribs is consumed in a few moments.

Whilst Potitus was undergoing this torture he seemed full of joy. The people could not understand it. Through the whole of the amphitheatre were heard expressions of " How well he bears it !" " What courage, what endurance ! he doesn't even complain." "Surely the God of Peter is with that youth ! "

The Emperor thought he had now at least subdued Potitus. He ordered him to be taken from the rack, and asked him which would he choose—to sacrifice or to die ? Potitus seemed as if he had been lying on a bed of roses. Almighty God had nulled all pain, and by a miracle preserved his limbs from the slightest deformation. Once more he scoffed at the threats of the Emperor, and defied his efforts to torture him or take away his life. Antoninus ordered some wild beasts to be let loose on him to devour him. They came bounding into the arena, but forgetting their native ferocity commenced to lick the feet of the holy youth.* They gathered round him in respect, and lay down on the sand of the arena in different postures, so as to form a circle.

The scene was strange and beautiful. Potitus was on his knees in the middle of them, and his hands and eyes were raised towards heaven in prayer ; the animals seemed to fear to make the least noise that might disturb him in his communion with their common Lord and Creator. The Emperor was surprised beyond measure, and little Agnes shed tears of joy. The people gazed for a few minutes on

---

* Ad cujus vestigia itidem feræ venientes deposita omni ferina rabie et occurrentes humiles capite osculabantur pedes ejus, etc. - *Acts.*

the strange scene with breathless silence, then, as if by common accord, they broke into a shout of applause that rolled like the echo of thunder through the arches of the mighty amphitheatre. When silence was restored, Potitus rose from his kneeling position and moved towards the Emperor; the animals followed, and kept close to him as if they loved to be in his company. Patting a monstrous lion on the head, he said, smiling, to the Emperor:

" Now, where are your threats ? Do you not see there is a God who can deliver me from you ? That God is Jesus whom I serve."

Antoninus was humbled, shamed, maddened. He heeded not the question of the holy youth, but commanded some gladiators to enter the arena and slay him. A scene still more extraordinary than that which we have just described ensued. The gladiators entered to slay Potitus. Four brutal wretches gathered round him. They wield their swords, but lo ! they are unable to touch him. An angel was there to turn their strokes aside, and they fell harmlessly on the air. They laboured with all their strength to strike him, but to no effect : he stood smiling in the midst of them, more like a beautiful phantom than a human being.* When the gladiators were so wearied that they could not wield their swords any longer, they gave up the fruitless task, and left the arena amidst the hisses and hootings of the excited people.

The scene of wonder is not yet over. The hardened heart of the Emperor is darker than ever ; the miracles which failed to convince him, excited him to greater rage,

---

* Nam sicut tentabant quodcumque ex membris ejus abscindere ita Domini virtus opitulabatur ut non ad exiguum attingere eum valebant.—*Acts.*

and, as if a demon sat in his place, he determined to attempt again the life of the holy youth. Rejected calls of grace deepened the guilt and blindness of the hardened sinner. Every new miracle worked by Potitus made him cry out more and more, it was by magic and by sorcery that he produced these wonderful effects. The same spirit characterizes unbelief in the present day; miracles as clear as the light of heaven, as incontestable as our own existence, are attributed to priestcraft, hallucination, or open falsehood.

There was the greatest commotion amongst the people. Shouts assailed the Emperor from every side. Every one seemed to be amazed at his defeat, and the reproaches which fell upon his ears drove him to desperation. He had another instrument of torture introduced in order to overcome Potitus, but this time the tables were completely turned on himself, and we have yet to record in this chapter one of the most extraordinary scenes that ever happened in the Coliseum.

The instrument he had now prepared was a pair of pincers with two large spikes, which were intended to pass through the head and meet in the very brain, so that there was no possibility of living after the application of this terrible torture. When the people saw the executioners coming into the arena once more, bearing this horrible instrument in their hands, they became silent, and leaned forward with the most intense anxiety to see the issue. Potitus freely offered his head to the executioners. The moment the spikes were applied, the holy youth prayed aloud that Almighty God would remove the instrument of torture from him and place it on the head of Antoninus. He had no sooner finished his prayer, than the instrument was lifted from his head before all the people, and carried by an invisible hand to the head of the Emperor.* There was great laughter and wonder amongst the people; the disorder lasted for a considerable time. When they were silent again, they heard the Emperor moaning in the most excruciating pain. All his attendants had gathered round him, and tried in vain to remove the spikes; he writhed and struggled as if in the agonies of death, and the senators and his attendants were filled with consternation. At length he cried out, in the most agonising pain, "Oh! save me, servant of God! save me! I know your God is powerful—oh! free me from this terrible pain."

Potitus said, " Why don't your gods free you, as my Lord Jesus Christ freed me ? "

But Antoninus still cried out louder, "Mercy, young man! mercy! for I am dying."

The senators and attendants in terror besought the young man to save the Emperor ; little Agnes too, in the impulse of filial love, raised her white hands in supplication for her father. There was a death-like stillness amongst the people as they watched what was passing. Potitus at length, taking compassion on the worthless Emperor, cried out in a loud voice:

"Well, I will cure him, if he will permit Agnes to become a Christian."

He assented. Before he had given the permission, little Agnes flew like a bird through the benches, and rushing into the arena, threw herself at the feet of the holy youth, breathless and unable to speak with joy. She knelt before him, and stretching out her arms, she looked

---

" Et fixit eum in caput Antonini imperatoris."—*Acts.*

up to him with tears flowing down her beautiful counte
nance, and cried out with vehemence, "Oh! baptize me!
baptize me!"

Potitus ordered some one near to bring him water
He addressed a few words to the lovely child as she still
knelt before him, and being convinced of her knowledge
of the faith, he baptized her before the whole concourse
of people. The moment the saving waters fell on the
forehead of the pagan child, the terrible spikes which
were piercing the brain of Antoninus were lifted from his
head by the same invisible hand that took them there,
and were flung into the arena with violence, bearing the
stains of his blood. Nothing could be heard but cries
of "Great is the God of Potitus!" The Emperor was
astounded at what had happened; he seemed like one
awakened from a terrible dream; the amphitheatre was
swimming round him, and his heart beat with fear and
anger. He had scarcely recovered from the shock of the
terrible pain he had just suffered, when he saw Potitus
leading Agnes towards him. The demon that ruled his
perverted spirit urged him to vent still further his impotent rage on the holy youth; but an invisible power
restrained him, and he was forced to hear Potitus speak.
They were his last words to the impious Antoninus; they
were short, powerful and prophetic.

"Antoninus, Emperor of the great Roman people! listen to me, a servant of Jesus Christ. I have conquered
thee in all thou hast prepared for me; now the scene is
over. Whilst thou dost persevere in thy impiety, I am
not to lose my crown; that crown can only come to me
by the sword, and in the place that I shall point out. The
mercy of God has to-day called this child to the know-

ledge and light of truth. Woe to thee, if thou dost interfere with her—that moment she will be taken from thee. Call thy lictors and let them tarry not. I long to be united to my Lord Jesus Christ." Then turning to Agnes, he said : " Farewell, my child ! and be faithful to the grace thou hast received to-day."

The Emperor, who was still maddened by his shame and defeat, was delighted at the hope of getting rid of the troublesome youth, and ordered the president, Gelasius, to see the sentence executed as Potitus wished. He was led away from the amphitheatre amidst the murmurs of all the people, and thus ended one of the most exrtaordinary scenes that ever passed within the walls of the Coliseum.

The Acts say that about two thousand persons were converted. All went to their homes from the amphitheatre struck with wonder at what they had seen, and filled with the greatest sympathy for the powerful but persecuted Christians. For days and weeks afterwards, those startling scenes in the Coliseum were the topic of conversation in the lounging rooms of the Baths and the benches of the Forum. The pagans endeavoured to explain all their mysteries by omnipotent magic, whilst the Christians sang their hymns of thanksgiving to the true God for the manifestation of His glory.

A few days afterwards, Gelasius and his troops returned with the news of the death of the holy youth. They reported that when his head was cut off, they saw his soul going to heaven in the form of a dove. The precise place of his martyrdom is unknown ; the Acts mention a place called Milianus, in Apulia, but all vestige of such a name has been long since lost ; even the river

Banus, on whose banks the martyrdom is said to have taken place, is not known.*

Although some doubt may be thrown on the place of his martyrdom, there is no question of the authenticity of the Acts. They are given in an epitomised form in nearly all the martyrologies ; also in Ferrarius Michaelus Monachus, Cæsar Eugenius Carraciolus, and De Vipera (S.J.), &c.

The Bollandists give two editions of his life in Acts, quoted from MSS. preserved in the monastery of St. Martin of Tours, and from a MS. preserved in the convent erected to his name at Naples by the saintly Bishop Severus. In the latter MS. there are some beautiful Latin verses of a very ancient date, referring to St. Potitus. The following are a few stanzas :—

> " O Stella Christi fulgida,
> Potite, martyr inclyte,
> Obscura culpæ nubila
> A mente nostra discute.

> " Tu, clarus inter martyres,
> Fulges ut inter sidera
> Sol, ac ut inter candida
> Ligustra candent lilia.

> " Luces ut ardent lampada,
> Humana lustrans pectora,
> Ut sol per orbem spargens,
> Humana siccans vulnera.

> " Non sic, Potite, cynnama
> Attrita sperant moribus,

The Roman Martyrology says in Sardinia, so also Baronius, An. 154. We are inclined to follow this opinion as the most probable, especially as his relics have been found under a church bearing his name near Cagliari.

Ut tu modestus florida
Ætate fragras sæculo.

"Post clara mortis funera,
Illustris inter angelos,
Tanto refulges lumine
Quanto per orbem nomine."

In the eleventh century the relics of this holy martyr were discovered, together with others, underneath an old church in Sardinia. Although there was no name on the sarcophagus, yet there was no mistaking the identity; for beside Potitus was laid the instrument which was applied to his head in the Coliseum, and miraculously transferred to the head of Antoninus. There was no other martyr of Sardinia punished in this way. Besides, there was a constant tradition that Potitus was buried under that church. It was in search of his body these discoveries were made. Jacobus Pintus, who gives an account of this discovery in his fifth Book *De Christo Crucifixo,* says: "In other places other sacred bodies were discovered, not without similar marks of sanctity and martyrdom, exhaling a most fragrant odour. Amongst the arguments or instruments of martyrdom, that especially was remarkable and interesting which was found in a larger and more precious sarcophagus; for, together with a great quantity of the bones, there lay the spikes that pierced from head to neck; and although there was no epitaph to record the martyr's name, it is well known there was no Sardinian martyr who suffered in this way except Potitus, whose relics, as is seen from all the martyrologies, were brought from Italy into Sardinia."— *Bollandists,* 13*th January.*

The reader, no doubt, will be anxious to hear some-

thing of the after history of Agnes. She was not destined to receive the martyr's crown. The few years of
her life were spent in peace in the imperial palace.

Antoninus dreaded to interfere with her ; he saw something supernatural about his daughter, which made him
look on her with awe and veneration. Every time she
flitted like an angel across his path, he thought of the
last terrible warning given him by Potitus. She was
permitted to live in the imperial palace ; by her virtues
and heroic example, she proved the divinity of her faith
as perfectly as if she were playing with lions in the arena
of the Coliseum. She passed her days unsullied by the
luxury and vanity of the pagan court. Like a freshly-
culled lily, floating in all its beauty and odour on the
muddy waters of the Tiber, she was carried into the great
ocean of eternity without a stain of blood or vice on the
angelic form that was restored to her by the SARDINIAN
YOUTH.

CHAPTER X.

ALEXANDER, BISHOP AND MARTYR.

1.

ALEXANDER is the third Bishop whom we find to have been exposed to the wild beasts in the Coliseum. He seems to have been fired with the zeal and love of an Ignatius, and raised to the wonderful and supernatural like Eleutherius. His Acts present us with another scene of baffled tyranny and triumphant grace ; and although we find repeated the same tale of wonder and mercy, yet, as with the annual return of spring, the flowers have ever new charms and nature new beauties, so each well-earned crown that we meet with in our path delights us with its wondrous fragrance and its surpassing beauty. Each martyrdom is like a garden decked with all the flowers and exhaling all the odours of sanctity and virtue. Stern facts only have come down to us through the lapse of centuries, yet they are caught up by the imagination like rugged cliffs in a mirage, and decorated with all the charms of poetry and romance. We might almost imagine that the same pen that wrote the biography of the Bible, in its rugged simplicity had been borrowed for the Acts of the Martyrs. The great heroes of those remote times had their long lives of eight hundred or nine hundred years summed up in these simple words, " he lived and died." Thus in the Acts of the Martyrs we frequently find short rapid sentences, and the briefest possible expressions : months, and even years sometimes, pass between events that are recorded in the same line, and, to a casual reader, they would seem to have passed in the same hour.

(The Acts of Alexander bear a very ancient date; they are simple and beautiful. They do not mention in what part of the reign of Antoninus the holy Bishop suffered. The Emperor reigned for twenty-three years, and it is probable twenty of these passed between the martyrdom of Potitus and Alexander. We are inclined to believe that Alexander suffered first, although we have accidentally placed the Acts of Potitus first. Both are well authenticated, and both suffered under Antoninus; their chronological position will not interfere with these interesting records.)

Our present sketch commences with a scene in a small town in Italy. The Acts introduce Alexander at once as a Bishop at his post in the midst of his people, combating the powers of darkness and spreading the glad tidings of the gospel. His sanctity and zeal, aided by a supernatural power of miracles, were fast breaking through the barriers of sin and infidelity, and raising the cross of the Crucified over the temples of the false gods.

Alexander was one of those holy men sent by Almighty God for the establishment of His Church. His preaching was confirmed by the most wonderful miracles; the promise of our Blessed Lord was fulfilled in him, that His disciples should perform even greater miracles than He himself. One morning, when he was engaged in prayer, he was disturbed by a pagan woman, who came to him wailing and crying, for her only son was dead. The poor mother had heard of the wonders worked by the Bishop. She was yet a pagan and unconverted; but in the deep sorrow of her disconsolate heart she madly seized the last hope that came to her with the name of the powerful Christian, and, throwing herself on her knees before him, begged of him to call her son back again to life. Alexander heard the voice of God calling him to promote His greater glory and save innumerable souls. He consoled the weeping mother, and bade her return to her house, promising he would follow immediately. After a few moments spent in prayer, he rose up and went to her house.

The boy had been dead for seve al hours. He was a beautiful child, cut off in the bloom of youth by an accident. He left his mother's house that morning full of health and spirits to play with his companions, but in a few hours was brought home dead. A large crowd of friends and sympathisers had already gathered round the couch on which he lay; some were looking sorrowfully on the calm features of the beautiful boy, others were slowly and solemnly repeating his name, according to the custom of the ancients, whilst others cast fresh flowers on his bed. His little companions cried lustily, for they loved him much. Near his pillow there was one in particular overcome with grief, who exclaimed from time to time, in the midst of convulsive sobs: "Poor Lucius! you said you would become a Christian when you'd get big." This was a Christian boy who used to serve the Bishop's mass every morning, and who afterwards became a priest.

When Alexander arrived, all became silent, and stood aside to allow him to pass. The Christians who were present saw in their saintly Bishop the representative of Him who gave joy to the weeping widow outside the gates of Nain. He approached the bed, and remained wrapt in prayer for a moment, then taking the boy's hand, said, in a loud voice, "Lucius, arise in the name of the Father, and of the Son, and of the Holy Ghost." Immediately the eyes moved, the hands and limbs were convulsed; life, which had entered the heart, was sending the vital stream through every fibre and vein ; the next moment the boy sat erect before the Bishop. His countenance changed from the marble tranquillity of death to an expression of terror and fright—he seemed to have been awakened from a frightful dream. Then a smile of joy lit up his countenance when he found himself in the land of the living again, and felt the warm kiss of his mother. Whilst greeting his companions, and receiving the congratulations of wondering friends, he suddenly lapsed into his feelings of terror. Putting his hand to his brow, he used incoherent expressions of fright, and speaking to himself, said : " Is it true ? Am I dreaming ? Where am I ?" Some thought he was still raving from the stunning effects of the fall that fractured his skull and took away his life, but the holy Bishop advancing once more to the couch on which he sat, calmly bade him say what he saw. The boy instantly cried out in a hasty and excited tone :—

" Hear me, O parents and friends ! I was taken by two Egyptians of frightful looks and full of anger, and they led me through a gloomy region to the brink of a dreadful pit, when there appeared a beautiful young man

with a shining countenance, who made the whole place
tremble as if shaken by an earthquake. He cried out
in a loud voice, ' Let go the boy, for he is called by the
servant of God, Alexander!' and behold I have been
brought back to my body." Then falling on his knees
before Alexander, he clasped his hands, and said with
great vehemence—" O Bishop of God ! baptize me in
the name of thy Lord, that I may never again see what
I saw this morning." A few days passed, and Lucius
and fourteen thousand others were regenerated in the
saving waters of Baptism.

Rumours of the wonderful doings were brought to
Rome. Antoninus, who was more a fanatic than a tyrant, sent an officer named Cornelianus with a hundred
and fifty men to seize the Bishop and bring him to Rome.
They found Alexander preaching to an immense concourse of people. A temporary altar had been erected
in an open plain, and he was surrounded by his faithful
flock. Seeing the great multitude of people surrounding
the Bishop, Cornelianus was afraid to seize him; he remained with his soldiers on the outskirts of the crowd
until the Bishop had offered the Holy Sacrifice. After
the celebration of the divine mysteries, the holy pastor
turned to his flock and announced to them it was the will
of God he should go to Rome to suffer for the faith and
Church of their Divine Master. More sad or startling
news could not have been given them ; every eye was wet
with tears ; some cried out loud whilst the Bishop was yet
speaking. Sublime and eloquent was the last warning
he gave them ; he poured out all the unction of his burning heart, and spake at length of the joys of heaven, and
the glory of suffering for Jesus Christ. When he had

given them his last blessing, he paused for a moment, and then changing his tone of voice, he said, slowly and majestically:

"The servants of the Emperor are already come to make me a prisoner of Jesus Christ; I command you to allow me to pass without any resistance. He who molests one of those men will be an enemy of the Great Master, who has told us to pray for our enemies." Pointing to the crucifixion on the altar, he said : " Remain you here in prayer before the great model of your patience whilst I go to my crown."

He then descended calmly from the altar and passed through his, flock, who were bathed in tears. There were hundreds of stalwart young men in that assembly, who might have offered effectual opposition to Cornelianus and his soldiers, but their faith and obedience to the Bishop tied their hands, and taught them the sublime morality of forbearance. A more touching scene is not recorded in the annals of sacred history. Grief, indignation, and all the passions of the soul were restrained by the noble power of patience. Their hearts were breaking to see their pastor and their father torn rudely from them as if he were a public malefactor, or an infamous conspirator against the throne of the Emperor. The self-possession and bravery of the pastor were reflected in the sublime forbearance of the people. The angels of God must have looked down with joy on a scene that was the nearest thing on earth to the perfection of heaven. Alexander, already a martyr in his heart, as firm as a rock, and as zealous as an apostle, thought more of his widowed people than of the racks, the cauldrons of boiling oil, and the roaring lions he knew were awaiting him in Rome, and giving one last, long and loving **look** on his weeping children, he raised his eyes, now sparkling with tears of affection, towards heaven, and breathed over the prostrate crowd this short but loving prayer, " O Lord! I leave them to thee."

He was accompanied to Rome by one of his priests, named Crescentianus. He followed him through all the different scenes of his martyrdom, and to him we are indebted for the beautiful Acts from which we are now quoting. Strange to say, Crescentianus did not say of what city Alexander was Bishop, nor have we any documents to indicate his see. It is generally presumed that it was not far from Rome, but from some expressions in the Acts, I am inclined to think his see was on the eastern coast of Italy.

On reaching Rome, Alexander was immediately presented to the Emperor. He was surrounded by soldiers, and his hands were tied behind his back. Antoninus sat on his throne silent and thoughtful, giving evident signs of uneasiness. Perhaps the recollection of past defeats deterred him from the risk of additional shame. Well he remembered the invincible spirit of the Christians, and the extraordinary power that made them terrible. He felt a supernatural awe steal over him when the Bishop appeared ; fear calmed the fanaticism of his blind devotion to the worship of the gods. He quailed **under the** steady gaze of his handcuffed victim, and would have given half his empire to purchase his apostasy, to save himself from the anticipated opprobrium of another humiliation and defeat. His biographers, and even contemporary writers, tell us that he was not a man of bloodshed or cruelty. He shuddered at the horrors of the reigns of Nero and Domitian ; but he felt some invisible power urging him on to persecute the Christians. Theirs was the only blood that stained his hands ; they were the terror of his dreams by night, the remorse of his conscience by day, and the mystery of his life. His interrogatory of the holy Bishop is a tissue of pride, hypocrisy and cowardice.

" Are you Alexander," he commenced, in a haughty tone, " who is bringing ruin on the East, deceiving men, and persuading them to believe in a desperate man who was slain by his companions ? If he were God, would he have suffered like a man ? "

" Yes ! He would have suffered as a man," said Alexander, taking up the last part of the Emperor's address as involving an attack on the great mystery of the incarnation. " It was for that purpose He came down from heaven, took on Himself human nature, that He might suffer for and redeem the creature He made."

Antoninus was silent for a moment ; he vainly tried to fathom the great mystery contained in the words of the Bishop ; the brightest pagan intellect could never grasp the sublimity of Catholic truth ; faith is alone the key that unlocks its treasures to the mind of fallen man. The Emperor was a philosopher and thought he knew a great deal, but finding the Christian prisoner before him so familiar with things he never heard before, he endeavoured to hide the blush that mantled his brow, and in a hurried and confused way resumed his address.

" I don't want to have much to say to you, young man, but come, deny your God, and offer sacrifice to our deities, and I will reward you by giving you an office of honour in my own palace ; but if you refuse, I will put you to the torture, and your God will not be able to take you out of my hands."

"Was it to make one worship those dumb stones you brought me here?" asked the holy martyr, indignantly. "Then, Antoninus, if you are resolved to torture me, do so at once, for I will always put my trust in Him who reigns above; I will never burn incense to a senseless idol."

"Let this insolent man be beaten with rods," said Antoninus, angrily; "he does not know to whom he is speaking. You have insulted me, who am the ruler of the world!"

Alexander smiled, and said, majestically : "Do not boast of thy power. A few days and thou wilt go where thou dost not wish ; thou wilt have less power than the worm we crush to death beneath our feet."

Whilst he was thus speaking, the lictors were untying their fasces, and picking out some of the strongest rods that guarded the axe. A soldier had approached to tear off the garments of the Bishop, when the Emperor, who seemed undecided and irresolute, cried out :

"Hold! let me see! Take him to prison ; give him four days to think over his folly, that he may give up the worship of his vanity, and come of his own accord to worship our gods."

"Look upon the four days as already passed," exclaimed the Bishop ; "and do with me now what thou intendest."

Alexander was led away to prison. He was patient and cheerful. The horrors of a Roman dungeon were not unknown to him, yet there was no expression of reluctance in his countenance, not a word escaped his lips indicative of fear. He spoke freely with his guards, and surprised them by his indifference. He seemed to consider himself their guest, and chatted as freely as if they were accompanying him to some delicious suburban villa to pass a few days in retirement. When they reached the prison, they pushed him rudely in, and drew the heavy bolt across the iron door, then grinned sarcastically at each other as if they had caught and subdued the wildest lion of the African deserts. They little thought the power of the God of the Christians could pass through iron doors; they go to sleep with the keys of the prison door under their pillow, yet another hour will find their prison empty and their victim escaped.

Poor Crescentianus, the faithful priest of the noble Bishop, followed as far as he could prudently go; but when he saw him cast into a gloomy dungeon, and heard the door ring as it was closed and the lock grate as the heavy bolt was drawn into its marble socket, he was filled with grief, and went away from the sad scene with a heavy and sorrowful heart. He rambled on through Forum and square and crowded piazzas, unmindful of everything, and wrapt in silence and gloom. The noise of the city was irksome; he longed to find some retired shady spot, where he could indulge in the consolation of tears in solitude and silence. Thus he strolled on until he passed through the gates, and felt the fresh breeze of the Sabine hills. He threw himself down under the shade of a large tree, and soon fell into a slumber.

Immediately a strange vision passed before him. He thought he saw Alexander kneeling in one corner of his loathsome prison; beside him was an angel of light, who joined him in singing alternately the verses of a hymn then commonly in use amongst the Christians. After this, he saw the angel untie his bonds, and lead him towards the door of the prison. The heavy door flew open, and they went through: the guards were all asleep, and they passed by unnoticed. The angel led him through the Forum, and those streets which lead to the Porta Capena.* Crescentianus, still asleep, thought he was then passing over every inch of the ground he had just walked. They were engaged in the most cheerful conversation, and the brilliant light that shone from the countenance of the angel made everything around brighter than day. The people crossed on either side, but seemed not to see them. At length they passed under the gate, and every step brought them nearer to where he was. He thought he could hear them talking when the angel suddenly stopped, and pointed out where he was sleeping, and, singing Alleluia in the most exquisite manner, began to rise gradually towards heaven. Alexander was riveted to the spot, and remained for a few moments gazing in the direction whence the lovely spirit had disappeared. Crescentianus, still in his dream, thought he saw the holy Bishop come towards him; his heart begins to leap—now he is nearer—another moment and he sees the venerable form of the Bishop bending over him. Starting from his dream, Crescentianus awoke, sprang to his feet, and cried out, " Alexander ! "

It was no dream. Alexander was really there. That moment they were clasped in each other's arms.

* The gate that led to the Appian Way.

Alexander told the good priest how the angel came to him in prison, delivered him, and led him within a few yards of the spot on which they were standing ; and the priest, in tears of joy, recognised that his vision was not a disappointing dream, but a consoling reality. They moved off together along the Appian Way, expatiating on the mercies of God. Alexander spoke with much fervour on what the angel told him ; how he was to be taken back again to the hands of his persecutors, and to suffer martyrdom for the faith ; that he was liberated from prison for a few days in order to confound the pagans, and to carry spiritual relief to some poor Christians dwelling in a small town in the vicinity of the city, who were wavering in their faith. Thus the joy and love of their hearts made them unconscious of the fatigues of the journey ; they did not stop until they arrived at the town pointed out by the angel.

Next morning the governor of the prison came in fear and trembling to announce to the Emperor that, by some unknown means, the prisoner Alexander had escaped. The wretched man did not know but that his own head would have to pay the penalty. Antoninus was more annoyed than surprised. The Christians were a puzzle to him ; he dreaded them, whilst he persecuted them with fiendish hatred. His answer to the governor was, Alexander must be brought before him at the end of four days ; otherwise, his own head would be the atonement to the offended gods. The governor received the message with terror, yet it was a relief to his terrified soul, although the sword of the executioner still hung over his head ; he seized the hope that a few days' respite afforded, and on his way back to his house, he planned his arrangements to search the city for his victim. But Alexander was like a city on a mountain, or a light in the most conspicuous part of the house ; the governor had no difficulty in hearing and discovering the abode of this great servant of God.

A couple of days have passed, and Alexander and the holy priest Crescentianus have converted the little town on the Appian Way to which they were sent by the angel. Miracles of all kinds confirmed their preaching : the light of heaven was poured on the sightless eye-balls ; and the lame were made to bound like the deer ; even the dead were called from more than four days' corruption, and appeared in Rome to their astonished friends, to tell how Alexander brought them back to life. Fame flew with untiring wing to every triclinium of the city— from the Forum to the baths, and from the baths to the Palatine. Immediately another troop of soldiers was sent to seize the Bishop ; and on the morning of the fourth day he was brought to Rome, secured by heavy chains, and surrounded by a cruel and demoniacal mob. The governor of the prison had saved his head, but heaven had gained a martyr.

The morning Alexander was brought to Rome, it happened that the Emperor and an immense concourse of people had assembled outside the city, in a field on the Claudian Road, to witness an exhibition of wild animals and athletic sports. The animals had just arrived from the East, and were intended for the games of the Coliseum. Whilst the ovariums were being prepared, they were exhibited here, to the great amusement and delight of the people.

The governor of the prison, who was trembling lest

some Christian magic should deprive him of his victim once more, rubbed his hands with glee when he saw Alexander in chains, and stoutly guarded by fifty armed soldiers. He ordered the saint to be brought at once to the Via Claudia, whilst he followed in his chariot, feeling the joy of a man who had just come out of a dungeon, after having escaped the sentence of death.

They marched about two miles outside the Flaminian gate, crossed the Milvian Bridge, and entered the field where the Emperor and the people had assembled—the same field, probably, which was in latter times the exercising ground for the Pontifical troops.

In the midst of the sports a rumour passes through the crowd—the Emperor has been called—something has happened. Some say fresh animals have arrived, and he wishes to see them at once ; others, that important news has come from the city, and he is returning to hear it. They see him moving with his suite towards a temporary dais erected at the end of the field, where he might rest and take refreshments. What is it ? is asked by a thousand voices at the same moment, as they see a troop of soldiers approaching from the Tiber ; in the front rank there walks a young man in the bloom of youth, in a strange but poor dress, and bound as a criminal. All eyes are bent on him. What can he have done ? Soldiers, too ! And there goes the governor of the Tullian ! Their wondering questions were not answered, but their curiosity was increased when some one said he was the Christian who had escaped from prison a few days ago. They all rushed round the shaded balcony of the Emperor, to witness the result of his examination.

Alexander was tranquil and cheerful. He was boomed and guarded : he knew that every eye was upon him. There was none of that false confidence, and apparent indifference to fate, which animate political prisoners, led through an excited and shouting mob to the tribunal of the state ; he had closed his eyes and ears to earthly sounds, his heart was away at the throne of God, imploring strength for his coming struggle ; nobility, majesty, and angelic sweetness were all blended in his countenance; the eye that looked at him through curiosity remained fixed with reverential awe. Amongst the crowd, there followed the faithful Crescentianus—he who knows no fear, defies death—and the holy priest recorded for posterity what he saw and heard. "Anxiously listening," says the good Crescentianus, "I heard Antoninus say—

"'Well, Alexander, hast thou consented to become our friend ?'

"Alexander, after a moment's pause, replied, 'Do not tempt my Lord Jesus Christ; thy father the devil once tempted Him, and said : "If thou be the Christ, turn those stones into bread;" and the Lord said : "Away! begone, Satan, the Lord thy God shalt thou adore, and Him alone shalt thou serve." So I say to you, thou shalt not tempt the servant of Christ.' "

At that moment, a terrible flash of lightning startled the crowd. A dark, heavy thunder-cloud had been passing overhead, and, as if in indignation at the insult offered to a servant of the great God, poured down its torrents of rain upon the multitude. The people ran everywhere for shelter. Frequent and prolonged flashes of forked lightning lit up Monte Mario and the Saxa Rubra with a lurid glare, and the earth shook with the most terrible thunder. Terror gave additional confusion to the scene ; the people ran to and fro, mingling their shouts with the screams of the animals, whilst some seemed to lose their senses with fright ; many were struck dead by the lightning, others were trampled to death by the crowd, as they madly rushed towards the city. Antoninus, who, a moment before, had been thinking of exposing Alexander at once to the hungry animals, was too terrified to carry his project into execution. By giving orders to have the prisoner transferred to his tribunal in the city, he was but obeying the unseen Providence of God, who wished to confound still more the folly of idolatry, and manifest His own omnipotence and divinity. The assembly broke up ; and the moment Alexander left the tribunal, the storm ceased, the sky became beautiful and clear, and the bright rainbow of heaven showed, to the prophetic eye of the holy Bishop, the sunshine of peace and triumph that would soon shine on the Church after the storm of persecution had passed away.

Next morning the city was in great excitement. The thunderstorm, which was perhaps but a natural contingency, was magnified into a masterpiece of witchcraft and skill on the part of the Christians.

In proportion as curiosity drew them round Alexander in greater numbers, their fear and respect were also increased. Antoninus was confused. He was enraged by the anticipation of a defeat, for he knew there was something extraordinary about the Christians. A private examination and execution were now impossible ; for long before the usual time for the trial and condemnation of Christian criminals, the Forum was filled with an eager and curious crowd. There was no need of a crier on this

occasion, to call them to witness the terrible fate of the
Christians. They poured in from every part of the city
in immense masses; the humble servant of God was to
be like Himself, for the resurrection of many, and for the
greater condemnation of the hardened and unconverted.

At length the Emperor arrived. Alexander was brought
before him. He had still that mild but inflexible look of
determination which, from the first day he saw him, to
the Emperor seemed superhuman. After he had taken
his seat, and silence was proclaimed, Antoninus commenced a long oration about the great Apollo and the
invincible Jupiter. He concluded with a touching appeal
to the human feelings of the Saint; he offered liberty, a
post of honour in his palace, friendship with Cæsar,
wealth, marble halls and boundless vineyards—everything
that the pagan world coveted; but the return for all this
—the necessary condition—was apostasy. Alas! how
many now-a-days are caught with the promises of the
world, and sell their faith and eternal happiness for a few
days of favour with Cæsar!

But Alexander seemed too indignant to answer. He
whispered to one of his guards near him something equi-
valent to this: "Tell the Emperor he is a fool for his
pains." The crowd knew nothing of what he said, but
saw a person whispering to Antoninus in a low voice.
His countenance became flushed with rage; he stamped
his foot, and, calling Cornelianus, cried out, angrily, "Let
him be put on the rack, and burn his sides with torches."

In those days of terror, the rack, the cauldron, and the
axe were always at hand; the torturers and the headsmen—
demons in human form—were always at their post when
a Christian victim was to be tortured or executed. A

few seconds after this order had been issued, a cumbrous machine was wheeled into the presence of the Emperor. Its ropes, wheels, and crossbar handles left no doubt as to its name and efficiency to torture the human frame. Another moment and the Bishop was stripped, the loops were passed round his hands and feet, and the rough arm of a lictor pushed him back on the machine. All were silent, and watched with breathless anxiety for the tightening ropes, the stretching limbs, the convulsed frame—but, oh, wonder ! the ropes are stretched to their utmost limits, and the Saint's body seems to have stretched with them, yet no pain, no moans, no contortion of the placid looks ; a smile plays around his lips, and joy beams in his bright eye. Burning torches are applied to his naked sides, but his flesh is not consumed, he feels no pain. The martyr himself compared the sensation to cold water poured over his body and washed off with the most delicate sponge. After half-an-hour of fruitless efforts to dislocate his bones, and burn his sides the Emperor had him taken off and once more said to him : "Now, see how long the gods are waiting for thee, and thou wilt not submit. Now I swear to thee by Jupiter, the only invincible god, and Apollo, who possesses the world and rules every age, if thou wilt voluntarily sacrifice to them I will esteem thee as a brother and give thee immense riches."

Contrary to the expectation of all, and even of the Emperor himself, Alexander replied : " Then where are your gods ? let us see if they prove their divinity that we may sacrifice to them."

If the governor of a besieged city on the point of yield ing through starvation saw the enemy retire on the prom-

ise of a slight reward, he could not have felt more joy
than Antoninus when the Christian Bishop consented, as
he thought, to offer sacrifice to his gods.   He ordered
him to be taken immediately to the temple of Apollo ; a
crier went before, declaring the victory of the Emperor ;
and the people, who the Acts say were about 3000, moved
en masse to the scene of expected apostasy and perversion.
But they were doomed to be disappointed. Let us follow
the crowd, and see once more how great is the God of
the Christians.

We have already mentioned where the temple of
Apollo is supposed to have been situated.   The procession moved along the Via Sacra through the triumphal arch of Titus, and, turning immediately to the right,
passed along the Via Nuova—the massive pavements
of which are still to be seen—and thus reached the
temple of the god Apollo on the southern part of the
Golden House.   Many of the people had run thither
immediately to secure a good place ; and when the Emperor and the holy Bishop, still guarded by the soldiers,
had arrived the lictors had to make passage through the
crowd.   Antoninus entered the temple first, and, in a
studied speech, thanked Apollo for his triumph over the
Christian. The fire, the incense, and the tripod were ready,
and a garland of fresh flowers was put on the brow of
the marble statue.   The Emperor beckoned to Alexander
to come forward ; he advanced majestically, knelt and
prayed.   The reader knows what is going to happen—
yes ! down came the idol and part of the temple, breaking
all before it—in a moment all was smoke, confusion and
ruin.   The murmur of the people was like the thunder
of the fall.   Alexander rose, smiled, and pointed to the

débris of the statue and temple of the mighty Apollo, as much as to say, " These are the gods you worship."

But as gladiators who contend with each other are more maddened by every defeat, so Antoninus became more enraged each time he was baffled by the Christian. He slunk away from the scene of the fallen temple as if every stone had a tongue to hoot him. It cost him little to blaspheme the god he pretended to fear ; in a fit of rage he determined once more to avenge himself on the Christian. What is the most terrible and disgraceful death he can inflict on Alexander ? To be torn to pieces like a slave by the wild beasts in the Coliseum. Such is to be the case : and as the enraged Antoninus moved towards his marble halls, he called Cornelianus, told him to guard his prisoner well till the morrow, and then to have him devoured by hungry bears and lions before the whole people in the amphitheatre.

2.

Once more we find ourselves in the Coliseum. More beautiful in its renovated splendour, it seems to have been built but yesterday, and to be commencing a new and more bloody career. The same scene presents itself to our view—crowded seats ; the people shouting ; every now and then a voice louder than the rest sends a sharp, shrill sound ringing through every bench, and re-echoing from the awning to the arena and back again. It meant " The Christians to the lions ! " The Emperor arrives. Trumpets, drums and clashing of arms mingled with the roars of animals and men : it was the homage of Rome to its terrestrial Jupiter.

Antoninus entered with a gloomy frown upon his brow. The adulations and absurd praises, vociferously clamoured forth by his subjects, remind him how false his greatness, how palpable his weakness, since he cannot conquer one man—a weak, young, unarmed captive! Blind, abandoned, and already judged, he could not see where thousands saw; yet historians say he had a noble soul! Perhaps they only meant by contrast. That soul was wrapped in a mist darker and denser than the cloud which the sun cannot penetrate. But as the impiety of the Jews was the instrument of the mercy of God, so the blindness of the Roman Emperors has been the source of everlasting glory to many.

Alexander is led in. Venerable, though young; beautiful, though austere; joy is stamped on his features; confidence is seen in his gait; his whole appearance is a defiance of death—the bravery of independence inspired by martyrdom and anticipated triumph. Hark! the animals are growling, as the apertures of their dungeons are opened; they are greeting some passing gleam of the light of heaven through the unbarred gates, or, perhaps, some favourite keeper whom they dare not touch. The wildest and best are permitted to seek the momentary freedom of a larger cage; a dainty feast of human blood they wish to give them.

Two bears rush into the arena, but an invisible power arrests their progress; they stand motionless, looking towards the martyr as if some wondrous light terrified and dazzled them. They will not move. Two more enter; they join their companions, and look with awe on the martyr of God. But the strangest thing in the annals of the wonders of the Coliseum is yet to be told

Alexander moves from the centre towards the throne of Cæsar, and, behold ! the bears follow and lick the print of his footsteps. "Ubi ambulaverat famulus Dei vestigia pedum ejus lingebant," says Crescentianus, an eye-witness.

Two lions were let loose, and with roars bounded towards him. But they likewise bowed themselves down before the great servant of God, and licked his feet. "Cumque venissent duo leones, humiliaverunt se ad pedes ejus plantasque lingebant."

Who could describe the noise, the shouts, the yells of the people ? Greater than any god must have been the thing called magic that could work such wonders. But the Christians knew it was the omnipotence of God ; their cry of praise fell like music on the ear of Alexander ; he rejoiced that there were even a few in the mighty mass of infidelity that surrounded him to join in thanking their common God.

Cornelianus, who had the care of the prisoner, knew the pleasure he should give the Emperor by the destruction of Alexander. He prudently (as he thought) anticipated the reluctance of the beasts to touch him ; these dumb animals were believed to be influenced by the dark arts of magic. He had in readiness the furnace burning under an enormous pan of heated oil ; and with the permission of the Emperor, it was wheeled into the arena. Louder and deeper became the murmurs of the excited people as they saw the burning cauldron take the place of the brutes, who had been coaxed away by large lumps of carrion flesh But need we delay to tell of another triumph, another defeat, another miracle ? Alexander was put into the burning mass : it was immediately extinguished.   Further and louder cries rang out from the benches ; the blasphemies of the pagans were not louder than the sweet " Deo gratias " of the faithful few.

We have remarked in former narratives, that these extraordinary miracles in the Coliseum were not without fruit.   Whilst thousands were left beyond any further doubt, there was generally a harvest of immediate conversion.   The saints in the amphitheatre were like the apostles, when they came out of the upper room in Jerusalem ; every word they spoke was an argument that appealed to the intelligence, and like an arrow pierced through the heart, the seat of the will, the affections, and the passions, which it led captive to the altar of eternal truth.   When the Apostles passed away, Almighty God still continued the ministry in all its original splendour of miracles and attraction.   The Flavian amphitheatre at Rome was, in its day, one of the spots chosen by Him for the continued Apostolate of His Church.   How venerable must its majestic walls appear to the eyes of the student of the Church's history !   Imperishable records, telling of conversions, of wonders, of mighty words, and examples of the martyrs of Christ.   Here the great Spirit of God breathed conviction and love, wheresoever it wished.   Pagans, and persecutors, and blasphemers, with hearts harder than the statues of their gods, entered the Coliseum in the morning, to gloat over scenes of cruelty and bloodshed ; before sunset, they were transferred, like the good thief, from the midst of their infamy and shame, to the joys of paradise.   Alexander will not be without a large and beautiful harvest of souls, and, even like his predecessors, who combated the powers of darkness in the arena of the Coliseum, he will have com-

panions in his glory. Let us continue the beautiful records of the Acts.

Antoninus, seeing his victim still unhurt and indomitable, was carried away by his blind fury ; and, without
stopping to consider whether he could succeed or not,
ordered Cornelianus to have him beheaded by the public
executioner. Cornelianus commanded silence. He read
aloud to the assembled thousands the sentence of the
Emperor ; that Alexander, the contumacious Christian,
was to be beheaded at the twentieth milestone on the
Via Claudia.

He had scarcely finished the last word of the sentence,
when there was a commotion near the Emperor's seat ; a
young man was struggling in the arms of another ; every
one was silent, and all eyes turned towards the scene.
At length he overpowered his antagonist, and rushed
towards the Emperor. It was Herculanus, a courtier of
the royal suite, and a particular favourite of Antoninus.
Almost breathless, he cried out in a clear voice:

" Cruel and insensate tyrant ! how has God blinded
thine eyes that thou mayest not see, and hardened thy
heart that thou mayest not understand, the greatness of
His power ? Behold this Christian: he has come forth
unhurt from all his trials ; no marks of the lash appear
on his body ; the rack and the burning torches had no
power to hurt him ; when torn by hooks, he did not
breathe a word ; the gods of Rome could not stand before him, and their temples fell to pieces at his wish ; the
lions crouched at his feet, and the bears licked his footsteps ; he came out of the boiling oil more radiant than
when he was put into it ; and now that he is ordered to
be beheaded, he goes to death with joy in his heart, and

a smile on his face.   Who can any longer doubt but **that** He in whom Alexander trusts is the only true God ? "

Having uttered these last words, he leaped into the arena to embrace the martyr, before all the people.   The young man had watched every triumph of the servant of God ; each one of them was a powerful argument in itself, but when put together they carried conviction, even in spite of prejudice, irresistibly to the mind.   He had from the commencement determined to become a Christian, but the scenes he witnessed in the Coliseum had worked up his feelings to a pitch of enthusiam which he could no longer control.   He had communicated his conviction to a friend ; who, knowing the terrible consequences which would follow from his public profession of Christianity, endeavoured to hold him back: **this was** the cause of the struggle between them.

Antoninus was thunderstruck at this sudden change in his friend, so that for a moment he was unable to utter a word.   He looked on them embracing each other in the arena, and then, assuming an air of indifference, ad dressed the young man as follows :—" How comes it Herculanus, that you entertain these sentiments, you who up to this moment held the Christians in hatred ? "

Herculanus answered boldly—

" Antoninus, I never hated the Christians.   For fourteen years I have been in your service, and have accompanied you to the temple ; but I prayed secretly in my heart to Christ, the great God of the Christians."

The Emperor muttered something hastily to Cornelianus, and left the Coliseum.   His orders were that both should be beheaded.

They were executed at different times and different

places. The Acts we have been quoting record the death of Alexander in a few short sentences. They are not easily understood. It would seem that Crescentianus, the friend and biographer of the holy Bishop, was so overcome with grief and sorrow, that he expressed himself with brevity and obscurity. However, by the aid of the Martyrology of Ado, and the epitomized records of Petrus de Natalibus, we are enabled to give the reader some interesting details, and so bring this wondrous story to a close.

Alexander was martyred on the Via Claudia, about five miles from the present town of Bracciano, near the beautiful lake of the same name. He was led out under an escort of soldiers to the twentieth milestone ; but why he was taken so far, and to this particular place, may be deduced from the following facts :—

At the time the events we have recorded were passing, the Emperor Antoninus was engaged in laying out a magnificent villa on the Claudian Way. The villas or suburban residences of the ancient Romans were superb adjuncts to the palaces of the nobility. For miles around the city, every spot that was beautiful in nature was decorated with marble mansions and artificial gardens. On the gentle declivities of the Alban hills, amid the olive groves of the Sabine, and on the very cliffs of the Apennines, the lordly mansion of the Roman patrician rose in stupendous grandeur, overlooking a beautiful solitude, and forming an oasis of summer repose for the luxurious and wealthy citizen. Antoninus selected the green slopes that surrounded Lake Bracciano, and erected a villa equal in magnificence to that of Adrian near Tibur. The ruins of this villa are still to be seen near Bracciano. Arrenghi, in his work on Subterranean Rome, in the fortieth chapter, has alluded to these ruins thus :—" Quo potissimum loco spectatissimæ quondam villæ. Veri imperatoris restigia ingentis quidem magnitudinis conspiciuntur."

It was to this spot Alexander was led out to be martyred.   Ado relates how a poor woman gave him a napkin to bind his eyes before his execution, as was the custom in cases of decapitation : it was brought back to her by an angel after the martyrdom of the holy Bishop. A similar fact is recorded of St. Plautilla, when St. Paul was going to be beheaded, and the towel or handkerchief was miraculously restored to her.   At the moment that the executioner's axe fell on the neck of Alexander, the earth was shaken by an earthquake ; a great number of houses in the little town of Bracciano fell, and the villa and baths of the Emperor were nearly destroyed.   Many of the inhabitants were killed in the ruins.

The faithful Crescentianus was at hand to bury the body. He built a new crypt near the scene of his triumph ; and having embalmed the venerable remains, he put on the slab these words, " Hic requiescit sanctus et venerabilis Martyr Alexander Episcopus cujus depositio celebratur undecimo Kal. Oct." (" Here rests the holy and venerable martyr Alexander, Bishop, whose deposition is celebrated the eleventh of the Kalends of October.")

The Acts record the wonderful conversion of Cornelianus, which we will give here in a few words.

Seven days after the martyrdom of the saint, Cornelianus came to the place where he was buried, and seeing the word *martyr* on his tomb, he was filled with anger : he took up a heavy instrument and stretched out his arm to break the slab, when that moment his arm was withered, and he fell insensible to the ground. He writhed and screamed in agony. The people gathered round him; his wife and his own family, on witnessing his condition, broke out into loud lamentation, and terror seized on every one present. They spoke to him, but he made no answer, for he had lost his senses. He was carried to his villa, and every means employed to restore him but in vain; his malady seemed to increase. In paroxysms of pain, he cried out: " O Alexander ! you are burning me ; I beseech you to assist me." When they heard him calling out for the assistance of the Christian whom he had put to death, they were surprised, and thought it was the effect of his madness. But there was a stranger looking on ; nobody knew who he was ; he whispered into the ear of the afflicted wife : " Take him to the tomb of Alexander again and he will be cured." She did so ; and no sooner did they put his withered arm against the tomb of the Saint, than it was restored, and Cornelianus came to himself again.

" On the following day," say the Acts, " he sent for Pothasius and his daughter, and related to them all that happened to the martyr, and what he had suffered on his account, and Pothasius wrote the words dictated by him." This document was preserved in the imperial archives. The priest Crescentianus says he saw it, and made some additions to it from what he saw. After the death of the Emperor Antoninus, which happened soon after the martyrdom of Alexander, Cornelianus gave the Christians a large piece of ground round the tomb of the Saint. His body was removed by Crescentianus to the seventh milestone on the same Claudian Way, and here there immediately sprang up a church and cemetery. All traces of these have long since passed away, for some of the most terrible of the persecutions of the Christians have yet to come ; and in the storms that afterwards blew over the Church, the sanctuary and altar were swept away ; but the faith was preached and flourished in the secret recesses of the Catacombs.

CHAPTER XI.

1.

THE Senate was the grandest institution of pagan Rome. Outside the hierarchy of the Catholic Church, there never was an assembly more powerful, more united, more lasting. It has passed through the wars, the storms and vicissitudes of twenty-five centuries, and still exists. Springing from obscurity, it moved insensibly into power, until it ruled the world. It rose amid a band of fugitives, truant slaves, and highwaymen—was founded by Romulus about 750 B.C. It consisted first of a hundred of the oldest and most respectable men of the little colony of exiles and slaves that settled down among the Seven Hills; hence its name of *Senate*, or assembly of old men or fathers. It was increased to two hundred when the rape of the Sabines brought a union between the two tribes. Under Tarquin the number was raised to three hundred, and under the Emperors, it reached as high as a thousand. All power was placed in their hands. The chief magistrate, although he bore the title of king, was but the commander of the army, and presided over the religion of the state. The Senate declared war or peace, and treated with the ambassadors of other nations. They wore a different kind of dress from the ordinary people; they had a special place appointed for them in the Coliseum and in all public functions; they were forbidden to traffic or intermarry with the persons of base extraction. Amongst the prohibited were actresses, and their daughters and grand-daughters. An ancient writer gives a detailed idea of the powers reserved to the Senate. In the days of its glory it was the sole source and centre of the power and greatness of Rome. "Nothing," says Polybius, "could go in or out of the treasury without its consent; it was the highest administration of the state. It judged the differences which arose between the cities and provinces that submitted to the Empire; it corrected or defended them when necessary. It enrolled the army and supplied their pay; it sent its consuls to the battle-field, and recalled them at will, or sent other generals to replace them; it declared the triumph and measured the glory of the conqueror; no public monument could be raised to the memory of the great without its consent. It was in fine the grand court of appeal for the nations of the earth—the sole representative of the Roman people."

If we add to their unlimited legal power the ascendancy that the senators of Rome must have naturally gained from their wealth, their personal merit, their patriotism, and their union, we can easily understand how they influenced the destinies of so many nations.

When we read the annals of this great institution, we are struck with the gravity of its debates, and the boldness and independence of its acts, ever mingled and directed by prudence and foresight. No authority was recognised among them but reason ; instead of party spirit, jealousy, and partiality, one grand and noble feeling pre-sided over their assembly, and guided their actions—it was the public good. This was the secret of their triumph and their power.

2.

The early history of the Senate is wrapt up in the history of Rome itself, and is inseparable from it. But, as the events we are about to relate took place in that era of Rome in which the Coliseum flourished, we must glance at its character at that time during those days of persecution.

After the political convulsions that shook the Empire, drove Cicero in exile, and placed Cæsar at the head of affairs, the Senate received a blow from which it never recovered. The form of the Roman government was completely changed ; the people, who had conquered the patricians, yielded up all their rights to their chief, and the whole power of the Empire became concentrated in one man. Cæsar assumed the title of Dictator and Em-peror, and therewith the rights of the Supreme Pontiff, the authority of the censors, and of the prætorship. Thus he controlled the treasury—had the right of declar-ing peace or war—the disposition of the provinces, and the election of the magistrates. His ambition was fatal to the power of the Senate, and although it continued its meetings, and sustained the splendour of its former prestige, yet it was nothing more than a political assembly, a grand council of the state, that enjoyed only as much power as its ambitious chief consented to give.

It is not, however, to be supposed that the **Senators** submitted to these changes without a murmur.   A spirit of envy and indignation showed itself in their public and private actions ; and the first Emperor was too sharp-sighted not to see a terrible revenge flashing from a hundred poniards in the very halls of the Senate.   A policy of conciliation only retarded the fatal blow.   He knew their power even in the very memories of the past ; and although he had triumphed over them as the idol of a mob, yet he could not afford to trample on the patricians and lose their support.

His policy was to neutralise the opposition of the inheritors of the old patrician power, by adding to their number from his own most devoted followers, and he immediately raised the Senate to nine hundred ; he increased in proportion the number of magistrates, and filled some of the most important offices with his own adherents.   It was by this means that men from the provinces of Etruria and Lucania, and Venetians, Insubrians, and others, barbarian and illiterate, were poured in to deteriorate and corrupt the great patriarchal institution of the Empress City.   This roused more than ever the indignation of the aristocratic party, and even the great Cicero murmured, and his powerful pen accelerated the ruin that was coming.   Suetonius tells us, that nothing could be heard but verses and songs ridiculing the new senators ; galling insinuations, that they were a conquered race of barbarians, and that Cæsar had made them change their skins for the *laticlave.*   On the Pasquin of that time (most probably the same old disfigured statue that stands at one of the angles of the Braschi Palace) were put up notices to this effect : " Let **no one** show the strangers the way to the Forum."

The indignation of the old patricians went on increasing. Though robbed and humbled, they were resolute
and determined. Their discontent at last burst out into
passion and fury, and, led on by the impetuous Brutus,
they resolved on Cæsar's death. He fell. His bleeding
body was still lying at the base of Pompey's statue in
the Forum, whilst the forty wretches who had assassinated him rushed through the streets with their daggers
in their hands, still reeking with the blood of the Dictator, and crying out : " Death to all tyrants." Yet their
triumph was but temporary. That venerable body did
not recover its power and prestige by violence and bloodshed ; they will not recover it now ; the decrees of Providence are against it ; it may exist, but will never again
rule the world.

The revolution of the *Ides of March,* as it is called,
robbed the world of its greatest man. Brutus boasted
of having slain a tyrant, but the provinces wept over
Cæsar's death. The cry of grief and public mourning
that rose through the whole Empire was the condemnation of the murderers. It was evident to all that the
jealousy and ambition of a body of factious citizens
caused the death of Cæsar, not the true love of liberty,
nor zeal for the welfare of the state. " They called themselves slayers of a tyrant," says Dion Cassius, a senator
himself, who lived about a century afterwards, " but they
were nothing more than assassins and murderers " (No.
xliv. 1).

Cæsar was beloved in the provinces. Its magistrates,
the army, and even the greater part of the Senate, lamented
his fall. The outer world cared nothing about the supre-
macy of the Senate. What advantage did they reap from

the politics or agitations of the Roman Forum ? **As long** as they enjoyed liberty, prosperity and justice from their acknowledged chief, why should they espouse the cause of the Senate ?   Moreover, the assembly itself had fallen from its pristine integrity.   Its effeminacy, its partiality, and departure from the rigour and patriotism of its ancient institution, drew on it contempt rather than submission and admiration.   Long before the monarchy of Cæsar, the great Cicero spoke these remarkable words, indicating its moral as well as political degeneration :—" It is on account of our vices, and not from any stroke of fortune, that, although we preserve the name of a republic, we have long since lost the reality."—" Nostris, non casu aliquo, rempublicam verbo retinemus, reipsa vero jam pridem amisimus."—*De Repub.* v. i.

The blood of Cæsar was shed in vain ; the anarchical faction of the Senate never held the reins of govern·ment ; the poniards that slew him commenced for the Senate the most terrible and disastrous period of its career.   In the civil wars and convulsions that followed, they not only lost the last vestige of their former power, but became the victims of the caprice or revenge of the ambitious aspirants to the supreme power of the Empire.

Augustus assumed the sceptre of Cæsar.   His reorganisation of the Senate was one of the most splendid, because most difficult, feats of his successful reign.   By his influence he caused nearly two hundred of its members, who were not fitted by birth or talent for their high position and honours, to resign their places.   He calmed their suspicions, and concealed his ambition by assuming the humble title of *Prince of the Senate.*   Nevertheless, during the time that was occupied in this work of reformation, he never appeared amongst them without having near him nine or ten of his most faithful adherents, who were secretly armed, and he himself carried his dagger under his toga. He prudently feared their resentment. Eleven years afterwards, in the year 18 before Christ, he completed the organisation, and reduced their number to six hundred; and thus commenced the imperial Senate.

It is unnecessary to follow the noble institution in its after career of servility and degradation during the reign of the succeeding Emperors.

After the abdication of Diocletian, and the triumph of Constantine, the Senate struggled on in its hereditary existence. Its name was torn from the Capitol and the military standards : in its place was substituted the more formidable and imperishable sign of redemption. The statue and altar of Victory, which presided as a tutelary deity over its assemblies, were removed under Constance, brought back under the apostate Julian, and finally destroyed by their own unanimous consent. There were still many among them who clung to the old rites of paganism ; but, ever docile to the command of the Emperors, under Theodosius the worship of the gods of the Capitol was proscribed, and Christianity declared to be the religion of the *Senate and Roman people.* "It was then," says the sublime Prudens, "that we saw those venerable fathers, those most brilliant lights of the world, the noble council of Catos, cast off the insignia of the old priesthood, and humbly clothe themselves in the white robe of catechumens."

" Exultare patres videas, pulcherrima mundi
Lumina, conciliumque senum gestire Catonum,

Candidiore toga niveum pietatis amictum
Sumere, et exuvias deponere pontificales."

Whilst, however, the power and independence of the Senate had passed away, it must not be forgotten that it was still the highest and most influential body in the Empire. Its members were the nobles of the land, and possessed immense wealth. According to Dion Cassius, a senator's fortune amounted to a million sesterces ; and if we believe Suetonius, some of them had annually a return equal to two million sesterces, about £105,000, which should be multiplied by ten to arrive at even a proximate idea of the value of money at that time. In a city of at least 3,000,000 of people, they were the principal and leading members. The usurpers of the imperial throne persecuted them, because they knew and feared their power. Moreover, when historians make sweeping assertions respecting the immorality and effeminacy of the great assembly, there must have been amongst them brilliant exceptions. History itself records names of honour and worth which flourished in the Senate in its very worst days ; many of these were Christians, and even martyrs, who shed their blood in the Coliseum in defence of the faith.

3.

Our next martyrdom will be a scene from the horrors of the reign of the Emperor Commodus. A more worthless tyrant could not have sat on the imperial throne. His insane ambition urged him to the assumption of divine honours. Not content with this, he had a throne erected in the midst of the Senate, and clothing himself in a lion's skin, and carrying a great club in his hand, he commanded the senators to offer sacrifice to him as if he were Hercules, the son of Jupiter. He issued a decree summoning a general assembly of the Senate in the Temple of the Earth. A crier was sent to all the neighbouring towns and villages to publish the decree, and all were to attend under pain of death. The people even in Rome itself were not aware of the cause of this extraordinary assembly of the Senate. They imagined that some terrible calamity was threatening the Empire, that a formidable revolution had broken out, and that the tide of war had rolled up to the very gates of the imperial city. The senators believing their counsel and advice were required for the public good, hastened in from their suburban retreats, and although in the middle of the summer heats, left their villas and farms and families, and poured in hundreds along the dusty Via Tiburtina and the sepulchral Appian and Latin Ways.

From the time of Augustus, the ordinary proceedings of the Senate commenced by sacrificing to Jupiter or Victory, whose statue was placed in their halls. Hence, as Baronius says (anno 192), no senator could remain a member of the body after he had become a Christian ; he was obliged to renounce the title or withdraw himself by voluntary exile.

The monstrous absurdities of Commodus, and the zeal of the Christians, led many of the pagans to the fold of the Church. We find in the Acts of Eusebius and his companions, that they went through the streets appealing to the ridicule and shame of the people. The sublime doctrines and morality of Christianity were at all times more beautiful and more powerful than the ridiculous and unmeaning worship of paganism. When the command was sent forth for them to worship a wretch like Commodus, many opened their eyes to the folly of their idolatry, yielded to the call of grace, and became Christians. Amongst these were some of the senators. Apollonius and Julius appear on the list of the undaunted men who dared to deny the divinity of the Emperor. The sword was the only thunder the revengeful god could command and he used it to show his weakness. Apollonius suffered about three years before Julius. His martyrdom did not take place in the Coliseum, but we will translate an interesting paragraph about him from the Fifth Book of Eusebius, as quoted by Baronius under the year 189. After speaking of the peace which the Church enjoyed before this time, he adds :—

" But this peace was not pleasing to the devil ; he endeavoured to disturb us by many stratagems ; and he succeeded in bringing to judgment and trial Apollonius, a man most celebrated amongst the faithful for his studies of polite literature and philosophy. One of his servants, a depraved wretch, was induced to betray him (for which he suffered severely). When the martyr, most dear to God, was asked by the judge to give his fellow fathers of the Senate a reason for embracing Christianity, he read for them a long and learned apology for the faith of Christ ; but they pronounced sentence against him, and he lost his life by a stroke of the axe ; for there was an old law amongst them that any Senator that was accused of being a Christian, and would not change his profession, was no longer free."

The morning of the grand assembly of the Senate had arrived. The city was alive with excitement. The venerable leaders of the community were full of hope that a better time was coming, that they were about to be restored to their ancient rights. It was the first time in this reign that they had been solemnly called together, and these meetings had become exceedingly rare. Each senator, attired in his best laticlave, brought his children with him to the temple of the goddess of the Earth, which stood under the shadow of the lofty arches of the amphitheatre. Along the Via Sacra, and around the triumphal arch of Titus, little knots of white-bearded senators were discussing the probable cause that induced the Emperor to reinstate the Senate. Some said it was fear, because of the death of Perrenius, their chief, and the warning the gods had given him, made him anxious to conciliate the Senate by restoring them to their power in the Empire. " I was present," said an aged citizen, to some of his friends, who had just come from Tiburtium, " when in the midst of the entertainments of the theatre a stranger suddenly entered. He was dressed as a philo-sopher, with the staff of a pilgrim in his hand, and a bag flung over his shoulder. Approaching the throne of the Emperor, and commanding silence with his hand, ' This is not the time, Commodus,' spoke the stranger, ' to in-dulge in theatrical shows and vain delights ; for the sword of Perrenius hangs over thy head, and if thou dost not take care, thou art already lost ; for he has bribed thy enemies, and corrupted the army in Illyria. Tremble for danger is at thy door !' The Emperor trembled in-deed," continued the aged senator ; " and to appease him, we all cried out, ' Death to Perrenius !' He was slain ; but the Emperor has never been the same since that day. He has become more cruel, more suspicious and unbear-able ; and I greatly suspect he has some deep plot in calling us together here to-day.   I come with my trusty dagger !" Saying this, he drew a beautifully gilt poniard from under the folds of his toga, and showed it to his companion as one of the treasures left him by his grand-sires.

The speaker was the same who drew his dagger some time afterwards under one of the arches of the Coliseum . and brandishing it in the face of Commodus, exclaimed, " Behold what the Senate has prepared for you ! "

Another said he thought it was because the terrible plague, that had broken out in Etruria and Cisalpine Gaul, was fast extending towards the city, and bearing desolation in its path.   He had heard that the Supreme Pontiff of the Capitol had suggested sacrifices to the angry Jove ; he thought that, perhaps, the Senate might have been assembled for that purpose.

" Not at all," interrupted a tall, thin senator, who was dressed as a military commander, who seemed a man of great importance, and spoke with a sarcastic smile, " not at all ; he thinks more of the harlots of his baths and lupanars than of his suffering subjects.   It is money he wants.   I heard from his comptroller that he hasn't an obolus to pay Charon for his ferry over the Styx. Sacrifice ! why, it will be only to offer sacrifice to himself, as the god Hercules and the son of Jupiter."   They all laughed as if he had made a good joke ; but a young man near him, who was silent and thoughtful during the conversation, felt a thrill of horror pass through him as Vitellius, the commander of the foot, spoke.   He concealed his indignation, and they all moved together towards the temple of the planetary goddess.

A strange scene once took place in a lunatic asylum in

England. A madman told all his companions, who were not so mad as himself, that he was God. Being a very violent character, he kept them all in fear, and they con-sented to call him God. One day, when there happened to be an insufficient number of attendants in the room, this madman got up on a chair and commanded all the other madmen to come and adore him. Whether through fear or frolic, they actually gathered around him and pre-tended to adore him. Some kissed the ground, others his feet ; one said he was the Archangel Michael, and brought the homage of all the other angels ; another said he was king of the earth, and brought the acknowledgment of all creatures. Thus the strange farce was going on, when other attendants came in, and removed the deluded man to the dismal solitude of seclusion.

This is almost precisely a picture of the terrible scene that was witnessed in Rome in the year of our Lord 192 ; not amongst madmen, but amongst the most educated, the most wealthy and most powerful members of the great Empire. The Temple of the Earth was dressed out with evergreens and flowers ; around the walls were rude pictures representing the fabulous deeds of Hercules ; an immense fire of faggots of costly wood blazed in the centre of the temple ; the priests were standing by in fantastic robes of yellow and gold, and the high Pontiff held a golden tripod in his right hand ; all was ready for sacrifice. But who was the god that had usurped the throne of the bountiful planet ? It was the living Hercules clothed in a lion's skin, and holding a massive club in his hand ; it was Commodus.

The senators entered one by one. They were imme-diately struck with fear and amazement. Some were seized with laughter, as if the whole thing were a joke, for which they afterwards paid dearly; others turned pale with consternation, for armed lictors were scattered through the temple, and the severe looks of the tyrant trying to assume the majesty of a real Hercules cast a funereal gloom over the proceedings. His diminutive figure, his bloated and ill-formed features, above all, his shameful and disgraceful life, made a sorry contrast with the splendid and gigantic hero called Hercules in the fables of mythology.

The proud wretch addressed the conscript fathers; he declared that he had called them together for the purpose of announcing that henceforward he was to be worshipped as the son of Jupiter. No historian has left us an account of the words he used—who could chronicle such nonsense and impiety? But the Senate, the weak, fallen Senate, went through the blasphemous farce of incense and adulation as to a god. Scenes like these frequently occurred in the great Babylon of pagan Rome, and show to what a depth man had descended in the darkness of idolatry and infidelity.

Strange as it may appear, Christianity had a long and terrible struggle with the powers of hell. Eighteen centuries have rolled over, and it is still on the battle-field—by trials, tribulations, and sufferings of every stamp it is slowly but surely pushing on its standard of the cross. Its complete triumph is to be commemorated, after the last day, in heaven. But in the second century of the Church, from which we record these events, the hatred of Christianity was so intense that, notwithstanding the force of reason that sustained it, and the incontestable miracles confirming its divinity, the degraded and cowardly Senate preferred rather to worship the proud and lascivious Commodus, than to expose themselves to danger. Alas! this was true of the Senate, but there was one exception. This was Julius. Over seven hundred aged men lent themselves to the silly mockery—Julius alone had the courage to express his contempt, and to refuse to bend his knee.

When it was announced to the Emperor that Julius would not come forward to offer incense to his divinity, Commodus commanded him to be brought before him by the lictors. All eyes were turned on the senator as he walked up between the lictors to the tribune of the temple, where the Emperor's throne was placed. The buzz of conversation ceased, and those who had been secretly casting ridicule and contempt on their demented ruler turned in eager silence to watch the fate of Julius.

"How have you become so mad," asked Commodus, "as not to sacrifice to Jupiter and his son Hercules?" (We quote from the Acts given by the Bollandists.)

Julius seemed for a moment too indignant to answer, but looking with brave contempt on the proud tryant, said : " You will perish like them, because you lie like them."

This was enough. The tyrant called Vitellius, the commander of the foot, and bade him take the insolent senator from his sight, exclaiming, angrily : " Confiscate his goods even to the last farthing, and scourge him until he sacrifice to our divinity."

The judgments of God are different from those of men. If our merciful and loving Father were capable of the passion of anger, and punished at the moment every insult offered to His Divine Majesty, the human race would have been long ago extinct. Commodus could not have employed a more cruel or worthless wretch to discharge his orders than Vitellius. He had Julius led away in chains and cast into prison, most probably the Mamertine, to await his pleasure.

After some days of confinement—deprived of food and every external comfort—he was brought before Vitellius in the same temple. Julius was ordered to be brought in, naked and covered with chains. When he had come before the seat of the judge, and under the statue that the impious Commodus had erected, Vitellius said to the martyr of Christ : " Do you still persist in your folly ? Will you not now obey the orders of the Emperor, and sacrifice to the gods Jupiter and his son Hercules ? "

" Never ! " answered Julius ; " you and your prince will perish alike."

" And who will save you, and make us perish ? " asked Vitellius, sarcastically.

" Jesus Christ," said Julius, raising his finger solemnly towards heaven ; adding, after a moment's pause, " He who condemns thee and thy foolish sovereign to eternal ruin."

Vitellius ordered him to be taken out to the Petra Scelerata and scourged ; but the body of the holy martyr was exhausted through want, and whilst the brutal executioners were beating him with their heavy whips, he expired. The wretched judge endeavoured to vent on his lifeless remains the anger and revenge that the premature death of his victim had left unsatiated ; he ordered the body of Julius to be cast before the statue of

the sun, and almost under the arches of the Coliseum,
that the dogs might devour him, and that the people
who poured into the amphitheatre might see his infamy.
What could the poor people expect. when such terrible
judgment was wreaked on the very senators themselves?
Guards were set to watch the body, that no one might
remove it, and a notice was put up on the walls of the
Coliseum that he had been put to death for not sacrificing to the divinity of the great god who had just come
amongst them. Angels watched over those precious relics ; no insult was offered ; the people trembled, and
passed on. Thousands pitied the fate of the brave man
who had had the courage to withstand the absurdities of the
impious and cruel Emperor ; greater contempt and greater
hatred for the tyrant-god who thus gloried in the blood of
human victims was the result produced by the cruelty of
Vitellius. The following night, when the guards were
asleep, Eusebius and his companions stole out from the
arches of the Coliseum, and took away the remains of the
holy martyr, and buried them in the catacombs or cemetery of Calepodius on the Via Aurelia. The greater portion of his body is at present in the Church of St. Ignatius in Rome.

CHAPTER XII.

ST. MARINUS.

FURTHER on in the history of Rome, we have another extraordinary case of a little boy, the son of a senator, exposed to the wild beasts in the Coliseum. . Neither age, nor condition, nor sex were safeguards against cruelty and tyranny. It is now-a-days the amusement and the wonder of the hippodromes of London and Paris to see little boys performing extraordinary feats of agility and skill, springing and tumbling as if their bodies were made of india-rubber, seeming to baffle the laws of gravity, and to fly in the air. Shouts of applause greet the young gymnast as he retires with a graceful bow. The Coliseum too has had its youthful prodigies. Not indeed that they were train ed to amuse the Roman people with surprising feats on tight-ropes, or throwing summersaults in the air, but were cast into the arena to be devoured by wild beasts, and thus caused the amusement of the unfeeling mob. Their courage, their skill and success were of a higher order than physical dexterity ; their reward was not the miserable wages of an employer, nor the shouts of an admiring audience ; but heaven, eternal life, and God. Let us cull one of these touching scenes from the history of the Coliseum.

A strange accident had placed the brothers Carinus and Numerianus at the head of affairs. In the year 283, their father, Carus, set out on an expedition against the Persians. He was a rude, rough soldier, and was successful in arms. Civil war had weakened the restless East, and Carus penetrated easily to the very heart of the enemies' territory. Having conquered Seleucia, and taken possession of Ctesiphon, he encamped near the river Tigris. Strange to say, there was an order from the oracles that the Roman arms were not to pass so far as this in the Persian territory. We will not stay to examine the origin of this superstition ; but the fact was, the very first day of their encampment, they nearly all perished in a terrible storm. A sudden night darkened the heavens, and the lightning fell in the middle of the camp, killing many, and setting everything in flames. Amongst the victims of this terrible storm was the Emperor Carus. Amidst the confusion of the darkness and the noise of the thunder, his tent was seen to blaze up with an immense flame, and the soldiers ran to and fro, crying out : " The Emperor is dead." His two sons, Carinus and Numerianus, were declared Emperors. The first remained in charge of the West, the other took the control of the East.

Carinus had a short, but cruel and bloody reign. He was not what his name expresses ; for history brands him with brutality and ignorance. Not that he adopted a uniform system of persecution, but rather used the sword against the Christians under the impulses of caprice and fashion. He had friends amongst them, and perhaps rather tolerated the cruelties of his tyrannical officials, than inflicted them himself ; yet he was an angel of mercy compared to the demon that followed him in the terrible war against the Crucified. The event that rid the world of the Emperor Carinus gave the reins of government to Diocletian, the worst and most brutal persecutor of the Church. Under Numerianus and Carinus, innumerable martyrs were sent to heaven. Amongst them was the brave boy Marinus—one of the saints of the Coliseum.

Marinus was a child of about ten years of age. It was discovered that he was a Christian ; he was seized, brought before Martianus, the prefect, scourged, and cast into prison.

In short, rapid sentences like these, the Acts give us the preliminary notice of our young martyr. But they speak volumes. What must have been the training of that child ! What must have been the spotless innocence of his untainted soul! Fancy wafts us across the lapse of centuries, and we imagine we are standing in the marble Forum of the mighty city. A crowd approaches, and some rough, rude soldiers are leading a beautiful boy to the court of the prefect. Heavy chains weigh down his little hands, and the large gold band round his purple laticlave tells of his being the son of a senator. What crime has he committed ? Could one so young and beautiful be a murderer and an assassin ? But the murmur passes through the ever-increasing crowd—he is a Christian. Enter the hall where the prefect has his tribunal (probably the Temple of the Earth); you hear no idle remonstrance from the youthful prisoner—no childish fear—no imploring sobs ; but brave and undaunted the little fellow stands erect before the tyrant. Whence that eloquence—that profound depth of learning and thought —the angelic sounds of his voice ? Behold the supernatural aid promised to those dragged before princes and tyrants—behold " wisdom perfected in the mouths of the innocent."

The judge is confounded—silenced by a boy. He vents his impotent rage, and orders Marinus to be flogged. The rough, cruel lictors tear off his little dress, and soon his snow-white and unwrinkled shoulders are red and blue from the galling lash. No heart-rending cries, scarcely a movement, save the convulsive shock which each stinging blow sends through his delicate frame. " Will you sacrifice ?" rings through the hall at intervals ; the answer is a low, sweet murmur of the sacred name of Jesus. Baffled and enraged, the tyrant ordered him to be cast into prison, to prepare some infernal machines of torture to shake the constancy of the heavenly child.

Poor Marinus ! In pain and suffering he passed the night in the darksome prison, no one to dress his wounds, not even a drop of water to cool his feverish tongue. He was accustomed to a beautiful room and a bed of down ; now he lays his aching bones on the cold, damp stones. Does he think of mother and playmates ? Do boyish fancies summon up the phantoms of fright ? Do pain and fear make him doubt of God ? No. Angels are around him ; his heart is light and cheerful, his interior joy absorbs the sensibilities of the flesh, and makes him forget the pain. The morning sun dawns, its meridian will have witnessed a greater defeat for the powers of darkness—a greater triumph for the senator's boy.

The judge has once more taken his seat, and Marinus is brought before him. The rack, the fire, and instruments of torture are prepared. Our little martyr sees them all, he knows they are prepared for him, but he is neither frightened nor dismayed. Though young in years,

he is old in the sublime lessons of the Gospel ; **he is**
prepared to die for Christ.   Finding he is still immovable
in his resolve, the wicked judge orders him to be stretched
on the rack.   But behold, Almighty God will not permit
His chaste and innocent servant to be dislocated or torn
by the brutality of the pagan.   No sooner have the executioners stretched his little body on the dreadful rack,
and are about to turn the wheels to tighten the ropes,
than the machine is struck by the lightning of heaven—
broken up into a thousand fragments, and the lictors and
bystanders felled to the ground ; whilst Marinus stands
unbound and unhurt in the midst of the fragments, pointing with one finger towards the wreck of the instrument
of torture, and with the other towards Him who is the
shield and strength of the oppressed.

The miracle, instead of terrifying and converting the
impious Martianus, made him more anxious to take the
boy's life ; but once more he will be foiled in his cruelty.
He had Marinus cast into a large cauldron, under which
he had placed an enormous fire.   But Marinus thought
he lay on a bed of roses, and the intense heat that made
the iron red-hot was to him a zephyr of odoriferous dew.
The tyrant, seeing it availed nothing, had him thrown
into an oven and gave orders that he should be kept in it
under a red heat until the following day.   But Almighty
God protected and consoled little Marinus ; and the next
morning, when they opened the oven, expecting to see
him burnt to a cinder, they found him with his little
hands folded in the attitude of prayer, and singing hymns
of praise to God.   When this was reported to the impious Martianus, he stamped his feet with rage, and commanded that he should be thrown to the wild beasts in

the Coliseum, that the hungry lions might rid him of the troublesome child. But once more the power of God will be displayed in the weak and innocent victim, and He who reigns above will laugh at the machinations of His enemies.

The scene in the Coliseum was extraordinary. A lion was let out first. It ran immediately towards the trembling child; but lying down before him, it seemed to reverence Marinus; then rising up, it placed its great paws on the little fellow's shoulders and began to lick his face. A leopard was let out, and it lay at his feet and began to lick them; then a female leopard and a tiger were let loose; but they all vied with each other in showing their respect. The people shouted; and the keepers tried to irritate them, but had to fly from the arena, for the animals threatened to turn on them. Occasionally the lion and tiger would go over to that portion of the Coliseum where the wretched Martianus was sitting, and looking towards him, would growl angrily, and then hurry back to the centre to lavish their caresses on the Christian child. Marinus spoke to them, and patted them as he was wont to treat the pet animals in his father's house. The Coliseum rang with mingled shouts of "Libertas," "Maleficium," "Mors," "Ut quid plus ?" &c., and similar expressions familiar to the crowds of the amphitheatre. The prefect, confused and defeated, scarcely knew what to do. Whilst the uproar was increasing among the populace, he ordered the lictors to remove the martyr, but they refused to enter the arena whilst the animals were free—even the keepers knew they would be torn to pieces if they interfered with the extraordinary child. At length signs were made to

Marinus to come out, and the noble child led the animals
to their den; and no sooner were the heavy gates closed
on them, than the lictors rushed on the helpless boy, and
putting heavy chains on his little hands, led him away as
if he were an infamous criminal.

But our tale of wonder, of triumph, and of cruelty, is
not yet finished.   Other miracles must render still more
celebrated the name of this infant Thaumaturgus.   All
Rome must witness him once more, as a proof of the
divinity of the Christian religion.   After his miraculous
preservation in the Coliseum, the public mind was filled
with interest about his future fate.   Martianus feared
lest the sympathy of the people might rouse their indignation against himself, and he hastened to convince them
of the justice of his cruelty to Marinus.   He ordered
him to be led immediately to the statue of Serapis, for
the purpose of offering sacrifice.   Thousands had already
poured out of the Coliseum, and were rushing up to get
a nearer view of the little hero, and join the immense
crowd that was moving towards the statue of the pagan
god, whose idol was raised in the vicinity of the amphitheatre.

An immense concourse had already taken up every
available spot around the statue of the idol; all were
filled with anxiety to see what would be the end of the
senator's son.   His beautiful and comely features, his
youth, his modesty, and his rank, had excited universal
admiration.   Some Christians were in the crowd, and
they almost wept aloud for joy at the constancy and
triumph of the little martyr.   Arrived at the statue of
Serapis, Marinus was led into the middle of the circle
which the troops had made amongst the people.   A

large pan of charcoal was burning at the foot of the statue, and the high priest of the Capitol stood near, holding the tripod in one hand and a box of incense in the other. Silence was commanded by a crier, and Mar tianus, in a coarse, loud voice, commanded the boy to offer sacrifice.

Behold! Marinus is kneeling. Has he consented to pray to the senseless idol? Is he afraid of further trials? or has the grace of God abandoned him? A breathless stillness reigns around; the tyrant prefect believes he has at length subdued the proud spirit of the Christian child. Foolish thought; Marinus was praying to the true God; his prayer had already pierced the clouds of heaven—its answer was the bolt of lightning that struck the idol of Serapis; the people saw their god broken to pieces at the feet of a child. Some ran away terrified, others were riveted to the ground in wonder, whilst others cried out: "Great is the God of the Christians!" Many were brought to the light of the faith on that day, for God maketh use of the weak things of this world to confound the strong.

Martianus had the martyr removed to prison. Almighty God heard the child's prayer to deliver him from the hands of his enemies, and prepared for him an everlast- ing crown. The prefect tried once more to take the little fellow's life, and ordered him to be beheaded; this time he succeeded, and on the 26th of December, 284 of Christ, the pure soul of the brave Marinus took its flight to the realms of bliss. The wretched prefect ordered his body to be cast amongst the slaves, criminals and gladiators who had been slain in the Coliseum. But the Christians were on the alert, and came to take it away by night. Finding guards had been set to watch, they prayed; and God, who has a special providence over the relics of His saints, came to their assistance. He sent a terrible storm of thunder and lightning, and so frightened the pagan guards that they fled from the Coliseum, and the Christians quietly removed the precious remains of the young martyr to the Catacombs.

These relics have found their way back again, after the lapse of sixteen centuries, almost to the same spot from which they were taken by the Christians. On the ruins of the superb temple of Venus and Rome, designed and raised by the extravagant Adrian, there sprung up in the middle ages a beautiful little church, dedicated to the Blessed Virgin. It is now better known as the church of St. Frances of Rome. This church is but a few yards from the Coliseum, and consequently quite near the site of the spoliarium where the bodies that were slain in the Coliseum were kept before burial. In this little church are now preserved the remains of Marinus, the Christian child-martyr.*

---

* For the facts connected with the martyrdom of St. Marinus, see Rom. Martyrology, Dec. 26; Ferrari, Cat. Sanct., same day; Mombritium, tom. ii. ; Petrus de Cat., lib. i. cap. 6, &c.

CHAPTER XIII.

ST. MARTINA.

THERE is nothing more delicate, more defenceless, or more beautiful, than the young girl whose virtue has never been sullied by the corrupt influence of the world. The peerless soul of the virgin is the brightest spot on earth, and the most pleasing to God. He has frequently, in the histo ry of the world, chosen the weak and humble frame of girlhood for the most extraordinary manifestations of H is power or of His goodness. He has sent, from time to time, beings who seemed to be angels clothed in human form, to attract us by the loveliness of virtue, and to show us the great mystery of love in which He unites Himself to the human soul. God has ever been wonderful in His saints—H e gave them His power when they asked it, and those extraordinary suspensions of the laws of nature which we call miracles were ordinary actions to them. But there was nothing so consoling as the power, the consolation and protection He imparted to the defenceless daughters of the Church in the terrible times of persecution. When dragged before tyrants for their faith and their virtue, He Himself took them as it were into His own hands, and made them not only triumph over the brutal rage of the pagan, but made them apostles and witnesses of the divinity of Christianity, the example, the glory, the crown of His Church. Their virginal chastity was more dear to Him than the stars of heaven, and He invariably smote with the lightning of vengeance the wretch that would dare to cast an unchaste look on those angels in human form. Although He permitted them to fall under the axe of the lictor, it was that their death might be the triumph of their chastity and their faith, and the commencement of their ineffable reward in the paradise of God. Neither persecutions, nor sufferings, nor torments of the most dreadful kind, nor yet the more powerful blandishments of the attractive but false joys of life, could ever induce the Christian female of the first centuries to yield up her right to the sublimest titles that heaven has given to earth—Christian and Virgin. The triumph of the youthful martyrs was the most perfect and absolute that history knows ; but could it be otherwise ? It was the triumph of Him who reigns in the highest heavens, who laughs at the malice of His enemies, and against whom nations rage in vain.

But whilst we look back in admiration at the thrilling and sublime lessons of heroism and virtue given to us by the Christian heroes of the early ages, a secret feeling of regret steals over us that these days of triumph are gone. The seductions, the blandishments, the immoralities of our days of peace and repose have been more destructive than the fire, or sword, or wild beasts of the pagans. It is rare to find now-a-days a true virgin—one who would suffer death rather than permit the slightest breath of corruption to sully the brilliancy of the gem of chastity. Alas ! what the rack, the scourge, or brutal violence could not touch in the days of the past, may now be blasted by a look, a squeeze of the hand, or a playful liberty, the corrupt influence of the worldly, and very often even irreligious, education permitted by the careless and indifferent parents of these times, has swept away the safeguards of modesty, and our children have lost their treasure ere they have known to prize it. But woe to the wretch who allows himself to become the instrument of Satan for the destruction of innocence! He will sink into the awful torments of hell, deeper than the impious Ulpian, who plotted the ruin and shed the blood of the Virgin Martina. Let us come to her interesting history.

Although Martina suffered under Alexander Severus, he was not guilty of her blood. Severus was but a boy of thirteen when he came to the throne, but he had a mother who has been extolled by both pagan and Christian historians as the honour and glory of the Empire. Giulia Mamea was one of the few remarkable women that figure in the history of these times; she enjoyed the friendship of Origen, and it was the wisdom and knowledge of this great master, aided by her natural virtue and talent, that rendered the reign of Alexander Severus one of the most popular and prosperous the Romans had seen for more than a hundred years. There is every reason to believe that she had embraced Christianity before she was murdered, together with her son, by the infamous Maximinian. The virtues of this young Emperor formed a contrast with the vices of his predecessors. He was attached to the Christians, and had an image of Jesus Christ among the penates or gods of his own palace. It is recorded that he even intended to

erect a temple to Him, and have Him recognised by the
Senate as one of the gods of Rome. But he was dis-
suaded from his purpose by one of his courtiers. What
Sejanus was in the reign of Tiberius, this unworthy
favourite was to the Emperor Severus; he bore, moreover, the name of a tyrant, whose cruelty and impiety he
seemed to imitate; this was Domitian Ulpian. The
clemency of the mother and her son, and the fear of
losing the imperial favour, made him restrain his hatred
of the unoffending Christians; yet he endeavoured to
vilify and misrepresent them, and even compiled a book
of all the laws and condemnations issued by former
Emperors against them; and sending a copy to each of
the governors of the provinces, directed them to enforce
these laws of the Empire, promising to hold them harm-
less for so doing. As he was the highest in esteem and
learning, he was appointed prefect during the absence
of Giulia Mamea and her son, and he availed himself of
his brief reign of power to vent his rage against the
Christians. Some of the noblest and wealthiest virgins
of the Empire were the first victims of his rage. The
young, the beautiful and virtuous Martina was one of
these victims.

Martina was the only child of one of the consuls of the
Empire. She lost her parents in her infancy, and in-
herited an immense fortune. Sentiments of virtue and
piety had been instilled into her young mind by her
Christian parents, so that she had learned almost in infancy the sublime lessons of the Christian school. Knowing the danger of riches, and wishing to give herself entirely to God, one of her first acts was to distribute her
wealth to the poor. Her fortune and position were well

know to Ulpian, but as soon as the fame of her extraordinary charity reached his ears, he suspected her to be a Christian. The sublime self-denial and charity taught by the law of Christ was considered foolishness by the pagans, and, as our Blessed Lord had intended, His disciples were known by their charity. Ulpian had for some time cast an evil eye on the orphan virgin, and finding all his designs on her wealth and virtue thwarted and rejected with indignation by Martina, his guilty passion turned into rage and cruelty, and he ordered her to be brought to the temple to offer sacrifice to the gods, so that in case of a refusal, she might fall completely under his power.

Two lictors were sent from the imperial palace to seize the Christian virgin, and bring her before the prefect. She refused to offer sacrifice to the idols of Rome. Ulpian determined, in the foolish pride of his heart, to conquer the resolution of the young girl, and he ordered the lictors to scourge her until she should consent to offer sacrifice to the gods. Her delicate and tender flesh was torn with whips loaded with iron. But God was pleased to favour His spouse with consolations which rendered her insensible to the excruciating tortures of her body. Finding she would not yield, he ordered her to be suspended from the yoke, and her flesh to be torn with iron hooks and other instruments of torture. Several hours were spent in vain by the brutal executioners to shake the resolution of the tender virgin, and when they had given up their fruitless task, they left the delicate frame of their victim torn, bleeding, and exhausted. The hour of triumph had come for Martina, and that of retribution for her executioners. Not that her prayers had called

down the lightning of heaven to smite the inhuman
wretches that scourged her, but, in the midst of her sufferings, she poured forth the prayer of Christian charity
for the conversion of her executioners.

She was led once more by the orders of Ulpian to the
temples of Diana and Apollo to offer sacrifice, when, behold, a fire descends from heaven and consumes them
to ashes, the very statues of these false deities melt at
the secret wish of Martina. The same power that destroyed the idols sent a ray of light into the hearts of her
executioners ; they immediately recognised the great and
true God, and declared themselves Christians ; they suffered a glorious martyrdom in the very presence of Martina, who was reserved for greater triumphs. The tyrant
prefect, who was hardened by vice and blinded by passion,
sought only how he could inflict new torments on the
Christian virgin ; and knowing her tender flesh was torn
by the scourges, and was still fresh and bleeding, he ordered boiling oil and pitch to be poured over her lacerated
body ; but he might as well have tried to remove the
seven hills of Rome as make Martina change her faith.
That which the tyrant intended as a fresh punishment
became a source of her greater glory and triumph. They
saw her surrounded with a halo of glory, a delicious
odour issued from her wounds, and at times she was
raised from the ground in an ecstasy of heavenly joy.

When all these things were reported to Ulpian he was
filled with confusion and rage, and he determined to have
her devoured by the wild beasts in the amphitheatre, and
before the entire populace of Rome. This he imagined
was the most degrading death he could select for her ;
because she was a noble lady of the first blood of the

Empire, and none but slaves and criminals of the worst
kind were subjected to this ignominious fate ; but God
intended it to show His power in His humble servant.

Martina spent the night in the gloomy prison of the
Mamertine. She enjoyed the consolations of divine love
in her soul, and angels were sent to keep her company.
It was near midday on the 10th of February of the year
228 when the noble virgin was taken from the prison to
the amphitheatre. Every bench is full, the last loud
burst of applause has died away through the palaces and
seven hills of the city ; the combat between the gladiators
is over, and the " editor " of the games announces, in
the midst of breathless silence, that the next amusement
will consist in exposing to the wild beasts a Christian
maiden who has refused to sacrifice to the gods of the
Empire. A terrible burst of applause shakes the walls
of the mighty edifice ; some poor Christians were present in disguise ; they had heard that their beloved bene-
factress had fallen into the hands of the tyrant, and was
condemned to the beasts. They bend their heads in
silent prayer that God would strengthen His servant, and
they wipe away the warm tear that is stealing down the
cheek.

The order is given, and the soldiers lead Martina into
the arena. She is a young girl, probably of thirteen or
fourteen years of age ; her arms are crossed on her breast,
and a blush of modesty has crimsoned her cheek, as she
knows the rude crowd are gazing on her. The white sand
of the arena scarcely yields to her delicate tread ; she steps
over a pool of fresh blood—the life-stream of the last gladiator that has fallen ; a shudder passes through her frame,
but a short prayer for strength has calmed her throbbing

heart. Her hair is long and beautiful, but untressed ; she is cheerful, and walks with an air of fortitude and confidence. The word flies through the assembled thousands that she is the daughter of a consul, and the interest and delight of the brutal populace increase in proportion as they recognise her nobility and beauty.

But there bounds a captive lion into the arena. He looks around in surprise, the human element is too near him ; with the thunder of his mighty roar, with which he has often wakened up his native forests, he laments his captivity, for he sees he is still a prisoner. His eyes are darting fire with hunger, rage and disappointment. Suddenly he sees a figure in his own domain—'tis Martina kneeling and wrapt in prayer. Hunger recalls his native ferocity, and, with bristling mane, he prepares for a desperate bound towards her. A death-like stillness reigns around ; every head is stretched forward, every eye fixed on the arena ; an involuntary shudder passes through every frame, for they fancy each moment the lion is devouring his victim.

But lo ! what do they see ? The king of the forest is gambolling around the little girl ; he licks her feet ;* she strokes him on the head and mane : he lies down beside her like a lapdog caressed by its mistress. There was a great and unseen Spectator looking at Martina in the Coliseum ; it was He who closed the mouth of the lions when Daniel was cast into their den.

Another lion was let loose, and it acted in the same manner. Martina called on the pagans to recognise the

---

* Et cursum arripiens ambulavit ad Sanctam et inclinans se osculabatur pedes ejus.—*Acts, Bollandists,* &c.

power of the God of the Christians, and thousands of the people left the Coliseum that morning proclaiming the sanctity of the noble virgin, whilst others determined to abandon immediately the worship of the false gods. Not so Ulpian. He writhed with disappointment and passion at his public defeat; he attributed her preservation to witchcraft, and ordered the virgin to be burned alive. But the flames had no power to touch her; not even a shred of her garment was burnt. Yet it was the will of Almighty God that Martina should receive the crown of Martyrdom, and when He had sufficiently proved to the wicked and cruel people of Rome their inability to contend against Him, He heard the prayer of His spouse to take her to Himself. Her martyrdom was effected thus.

There was at a short distance from the Coliseum an edifice which served as an auxiliary in its religious character. The amphitheatre may be regarded in some respect as a great temple. It was dedicated to Jupiter, and Bacchus, and Apollo; the very games and spectacles were frequently celebrated in honour of some of the gods. A smaller temple, which stood about two hundred yards from the amphitheatre itself, served for the ordinary rites and sacrifices. This temple was dedicated to the goddess of the Earth. Antiquarians say it stood where we now see the remnants of a tower of the middle ages designated "Torre dei Conti," between the Piazza delle Carette and the Via Alessandria. This spot, now neglected and almost unknown, has some sacred memories hovering around it that must render it dear to the Christian pilgrim to the Eternal City. Here many martyrs won their imperishable crown. This temple is said to have served from time to time for the assemblies of the

Senate, and for the tribunal chair of a prætor; being in the very heart of the ancient city, and near the Coliseum, it was the spot to which the Christians were most frequently taken to offer sacrifice. Before this temple was a monument which witnessed the cruellest and bloodiest scenes of those terrible times. Its very name of *Accursed* or *Criminal Stone* (Petra Scelerata) tells of the horror in which it was held by the people themselves. It was a sort of elevated stage, on which there was an immense slab of marble where public malefactors and criminals were generally executed. It is unnecessary to remind our reader that in the days of persecution the Christians were put on a par with the lowest class of criminals; and here some of the noblest blood of the early Church was shed in testimony of our faith. Here were martyred the Popes Sixtus and Cornelius, and the Persian martyrs Abdon and Sennen. The senator Julius was dragged here naked and in chains, and was flogged until death relea ed his spirit from the prison of flesh; his body was left exposed to the public gaze for several days. From this spot a whole host of Christian martyrs were sent to heaven; not the least remarkable was Martina.

Having been condemned by Ulpian to be beheaded, she was taken here to be executed. A herald first mounted the Petra Scelerata, as was the custom, and announced to the people that Martina was condemned because she was a Christian. The moment the fatal stroke had fallen on her neck, a voice was heard calling her to everlasting joy, and the whole city was shaken by an earthquake, so that many temples were ruined, and great numbers of the people were converted.

When the storm of persecution had passed over, and the labarum of Constantine was planted with universal joy on the Capitol, the sacred memories and traditions of the Christians found expression in all the pomp of ex·ternal worship. They had watched in silent and jealous care the spots where the martyrs had shed their blood, and the moment liberty was proclaimed on the bronze plates on the walls of the Capitol, they flocked in hundreds to these sacred places ; and in a short time superb edifices sprang up to commemorate the triumph of the martyred heroes. Nearly all the great churches of Rome have some sacred reminiscences around their foundations that lead us back to the scenes of the first three centuries. St. Peter's, the noblest and most complete building ever raised by man, has been erected on the spot where the great apostle was martyred, or, as some say more correctly, the crypt where his body was preserved. There are records of a sanctuary and pilgrimages, and even martyr-doms, from the first century around this sacred shrine, that modern devotion has enriched with all the magnifi·cence that wealth and art can produce. Amongst the Saints whose memory the ancient Christians of Rome loved and venerated with a special devotion, there were three virgins who bore an extraordinary similarity to each other in age, condition, sufferings and miracles. They were Prisca, Martina and Agnes. They were all of con-sular or noble families, They were persecuted for the faith at the tender age of thirteen ; each of them suffered attacks on their chastity as well as their faith, and Almighty God made them the instruments of the most stupendous miracles, the defeat and confusion of their per·secutors, and the conversion of innumerable souls. Three beautiful churches, which now form the three points of a triangle, sprang up over the places where they were martyred, or their relics were preserved; through the long lapse of seventeen centuries, and the ever-swelling tide of war and destruction that has since then rolled around the fallen yet everlasting city, the records, the relics and the imperishable devotion of the people have been preserved; they have passed from generation to generation, and are to this very day the honour and the pride of faithful Christian Rome.

Almost in the heart of the ancient Forum there was erected a beautiful little church, and dedicated to the virgin Martina. When after the lapse of nearly ten centuries, the walls of this little church were tottering through decay, the devotion and memory of the Saint were as fresh and strong as in the days that saw the erection of this monument of piety. It was rebuilt in the thirteenth, and again in the sixteenth century, when the relics of the saint, together with those of three other martyrs, were found. The subterranean chapel of this little church is a gem of architectural beauty; it was the design and gift of the celebrated artist Pietro da Cortona. Here we have often knelt at the shrine of the young, beautiful and virtuous Martina, and prayed that, through her intercession, there might be reflected in our actions that sublime virtue that shone so brilliantly in her life.

CHAPTER XIV.

THE PERSIAN KINGS.

THE Coliseum has been steeped even with the blood of kings. Slaves, soldiers, generals, noble virgins, senators, bishops and kings, all have sanctified its arena with their miracles or their blood. But by what strange combination of circumstances was it that the life-stream of crowned heads should deepen the crimson dye of that terrible spot? Were they pagans and tyrants who were dragged here by ruthless and revengeful mobs and pierced by a thousand daggers or torn to pieces by men maddened like lions, in retribution of their cruelty and crimes? No; it is not so; we are still in the days of the terrible persecutions of the early Church, and the subjects of the present chapter are Christian martyrs, who suffered for the faith in the Coliseum in the first half of the third century. Before relating the circumstances of their martyrdom, it may be useful to make a few historical remarks, taken from the annals of those times.

The power of the Empire is sinking fast. The mighty wave of time is rolling sensibly over the city of gold and marble, and the great dynasty that was thought to be imperishable is showing signs of decay. Almighty God has passed sentence on the impious city, and in the most dreadful of all His judgments, He allows its blinded inhabitants not only to accelerate, but also to increase its terrible retribution. The picture of crime, of cruelty, and of bloodshed which represents the last half century preceding the triumph of Constantine, is the darkest and most thrilling, not only in the history of Rome, but of the world itself. At the time we are now writing of (A. D. 240), the whole empire was shaken by internal convulsions and civil wars. In the brief space of three years, four Emperors, after sitting for a short time in anxiety and misery on the throne of the Cæsars, were dragged by violence from their ill-gotten power, and closed their short-lived career of ambition and crime by a terrible and well-merited death. But all this internal trouble and confusion naturally impeded the progress of Christianity, Almighty God was pleased to give His apostles and servants an opportunity of scattering the holy seeds of the gospel ; and that they might take firm root in the souls of men, He sent a few years of sunshine and calm. To use a homely simile, the little bark of Peter, tossed about by so many tempests and adverse winds, was brought into port to prepare its rigging and sails for another and more terrible storm ; billows of blood will flow around her before long. Not only did the protecting providence of God give peace and calm to the Empire, but it placed a Christian Emperor on the throne of the Cæsars. We do not allude to Constantine, nor to the Emperors who reigned after the final triumph of the Church ; we are still seventy years before the dawn of that bright period, and there are five of the most cruel and bloodthirsty persecutions the Church ever suffered yet before

her ; but we allude to the Emperor Philip, who succeeded
Gordianus III.   He was not only favourable and generous towards the Christians, but was himself a Christian.

When the Emperor Gordianus III. ascended the
throne, he was but a young man, under the guidance of
his preceptor, Misithes.   He had a prosperous reign of
six years.   His docility, natural probity, and amiable
disposition, united with the skill and prudence of his
virtuous preceptor, made him dear to the whole Empire.
Even the success and triumph which fortune had given
to his military enterprises, made his reign a real sunshine in those days of revolt and trouble.   In the year
243, whilst away on an expedition against the Goths,
and the ever restless and unsubdued Persians, his good
preceptor died, and Julius Philippus succeeded Misithes
in the prætorship, one of the most important offices in
the state.   Ambition entered the heart of Philip, and he
determined to obtain the command of the Empire.   He
knew Gordian was too much beloved by the soldiers
to make them betray him, and he resolved upon his
assassination.   For this purpose he hired a wretch, and
the bloody deed was effected.   Philip was declared
Emperor in 244.   On Easter Eve in the same year,
Philip was in Antioch with his wife, Severa, and they
repaired to the Catholic church to join in the public
prayers in preparation for the great festival.   The holy
Bishop Babilas was at this time in the see of Antioch ;
and having heard that the Emperor was coming to the
church, he stood at the porch, and refused him admission.
With the courage and zeal of an apostle, he bade the
Emperor go and do penance, for the blood of his
murdered victim called to heaven for vengeance.   The

holy Bishop repulsed him with his own hand, and would
not permit him to enter except in the garb of a public
penitent of the Church.   Philip humbled himself before
the aged Bishop; he confessed his crimes, and voluntarily accepted the penance which the minister of God
imposed on him, and thus was permitted to enter the
Church of the true God, before whom the crown and
tattered garment are alike.   Eusebius, in his sixth book
and thirty-fourth chapter, speaking of this strange event,
says:—"Gordian ruled the Roman Empire for six full
years; Philip, together with his son Philip, succeeded
to him.   He, being a Christian (the report is), wished
to take part in the prayers of the Church on the eve of
the Pasch with the rest of the people; but the Bishop
who then ruled the Church would not allow him to enter
until he had made confession of his crimes, and placed
himself amongst the public penitents. . . And the
Emperor is said cheerfully to have submitted; and by
his penance to have shown a sincere and religious fear of
God."

We cannot pass over the authority, much less the
beautiful and powerful eloquence, of the great Chrysostom, in his panegyric on Babilas.   Speaking of his
brave and intrepid reproof of the sinful Emperor, he
compares him to the Apostle St. John ; and alludes to the
Emperor in words that leave no doubt of the tradition
of the time in which he flourished.   "Nor was he the
mere tetrarch of a few cities," says St. Crysostom, speaking
of Philip (in Lib. in S. Bab. et Contra Gentiles, No. 6),
"nor the king of one nation only, but the ruler of the
greater portion of the world—of nations, of cities, and
a countless army, formidable on every side, from the

boundless immensity of the empire and the severity
its power; yet he was expelled from the church by the
intrepid pastor, like a bad sheep that is driven from the
flock. The subject becomes the ruler, and pronounces
sentence of condemnation against him who commanded
all. Alone and unarmed, his undaunted soul was.filled
with apostolic confidence. With what zeal was the
ancient Bishop fired! He commanded the satellites of
the Emperor to depart. How fearlessly he spoke, and
placed his right hand on that breast that was still glowing
and bleeding with the remorse of recent guilt! How
he treated the murderer according to his merits!" &c.

It is not our intention at present to discuss the
question that has been raised by modern historians,
whether Philip was a Christian or not. Nearly all the
histories of the ancient Church written in the English
language, slur over the fact as if too extraordinary to be
true, or too doubtful to be entertained for a moment.
Yet the whole weight of ancient authority is in its favour.
Men like Eusebius, St. John Chrysostom, Orosius, St.
Vincent of Lerius, and Cassiodorus, were not likely to be
the dupes of an idle tradition; the fact is mentioned by
numerous authors. Amongst others, Baronius writes as
follows :—

"Pontius was raised to the prefectship, and was the
friend and familiar of the Philips, the Emperors. On
occasion of the celebration of the thousandth anniversary
of the foundation of the city, they said to him : 'Let us
go and propitiate the great gods who have brought us
to this thousandth anniversary of the Roman city.' But
Pontius by many stratagems endeavoured to escape,
whilst they were forcing him as a friend to offer sacrifice.

Believing an opportunity was given to him by God, he said : 'Most devout Emperors ! Since God has honoured you with an august power over men, why do you not sacrifice to Him who has conferred such a favour upon you ?' Philip the Emperor replied : 'That is precisely the reason why I wish to offer sacrifice to the great god Jupiter; because all my power is given to me by him.' Pontius, smiling, said : 'Be not deceived, O Emperor, there is an omnipotent God in the heavens, who built up everything by His holy Word, and gave life by His Spirit !' Moved by these and similar exhortations of the Saint, the Emperors believed and were baptized by Pope St. Fabian. Then Fabian and Pontius broke to pieces the idols in the temple of Jupiter, and razed the temple itself to the ground ; many of the people, being converted to the Lord, were purified by the saving waters." (See Baronius, A.D. 246, No. 9 ; and the Bollandists, 14th of May, &c.)

Whether he was a Christian or not, it is certain the Church enjoyed a profound peace. For nearly thirty years she had been gathering strength, as the persecutions from the time of Severus were only partial, and fell more on individuals than on the great bulk of the people.

On every side schools and great centres of learning sprang up, and the Church seemed to be lifting up her head with honour and triumph. The East was specially gifted with men who shone like stars of science and eloquence. Some of the greatest names in the history of the Church flourished in this period. The great Pope Fabian was in the chair of St. Peter's ; there was Babilas in Antioch, Dionysius of Alexandria, the eloquent Cyprian at

Carthage, the Thaumaturgus, or wonder-working Gregory of Neo-Cæsarea, and St. Firmilian of Cappadocia Then there were Origen, Pionius, and many others, who adorned the different grades of the hierarchy with learning and zeal.

Churches sprang up in every place, and assemblies were held in public ; the principal emoluments of the Empire were conferred on Christians. St. Gregory of Nyssa, speaking of St. Gregory Thaumaturgus, says that, " By the preaching and zeal of that great Bishop, not only his city, but the whole country round, had embraced the true faith ; the altars and temples of the false gods were hurled to the ground, and there churches erected, and the people were purified from the contamination of unclean sacrifices." (In Oratione de St. Greg. Thaum., towards the end.)

Thus the faith had spread far through the East ; Cappadocia, Pannonia, and Syria were nearly entirely Catholic ; and Persia, on the confines of those territories, was also bearing fruit to the preaching of the Apostle St. Thomas, and was at this time, like its sister provinces around, a most flourishing portion of the garden of the Church. Kings and nobles had embraced the faith, and when the persecution broke out, Persia sent many noble martyrs to heaven. Among these, the virtues and constancy of the two kings or petty rulers who form the subject of this notice were not the least remarkable. They were seized in the persecution of 250, brought to Rome, and martyred in the Coliseum.

The hour of sunshine and peace is now drawing to a close, and the year 250 opened, even on its first day, with one of the most terrible persecutions that the

Church had suffered.   The blessings and repose of peace had relaxed the morals of the Christians, and it pleased Almighty God to purify them once more by the fire of persecution.   The great Bishop of Carthage, who was secreted in exile during the few months that the storm raged, describes the sad causes that drew once more the terrible sword over the Christian community. " Almighty God," says the great doctor, " wished to prove His family ; for the blessings of a long peace had corrupted the divine discipline given to us ; our sleeping and prostrate faith roused, if I may so speak, the celestial anger.   And although we deserved more for our sins, yet the clement and merciful Lord so acted that what has passed has been more a probation than a persecution.   The whole world was wrapt in temporal interests, and Christ ians forgot the glorious things that were done in the days of the apostles ; instead of rivalling their brilliant exam ple, they burned with the desire of the empty riches of the world, and strained every nerve to increase their wealth.   Piety and religion were banished from the lives of the priests, and fidelity and integrity were no longer found in the ministers of the altar ; charity and discipline of morals were no longer visible in their flocks.   The men combed their beards, and the women painted their faces ; their very eyes were tinted, and *their hair told a lie.*   To deceive the simple, they used fraud and subtlety, and even Christians deceived each other by knavery and underhand dealing.   They intermarried with unbelievers and prostituted the members of Jesus Christ to pagans. They scoffed at their prelates in their pride, and they tore each other to pieces with envenomed tongues, and seemed to destroy each other with a fatal hatred.   They despised the simplicity and humility demanded by faith, and permitted themselves to be guided by the impulses of worthless vanity ; they contemned the world only in words. Did we not deserve, then, the dreadful horrors of persecution that have burst upon us ? "

The instrument of God's anger was Decius. He permitted this cruel usurper to hold for one year the power of the Cæsars, for the glory and purification of His Church. Our blessed Lord had said in the garden of Gethsemane, that all that take the sword shall perish with the sword (Matt. xxvi. 52). In His eternal decrees, He had prepared His judgment for Philip, who had unjustly drawn his sword against Gordian ; and by the hand of a usurper he too must die. Towards the end of the year 249, intelligence was brought from the East to Rome that Iotapian and Priscus had been declared Emperors by a part of the army. The revolt was soon quelled and the usurpers killed ; but the spirit of revolution had spread like a pestilence, and another and more formidable rival appeared in Decius, who was declared Emperor by the great bulk of the army, then on the confines of Pannonia. Philip met him with a much larger force near the walls of Verona ; a desperate battle ensued, in which the Emperor was slain. No sooner was the news of his defeat brought to Rome, than the prætorians murdered the son of Philip, and declared Decius Emperor ; but they little knew the character of the man to whom they were committing their property, their honour, and their lives. He entered Rome in triumph, and one of his first imperial acts was to issue edicts against the Christians.

Decius seemed determined to destroy the very name

of Christian, and his edicts were as cruel as those which had issued from Nero or Domitian. He affected an in dignation that almost amounted to frenzy against the Romans, because they had abandoned the worship of their gods, and permitted the progress of the hated Christianity. " He imagined," says St. Gregory of Nyssa, " by cruelty and bloodshed to resist the power of God, to overturn the Church of Christ, and prevent the further preaching of the mysteries of the gospel. Then he sent edicts to all the rulers of the provinces, threatening them with the most dreadful torments if they did not endeavour to exterminate the Christian name, and bring the people back again to the worship of the devils of the Empire."

He found willing agents in his magistrates, and so warmly did they take up the terrible declaration against the unoffending Christians, that, according to the same authority, all public business was suspended for some time that they might carry out the terrible decrees. The prisons could not hold the multitudes that were seized ; and whilst some were put to death by the most cruel torments in the public squares, others found a home in the deserts. " Nor was there mercy for childhood or age, but all, as in a city taken by a cruel and enraged enemy, were handed over to torture and death ; not even the natural weakness of the female sex was pitied, that they at least might be freed from excruciating tortures ; the same terrible law of cruelty raged against everything that was considered adverse to the idols." (St. Greg. of Nyssa, towards the end of sermon on St. Greg. Thauma-turgus.)

It seems somewhat doubtful whether our Saints, Abdon

and Sennen, who suffered in the Coliseum during this persecution, were brought from Persia by force, or had come, like many other Persian nobles, through a sense of devotion or curiosity, to the great Roman capital. The Acts adopted by the Bollandists state that they were brought thither in chains by Decius himself. The Emperor was not in Persia, although he set out on an expedition towards the East, in which he was slain; but this might have happened under Gordian, as Decius was then a commander of the army, and subdued a revolt on the confines of Persia. The remainder of the Acts is received as genuine. As they tell the tale of the sufferings of those noble youths in beautiful and simple language, we will give them almost word for word.

When Decius arrived in Rome, he ordered the Senate to be assembled, and the Persian youths to be brought before him. They were brought in chains, and bore the marks of the cruelty with which they had been treated; they wore the royal insignia of their power, the gold and precious stones and splendour of their embroidered garments contrasting sadly with the heavy chains of criminals that bound their hands and feet. The whole Senate looked on them with pity. Almighty God had cast around His servants a majesty and a celestial beauty that struck the bystanders with awe and respect.

Decius, rising up, addressed the Senate in these words: "Conscript fathers! be it known to your august assembly, that the gods and goddesses have delivered into our hands the most inveterate enemies of the Empire. Behold the wretches before you." And when a murmur had passed through the assembly, all were silent through fear, they seemed to regard the young noblemen with sympathy. Then Decius commanded the high priest named Claudius to be brought from the Capitol in order to make them sacrifice.

When he was come, Decius said to them : " If you sacrifice now, you can remain in the liberty of kings, and enjoy your possessions in increased honour and power under the great Empire of Rome. Take care how you refuse."

But Abdon answered for himself and his companion, and said: "We have offered sacrifice and homage, though unworthily, to our Lord Jesus Christ; we shall never sacrifice to your false gods."

Decius cried out to the lictors and attendants : " Let the severest torments be prepared for these wretches, and let fierce lions and bears tear them to pieces."

Abdon bravely answered : " Do not delay the execution of thy sentence ; we are longing to possess our Lord Jesus Christ, who is able, when he willeth, to destroy thyself and thy wicked machinations against His Church."

Decius ordered a public manifestation to be made in the amphitheatre, that all might see the fate of the royal Christians. On the day appointed they were brought before the Temple of the Sun, to try if they would offer sacrifice. They were roughly dragged before the idol by the soldiers, but they spat on it with contempt. They were then stript of their garments, and scourged. After this they were brought into the Coliseum to be devoured by wild beasts. Whilst entering into the arena they said aloud : " Thanks be to God, we are going to our crown ; " and making the sign of the cross, they began to pray. Some bears and two lions were let into the arena, but they came bellowing to the feet of the martyrs, and not ɔnly would not touch them, but would not leave them, and even prevented the keepers from approaching the holy servants of God. Seeing this, Valerian cried out : " They have some magic power about them ; let the gladiators slay them." The gladiators entered with spears and slew them ; their bodies were tied together, and were cast before the Temple of the Sun, alongside the amphitheatre, and were left there as a terror to the Christians for three days. On the third night, the Christian Quirinus, sub-deacon,who remained near the amphitheatre all the time, watching an opportunity to take the bodies, succeeded in bringing them to his own house. He respectfully wrapped them in fine linen, and enclosed them in a leaden case. Their bodies were thus preserved until the time of Constantine.

The spot where they are supposed to have been laid is now under the Passionists' garden on the Cœlian. But God would not have the remains or the memory of such great martyrs entirely lost to the world. During the reign of Constantine, when He had displayed to His infant Church in Rome the rainbow of peace and prosperity, He admonished a holy priest in a vision where he would find the remains of SS. Abdon and Sennen, and they were removed to the cemetery of Pontiano, or *ad Ursum Pileatum*, as it was known in the early days of the Church. The beautiful and ancient Church of St. Bibiana is erected over this cemetery. When Gregory **IV.** was restoring the venerable Church of St. Mark in the ninth century, he had the bodies of these two great saints removed, and they are justly enumerated amongst the great treasures with which Gregory enriched that church. Relics were sent to Florence, and some also to France ;

but the larger portion of their remains is still **preserved** in the confessional of St. Mark's, awaiting the hour **in** which they will be united again to the brave spirits that animated them, to assist in the judgment **of the wicke**d world that condemned them.

CHAPTER XV.

THE ACTS OF POPE STEPHEN.

1.

THE events we are about to relate took place in the year 259 of the Christian era. The Emperors Valerian and Gallienus had usurped the throne, and under their tyrannical rule a terrible persecution burst upon the Church. Scarcely in any other reign of the two hundred and fifty years that had passed over the Church are there to be found such visible interpositions of Divine Providence for the glory of His martyrs and the humiliation of His enemies. The thunders of heaven rolled over the heads of the persecutors, the earth shook beneath their feet, and their idols were melted like lead in a furnace at the prayers of the martyrs; yet the stream of blood flowed on, and the angels were daily and hourly carrying aloft the peerless spirits of the triumphant Christians to the abodes of peace and joy.

There never was a time in the history of the Empire when the people were so visited by public calamities as during the reigns of Gallus and Valerian. Inundations, fires and earthquakes had decimated whole provinces, and destroyed cultivated lands and beautiful cities;

famine and pestilence joined in the war of extermination, and the sighs of grief were heard on every side. As
might have been expected, the Christians were blamed
for all the calamities of the Empire. The Evil One spoke
through the oracles on the Capitol, and fired the public
mind against the "detested religion," which was now
spreading on every side. The persecution came; but the
circumstances that brought it about were peculiar.

For the first three years of his reign, the rule of the
Emperor Valerian was mild and pacific. He was in a
particular manner partial to the Christians. In public
and private he showed them respect and favour, and
the Church flourished on every side. "Before the persecution," says Eusebius, the great historian of the early
history of the Church, "Valerian was gentle and kind
towards the servants of God. Not one of the former
Emperors—not even he who was publicly recognised as
a Christian (Philip, A.D. 244)—showed such favour towards us as this prince in the commencement of his reign.
His household was filled with Christians, and appeared
to be a Church of Jesus Christ rather than a palace of
the Roman Emperor." (Book vii., chap. x.)

Amongst the courtiers was a man named Macrian.
He was of low birth, but had some pretensions to
learning; being well skilled in sorcery and magic, he
ingratiated himself into favour with the Emperor.
Avarice, ambition and cruelty had taken possession of
his soul. He aimed at the supreme power, and longed
to gratify the base propensities of his heart, by shedding
the blood of the Christians, whom he hated without a
cause. It is supposed that the demons, who are permitted to influence men through the black art, intimated

to Macrian that he could never attain the realization of
his ambitious hopes as long as Valerian was a friend to
the Christians. He set himself with cruel ingenuity to
pervert the noble and generous disposition of the peaceful Emperor, and history tells the terrible tale of his success. He commenced by telling him of the wonders of
magic ; how it could unveil th e future and guide the
present in the paths of the highest prosperity, and was
the talisman of wealth, power and glory. The unthink-
ing Valerian was caught like a fly in poisoned honey.
Under the counsels of his impious preceptor, he began
to believe that lessons of wisdom were written on the
entrails of new-born infants, and that the terrible secrets
of the unknown future might be deciphered in the life-
streams of the heart's blood. His first victim was a new-
born child. In blinded fanaticism he bent over the
reeking entrails of the infant to trace in its scarlet fibres
the language of prophecy and knowledge. The jaundiced
eye sees everything one colour ; so when passion rules
predominant in the soul, every thought is moulded to its
form, and the noble faculties of the intellect and will lend
their services to its gratification. Thus Valerian thought
he saw in the horrible practices of magic the unveiled
sources of knowledge and power. It is not to be wondered at that, under the guidance of the impious
Macrian, he found out that the gods (the devils) were
not pleased with the Christian sect ; and, as one abyss
calls on another, he fell into the lowest depths of cruelty,
intolerance and fanaticism. The end of the year 251
found Valerian one of the most cruel and unfeeling persecutors of the Church.

During the days of peace that preceded this persecution, Almighty God vouchsafed to the holy St. Cyprian, Bishop of Carthage, a knowledge of the terrible time that was coming. The learned Bishop wrote to several Churches to prepare them for the storm. In his sublime exhortation to martyrdom, in his letter to the Thibaritans, he says : " Instructed by the light which the Lord has deigned to give us, we must forewarn your souls by the solicitude of our admonition ; for you must know, and hold for certain, that a day of terrible trial is about to dawn—the time of Antichrist is at hand. We must all stand prepared for the battle, and think of naught but the crown of glory, and the ineffable reward that will follow a brave confession of the faith. Nor are the trials that are coming like the past ; a severer and bloodier combat awaits us, for which the soldiers of Christ must prepare by unflinching faith and unsullied virtue, remembering they daily consume the blood of Christ, that they may shed their blood for Him." (St. Cyprian, Epis. 56, ad Thibaritanos, de Exhortat. Mart.)

When the clouds that threatened the storm to the prophetic eye of Cyprian burst in the following year over the world in all the horrors of a bloody persecution, the great doctor himself was one of its most remarkable victims. He tells us, in another part of his works, when the persecution broke out, how the infuriate mob called aloud in the amphitheatre of Carthage that he should be cast to the lions. As the highest buildings are most exposed to the lightning so the Bishops and Fathers of the Church were the first victims of the persecution. In Rome, the great Pope Stephen was martyred whilst celebrating mass in the Catacombs. It is from the Acts of this Holy Pontiff we will quote just now some of the scenes connected with the Coliseum during this persecution.

Although Almighty God permitted the persecution to try His Church, yet He prepared a terrible retribution for the injustice of His enemies. All the persecutors came to an untimely and miserable end. Perhaps not one of those tyrants who shed Christian blood was so humbled or accursed as Valerian. "They have chosen their own way," says Almighty God, through the prophet Isaias, "and the abominations which their heart desired; but I will show up their folly, and will repay them for their sins." (Isaias lxvi. 3, 4.) The whole Empire participated in the curse that fell on the impious Valerian; the accumulated evils of plagues, famines, earthquakes, and civil wars swept like a tempest over the world, decimating the human race, and spreading terror and confusion on every side. The barbarians who were on the borders of the provinces rushed in, as if by a preconcerted plan, on different portions of the Empire, and commenced to pillage and plunder all before them. Valerian was forced to turn his attention to more formidable enemies than the unoffending Christians. He organised the troops for war, he sent his son Gallienus against the Germans, and his best and bravest captains to other portions of the Empire; whilst he himself took the lead of the army against the Persians, who were now, as for many years past, the most formidable enemies of the Empire. Sapor, the King of the Persians, routed and destroyed the Roman army, and took the Emperor prisoner; a terrible hour of retaliation had come for the cruel Valerian. He was dragged before the haughty Persian in chains, and still clothed in his magnificent robes of purple and gold. After having insulted him in the most cruel and barbarous manner, he was made to walk before the chariot of the Persian king, and thus brought through all the towns of the kingdom, to be insulted and ill-treated by the entire Persian people. The vilest slave could not have been treated with more contempt. Every time that Sapor wished to enter his chariot or mount his horse, Valerian was brought out and made to stoop down with his face towards the ground, so that the barbarian king might make a footstool of his back. After several years passed in the most horrible servility, in hunger, insult and unceasing pain, a fate still more terrible awaited him. When his natural strength was failing, it was determined to anticipate death by the last and cruellest act of their revenge. He was flayed alive, and his skin, stuffed with straw, was hung up in one of their temples as a monument of their triumph and revenge. Thus shall they perish who raise their arm against God!

2.

Whilst Valerian was prosecuting his horrible and impure studies in magic, the Christians were aware of the change that had come over his character, and prepared themselves for the impending storm. The Catacombs were opened again, and provisions were brought to those dreary abodes of the dead; the altar and the tabernacle were shorn of their ornaments, and the dread mysteries were celebrated once more by the tombs of the martyrs in the gloomy passages under ground. The catechumens were all baptized, and the faithful were exhorted and fortified by frequent Communion and unceasing prayer. Valerian showed by many signs his altered feelings towards the Christians, and whilst he was premeditating a dreadful carnage of the followers of Christ, an heroic act of zeal and courage by one of the domestics of the palace roused the latent fire of his cruel and perverted heart, and unsheathed the sword for the bloodshed of thousands.

One day a poor woman was seen weeping and distracted with grief outside the gates of the royal palace. A Christian servant of the household was passing, and learned that she was robbed of her child by the Emperor, and she knew they were cutting it to pieces inside. The Christian went to the apartments of the Emperor, and found him with the impious Macrian bending over the lifeless body of a beautiful infant; their hands were stained with blood; they looked more like furies than men. Roused to holy indignation at the dreadful sight, the fearless servant of God reproved the Emperor for his impiety. She threatened him with the judgments of the Eternal God, and made him tremble at the terrible retribution that hangs over the murderer and the oppressor of the poor; but the spirit of evil had already taken possession of the wretched Valerian; the language of reproof grated harshly on his haughty soul and, bursting into rage, he ordered the lictors to remove and torture the Christian that dared to correct him. In the same breath in which he condemned his first martyr, he ordered the bronze plates that announced the decrees of persecution and bloodshed to be hung from the walls of the Capitol and the columns of the Forum.

Pope Stephen called his trembling flock around him, and exhorted them to martyrdom; by holy admonitions and by love of sacred writ he imbued their minds with sentiments of pious confidence.   Amongst other things, say the Acts of the martyrdom of this holy Pontiff, which we quote from Baronius, (A.D. 259) he addressed them in these words: " My beloved little children, listen to me a sinner. While there is yet time, let us be instant in good works, and that not only to our neighbours, but to ourselves ; and, in the first place, let me admonish each one to take up his cross and follow our Lord Jesus Christ, who has vouchsafed to say to us, ' He that loves his life shall lose it, but he that loses his life for my sake shall find it in eternity.' Wherefore, I beseech you all to be most solicitous, not only for your own, but for your neighbours' salvation ; so that if any among you have friends or relations still in heathenism, let him hasten to conduct them hither to receive baptism at our hands."

Among the Christians who were listening to the address of the holy father, there was a saintly and venerable man named Hippolytus, who had been a wealthy Roman citizen, but gave all his substance to the poor, and was now leading a solitary life in the Catacombs on the Appian Way. When Stephen had ceased to address the Christians, Hippolytus cast himself at his feet, and said: "Good father, may it please you, there are my nephew and his sister, both. Gentiles, whom I myself reared—a little boy about ten years of age, and the girl thirteen ; their mother, a Gentile, is called Paulina ; their father, who sends them both to me from time to time, is named Adrias." Then the blessed Stephen exhorted him to detain the children when next sent, that thereby the parents also might be brought to visit him.

After two days the above-mentioned children came to Hippolytus, bringing certain cakes of bread. He detained them, and sent word to the blessed Stephen, who coming embraced the little ones and cherished them. Full of solicitude about their children, the parents came in haste to seek them. Then Stephen addressed them on the terrors of the future and tremendous judgment, earnestly exhorting them to abandon the idols, as did Hippolytus also. Adrias, the father of the children, said that he dreaded being despoiled of his property and put to death —the lot prepared for all who professed themselves Christians. Paulina, sister of Hippolytus, said the same, and rebuked him for urging such a course, for she hated the religion of the Christians. They departed, leaving those in the Catacombs who had exhorted them without success, but not without hope.

Then the blessed Stephen, calling the learned priest Eusebius and the deacon Marcellus, sent them to Adrias and Paulina, to invite them again to the Catacomb where Hippolytus abode ; and when they were come, Eusebius said to them: "Christ expects you, that He may introduce you into the kingdom of heaven." And when Paulina began to insist on the glory of this world and the miserable lot of the Christians, he portrayed to them the ineffable glories of heaven, which they could not attain except through faith and baptism. Paulina declined to decide till the next day. The same night there came a Christian father and mother with their son, who was a paralytic, to Eusebius in the Catacombs, to have him baptized ; who, praying over him, baptized him ; whereupon he was cured, and his tongue being loosened, he gave praise to God. Then Eusebius offered up the Holy Sacrifice, and all participated in the body and blood of Christ. When Stephen the Bishop heard of this, he came, and they rejoiced together.

But when it was morning, Adrias and Paulina returned, and on hearing of the cure of the boy, being filled with admiration, they prostrated themselves with great contrition, praying the Pontiff to baptize them. Seeing this, Hippolytus gave thanks to God, and cried out: "Holy father, do not defer their baptism." Stephen answered: "Let then the necessary solemnities be completed, and put to them the prescribed questions, that it may be seen if they truly believe and have no longer any trepidation at heart." After the interrogation, he enjoined them a fast, and having instructed all the catechumens, he baptized them in the name of the Trinity, and placing on them the sign of the cross, he called the boy Neone, and the girl Mary, and he offered the Holy Sacrifice for them. When all had communicated, the blessed Stephen departed. The newly-baptized remained, and dwelt with Hippolytus, Eusebius and Marcellus in the Catacombs, but the property which they had in the city they distributed among the poor.

As soon as the news of this transaction came to the ears of the Emperor, orders were issued to seek out the converts, and a reward of half their property was offered to any one who should detect them. It was then that Maximus, a writer in one of the government offices, had recourse to a device to find them out. He feigned himself a Christian that begged alms, and coming to a place called *Area Carbonaria*, on the Cœlian Hill, remained there begging until he saw Adrias passing by, to whom he thus addressed himself in order to obtain a proof of his being a Christian :—"For Christ's sake, in whom I believe, I beseech you, take pity on my distress." Then Adrias, taking pity on him, bid him follow. But when they were entering the house, Maximus was seized by a demon, and cried out : " Man of God ! I am an informer. I see above me an immense fire ; oh ! pray for me ; I am tortured by the flames ! " Afterwards, when they had interceded for him with tears, he fell prostrate on the ground, and was cured; and when they lifted him up he exclaimed : " Perish the worshippers of idols ; let me be baptized ! " They took him to the blessed Stephen, who, having instructed him, at length baptized him, and he prayed to remain some days with Stephen the Bishop after he was made a Christian.

When Maximus did not return, search was made for him, and some of his fellow-clerks were sent from the same department to his house. They found him prostrate in prayer. Laying hands on him, they brought him before Valerian, who said to him : " Hast thou been so blinded by bribes as to deceive me ?"

" True," replied Maximus, " hitherto I have been blind ; but now, being illuminated, I see."

" In what light ?" said the Emperor.

" In the faith of the Lord Jesus Christ," replied Maximus.

Then Valerian in a rage ordered him to be precipitated from one of the bridges of the Tiber. His body was afterwards buried by Eusebius in the Catacombs on the Appian Way.*

* The little chapel in which Maximus was interred is still shown in the Catacombs of St. Sebastian on the Appian Way. As these Catacombs are left publicly open for strangers, there are none so well known in the Eternal City. The stone with the inscription " Locus Maximi," is still preserved in the same spot. It was in this gloomy subterranean chapel that St Philip Neri used to spend whole nights in prayer.

After this, Valerian sent a body of seventy soldiers with orders to use every diligence till they had found Eusebius and the others. When the holy priest, together with Adrias, Paulina, and the children, as also the venerable Hippolytus, were discovered, they were led in bonds to the Forum of Trajan. The deacon Marcellus gave vent to complaints against the Emperor, for his cruelties against the friends of truth, and being denounced for this by Secundinus Togatus, he also was seized.

Eusebius the priest was the first who was interrogated by the judge: "Are you the disturber of the city?—But, first, what is your name?"

"I am called Eusebius, and a priest."

Then the judge ordered him to be set aside, and Adrias to be brought in; who, being first questioned as to his name, and then as to how he came by the abundance of wealth and affluence with which he seduced the people, replied: "In the name of the Lord Jesus Christ, I inherit it from the industry of my parents."

"Therefore make use of your inheritance, and do not waste it in subverting others," said the judge.

"I do expend it truly, and without deception, for the advantage of myself and my children."

"Hast thou children and a wife?"

"They are here with me in chains."

"Let them be brought in," said the judge.

Then Paulina with her children, Neone and **Mary,** were brought within the veil, followed by Marcellus **the** deacon and Hippolytus; when the judge said—

"Is this your wife? and are these your children?"

"They are," said Adrias.

"And who are those other two?"

" **That** is Marcellus the deacon, and this is my brother Hippolytus, a faithful servant of Christ."

Turning to them, the judge said : " Declare with your own mouths by what names you are called ? "

Marcellus said : " I am called Marcellus the deacon."

" You," said he to Hippolytus, " what is your name ? "

" Hippolytus, servant of the servants of Christ."

The judge then ordered Paulina and her children to be taken aside, and then said to Adrias: " Tell me where your treasures are, and let you and those who have been led in with you offer sacrifice to the gods, and save your lives, which otherwise you will speedily lose."

" We," replied Hippolytus, " have already cast away vain idols, and have found the Lord of heaven and earth, Christ the Son of God, in whom we believe.

Then the judge ordered all to be led to the public prison and not to be separated : they were led to the Mamertine keep.

After three days, the prefect, assisted by Probus, held his court in the Temple of the Earth, where he had ordered instruments of torture of all descriptions to be kept in readiness. Adrias was brought in first, and was interrogated about his property. When nothing satisfactory was elicited, the altar was lit up before the goddess Minerva, and they were ordered to offer incense. But all rejecting the proposal with horror, laughed at the judge for asking them. They were then ordered to be stripped, and being extended naked on the rack, were beaten with sticks. Then the blessed Paulina, being very severely beaten, resigned her soul to God. Seeing this, the judge ordered Eusebius and Marcellus to be beheaded. The sentence was executed at the Petra

Scelerata, near the Coliseum, on the 13th of the kalends of November. Their bodies were left for the dogs; that of St. Paulina was cast out of the pavement; and all three were collected by another Hippolytus, a deacon, and buried in the Catacombs on the Appian Way, where they had so often met.

Secundinus after this brought Adrias and his children with Hippolytus home to his own house, leaving nothing untried to discover the money; but their answer was: " What we had, we expended on the poor; our treasures are our souls, which we can on no account afford to lose; obey your commission." Then Secundinus had the children tortured; to whom their father said: " Be constant, my children." While they were under the strokes, they said nothing but " Christ, assist us."

After this he commanded Adrias and Hippolytus to be submitted to torments, directing their sides to be burned with torches; and when they had been tortured in various ways and could in nowise be induced to sacrifice, or even to say that they consented to it, Secundinus said: " Quickly lift the children Neone and Mary from the ground, and carrying them to the Petra Scelerata, slay them before their father's eyes." When this had been done, their bodies were flung on the public place (*i.e.*, alongside the amphitheatre). They were carried away at night by the faithful, and interred in the same catacomb with their mother on the Appian Way.

When Secundinus had announced all to Valerian, after eight days, he directed his throne to be prepared in the circus. Flaminius and Hippolytus and Adrias, bound in chains, were conducted, with a herald crying out before them : " These are the guilty wretches, the guilty wretches that overthrow the city ; " and when they had arrived before the tribunal, the judge began again to question them about the money, saying : " Give up the money by which you used to lead the people into error."

" We preach Christ," replied Adrias, " who deigned to liberate us from error, not for the destruction of men, but that we may have life."

When Secundinus Togatus saw his words availed nothing, he directed their jaws to be beaten for a long time with leaden sticks, while the crier made proclamation to them : " Sacrifice to the gods by burning incense ;" for he had ordered a lighted tripod to be placed there for the purpose.

Hippolytus, streaming with blood, cried out : " Execute your office, unhappy man, and cease not ! "

Then Secundinus ordered the executioners to cease beating them, and said : " Now at least take pity on yourselves ; you see I pity your foolishness."

They answered : " We are ready to bear any torments rather than do what you or the Emperor wish us." Secundinus reported this to the Emperor Valerian, who ordered them to be forthwith destroyed in the presence of the people.

Then Secundinus commanded them to be taken to the bridge of Antoninus, and to be beaten to death ; where, after suffering a long time, they gave up the ghost, and their bodies were left in the same place near the island Lycaonia. Hippolytus, a deacon of the Roman Church, came by night and removed their bodies to the same crypt on the Appian Way (5th Ides of December) where the other Saints had been placed. (See Baronius, under the year 259, No. 8 and following.)

From the Acts we have beer quoting, we find that no sooner had the Catacombs been consecrated by the sacred remains of the martyrs than they became the voluntary homes of the living. Whilst peace reigned in the Empire and the dread sacrifice was offered in little churches in the very heart of the city, some of the fervent Christians retired to the Catacombs for prayer and solitude. Such was the case with Hippolytus, the brother of Paulina, whose terrible death we have just recorded. We have in the same Acts a beautiful account of a Grecian woman and her daughter who spent some years in one of the crypts on the Appian way, remaining in prayer by the tombs of the martyrs long after the sword of persecution had been returned to its scabbard. These were relatives of Adrias and Paulina, and were likewise Christians. Having arrived in Rome, they learned that their kinsfolk were martyred; they went in great joy to the little chapel in the Catacombs of St. Sebastian (as they are now called), where these martyrs were buried, and there passed thirteen years in vigils and prayers, until it pleased God to call them to Himself, and they were interred in the same crypt.

3.

Nearly a year had passed since the scenes described above took place. The persecution still raged, but was losing the virulence of its first outbreak. The Evil One, who had taken possession of the heart of Valerian, urged him on to still greater cruelties, and to deeper and more intense hatred against the Christians. Consequently, he issued a new edict, more formidable and cruel than the preceding. Informers were promised a reward of all the

property of the Christians they should betray ; and Valerian himself sent secret orders to the rulers of the provinces, that although he publicly commanded only the
death of the principal Christians, he in reality wished
the entire extermination of the sect. Thus in the following year, the persecution raged more fiercely than ever ;
and we must now return to the second part of the
beautiful Acts we have just quoted, and continue the
tale of bloodshed and horror that passed under the walls
of the Coliseum seventeen centuries ago.

When the edict was published, the blessed Stephen,
having assembled all the clergy, thus addressed them :
" Brethren and fellow-soldiers, you have heard of the
cruel and diabolical mandates that have been issued, that
if any Gentile deliver up a Christian, he shall receive his
entire property. Do you, therefore, brethren, reject the
goods of this world with contempt, that you may receive
a celestial kingdom ; fear not the princes of this world,
but pray to the Lord God of heaven, and to Jesus Christ
His Son, who can rescue us from the hands of our enemies,
and from the malice of Satan, to associate us to His
grace."

Then the presbyter Bonus, answering, said : " Not only
are we prepared to relinquish earthly possessions, but
even to pour out our blood for the name of our Lord
Jesus Christ, so that we may deserve to obtain His grace."
And having spoken thus, all the clergy prostrated themselves at the feet of the blessed Stephen, and told him
there were some Gentile children and others of their
neighbours not yet baptized, whom they prayed permission to bring ; wherefore he directed that all should
assemble the next day in the crypt of Nepotiana.

When the next day came, there were found assembled catechumens of both sexes to the number of one hundred and eight ; all of whom the same Stephen baptized, and offered for them sacrifice, of which they all partook. Whilst the Pontiff held his station in this Catacomb, arranging the affairs of the Church, teaching, exhorting, holding councils, and celebrating mass, through the crypts of the martyrs, multitudes of the Gentiles resorted to him to be instructed and baptized.

The servant of one of these, Sempronius, had been seized, and was questioned in every way to force him to disclose how he had disposed of his master's riches ; and amongst other things, when the idol of Mars, with a tripod, was placed before him that he might sacrifice, he said : " May the Lord Jesus Christ, Son of the living God, destroy thee !" and forthwith the idol melted.   Amazed at this, Olympius, the officer charged with his execution, ordered him to be brought to his own dwelling, threatening to exhaust every species of torment on him that night.

On coming home, he told his wife, Exuperia, how the idol melted at the name of Christ.   " If, then," said she, " so great be the virtue of that name as thou narratest, it is better for us to abandon gods who cannot defend either us or themselves, and seek Him who gave sight to the daughter of Nemesius."   Olympius then told his domestic, Tertullian, to treat Sempronius with honour, and to try and discover where the treasures were of Nemesius, his master.   But that same night, he with his wife Exuperia, along with their son, came to Sempronius, and falling at his feet, said : " We recognise the power of Christ ; we seek to be baptized by thee."

Sempronius said to Olympius : " If you do penance with your wife and son, all shall be administered to you in due season."

" Thou shalt have proof even now," said Olympius, " that from my whole heart I believe in the Lord whom thou preachest ; " and so saying, he opened a room where he had idols of gold and silver and marble, and told Sempronius he was ready to do with them whatsoever he should direct.

" Then," said Sempronius, " destroy every one of them with your own hands—the gold and silver ones melt down with fire, and distribute them to the poor ; and then I shall know that thou believest with thy whole heart."

When Olympius had done so, a voice was heard saying : " Let my Spirit rest in thee." On hearing this, Olympius and his wife began to be strengthened more and more, and to glow with a fervent longing to be baptized.

Sempronius communicated these things to Nemesius, now at liberty, who went in haste to inform the blessed Stephen, who returned thanks to Almighty God, and went in the night to the house of Olympius, who fell at his feet, together with his wife and son, pointing to the fragments of his idols as a token of his sincerity. Seeing this, the blessed Stephen gave thanks to God, and commenced to catechise them on ecclesiastical tradition. He then baptized them and all of their household that believed, together with their son, whom he called Theo- dulus, and offered sacrifice for their redemption.

After the third day, this news was brought to Valerian and Gallienus, who forthwith ordered Nemesius and his daughter Lucilla, whose sight had been restored, to be slain at the Temple of Mars on the Appian Way, while Sempronius, Olympius, Exuperia, and Theodulus were burned to death near the amphitheatre. They expired singing the praises of Christ, who had vouchsafed to associate them with His martyrs; and their remains having been collected by the clergy were consigned to the tomb by the blessed Stephen with the accustomed hymns.

After some days, special edicts were issued for the apprehension and punishment of Stephen and the clergy of the Roman Church. Twelve of the latter were immediately seized and put to death without any hearing. Amongst them was that venerable priest named Bonus, or the Good, who had made that glorious declaration when the clergy were addressed in the Catacombs by Pope Stephen. Their bodies were collected, and laid near those of two other holy martyrs in a crypt near the Via Latina, by Tertullian, freedman of Olympius. On learning this, the blessed Stephen sent for Tertullian, and having instructed him regarding the kingdom of God and life eternal, baptized him, and gave him in charge, while yet in his white robes, to a priest, who specially enjoined him to seek out the bodies of the holy martyrs. After two days, he was taken and brought before Valerian, by whom he was interrogated as to the property of Olympius; and having answered, and sustained every species of torture with heroic constancy, he was finally beheaded at the second milestone on the Via Latina. His remains were collected by the blessed Stephen and interred in the same crypt.

The next day soldiers were sent to seize Stephen, and the clergy who were with him; and when they had led him into the presence of Valerian, the Emperor said: "Is it you who are endeavouring to overthrow the Republic, and by your persuasion to induce the people to abandon the worship of the gods ?"

To which Stephen replied : " I indeed do not overthrow the Republic ; but I admonish and exhort the people that, forsaking the demons whom they worship in their idols, they would pay homage to the true God, and Jesus Christ, whom He has sent." Then Valerian commanded him to be led to the Temple of Mars, where his sentence was to be read from the tablets.

Blessed Stephen, being led out of the city on the Via Appia, when he had come to the Temple of Mars, said, lifting his eyes to heaven : " Lord God and Father, who didst destroy the tower of confusion at Babel, destroy this place in which the devil deceives people to superstition." It then began to thunder ; and the lightning flashes struck the temple, which in part fell to the ground. The soldiers having fled, Stephen, who remained alone, went with his attendant priests and deacons to the neighbouring cemetery of Lucina, where he encouraged the Christians to martyrdom by many exhortations. After this, he offered sacrifice to the Omnipotent God. The soldiers who were sent in pursuit, found him in the act of celebrating mass ; but, without being terrified, he continued intrepidly the mysteries which he had commenced, until they struck off his head as he sat in the pontifical chair before the altar, on the 4th of the Nones of August. Great were the lamentations made by the Christians at being deprived of so great a pastor, and they interred his body, with the chair drenched with his blood, in the same crypt, in the place called the cemetery of Callistus. (See Baronius, An. 260.)

The relics of Hippolytus, Adrias, Paulina, and the children Neone and Mary, are preserved under the high altar of the beautiful little church of St. Agatha, in Suburra. It is now the collegiate chapel of the Irish students at Rome, to whom it was given, together with the spacious college attached, by Gregory XVI., " whose memory is in benediction." The faithful children of St. Patrick kneel around this venerable shrine, and learn in prayer that spirit of martyrdom which is still necessary for their own suffering country. Ireland, too, has had her martyrs ; and the shrine of the victims of the early persecutions of the Church must forcibly recall to the memory of the exiled Levite the history of his suffering country. His faith sees the brighter side of the cloud that passed over Ireland in the penal times ; his fathers stand with the heroes of Rome amid the bright galaxy of heaven's martyrs ; his country is numbered amongst the nations favoured by God.

CHAPTER XVI.

WHILST the impious Valerian was paying the penalty of his crimes under the galling lash of the victorious Persian King, Sapor, his worth-'ess and debauched son, Gallienus, continued the reign of tyranny over the Empire. Without affection for his father, and without interest in the Empire, he gave him-self up to the most shameful excesses and debaucheries.

Five usurpers rose almost simultaneously to wrest from him the reins of government. Amongst them was the impious Macrian, whose wicked counsel had brought Valerian into hostility against the Christians, and drawn down so terrible a retribution from heaven on that ill-fated Emperor. The most successful of the rivals of Gallienus was the soldier Claudius. He rose from a tribune under Valerian to be commander of a camp; his triumph over the Goths made him famous; praises were poured on him, statues erected to his name, and he was the idol of his army. His ambition kept pace with his fortune; he aimed at supreme control.

He was a crafty man, and resorted to a stratagem that proved successful in removing his rival. He wrote out the names of some of the bravest and most daring officers in the army of Gallienus, and imitated perfectly the characters and handwriting of the Emperor. This document, which was a pretended list of those whom the tyrant intended to put to death, was sent by a confidant to the camp of Gallienus, who was then besieging the usurper Aureolus in the city of Milan. It was picked up by one of the intended victims. He called the others around him—they resolved to kill Gallienus that night. When all was dark, they raised a false alarm, the soldiers were called to arms, and in the confusion, the wretched Emperor was pierced through the body with a javelin, and an officer cut his head in two with his sword. Claudius was declared Emperor by his own army; defeated Aureolus; and came to Rome to steep his hands in the blood of the Christians, to stain his name with eternal infamy.

His predecessor was too intemperate to be formidable. Cruelty, bloodshed, and wholesale immolation of innocent victims are not the stains found in that page of history in which his name is mentioned. His impurity, intemperance, and the open indulgence of brutal passions, did not allow him even a sober moment to molest the Christians. Yet the old laws of persecution were still in force ; there were judges and governors who used the terrible edicts to gratify the whims of cruel caprice, and remove those whom they considered obnoxious. Many martyrdoms are recorded in the provinces; whilst in Rome the persecution raged without the horrors of bloodshed. The Christians suffered, but not in the Coliseum, or at the Petra Scelerata ; they were not torn to pieces with knotted scourges, or cast into cauldrons of boiling oil ; they were not flung into the Tiber, nor beheaded at the third or seventh milestone ; but another, and, to the Christians themselves, a more tedious persecution raged against them. They were cast into loathsome prisons, chained to the galleys, or made to work like public malefactors in the woods and sandpits in the neighbourhood of the city. Thus when Claudius entered Rome he had his victims prepared for him ; his short and bloody reign opens with one of the most heart-rending and cruel scenes we have found in the Coliseum's tales of horrors.

In the Acts of the Persian nobles Marius and Martha and sons, as given in the Bollandists under the nineteenth of January (and first of March), we read the following :—

"At the same time Claudius ordered that if any Christians should be found either in prison or at large, they should be punished without trial. When this law was promulgated, there were detained in the Via Salaria two hundred and sixty Christians, who, for the name of Christ, were condemned to work in the sandpits ; these he had confined in a potter's store, and then ordered to be taken to the amphitheatre to be slain with arrows. When this happened, Marius and Martha his wife, together with their sons Audifax and Abacuc, were very much afflicted —came to the place where they were slain, bringing with them the blessed John the priest, and found fire was placed over the holy bodies. They then commenced to remove the bodies, and bury them with liniments and spices, for they were very rich ; and as many as they could rescue they buried in the crypt on the Via Salaria, near the *Clivum Cucumeris.* They buried also at the same time a certain tribune of Claudius, named Blastus, and in the same place they spent many days with blessed John in fasting and prayer."

The imagination must fill up the horrid details of this dreadful massacre. According to the Acts they were shot with arrows in the Coliseum The brutal soldiery were permitted to take the place of the spectators, and to let fly their arrows on their companions who were forced into the arena. The corps of archers was always the most savage and brutal of the soldiers : from their body the public executioners were generally chosen ; their intemperate habits, their rough, brutal appearance, and their want of the common feelings of humanity, made them hateful to the pagans themselves ; they were meet instruments in the hands of tyrants for the torture of Christians.

It is terrible to contemplate these brave soldiers, unarmed, bound and silent, awaiting the fatal darts that were to pierce them through. In vain we look for anything in the horrors of shipwreck or the battlefield to compare to this scene. In the former its terrors are more in anticipation than in reality ; the wave that engulphs its victim, hides for ever the agonies of death ; an occasional scream from a struggling victim breaks through the storm ; but then, a moment, and all is over, not a vestige of the wreck is seen, the mighty billows roll on and the wind howls as before. Not so in the scene before us in the Coliseum. For hours the sigh of the dying mingles with the rude laugh of the archers. Here a group are on their knees, hands clasped and in prayer ; the hum of the flying arrows is their death-knell ; they fall one by one : there two friends have clasped each other in the last deadly embrace ; they have fallen together, and their blood mingles in the same stream. Never was greater battle won by the brave ; their courage was a defiance of death —the spoils of their victory th e richest ever won.

Were these poor soldiers strangers to all the ties of nature, and the passions of the soul ? Certainly not. The grace to suffer martyrdom does not mean a benumbing of the human sensibilities ; with them affection, fear, and pain are felt as strongly as in the heart of the dying soldier on the field of battle. Home, family and friends were loved by the martyr ; but the supernatural unction of grace deadened the pang of separation ; the aged parents, the beloved spouse and the tender children were cheerfully given up to that paternal Providence that blesses with the same stroke that it chastises. Without a murmur, without a sigh of regret, they awaited their crown.

From the horrors of this massacre we are wrapt in spirit to another scene, bright and consoling. Away above the mighty vault of the amphitheatre, we see thousands of brilliant spirits soaring over the dying soldiers, bearing crowns of unfading laurel, and wafting the liberated souls to eternal joy. When the great ruin is lit up on a summer's evening by millions of fire-flies sailing like floating stars in the dark sky, it brings to mind the bright angels sent from on high to greet those martyred soldiers. Terrible was the contrast between the gloom of the carnage in the material world, and the joy it brought in the regions of true bliss. Centuries of immutable joy have rolled over those heroes of the Coliseum ; short their battle but long and eternal their reward. The woes of earth are momentary pangs ; beyond the grave they become specks in the distant horizon of the past ; the excruciating torments of martyrdom, which at first cause a shudder, are but seconds of transition to eternal joy. It is not, then, with sentiments of pity or indignation that we withdraw our thoughts from this scene of blood ; we look up from our lowliness to the bright galaxy of martyred spirits in the regions above, and we ask them to allow the struggling wayfarers in this valley of tears to join in their unceasing hymns of gratitude to the goodness and mercy of God.

CHAPTER XVII.

THE ACTS OF ST. PRISCA.

1.

A T the time when Claudius was Cæsar, he issued a new and most impious edict to the whole world, that the Christians should offer sacrifice to the gods or be put to death. He ordered his presidents and judges to carry out his law, that he might destroy the worship of the Christians ; he enjoined on them, moreover, that those consenting to sacrifice should be considered worthy of great honour, while non-conformists should be treated with the utmost cruelty. In order to manifest the earnestness of his zeal, and to commence the observance of his impious law, this Emperor Claudius held sacrifices in the Temple of Apollo, and at the same time ordered the soldiers to seize all who were known to be Christians, men and women, and by dint of terror and direful tortures force them to sacrifice to the gods.*

2. There were then malignant men who ardently desired to destroy the Christian worship ; and coming to a

---

* The context of this chapter is almost a literal translation from the original Acts.

certain church, they found the blessed Prisca praying
She was of noble blood ; her father had been thrice consul,
and was exceedingly rich. This holy child was in her
eleventh year, and was adorned with the grace of God
and the most perfect purity of morals.*   The ministers
of the Emperor said to her : " Our Emperor Cl audius has
commanded you to sacrifice voluntarily to the gods." The
blessed Prisca said with a joyful heart : " First let me
enter the holy universal Church, that I may co mmend
myself to my Lord Jesus Christ, and then we will go in
peace.   It is necessary that, in the name of our Lord,
I confound your unworthy Emperor, and assist in the
triumph of Jesus."   And returning to the church, she
completed her prayers.

3. Having finished her petition, she went with them,
to the Emperor.   The ministers, entering into the apartments of Claudius, said to him : "This girl is willing to
obey the commands of your majesty."   On hearing this
he rejoiced exceedingly, and ordered her to be brought
into his presence.   When she was brought into the
palace before him, he said : " Thou art great, O god
Apollo ! and glorious above all the gods, who has brought
me this illustrious virgin, so beautiful and with such good
dispositions."   Then, turning to the blessed Prisca, he
said : " I have arranged to have you brought to me, to
make you my mistress, and the sharer in the power of
my kingdom."   To this Prisca said : "But I will sacrifice
without blood, and only to the immaculate God, my Lord
Jesus Christ."

4. The Emperor, hearing these things, and not under-

* Hæc in undecimo anno erat bonorum operum, et gratia Dei
moribus ornat."—*Acts Bollandists*, April 18, No. 2.

standing their meaning, ordered her to be led to the Temple of Apollo that she might sacrifice to him. The holy virgin being ordered to enter the temple, said with a cheerful countenance to the Emperor : " Do thou also enter, thou and all the priests of Apollo, that you may see how the omnipotent and immaculate Lord is pleased with the sacrifices of His faithful." The Emperor ordered all who had gathered round to watch what she was going to do.

Blessed Prisca said : "Glory be to Thee, O glorious Father ! I invoke Thee, I implore Thee, cast down this motionless and dumb idol, the vile emblem of falsehood and corruption ; but do Thou, O Lord, hear me, a sinner, that this Emperor may know how vain is the hope he has placed in his idols, and that he ought to adore no other god but Thee alone."

When she had prayed thus, there was immediately a great earthquake, so that the whole city was shaken ; the statue of the god shook, and fell to the ground ; in like manner the fourth part of the temple was destroyed, and overwhelmed a multitude of people, together with the priests of the idol.*

The Emperor was terrified, and fled. Prisca said to him : " Stay, Emperor, and assist ; your Apollo is broken to pieces, and you may now gather up the fragments , moreover, his priests are destroyed in the same ruin ; let him come now and assist them."

5. And the demon who dwelt in the idol cried out with a loud voice : " O virgin Prisca ! handmaid of the

---

* " Et hæc ea orante, statim terræ motus factus est magnus, ita ut civitas concuteretur et corruit Apollo et comminutus est ; simili modo quarta pars templi destructa est et oppressit multitudinem paganorum cum sacerdotibus idolorum."—*Acts.* No. 4.

great God who reigns in heaven, thou who keepest His
commandments and hast stript me of my habitation!—
I have lived here for sixty-seven years, and under Claudius Cæsar twelve. Many martyrs have come and have
not exposed me. Having under me ninety-three other
most impious spirits, I order each of them to sacrifice to
me daily fifty souls of men.* O Emperor, persecutor of
the Christians! thou hast found a holy soul, through
whom thou wilt finish thy reign in disgrace." These
words were spoken with a loud voice and great lamentation; terrible darkness surrounded those who were
present, and they went away in great trepidation and
doubt.

6. The Emperor, not understanding that it was by the
divine power that the idol had been overthrown, ordered
her to be buffeted on the face; and when the executioners had beaten her for some time, they lost their strength
and cried out: " Woe unto us sinners! surely we suffer
more than this girl: she is not hurt, and we are in pain
We beseech thee, O Emperor, to have her taken from
us." But the Emperor, enraged against them, ordered
the face of the blessed Prisca to be beaten still more
Looking towards heaven, the holy virgin said—

" Blessed art Thou, O Lord Jesus Christ! for Thou
givest eternal peace to those who believe in Thee."
And when she had said this, she was surrounded with
a bright light, and a voice from heaven was heard saying—

" Daughter, be of good courage and fear nothing, for

---

* A similar thing is read in the Acts of Martina and Titiana, but
we must remember it is the proud spirit of lies that is speaking
His authority is not worth much.

I am the God whom thou invokest, and I will never abando n thee."

After these things the Emperor was enraged almost to madness.

7. The next day, sitting before his tribunal, the Emperor said : " Let that wicked little sorceress be brought in, that we may see some more of her charms."

When she was brought before him, he said to her: " Will you consent to live with me, and sacrifice to the gods ? "

But she firmly replied : " Cease, most impious of men, and son of a satanic father ! Are you not ashamed to insult a helpless girl and ill treat her thus, when you know she will never consent to sacrifice to your idols ? "

Then the Emperor in a fury ordered her to be stript and to be beaten with whips. The child's body appeared as white as snow, and so bright was the light that issued from her, that the eyes of the beholders were dazzled.* Whilst they were beating her, the holy virgin said : " I have cried with my voice to the Lord, and He heard me in the combat of my passion."

The Emperor, hearing her pray thus, said : " Do you think you will seduce me with your magic ? "

But blessed Prisca answered: " Thy father Satan is the prince of all darkness ; he loves fornicators and embraces magicians." The Emperor then ordered her to be beaten with rods, but the Saint, hearing this new punishment, smiled and said : " O unjust and impious man, enemy of

---

* " Tunc iratus imperator jussit expoliari eam et iterum cædi. Sancta autem videbatur candida sicut nix, cujus splendebat corpus in tantum quod nitor claritatis ejus caligare faciebat respicientes in eam."—*Acts*, cap. 11, No. 1.

God and inventor of evils! you are too blinded to know the blessings you are procuring for me from the Eternal Creator."

8. Then Limenius, a relative of the Emperor, said to him : " This contaminated child does not suffer these tor-ments on account of the glory of the Christians and the Crucified ; but, like a shining ray of the sun, hopes to obtain everything. Let your majesty command her to be cast into prison until to-morrow, and have her be-smeared with the oil of fat, and let us destroy this brightness."

The Emperor immediately ordered her to be cast into prison until the following day. While she was being led to prison, she cried out with a loud voice before all the people, saying : " I give Thee thanks, O my Lord Jesus Christ, and I implore Thy holy grace ; pre-serve me from this impious and impure Claudius, who despises Thy goodness." During the whole night, the holy child was glorifying God in prison, singing hymns ; and the voices of a multitude of persons were heard praising God along with her. When morning dawned, she was ordered to be let out of prison, but first to be smeared with oil and grease. But when Limenius was leaving the palace, he perceived a fragrant smell, as if the air were filled with the perfume of aromatics, and said to his companions : " Do you not perceive the beautiful scent ?"

But they replied : " The gods have made this beautiful scent for the beloved Prisca, for they all say her own gods appeared to her during the night."

When they arrived at the prison, they found the blessed Prisca sitting on a throne, and surrounded by a multitude of angels, whose brightness it would be impossible to describe. She held in her hand a tablet, and read these words : " How great are Thy works, O Lord ! Thou hast made all things with wisdom." (Ps. ciii. 24.)

But Limenius was terrified, and leaving the place, went to the palace to announce to the Emperor the great wonders of God. The Emperor commanded her to be taken to the temple to sacrifice, and, in case of refusal, to be exposed to the wild beasts. Prisca continued to pray : " I have run the way of Thy commandments, O Lord ; teach me Thy justifications, and I will learn the wonders of Thy divinity. Free me from the punishments of men, that I may keep Thy commandments."

9. The Emperor seeing her countenance more beautiful and cheerful than before, said to her : " Hast thou listened to good counsel, and consented to sacrifice to the benign gods ? "

But she said to him : " My conversion, Emperor, is complete ; thou wilt not persuade me to mingle in thy controversies, for I am freed from the impieties and seducing vanities of this world. I have received the commands of my Lord Jesus Christ. It is good for me to cling to Him, and place all my hope in Him, who contains all truth, to whom nothing is wanting, for He is omnipotent. The seduction of thy words are like arrows of darkness, that point out the way to eternal gloom. I rejoice rather in the death of the saints that surround me, and who have subdued thy father the devil."

10. The Emperor in anger said to her : " You shall not die, Prisca, if you come and sacrifice."

But she said to him : " Do you order me to enter the temple again ? "

To which the Emperor said, " Yes ; go in and sacrifice, that you may not be devoured by the wild beasts."

Prisca then said : " By the grace of my Lord Jesus Christ assisting me, His humble servant, I will go in as you order."

But the demon who inhabited the idol, knowing that the holy child was coming to banish him, cried out with a loud voice : " Woe to me ! where shall I fly from Thy Spirit, O God of heaven ? Fire is pursuing me from the four corners of the temple."

Prisca entered, making the sign of the cross, and pointing to the statue of the idol, said : " Emperor, look at this imposition : there are eyes that do not see, ears that do not hear, hands that do not feel, and feet that cannot walk—a statue decorated with contemptible vanity ; do you wish me to sacrifice to this ? "

The Emperor (not understanding what she meant) cried out: " May the gods live for ever ! thou hast consented to my request."

But the blessed Prisca approached the idol, and poured forth a prayer to the Lord, saying : " O Lord God, Eternal King ! Thou who stretchedst forth the heavens, and didst build up the earth ; Thou who settest limits to the waters of the ocean, and hast trampled on the Serpent's head ; Thou, O Lord, wilt not abandon me now ; hear my prayer, and destroy this idol made by the hands of men, and used by the demon as an instrument full of deceit and malice ; and let Claudius by different punishments know that Thou alone art blessed in eternity. Amen." Then she said with a loud voice : "I command thee to depart, thou who dwellest in this deaf and dumb idol." A noise as of thunder was immediately heard, and fire

fell from heaven, which consumed the priests of the temple ; a multitude of people were killed ; the purple on
the right arm of the Emperor was burnt, and the idol
was reduced to ashes.* Blessed Prisca said : " Glory be
to God in the highest, and peace on earth to men of good
will."

11. After this the Emperor was enraged, and without
adverting to the miracle which had taken place, or to the
power of the invisible God, said to the prefect : " Take
this magician, and tear her whole body to pieces with
sharp iron hooks, that she may no longer see the light of
this world. I am full of confusion and shame, and know
not what to do." The prefect, taking her, went immediately into the prætorium, and sitting on his tribunal,
ordered them to bring in Prisca, saying : " Introduce that
temple destroyer, that we may see what she will do."
Prisca entered the prætorium smiling.

" The prefect said, " You deride me, little sorceress,
because you are still alive ; by the most pure sun, I will
cast your entrails to the dogs, and then we shall see if
your Christ will have any comfort for you."

The blessed Prisca replied : " O impious man ! ought I
not to deride the power of your Emperor, who has been
conquered by a little girl through Jesus Christ, and then
delivers me up to you ? "

The prefect said : " He is ruler, and has power to
deliver you to me, that I may force you to sacrifice, or
take away your life."

---

* " Et mox tonitruum magnum factum est et cecidit ignis de cœlo
et combussit sacerdotes templi et multitudo populi mortua est, et
imperatoris partem dexteram purpuræ combussit, et idolum in favil
lam redegit."— *Acts,* last lines of No. 10.

Prisca said : "I will not sacrifice ; torment me as you please."

Then the prefect ordered her to be stretched on the rack, and her limbs to be cut with small knives. Whilst they were tormenting her, she cried with a loud voice : "O Lord Jesus, help me ; to Thee do I fly for succour."

12. The enraged prefect ordered her to be cast into prison ; but she, binding up her holy body, and fortifying herself with the hair of her head, went quickly into prison. The prefect, mounted on a horse, repaired to the prison, and found the holy girl, as before, sitting on a high throne, and her beautiful face shining like the sun.* In amazement he left the place, and shutting the prison door, he sealed it with his ring, and leaving fifty men to guard it, went to the Emperor. Blessed Prisca was in the meantime glorifying God, and singing His praises, and there was a great light in the cell in which she was confined. The prefect found the Emperor in his palace, who, on seeing him, wondered, and said : "What are you coming for ? "

He replied : "As your majesty ordered me, I have tortured the wicked little Prisca with iron swords and hooks, and I have tried to kill her, but, behold, she is still alive, and refuses to sacrifice. I have executed your commands ; you must now consider what other punishment you will order to be inflicted on her."

The Emperor said to him : " It is evident that she confides in her incantations. Let her be delivered to the wild beasts, that they may tear her to pieces."

The prefect was silent.

---

* There is extreme brevity used in this portion of the Acts. Circumstances that may have had days intervening are recorded as happening in the same hour.

13. When morning was come, he sent the executioners for her, and when she was brought in before him, he said : " The Emperor commands you to sacrifice ; if you refuse, you are to be exposed to the wild beasts."

Blessed Prisca, with a countenance shining like the light of the sun, answered: "In the name of the Lord Jesus Christ, who suffered for us who believe in Him, I am sure of conquering you."

Hearing this, the prefect was much irritated, and went to the Emperor, and said to him : " I beg of your majesty to come with me to the amphitheatre : " and they went towards it together. Then they had her cast between two wild beasts.

Blessed Prisca said : " Watch my sacrifice."

The prefect said, " Behold, O Emperor, this sorceress who overthrew our gods ; may she be torn to pieces by the beasts."

Amongst the animals was a savage lion, which had not been fed for four days.* The Emperor, sitting on his throne, was overcome with sadness, and ordered Prisca to be led into the arena. When she entered the Coliseum, a great noise was heard in the heavens which terrified the spectators.

The Emperor said to her : " Believe and consent to my wishes ; avert the terrible calamity that is hanging over you ; for I swear by the gods that I love you exceedingly."

The holy child raised her eyes to heaven, and said : " O Lord Jesus Christ, who hast manifested the knowledge

* " Erat autem et alius leo immanissimus qui quotidie comedebat septem oves. Hic non comederat per dies quatuor, ut devoraret B. Priscam."

of Thy divinity, and crowned Thy saints with glory, preserve me perfect in this combat to-day." Then turning towards the Emperor, she said : "O miserable wretch! know that I would rather be devoured by beasts, that I may merit eternal life with Christ, than fall into the snares of eternal death by yielding to thy seductions."

The Emperor then ordered the most ferocious lion to be let loose to devour her. The lion was roaring in his den, so that he terrified all the people. His keeper let him out, and he entered the arena bounding and roaring ; then he walked towards the Saint, not showing terror but love, and leaning forward, he adored her, and kissed her feet.* The blessed Prisca, praying to the Lord, said : "O God, Thou permittest me to combat like a criminal in this theatre of guilt, but Thou preservest my soul unsullied and undefiled." Then turning towards the Emperor, she said : "You see, O Emperor, you have but manifested our power over tortures and wild beasts, because Christ, who made heaven and earth, and everything in them, is always victorious ; to Him everything is subjected by the will of His Father."

The Emperor, seeing the meekness of the lion, and that it showed the reverence of love towards the Saint, said to her : "Humble yourself and acknowledge the gods, for they are helping you."

But Prisca replied : "They cannot help themselves, how then can they help me ? In the name of my Lord Jesus Christ, by my combat, and by my martyrdom, they are annihilated."

---

* "Et erat leo rugiens in cubili suo, ut omnes terreret. Ille qui eum nutriebat aperiit leoni et egressus leo rugiit cursum arripiens et ambulavit ad Sanctam, non terrorem ostendens sed dilectionem et inclinans se adorabat, osculabatur pedes ejus."

The Emperor commanded the lion to be taken back to his den ; but, before he left the arena, he attacked one of the relations of the Emperor, and killed him. The enraged Claudius ordered the blessed Prisca to be cast again into prison ; she was filled with the grace of God, and said : " Preserve me, O Lord, from the snares they have laid for me, and from the scandals of the workers of iniquity."

14. After three days the Emperor once more ordered a sacrifice to be offered in the temple, and sent for the holy virgin.   She came, and was resplendent as the sun.   Claudius said to her : " Believe and sacrifice, and you will be safe."   But she said : " I do sacrifice, and I believe in Jesus Christ."   Then the Emperor in anger ordered her to be suspended and torn with hooks. When she was drawn up, she said : " Thou hast rejoiced me, O Lord, in T hy holy will, and I will delight in the works of Thy hands ; Thy judgments, O Lord, are true eternal light ! " Saying these things, immediately the arms and bones of those who were tormenting her were afflicted with the sharpest pain, so that they cried out to the Emperor : " Free us, we beseech thee, from these pains ; the angels of God are tormenting us."

15. He then ordered her to be burnt by fire.   The attendants did as they were told, and kindled an immense fire and cast her into it.   With a loud voice she cried out : " O Lord, Thou who lookest down from heaven on those who believe and seek after Thee, help me, Thy handmaid ! " And immediately there came a great fall of rain and a furious whirlwind, which scattered the flames on every side, so as to burn those who stood round about.

But the Emperor was exceedingly dejected because he was conquered by a little girl.*

16. In his exasperation he ordered all her beautiful hair to be cut off. And when the attendants had cut off her hair, she said : " It is written by the Apostle, if a woman have a beautiful head of hair, it is her ornament ; you have taken from me that hair which God has given me ; God will take from you your kingdom."

He then directed that she should be taken to the temple, and he shut the door, and having sealed it with his ring, departed to his palace. The holy child remained there a day and a night praising and blessing God. Although the Emperor and priests were wont to go to the temple every day, they would by no means go whilst the blessed Prisca was there, for they heard the voices of a multitude of angels. Claudius said to those around him : " Our god whom we worship is great, for he has assembled all the other gods to instruct and comfort Prisca." On the third day he ordered a great sacrifice of oxen to be prepared. When the crowd opened the doors of the temple, they saw the blessed Prisca, sitting on a throne, and surrounded by a great crowd of angels, whose beauty was ineffable ; but their god they saw lying on the ground.† The terrified Emperor cried out : " Where is our god ? " To which Prisca said : " Do you not see him reduced to dust ? "

---

* " Et mox pluvia facta est magna, et sonitus venti, et dispersa est magna flamma et incendit qui circumstabant omnes. Imperator autem valde tristis erat quia vincebatur a puella."—*Acts*, No. 15.

† " Turbæ autem aperientes portam templi viderunt B. Priscam sedentem in sede et cum ea existentem cœtum Angelorum quorum pulchritudo enarrari non potest ; viderunt autem deum illorum in terram cecidisse."—*Acts*, No. 16

17. Then the Emperor, enraged beyond measure, ordered her to be led outside the city to be beheaded. The holy martyr Prisca, rejoicing, said : " O Lord Jesus Christ, Redeemer of all, I praise Thee, I adore Thee, I beseech Thee, I implore Thee, who hast liberated me from all the evils intended for me. Save me now, O Lord Jesus Christ, with whom there is no acceptation of persons ; perfect me in the confession of Thy name ; order me to be received into Thy glory, that I may happily escape the evils by which I am surrounded ; and reward the impious Claudius according to his works towards Thy helpless handmaid ! " And having said this she turned towards the executioners and addressed them thus : " Fulfil the orders you have received." And thus did the blessed Prisca end her life by the sword ; and a voice was heard from heaven, saying : "Because thou hast fought for My name, Prisca, enter into the kingdom of heaven with all My saints." And when this was said, the executioners fell on their faces and died.*

18. Then it was announced to the Bishop of Rome by a Christian who watched in concealment, how they led the blessed Prisca along the Ostian Way, to about the tenth milestone, and there beheaded her, and took away her life. The Bishop, having heard this, went with him to the place he mentioned, and they found her body between two eagles, one at her head and the other at her feet, guarding it, lest the beasts should touch it. There was a dazzling light round her head, and her face smiled

---

* " Et ita finivit vitam B. Prisca per gladium ; et vox de cœlo facta est, dicens, Quia certasti pro nomine meo, Prisca, ingredere in regnum cœlorum cum omnibus sanctis ; et, facta hac voce, carnifices ceciderunt in facies suas et mortui sunt."—*Acts*, No. 17.

in the Holy Spirit.* Then the Bishop himself and his companion dug a grave, and buried her in that spot.

19. When the Emperor heard all these things, he was struck the same day with terrible grief in his heart, and like a rabid dog ate his own flesh,† and groaning and trembling, he cried: "Have pity on me, thou God of the Christians! I know I have transgressed Thy precepts, O Christ, and blasphemed Thee; I have persecuted Thy name, and have ungratefully sinned against Thy hand-maid. I am justly afflicted by Thee; Thou rewardest me as I have deserved." He expired, convulsed and writhing in agony, and a terrible voice was heard saying, "Enter, Emperor, into the furnace of hell; go to exterior darkness, for gloomy places of pain are prepared for thee." There was a great earthquake, and there believed that day, of those who were in Rome, on account of the voice that was heard from heaven, more than five thousand, not counting women and children.‡ The martyrdom of the blessed Prisca took place on the 18th day of January.

20. After a short time, the faithful of Christ built a

---

* "Tunc episcopus, hoc cum audivit, ambulavit cum ipso qui ei nuntiaverat, et ibi eam invenerunt jacentem, unam quidem aquilam sedentem ad caput ejus et aliam ad pedes custodientem corpus ejus, ne a feris tangeretur. Caput vero lucidum splendida facie risit in Spiritu Sancto."—*Acts*, No. 18.

† "Percussus est dolore cordis eadem die, et, sicut rabidus canis, carnes suas comedebat."—*Acts*, No. 18.

‡ "Ingredere, imperator, in clibanum Gehennæ; vade in tenebras exteriores, tibi enim præparata sunt tenebrosa pœnarum loca. Factus est autem terræ motus magnus, et crediderunt in eadem die, de iis qui erant in urbe Roma, pro voce quæ facta est de cœlo, numero plusquam quinque millia, exceptis parvulis et mulieribus."—*Ib.* 19.

church in this place, and served God in it night and day. Her venerable body remained here until the consulate of Antonius (A.D. 275), when her burial-place was revealed to the most reverend and Holy Pope Eutychian, who gathered together the priests and faithful, and having prepared a sarcophagus of wonderful beauty went in procession to the spot. They dug up the earth and found it. With great devotion and reverence they raised the most holy and blessed body of Prisca, virgin and martyr; and singing hymns and sacred canticles, they took it to the city, and deposited it near the Roman arch in the church of the martyrs Aquila and Prisca, praising and glorifying God, who is in heaven, to whom is all honour and glory, who liveth with God the Father in the unity of the Holy Spirit through all ages. Amen.

The Acts of St. Tatiana, as narrated by the Bollandists, are precisely similar to those of St. Prisca. Whether they were two different saints, or the same called by another name, is doubtful. However, following the learned judgment of Papebrochius, we believe St. Tatiana was in reality another of the heroines of the Coliseum. She has a distinct festival in the Roman martyrology on the 12th of January.

CHAPTER XVIII.

CHRYSANTHUS AND DARIA.

1.

CHRYSANTHUS was the son of a senator from Alexandria named Polemius, who went to Rome during the reign of Numerian (A.D. 282), and was immediately enrolled in the senatorial body of the imperial city. The father and son were pagans, but that inscrutable Providence, which St. Paul compares to the potter, who destines some vessels for honour and some for dishonour, cast the light of faith into the heart of Chrysanthus, and made him not only a Christian, but a noble martyr of the Church of God. He was a young man, of ardent temperament, and whilst gifted with a powerful mind, was passionately fond of study. He went through all the systems of philosophy known in those days, studied eloquence under the first masters, and ere yet he stood on the threshold of manhood, his mind was developed by science and erudition. These pursuits were incompatible with the indulgence of the baser passions of nature, and Chrysanthus was virtuous without his knowing it. Almighty God looked on him with complacency, and by His divine grace brought him to the knowledge of the Christian faith. The means employed for his conversion were such as are common even in our days.

In his ardent thirst for knowledge, he read every book that came in his way. He had heard of the Christians. The wonderful things related of that persecuted sect roused his curiosity to the highest pitch. Their virtue and patience in suffering, and their extraordinary love for each other, struck the intelligent mind of the noble youth with amazement and delight. In a short time a few books of the Christians, and a copy of the sacred Scriptures, were put into his hands. He read them with avidity. Light was beaming from every page ; an unaccountable feeling of peace calmed his troubled heart. Night, noon and morning, he was wrapt in the study of that true philosophy which emanated from Eternal Wisdom itself. He wondered he had lived so long without knowing it—so sublime, so simple, so perfect, so beautiful, so terrible ; like the child's first vision of the ocean, no language could tell all he felt.

Chrysanthus became a Christian. He was led by the guidance of a supernatural power to an old hermit, named Carpophorus, and was instructed and baptized. After his baptism, his mind was filled with the light of heaven, and his heart glowed with the fire of zeal for the conversion of souls ; he longed to impart to others the joy that filled his own soul. In eight days after his baptism, we find him preaching in the public piazzas, as fearless as the Apostles when they came forth from the Cœnaculum of Jerusalem to commence the great work of the world's conversion. Numbers were converted by his powerful discourses ; but it pleased God that he should glorify His Church by his sufferings.

His father learned with rage that he had embraced Christianity. Like all pagans, he thought nothing was more mad or impious than to preach that a crucified man was the true God. He seized Chrysanthus and locked him up in a room in his own house; and endeavoured, by harsh treatment, to force him to return to the worship of the gods. He allowed no one to see him, and only gave him food once in the day; but the young man was happy, and unflinching in his resolution; he treated his cruel father with respect and reverence. Some days passed in this way, when the evil spirit, finding he was immovable in his faith, laid a wicked and dangerous snare for his virtue.

A friend of the senator Polemius came one day to see him. He found him sad and afflicted on account of the failure of his efforts to overcome his son's resolution. Polemius opened his mind to his friend, and asked his advice. A more insidious, wicked counsellor he could not have found; the devil seemed to have employed him to plot the ruin of Chrysanthus.

" If you wish to change the resolution of your son," said the stranger, " try him with pleasures rather than privations; tempt him with youth and beauty; pleasure will make him forget he is a Christian: you must know these trials which you inflict on him are considered by the Christians more honourable than painful."

Polemius thought this good advice, and determined to act upon it. He prepared his triclinium with the most beautiful hangings, loaded the tables with costly viands, and selected a number of handsome females, whom he dressed in gorgeous style; and when he had prepared everything that could please the senses or gratify

the passions, he introduced the holy youth, hoping first
to destroy his virtue, and then find an easy victim in his
faith. Chrysanthus entered the triclinium in surprise,
for he did not know what his father intended. A thous-
and lights were reflected from crystal lustres, the walls
were hung with priceless tapestry, and the odours of the
most delicious viands mingled with the perfumes of the
most beautiful flowers. Round the circular table were a
number of females reclining ; they were lewdly dressed,
and represented the goddesses of pagan mythology ; they
were fanning themselves in luxurious ease, and seemed
to be awaiting the arrival of the principal guest of the
evening, who was Chrysanthus. When he entered, they
all rose to pay him homage, the musicians played, and
incense was burned. The holy youth looked round him
in amazement ; suspicion passed in a moment to conviction ; he saw that a snare was laid for him. He had
scarcely entered the room when his father slipped from
behind him, left the room, and suddenly closed the door,
fastening it with a heavy bolt.

Chrysanthus prayed in his heart for strength, for he
knew he could not be continent unless the Lord assisted
him. His prayer was heard, and all the allurements and
temptations of the devil fell like spent arrows on the
shield of his faith. The Almighty worked a strange
miracle in his behalf. He was scarcely left alone in the
room, and had breathed a short prayer to the Most High,
when all the females fell into a sound sleep. He stood,
as it were, in the midst of a solitude, and kneeling apart
in the magnificent chamber, gave his soul to the sweet joy
of communion with God.

His father and the attendants were surprised at the

sudden silence that had come over the banquet-hall—not a whisper, not a move, all was still as death. At length, overcome with curiosity, Polemius stealthily opened the door, and looked in. He was struck with terror and amazement. The girls, musicians, and slaves, were lying on the benches or on the floor, as if dead, and Chrysanthus was kneeling, wrapt in prayer, in a corner of the room, with his arms crossed upon his breast. Was it a dream? was it magic? or was it a stratagem, organised by the cleverness of his Christian son, to trifle still further with his wishes and turn him to mockery? He was thunderstruck, and stood in fear and doubt on the threshold of the triclinium. He called all his domestics and attendants to look at the strange scene. Some wept because they thought the girls were dead; others fled in terror and called all the friends of the family; the house became a scene of confusion, whilst all was as calm as a tomb in the triclinium.

At length, after a day and a night had passed, the friends of Polemius assured him that it was all produced by magic and the black arts, which Chrysanthus had learned from the Christians; and after much deliberation, they determined to enter the room, and remove the females. When they brought them outside of the triclinium they immediately awoke; they were unconscious of what had happened, and wished to return to the banquet which they had not yet touched. They returned in spite of all remonstrance, and had scarcely entered the door when they fell down asleep again. Whilst some were amused and others were terrified, the devil was preparing another trial to shake the virtue of Chrysanthus.

Amongst the friends of Polemius there was a venerable

old man, much esteemed for his learning and prudence. Taking the senator aside, he said to him : " Polemius, I see through the dark arts of thy son ; he has been an apt disciple of Christian magic, and now he finds it easy to exercise his skill on those simple and weak girls ; but as these arts have no power over noble and educated minds, let us seek an intelligent, handsome person who can reason with him, and become his wife. I know one amongst the virgins of Minerva ; she is young, beautiful, and intelligent. The beauty of her countenance and the powers of her mind will surely triumph over Chrysanthus."

Polemius consented. He was so deeply biassed against Christianity that, if even the meanest unfortunate from the low lupanars of the city could have succeeded in withdrawing his son from the practice of virtue, he would have received her into his family, and made her heiress to the title and wealth of his senatorial rank. There were only two crimes in the category of the old senator : they were Christianity and cowardice in battle.

We will leave for a moment Polemius and his aged friend devising the best means to ruin the noble Chrysanthus and invite the reader to a different scene in another part of the city.

Amongst the peculiarities of pagan worship, it was usual for females to dedicate themselves in a particular manner to some goddess. They had gods, both male and female, to express every tendency of the mind ; every passion and every desire were personified in some divinity. Those things which are now-a-days the occupation of the leisure hours of the fair sex, such as music, poetry, needlework, &c., were in the days of the Roman Empire

works of religious homage offered to an imaginary tutelary divinity. The votaries of the different goddesses
assembled together from time to time in the vestibules
of their respective temples. These gatherings always
terminated with a splendid banquet, to which their
friends of the male sex were invited. Amongst the virgins of Minerva, as they were called, there was one of
those naturally virtuous, noble, generous souls, whom we
must now introduce to the reader as the heroine of this
interesting historical record.

Her name was Daria. She was just in the dawn of
womanhood, and surpassed all her companions in beauty
and grace. From her girlhood (she was probably at this
time sixteen) she had enrolled herself among the lovers
of Minerva, which was considered in those days an act
of great merit and virtue. Noble and generous, she was
beloved by all ; and in the dramatic representations common amongst children even in those remote times, she
was invariably elected to take the part of Pallas Minerva.

One morning Daria went with her companions to the
vestibule of the temple of Pallas Minerva. Antiquarians
pretend to be able to point out the very spot. It was
not far from the Coliseum. Perhaps the reader of these
lines may have been to Rome, and may have remembered passing in the Via Alessandria (leading from the
forum of Trajan to the Coliseum) the remains of a splendid portico of beautiful and rich carving, and the columns
nearly buried in the earth. It is called by the people in
the neighbourhood, *Le Colonnacce.* In Murray's "Guide
to Rome," they are spoken of thus :—" These columns
are more than half buried in the earth ; their height is
estimated at thirty-five feet, and their circumference at

eleven. They stand in front of a wall of poperino, on which the capital of a pilaster is still visible. The frieze is richly ornamented with sculptures representing the arts patronised by Minerva. In the attic above the two columns is a full-length statue of that goddess, and among the figures on the frieze are females weaving, others weighing the thread or measuring the webs, others again carrying the calathus ; and a sitting veiled figure of Pudicitia " (page 39).

Here it is most probable the young girls of the Minerva school were accustomed to meet, to assist each other in the study of the fine arts as represented on the beautiful frieze of the portico, the only existing remnant of the magnificent temple itself. Daria was gay and cheerful, and surrounded by a number of her companions, when the senator Polemius and his aged friend mounted the steps of the portico, and called her aside. Humble and unassuming in her thoughts, she was thunderstruck when she heard they had come to make her the spouse of Chrysanthus. She was not entitled to this position by birth or fortune, and she almost doubted the sincerity of the proposal ; but finding Polemius was really in earnest, for he entreated her with tears in his eyes, she thanked Minerva for her good fortune, and calling a faithful slave who always accompanied her, she hurried away to the house of the senator, without even telling her companions of the strange freak of fortune that was about to raise her from her humble position to be mistress in one of the first families of Rome. Bright were the castles of future bliss she painted before her happy mind, as she tripped gaily along by the side of the aged men. Little she thought of the designs of an all-seeing and loving

Providence, that was leading her from darkness to light, and was preparing for her joys and delights more beautiful and lasting than even her vivid fancy could paint.

Arrived at the palace of Polemius, they found the bustle and noise of the last few hours had subsided. Crysanthus had his copy of the Holy Scriptures brought to him in the triclinium, and was deeply engaged in study when his father returned. The girls endeavoured to dissuade Daria from going into the apartment, but she, apparently through confidence in her charms, but more truly led on by a supernatural influence, determined to discharge the commission given to her by his father, to offer herself to him as his bride. They dressed her out in the most gorgeous manner; jewels and diamonds of priceless worth sparkled on her snowy breast, and her beautiful hair was plaited with flowers and gold; the rouge of beauty and health on her cheeks required no artificial tint, for nature had given charms no art could imitate; the proud and wealthy Cleopatra, of Eastern fame, would have changed places with Daria. The senator embraced his old friend, and thanked him that he had recommended such a beautiful girl to become his daughter.

But Daria was made for heaven; a few hours will find her an angel. When she entered the triclinium, contrary to the expectation of all, she was not overcome with sleep; even Chrysanthus arose, received her kindly, and bade her be seated. He prayed for a moment in his heart, and then drawing near, he addressed her in these words: " Illustrious and beautiful virgin, if it be for the sake of a short-lived union with me, and to induce me, who am inflamed with the love of another, to abandon my resolution, that you have recourse to these costly ornaments and beautiful dresses, you are greatly deceived. Would you not rather seek the love of the Immortal Son of God ? Nor is such a task difficult if you wish it ; for if you preserve your body and soul free from stain, then the angels of God will caress you, the Apostles and martyrs will be your friends, Christ Himself will be your spouse, and He who is all-powerful will prepare for you a chamber of unsullied gems in His everlasting kingdom, He will preserve immortal the flower of your youthful beauty, and will inscribe your name for a rich dowry in the book of life."

Daria was much moved at these words. The shame of being considered a mere harlot roused the noblest feelings of her heart. The earnestness with which Chrysanthus spoke, and the sublime and mysterious promises of happiness without end, made her fling to the ground the mask of deceit and hypocrisy with which she thought to win his affections ; her answer was noble and sincere.

" Believe me, Chrysanthus !" said she, excitedly, " it was not the allurements of a base passion that brought me before you. I was urged, by the tears of your father, to bring you back to your family and the worship of our gods."

" Well, then," said Chrysanthus, " if you have any arguments by which you can induce me to change my resolution, I will patiently listen to you ; let us calmly weigh these things for our mutual advantage."

He drew nearer to her, and they commenced a very interesting and philosophical conversation, which we will give in an abbreviated form from the Acts, as in Surius (October 28)

" Nothing," said Daria, " can be more useful or neces sary to man than religion.   When we neglect this primary duty of our existence, we should fear to excite the anger of the gods."

" And what worship, most wise virgin," asked Chry-santhus, " should we give to the gods ? "

" That worship," she answered, " which will induce them to protect us."

" How can they protect us, whilst they themselves require the protection of a dog, lest they should be plundered by nocturnal thieves, and who have to be fastened to their pedestals by iron nails and lead, to prevent them falling and being broken to pieces ? "

" That is very true," replied Daria, " but if the unlettered multitude of men could worship without images, there would be no necessity for making them ; now, indeed, they are made of marble and silver and bronze, that worshippers may see with their own eyes those whom they should love, venerate, and fear."

" But let us consider a moment," said Chrysanthus, " what is said of those images, that we may see if they are worthy of our adoration.   Certainly, you would not consider that person or thing a god which does not show any external proof of glory or sanctity.   What signs of probity has the sword-bearing Saturn, who killed his own children the moment they were born, and devoured them, as his own worshippers have written of him ? What reason have you to praise Jove himself, who has committed crimes,homicides, and adulteries, equal in number to the days of his life ; plotting the ruin of his father ; the murderer of his children, the violator of matrons, the husband of his own sister, the usurper o kingdoms, and the inventor of magical arts? Since writers accuse him of these and similar impieties, not fit to be mentioned, how can you call him, and believe in your heart that he is a god? What more absurd, noble virgin, than to deify kings and generals, because they have been powerful and brave in deeds of war, whilst the very men who worship them saw them die like other mortals? What cause for divinity do you find in Mercury, whom poets and artists love to represent with the heads of pigs and monsters and outstretched wings; by whose magic arts the hidden treasures of the earth are discerned, and the poison of snakes destroyed, and yet he performs all his wonders by the power of demons, to whom he daily sacrifices a cow or a cock; are not such the fables told of him? Where is the sanctity of Hercules, who, fatigued in saving others from fire, at length by his own divine inspiration cast himself into the flames, and miserably perished with his club and his skin? In Apollo himself what virtue have you, either in his Dionysian sacrifices, or his intemperance and incontinency? It remains for us now to speak of the royal Juno, the stupid Pallas, and the lascivious Venus."

Daria started, for she had never heard her beloved Minerva called stupid before.

" Do we not find them," continued Chrysanthus, firmly, " proudly disputing amongst themselves which is the handsomest? Are not the works of poets and historians full of the wars and miseries brought on the human race on account of the slighted beauty of one of these vain goddesses? Since, then, none of these persons are worthy of divine honour, in whom will the human race, borne by the natural impulse of nature to religion, place its confidence, to worship as its god? Not surely in the minor gods, for they are but the slaves of the others. Does it not come to this, then noble virgin, if the greater and more powerful gods are so miserable and so impious, much more so will those be who worship them."

It might be thought that the power and eloquence of this address would have immediately overcome all the prejudices and vain confidence that Daria hitherto felt in paganism, but she was gifted with an intelligent and brilliant intellect, and her reply to the invectives of Chrysanthus was not only apt and beautiful, but rendered the debate extremely interesting, and henceforward deeply philosophical.

" But you are aware, Chrysanthus, that all these things are but the fictions of the poets, and not worthy of the consideration of serious minds. In the school of our philosophers, where prudent men treat of things as they really are, the gods are not clothed with the vices you mention ; their power and providence are expressed by symbolic names, which have given origin to fancies of poetry. Thus, allegorically, time has been called Saturn ; Jupiter is another term for heat and light, and the vivifying power of nature ; Juno is interpreted to mean air ; Venus, fire ; Neptune, the sea ; Ceres, the earth ; and so on with the rest. Do not these things serve us ? are they not worthy of honour ? "

" If these things be gods," said Chrysanthus, earnestly, " why then do you make images of them, and worship the representations of things you have always present ? The earth is never absent, fire is always at hand, the air surrounds us everywhere and always. How strange you should adore the images of those things, and not the things themselves! What king or ruler would order his people to despise himself, but to honour and adore his statue? Weigh for a moment the folly of this theory. Those who worship the earth, because of their veneration for its divinity, should endeavour to show in their manner respect and honour due to the goddess. Should they tear her to pieces by ploughs and spades, and trample her ignominiously under foot? There are others who deny she is a goddess at all, and lacerate her sides with ploughs and harrows, and show contempt rather than respect; yet, to which of these does she open her bosom with the abundance of her harvests and delicious fruits? To him, indeed, who blasphemes and outrages her great divinity. If she were really a goddess, would this be so? Thus the fisherman, who goes to sea to catch fish, despising its divinity, prospers better than the fool who stands on the beach to adore Neptune in the roaring billows. So with the other elements. They are directed by the divine providence of one great God, who created them for the benefit of man. They form but the parts of one great work, and are dependent on one another. The earth brings forth its harvests and its fruits; but take away the light of the sun, the moistening rains, and the refreshing dews, and it becomes barren and worthless. The sea rolls its mighty tide from shore to shore, and bears on its bosom the commerce of nations; it obeys fixed laws, and proclaims the power and glory of its Creator. He, then, who created the sun, the earth, the sea, the air, and animates all nature with the vitality of reproduction, is alone worthy of honour, reverence, and worship. The scholar does not reverence the letters or books of the preceptor, but the preceptor himself. The sick man does not praise the material drugs that cure him, but the genius and skill of the physician Thus, noble virgin, since those things which you mention as divine are inanimate and dependent, there must be another power to act on them, and animate them—that power is God!"

Daria was converted. Chrysanthus had scarcely finished his last sublime argument, when she threw herself at his feet, and begged to be instructed in the knowledge of the true God. While he was speaking, her heart was the battlefield of contending powers ; vanity and self-love had built their castles in her mind, and a deep seated prejudice seemed to have closed all the avenues of conviction ; but the Almighty, who influences, but does not force, the free-will, sent to her aid the powerful agents of reason and grace. The eloquence of Chrysanthus, far more skilled in knowledge than the young girl who ventured to reason with him, and the sweet, invisible promptings of divine grace, made her a willing captive to the gospel of love.

2.

Almighty God, having brought these two souls to the knowledge of the truth, destined them to be vessels of election to proclaim His glory, and procure the salvation of many souls. When Daria declared her willingness to become a Christian, Chrysanthus and herself entered into a holy alliance ; they adopted a pious stratagem for their mutual benefit and the salvation of others. It was agreed they should pass as man and wife before men, vowing their chastity at the same time to God. By this stratagem, Daria was allowed to go to her own house to prepare for baptism, and Chrysanthus was set free by his

father. There were great rejoicings at his supposed return ; and Polemius gave a magnificent entertainment to his friends. Chrysanthus went every day to see Daria, and as soon as she was prepared she was baptized, together with her mother, by the holy Pope Cajus. Immediately after her baptism, she received from the hands of the holy father the veil of virginity, after which, the Acts say, " She was a most holy virgin."

The fire of their zeal communicated itself to every one that came in contact with them ; through the same means by which they themselves were converted, many others were induced to give up the follies of paganism and embrace the Christian faith. Numbers of young people gave up the world and embraced chastity. Chrysanthus instructed the men, and Daria the women. The devil could not suffer this good to continue, and consequently raised a storm which brought them to the crown of martyrdom.

There were some wicked young men in the city, who had been casting evil eyes on some of the girls converted by Daria. Maddened by their loss, and instigated by the devil, they went to the prefect of the city and reported that, through the machinations of the persons named Chrysanthus and Daria, their betrothed wives were stolen away from them, and cajoled into the hated sect of Christianity. (Clamant adolescentes se deponsuras sibi mulieres amisisse, &c.) Some women also said the same of Chrysanthus, and the prefect Celerinus ordered them to be seized at once, and if they would not sacrifice to the gods, to be put to the torture. Claudius, a tribune of the soldiers, and a man in great repute on account of his magical skill, was deputed to see these orders exe cuted. It was a happy event for himself and his soldiers, as the sequel of our narrative will prove. He handed Chrysanthus to his brutal soldiers, with permission to torment him as they pleased, until he should consent to sacrifice.

It would be impossible to describe the innumerable tortures and insults offered to this noble youth, who rejoiced to imitate our blessed Lord in His sufferings as well as in His patience. They dragged him with violence to a temple of Jupiter outside the city walls, and here they tried every species of pain and indignity to induce him to sacrifice. Amongst other things they procured some thongs of skin and moistened them, then tied them as tight as they could round his arms and legs, hoping that when the wet leather should dry, it would so contract as to cut into the very bones ; but the moment they had wound them round the Saint, and skilfully knotted them, they broke and fell to the ground in pieces.

They then led him back to the city and cast him into a most vile prison, and tried to bind him again with a triple cord, which fell from him in like manner. They attributed all this to magic, and one soldier more impious than the rest, threw some filthy water over him, saying, to the great amusement of his companions: "Now your magical arts will no longer be of any use to you ;" but, instead of a disagreeable smell, there came a sweet odour as if they had sprinkled him with rose-water. He was next put naked into the skin of a calf, and left in an open square, to be worried by the dogs and scorched by the burning heat of the sun. But the servant of God suffered no inconvenience from this infliction—the dogs came near, snuffed the breeze as though some strange scent impregnated the air, and then retired quickly as if they had been beaten. Nor was his skin cracked or browned, but after a day and a night, during which they left him in this state, taking their turn in guard to watch him he was found more cheerful and more beautiful than before. They wondered exceedingly, and once more led him to prison, and hastened to tell Claudius, their tribune, all that had happened.

Claudius came in person to witness the wonders ; and, in the pride of his heart, thought he could explain to his ignorant soldiers the process of magic by which miracles were wrought. When he arrived at the prison, they found it illuminated as if a thousand lamps hung from its gloomy walls, and a most beautiful odour came forth like the breezes that pass over a garden in spring. Claudius ordered the Saint to be brought before him ; and, surrounded by his rude veterans, he haughtily addressed the servant of God in these words—

"By what power do you perform these wonders ? I have subdued all sorcerers and magicians, but I have never come across so much art as yours. As you seem to be an illustrious and wise man, all we will ask of you is, to renounce the wicked assembly of the Christians, who excite sedition and tumult in the Roman people ; sacrifice to the omnipotent gods ; and preserve yourself in the dignity of your birth and fortune."

Chrysanthus was praying in his heart for the conversion of this well-meaning but ignorant tribune. Assuming a tone of independence, and with a gentle reproof, the Saint replied—

"If you had but one spark of prudence you would

openly declare what you have partly confessed ; that it is not by magic I do these things, but by the power of the great God. You see me in the same manner as you see your own gods ; yet if you confess the truth, you will acknowledge they have not even the power of hearing or seeing that we have. You have a spirit within you that animates your body and gives you intelligence. What are these things you call gods but dust and lead ? "

Blasphemy against the gods of the Empire was severely punished by the old Roman law ; and Claudius, who heard them ridiculed by Chrysanthus, felt at the moment the truth of what he said. Nevertheless, yielding to the first impulses of his pagan heart, he ordered the Saint to be stripped and flogged. Rods as hard as iron were brought to inflict the severest punishment on him, but the moment they touched his flesh they became soft as paper. When the tribune saw this miracle he was greatly moved ; grace which had been knocking at his heart found admission, and he ordered the Saint to be unbound and clothed again. Every one was silent whilst the soldiers were dressing Chrysanthus ; they wondered what the tribune meant by treating him with such lenity, or what species of trial he was preparing to shake the constancy of the servant of God. But Claudius commanded silence and attention, and then solemnly addressed them in these words—

" You are aware, brave soldiers, that I understand all charms and magical arts ; this man, I see, does not perform these wonders through any magical art, but through the assistance of the divine power ; you have seen how the bonds with which we bound him were broken ; he has been exposed to the sun without any inconvenience, and his fetid prison was turned into a chamber of light and perfume, and now the rods of the hardest wood become soft as paper when used against him. Wherefore, since in these things there appears sincerity and truth, what remains for us but that we prostrate ourselves at his feet, asking pardon for the iniquities we have committed against him, and beg him to reconcile us to that God whose followers are victorious in every war? Just as this man conquers us, so would he overcome all the rulers and emperors in the world."

When he spoke thus, Claudius and all his brave soldiers knelt around Chrysanthus, and the noble tribune spoke for his companions in arms, and said aloud: "We know, holy youth, your God is the true God, and we beseech you to tell us something of Him, and reconcile us to Him." Chrysanthus wept for joy. His prayer was short and silent, but powerful; immediate and abundant was the response. That day he baptized the tribune with his wife and children together, and a whole cohort of soldiers. He passed some days in peace in the house of Claudius, instructing his neophytes, and preparing them for the trial their young faith would soon have to suffer.

In the meantime intelligence was brought to Numerian of what had happened. He commanded that Claudius should have a stone tied round his neck, and be cast into the sea, and all the soldiers that would not sacrifice to be beheaded. God infused so much grace into their souls, that they vehemently desired to die for His sake; the two sons of Claudius confessed themselves Christians, and suffered a glorious martyrdom; so also all the soldiers bravely exchanged a miserable life in this world for an eternal and happy existence in the blissful kingdom of God.

There happened to be, in the place where they were executed, an old monument appropriated by the Christians and used for a little church. It was on the Via Maura, and not far from the city. The Christians buried in this monument the bodies of Claudius and his soldiers. Hilaria, who was still alive, came here frequently to pray, and with many tears she besought our Lord to take her with her husband to the enjoyment of His presence. One day, when some pagans were passing, they discovered her praying, and knowing her to be a Christian, they resolved to seize her and take her before the Emperor. When they came toward her for this purpose, she begged of them to allow her to pray for one moment longer, and then she would go with them wherever they pleased. They consented, and she went into the interior of the monument, and stretching her arms towards heaven, she asked of Almighty God to save her from shame and the terrible trial she would have to suffer for the faith. God heard her prayers. When the pagans had waited a few minutes they became impatient, and going in to seize her, they found her on the ground lifeless. Her happy spirit had flown away to realms of bliss. The pagans were frightened and fled. Two of Hilaria's handmaids, who had been near, and were watching unobserved the whole proceedings, respectfully buried their good mistress in the same tomb beside her martyred husband and children.

But let us return to the heroes of this sketch. As it was known that Chrysanthus was the cause of the extra-ordinary conversion of the legion of Claudius, direr pun ishment was reserved for him. He was cast into the Mamertine prison, whilst they consulted as to what kind of death he should be put. The Acts say this was a most deep, gloomy, and horrible prison ; he was naked and bound with massive chains from head to foot. Nevertheless the light, the odour, and the joy that had heretofore brightened all the dungeons that were sancti‧ fied by his presence, did not abandon him in the Mamertine prison. Chrysanthus felt more happiness and more honour in being cast into the prison of SS. Peter and Paul than if they had declared him Emperor.

We must now retrace our steps for a moment, and watch the fate of the noble and beautiful Daria. As was ever the case in those days of infamy, the first tor‧ ment inflicted on the Christian maiden was that suggested by demons of hell—the lupanar. On the morning Daria was seized, she was brought before the Emperor himself on account of her surpassing beauty. The Acts pass over the interview, but it is evident that the noble contempt with which this pure soul despised the allurements and promises of the Emperor, brought on her his terrible in‧ dignation, and, in a fit of rage, he ordered her to be ex‧ posed in the most public lupanar in the city. This was under the arches of the Coliseum. Whilst Chrysanthus was performing wonders and baptizing hundreds of souls in one part of the city, Daria was the heroine of the most stupendous miracles under the arches of the amphitheatre. That Power which never abandons the helpless maiden unwillingly cast amongst the impious, knew how to pre‧ serve Daria. We will record the miracle of her preserva‧ tion in the precise words of the Acts.

" But to Daria aid was given by a lion which had fled

from the arena—having entered the chamber where she was exposed and praying, he placing himself in the middle. The citizens, unaware of this, sent unto the virgin a most impious and false young man.   But immediately he entered, the lion flew at him, threw him to the ground, and as he trampled on him, looked towards the virgin of Christ that she might order him what he was to do with the youth.   Perceiving what he had done, holy Daria said to the lion : ' I beseech you, by the Son of God, that you permit him to hear what I have to say.'   Then the lion, having left him free, watched at the door lest any one else would come in.

"Then Daria said to the youth : 'You see the very ferocity of the lion, having heard the name of Christ, worships God ; but you, unhappy young man, gifted with reason, are plunged into so many crimes and impieties ; you boast and glory in those very things you ought to be ashamed of.'   But the young man prostrated himself at her feet, and began to cry out : ' Let me but depart safe, and I will preach to everybody that the Christ whom you adore is the only true God.'   Daria then ordered the lion to let him pass.   And when the lion had left the door, he rushed through the streets crying out in a loud voice that Daria was a goddess.

" After this, when some daring men came from the arena to seize the lion, he, by divine power, cast every one of them to the ground, and held them at the feet of the holy virgin, not doing them any harm.   Daria then said to them : 'If you believe in Christ, you may go away in safety ; but if not, let your own gods free you.'   But they cried out with one voice : ' He that does not believe Christ to be the living and true God, let him not go out of this place alive ! ' And when they had said this, they went away crying out: ' Believe, O Romans ! there is no God but Christ, whom Daria preaches.'

" Then Celerinus, the prætor, ordered fire to be applied to the chamber where Daria was exposed. Seeing the fire, the lion was afraid, and showed signs of alarm by roaring. But Daria said to the beast : ' Be not afraid ; you will not perish by fire, nor will you be any more captured nor killed, but you will die a natural death. Cease then to fear, but go away in peace, for He whom you have honoured in me will protect you.' Having bowed his head, the lion went away, and passing through the middle of the city, no one touched him. All those who were saved from his mouth were baptized," (Surius, Oct. 28).

When all these things were announced to Numerian, he ordered Pontius, a prætor, to force Chrysanthus and Daria to sacrifice to the gods, or to put them to death by the severest torments. When the prætor had advised them, and tried in vain to make them sacrifice, he ordered Chrysanthus to be suspended in the armoury. But the instrument was instantly broken to pieces, and the torches were extinguished. Those, on the other hand, who touched Daria were struck with fear, and suffered intense pains. The prætor, seeing these things, went quickly to the Emperor to tell him ; but he, attributing them to magical arts, and not to divine interference, ordered them to be buried alive in a pit outside of the Salarian gate. His orders were obeyed, and it was the will of Almighty God that His servants should thus win their crown and come to Himself. Chrysanthus and Daria were led out of the city followed by a great crowd,

and when put into the large pit they sung a hymn together.   They were overwhelmed by the stones and earth
which the pagans cast on them, and finding their death
and their grave in the same spot, they passed away united
in spirit to the eternal nuptials of the Lamb of God.

Soon after their martyrdom, their tomb became the
scene of stupendous miracles and innumerable conversions.   The people flocked thither in fearless crowds,
so that it became publicly spoken of, and Numerian
ordered his soldiers to remove every vestige of the tomb,
so that the Christians could not assemble there in future.
The soldiers came one morning after the celebration of
the holy mysteries, and rushing on the congregation put
a great many to death.   Among those who thus fell on the
tomb of the martyrs was the priest Diodorus, the deacon
Marianus, and the clerics, and many whose names are
not known.

The Acts of these great saints conclude with these
words :—

"We, Varinus and Armenius, brothers, have written
these things as they happened, by the orders of the most
holy Pope Stephen, and we have sent (these Acts) to
every city, that all may know that the holy martyrs,
Chrysanthus and Daria, have received the crown of martyrdom in the celestial kingdom from God ; to whom be
glory and power, now and for evermore."

CHAPTER XIX.

THE PERSECUTION OF DIOCLETIAN.

THE persecution of Diocletian was by far the severest and most general of all the persecutions of the Church. A countless number of martyrs was sent to heaven, and the Church commenced, in the midst of all the cruelties and horrors of this visitation, that glorious career of triumph which diffused her influence and carried the blessings of the faith far beyond the limits of the great Roman Empire itself. The opening of the fourth century beheld the battle between herself and the powers of this world ; she triumphed, and holds to this day the power she gained. Before quoting any of the Acts of the glorious martyrs of this reign who suffered in the Coliseum, we will give our readers an outline of this terrible persecution ; how it was brought about, and the happy consequences that followed.

We will not tarry over the strange vicissitudes of fortune that placed such a man as Diocletian at the head of the Roman Empire. He was a slave, and born of a slave, and won his honour as a brave barbarian in the ranks of the army. He was named General by Probus, and on the death of Carinus was declared Cæsar by his own troops. His character was a compound of ignorance, pride, avarice, and cruelty. Superstition, which is ever the characteristic of weak minds, found its home and triumphed in his wicked, cowardly heart. He believed in the oracles, and had implicit faith in all they said. A strange coincidence gave him great reverence for these pagan delusions. A Gaulish Druidess told him, whilst he was yet a general, that he would become Emperor when he had slain a boar. He assassinated with his own hand the murderer of Numerian, and was soon after declared Emperor; this, he thought, was the fulfilment of the prophecy. It was the oracle of Apollo, as we shall see further on, that made him persecute the Christians.

Diocletian had a friend. He was an ignorant, low-born soldier, named Maximian, whom blind fortune had also favoured, and from being his companion in the army, he was raised to be part ruler in the Empire. Ignorant and cruel like Diocletian, he was a meet instrument in the hands of the powers of darkness, who were preparing for a tremendous onslaught on the Church of God. They divided the Empire between them. Diocletian preferred the luxury of the East, and left to Maximian the ill-fated West.

Strange to say, in the first years of Diocletian all was sunshine and calm in that part of the Empire which he retained for himself. Eusebius, in his eighth book, gives a glowing description of the prosperity of the Church in those regions. Whilst it is perfectly certain that Diocletian mistrusted and even hated the Christians, he seems to have refrained from molesting them though fear. Their numbers at this time were immense; public indignation against them had more or less subsided; the political disturbances of the last four years had turned the pagan mind towards passing events, whilst the ever-watchful and ever-active spirit of faith, taking advantage of the calm, walked abroad in search of souls, and publicly preached the gospel of the Lord. A few months' tranquillity was sufficient for the prostrate Church to rise from its ruins. The moment there was a lull in the storm of persecution, thousands were seen thronging round the cross, and catechumens and neophytes swelled the ranks of the Christians that were decimated during the struggle. Thus when Diocletian came to the throne, nearly half of the Empire were Christians. The Church of the East was particularly flourishing. Led on by the Basils, the Gregorys, and a host of martyred heroes, it had already struck its roots too deep in the soil to be blighted by this most terrible persecution the Church ever suffered. Even in Nicomedia, which bore the central shock of the tempest, she was only concealed when Diocletian and Galerius thought she was annihilated. So flourishing were the Christians, that even the wife and some of the children of the Emperor had embraced the faith,* and many of the officials of the imperial household openly professed Christianity.

" How so much glory and liberty were given to us before this persecution," says Eusebius, " I cannot explain. Perhaps it was the benignity of the Emperor, who even committed to us the care of provinces, removing all fear of having to sacrifice to the gods in consideration of the esteem in which he held our religion. What use is it to speak of the numbers in the imperial palaces, their wives, their children, and domestics, to

---

* This fact is now doubted through statements made in the newly discovered work, *De Morte Persecutorum.*

whom he gave liberty of openly worshipping God ?   Who could describe the innumerable crowd of men who daily flocked to the faith of Christ, the number of churches in every city, and the crowds of illustrious persons who gathered into the sacred edifices of the true God ?   The old churches were no longer sufficient, but new and larger ones were raised from their foundations.   Thus our holy faith progressed more and more every day, in spite of the malignity of demons and the plottings of wicked men, whilst the Lord deemed us worthy of the protection of His right hand." *   These last words of the great historian are ominous, for he is but writing his introduction to the most terrible of his oft-told tales of death and persecution.

Although Eusebius speaks in the strongest terms of the general peace of the Church, and the apparent partiality of the Emperor, we must not forget that Diocletian was a hypocrite, and acted in those first years of his reign with toleration towards the Christians rather through a low, cowardly policy, than through real favour and indulgence.   In certain parts even of the provinces reserved to himself, the persecution raged with more or less violence, according to the pleasure of the governors, and in virtue of the unrepealed edicts of Aurelian, still in force against the Christians.   In the province of Egea in Licia, and in the first year of his reign (285), we read of the martyrs Claudius, Asterius, Neone, and their companions.   There are monuments which show that the persecution still raged in other provinces.†   All this

* Eusebius, Hist. Eccl., lib. viii. cap. 1.

† Bollandists, August 23.   Also in Tillemont, tom. v. Persé-cution de l'Eglise sous Dioclétien, art. 2.

must have been known to Diocletian ; he permitted the persecution, where he could have so easily prevented it. However, this hypocrisy was a virtue compared to the bloodthirsty cruelty of his later years.

We must turn our eyes for a moment to Maximian. This wretch, raised so unexpectedly to the purple, set no bounds to his passions. He hated the Christians even more than Diocletian. One of his first acts was to put to death in Gaul a whole legion of Christian soldiers. They were the best and bravest soldiers in his army, and amounted to more than six thousand.* They were sent specially from the East to assist him in quelling disturbances of a formidable character. All over the West, the noblest and richest were brought to the axe to satiate the cruelty and avarice of this monster.

Nevertheless, the Church was advancing on every side, and Eusebius does not hesitate to call these days a calm. But, alas! that calm had an evil effect on the Church; the rigidity of the ancient morals became relaxed, and disorders were gradually creeping in. "The quiet liberty," says Eusebius, "granted to us by the Lord, that we might attend more tranquilly to the observance of His precepts, was abused by us. There crept among us the spirit of envy and ill feeling ; an intestine war raged ; the weapons with which we sought to injure each other were our detracting tongues ; fraud, falsehood and hypocrisy were usurping the control of the actions of men, and the scourge was already taken into the divine hands. We saw it fall somewhat heavily on those who served in the army, yet we were so callous to every

---

* See Ruinart, Acta S. Mauri et Sociorum.

warning of the gospel, that we did not endeavour by timely penance to avert from ourselves the threatened storm, which we saw gathering around us. Like blind and foolish people, who did not imagine that human events are directed and ordained by a superior Providence, for its own wise ends, we continued to tempt God by adding new and deeper crimes to our former guilt. At length, Almighty God, according to the prediction of Jeremias, covered the daughter of Sion with confusion, and cast to the ground the celestial glory of Israel, and in the day of His anger the Lord did not remember the footstool of His feet." *

The powers of darkness seemed to have measured every step, and to have advanced cautiously before coming down with all their fury on the sleeping camp of Israel. Another monster in human shape is sent on earth to have power; he surpasses either of the reigning Cæsars in villany, cruelty, and sin of every kind. This man was Galerius.

Diocletian, in whom timidity and fear had become imbecility, conceived the idea of dividing the Empire into two more parts. The constant disturbances of the barbarians who threatened on every side, and even some internal revolts, induced this short-sighted Emperor to adopt this suicidal policy. His idea was to nominate two additional Cæsars, who would have full power to defend and rule their relative districts, without bearing the name of Emperor. For this purpose he nominated Constantius Chlorus, a man of noble birth and deserving qualities, and Galerius, the son of a peasant, a soldier of fortune, but a tyrant and a bitter enemy of Christianity.

* In the first chap. of eighth book, as quoted above.

For some years Galerius was occupied in quelling the disturbances on the frontiers of the Empire. Through the prayers of the Christian soldiers in his army, he gained a complete triumph over the Persians. His pride, of course, was keeping pace with his fortune, and he returned so puffed up with his greatness, that he despised his benefactor, and determined to be Emperor himself. His mother was still alive. She, too, was cruel and super-stitious; the only education she gave her son was hatred of the Christians. On the return of Galerius from the East, she had scarcely embraced him when she com-menced to revile the Christians, and commanded her son to persecute them.

Galerius ruled in the province of Illyrium, and here he first drew his sword against the Church. He com-menced with his own household, and then with the army.[*] The slaves of his impious mother were burnt at the kitchen fires, whilst she herself looked on like a fury, in brutal glee. In the army, the first officers in power were ordered to put the Christians to death, but finding they were too numerous, and that two-thirds of their number would be destroyed, the order was modified, and only a few of the most remarkable were executed; at the same time all the others were debarred from any promotion or emolument arising from the service. When we say a few only were martyred, they were few compared to the great number who survived; nevertheless they may be counted by thousands. In the Acts of St. Andrew, who was

[*] " (Galerius Maximianus) diu ante reliquos imperatores, Christi-anos qui in exercitu militabant ac præsertim eos qui in palatio suo versabantur, per vim abducere a religione sua conatus est, &c.— *Euseb.*, cap. xviii.

tribune of a legion in the army of Galerius, we read that he was martyred about the year 300, together with three thousand companions.* But prudence restrained the sword of Galerius, and forbade the blow he intended to strike—the hour destined by Providence had not yet arrived, but was coming fast.

For four years he had desired the total extermination of the Christians. He knew by experience that they went like lambs to the slaughter; that they neither murmured nor revolted against the unjust sentence. With fiendish malice he conceived the idea of procuring a simultaneous and universal persecution throughout the entire Empire, to sweep for ever from the face of the earth the hated name of Christian. To effect this, he saw that an edict from Diocletian was necessary. He set out for Nicomedia, where Diocletian was residing, and did not leave till he had effected his purpose.

This was in the year 302. Nevertheless, Diocletian trembled at the thought of a wholesale slaughter of the Christians. His natural timidity tortured his mind with pictures of revolts, and insurrections, and civil war which might hurl him from his throne. Notwithstanding the supernatural warnings of his dreaded oracles, the ceaseless entreaties of Galerius and his impious mother, Diocletian feared to take the terrible step, and delayed, while he could, to sign the fatal edict. Galerius, seeing entreaty failed, assumed the haughty tone of defiance, and Diocletian at length consented, if the oracle of Apollo should recommend it. A seer was sent to the oracle, and a bribe from Galerius brought back the answer that the Christians were hostile to the gods. The die was

* *Bollandists,* 19th August.

cast. The month, the day, and the hour were named, when the three demons should be unchained, and the Church of God cast into desolation and woe. The Terminal Games, which were celebrated every year with great pomp, were at hand, and the first day of these games, the 23d of February 303, was selected for the commencement of the persecution. Messengers were despatched to the governors of the provinces to be in readiness, to prepare the rack, the furnace, and the sword for the servants of Christ. Many of them rejoiced at the prospect of this feast of blood. The extermination of a hated sect was ever welcome, but the hope of boundless wealth from the murdered Christians pouring into their coffers, and increased favour with the august Cæsar, produced in their corrupted hearts a zeal and a co-operation in the terrible cause that rendered this persecution not only the most general, but by far the most destructive, that ever passed over the Church.

The Christians knew the hour of trial was coming. Persecutions were not inaptly compared to the storms on the deep, and the Church was the little bark of Peter that was to brave the raging elements. There were signs in the heavens that told of the approaching struggle ; their future was dark and gloomy, like the horizon when the storm is coming up. The voices of the pastors rang through the churches like the shrill whoop of the seagull breasting the rising surges, and giving its well-known storm-cry. The women and children were sent to the cabins of the Catacombs for safety, whilst every loose spar was lashed to the bulwarks, and every sail was reefed. The bishops had gathered their trembling flocks together, and addressed them with a fervour and elo quence which made them martyrs in desire before the axe of the executioner brought them their crown. Whilst brave youths, with hearts of oak, like Sebastian and Pan·cratius, remained in the cities to bear the brunt of the fight, and to encourage their weaker brethren, tender maidens of noble blood, like Agnes and Prisca, buried themselves in the solitude of country villas, and prayed with fluttering hearts, like frightened doves sighing in their cots. The anticipation of evil is often more painful than the stroke itself. Before the terrible edict was promulgated many churches were abandoned, and the altar and sacrifice were removed to the private room of some obscure Christian, or to the archisoliums of the Catacombs. The timid Marcellinus was the pilot of the Church during the commencement of the storm—even he lost courage in the fury of the tempest ; he abandoned the helm for a moment, but claimed it again like Peter, and sank at his post. The pious matron Lucina had given her garden and villa outside the Porta Capena for a new cemetery, and as far as the time permitted, the Church in Rome was girded for the struggle.

At length the bloody edict is ready. A copy is sent from Nicomedia to Rome and Illyrium. Galerius, the prime mover of the persecution, so longed for the dawn of the dreadful day, that he determined to keep its vigil. The Christians had built a beautiful church on a hill that looked down on the city of Nicomedia. It could be seen from the windows of the palace where the Emperor lived. Scarcely had the morning of the 23d of February dawned when a troop of soldiers was sent to destroy the church. They seized everything that was inside—books, furniture and some vestments—and burned them in the piazza ;

then with yells and shouts, they levelled the building to the ground. The Emperor and Cæsar were enjoying the scene from a window in the palace, and rewarded the soldiers on their return for their noble and brave conduct. The next morning the parchment scroll that announced a crown of eternal glory for thousands of the chosen children of God was hung on the marble columns of the Forum of Nicomedia.

The edict should have been published at the same time throughout the Empire, but through some secret jealousy of the Senate, it was deferred in Rome until the 15th of the Kalends of May. The haughty Senate still clung to the rights of its original institution, and flattered itself that its nominal power was a reality. Nevertheless, like a dismantled and abandoned fortress, it cast its proud shadow on the plain as in the days of its glory, and impeded for a while the fall of the uplifted sword. But the demon was not to be robbed of his prey. The Roman mob were accustomed to obey his suggestions, and were willing agents for every insult offered to the true God. It was in one of the paroxysms of brutal excitement that the terrific shout which had so often echoed through the benches of the Coliseum was made to resound through the Circus Maximus. Infuriated myriads of the dregs of the people rose as if with a simultaneous impulse, and shouted : " Christiani tollantur ! " " Away with the Christians," was twelve times repeated by a chorus of a hundred thousand blood-thirsty voices. This was followed by cries, ten times repeated, of " Death and extermination to the Christians ! " Wherefore, it was agreed by the Senate that a persecution should be declared against the Christians, and it was decreed accordingly. (See Acts of St. Sabinus in Baronius, under the year 301.)

In Nicomedia, a wealthy Christian gentleman was passing through the Forum on the morning the edict was published. In the excess of his zeal he imprudently tore it to pieces, and scattered it to the wind. He was seized, and was roasted to death at a slow fire before the palace of Diocletian.* Galerius raged with more fury than ever; revenge and desperation gave a deeper dye to his natural cruelty. The first edict was too lenient for his purpose, and he will have another, written in characters of blood. The author of the "Death of the Persecutors of the Church" tells us how he procured the second edict.

"By the assistance of some confidents, he set fire to the royal palace. As soon as the conflagration was discovered, the agents of the impious Emperor commenced to cry out aloud that the Christians were the cause of the fire, and were the enemies of the sovereign; so that the flames of infernal hatred against the Christians burned more furiously in the hearts of the Gentiles than the material flames that were devastating the imperial dwelling." (De Morte Persecutorum, cap. xiii., also in Baronius, A.D. 201.)

Another and another edict followed the first they were more sweeping and more terrible than any law ever before published. They were directed in a particular manner against ecclesiastics, churches, sacred writings, and virgins. Horrible to relate, one of the enactments of these edicts was, that every young girl that would not sacrifice was to become public property.† But the light-

---

* In the Martyrologies of Ado and Usuardus this man is called John, and is commemorated on the 7th of September.

† See Acts of St. Theodora, April; also Tillemont, vol. **v. art. 19**; also Baronius, Anno 301, No. 31 and following.

nings of God were ever ready to defend His helpless
spouses; and wherever they attempted to put this im
pious law into execution, death and judgment were the
immediate issue. The machinations of the wicked Galerius
did not cease here. Seeing the success of his first stratagem, fifteen days had scarcely passed, when he set fire
again to the imperial palace, and throwing the blame on
the Christians, made Diocletian believe they were incen-
diaries who wished to burn him alive in his own palace.
Galerius fled in trepidation, as he said he was not safe
whilst there was a Christian in the palace. All these
plans had the desired effect on the weak-minded Diocletian, and from being a mere instrument in the hands of
his colleague, he became the most terrible enemy of the
Church, and surpassed, if such were possible, the cruelties of the other two.

"His fury against the Christians," says Lactantius,
"had now reached the highest; he no longer persecuted
a few, but every one and everywhere. He first obliged
Valeria, his daughter, and Prisca, his wife, to contami-
nate themselves with the Gentile sacrifices. He put to
death his favourite eunuchs, who had the direction of the
whole court and the immediate service of his own person;
priests and other ministers were seized and slaughtered
without any trial, and men and women of every age were
subjected to the most cruel torture. The number of the
accused being great, they were put to death in crowds.
Immense fires were kindled around them, and thus consumed them together. The Emperor's domestics were flung
into the sea with stones round their necks. In all the
temples of the gods, there were placed judges, whose sole
business was to make the people sacrifice; the public

prisons were full, and every new and unheard-of torture was tried to pervert the Christians or tear them to pieces." (As above, chap. xiv.)

The war of extermination is now fully declared, and the battle is raging over the whole Empire. The province of Gaul was the only spot that escaped its fury. It was at this time under Constantius Chlorus, the father of Constantine the Great. He was just, and unprejudiced against the Christians, and where he could, he prevented wholesale murder and slaughter. Some of the governors under him confiscated the goods of the Christians and occasionally put them to death; yet Gaul was spared the terrible horrors of the other portions of the Empire. The descriptions of this hour of trial left us by Lactantius, Eusebius, and the immortal Basil,* would fill volumes —volumes that would be sacred in the eyes of the Church, for in showing the virulence and universality of the persecution, they declare the glory and greater triumph of that divine institution which has survived it, and stands on the rock of ages as indestructible to-day as when the impious Galerius sought to annihilate it.

Everything that human and demoniacal malice could suggest was tried for the extermination of the Christians. " It was, moreover, proclaimed," writes a holy martyr quoted by Eusebius in his eighth book, " that no one should have any care or pity for us, but that all persons should so think of and behave themselves towards us as if we were no longer men." The eloquent Basil, in one of his sublime panegyrics on the Christian martyrs, says :

---

* Eusebius and Lactantius were eye-witnesses ; Basil saw the effects of the persecution, for he flourished in the first half of the fourth century.

'The houses of the Christians were wrecked, and laid in ruins ; their goods became the prey of rapine, their bodies of ferocious lictors, who tore them like wild beasts, dragging their matrons by their hair along the streets— callous alike to the claims of pity for the aged, or those still in tender years. The innocent were submitted to torments usually reserved only for the vilest criminals. The dungeons were crowded with the inmates of Christian homes that now lay desolate ; and the trackless deserts and the forest caves were filled with fugitives whose only crime was the worship of Jesus Christ. In these dark times the son betrayed his father, the sire impeached his own offspring, the servant sought his master's property by denouncing him, the brother sought a brother's blood—for none of the claims or ties of humanity seemed any longer to be recognised, so completely had all been blinded as if by a demoniac possession. Moreover, the house of prayer was profaned by impious hands ; the most holy altars were overturned ; nor was there any offering of the clean oblation, nor of incense ; no place was left for the divine mysteries ; all was profound tribulation, a thick darkness that shut out all comfort ; the sacerdotal colleges were dispersed ; no synod or council could meet for terror of the slaughter that raged on every side ; but the demons celebrated their orgies and polluted all things by the smoke and gore of their victims." (Orat. in Gordium Mart.)

Lactantius says : " The whole earth was afflicted and oppressed ; and three wild beasts of the most brutal character roared from east to west in their rage to devour the Christians. If I had a hundred tongues and a hundred mouths, if my voice were of iron, I could not relate the he rose of the Gentile cruelty, nor the names and quality of torments they used against the Christians " (De Morte Pers., cap. xvi.)

To find out the Christians, they had recourse to some malicious but ridiculous stratagems. Besides the court spies, whose name was legion, it was enacted that idols should be erected in all provision shops, so that not even the necessaries of life could be purchased without sacrificing to the demons. Every piazza, every fountain, every bakehouse, and every butcher's stall, had its little statue of some fabulous god, a pan of fire and a box of incense. Those who wished to buy must first burn some incense to the idol, and an officer of the government stood by to insist on the absurd homage intended for the demons. To such excess did they carry the rage for sacrifice, that old men who had not left their homes for years were dragged to the public squares to burn incense, and tender infants in their mothers' arms were made to join in this blasphemous mockery of the true God.*

If we were to recount the terrible sufferings of the Christians under the new and unheard-of tortures (as Lactantius calls them) invented by the persecutors, we should fill pages of horrible scenes that would send a cold thrill through every vein of our bodies. They would surpass everything the cruellest fancy ever imagined. Fire, water, iron, and the brutal strength of incarnate demons lent all their combinations to produce pain, to burn, to tear and destroy ; the highest science was to kill by the slowest tortures. The shame of being stript before brutal mobs was more painful to Christian youths of both sexes than the scourge of the rack. There was

* St. Optatus Milivitus, lib. i. and iii.

as little pity or mercy for the tender girl of eight years as for the old man of eighty.

To increase the horrors of these days the mangled bodies of their victims were deprived of burial, and often left for days in the public squares, or thrown into the fields outside the cities, to be devoured by dogs or birds of prey. Orders were issued to have these bodies guarded day and night, lest the Christians should take them away and honour them. " You might have seen," says Eusebius, " no small number of men executing this savage and barbarous command ; some of whom, as if this had been a matter of high concern and moment, watched on a tower, that the dead might not be stolen away. Also the wild beasts, dogs, and birds that prey on flesh, scattered here and there pieces of human bodies ; and the whole city was strewed round about with men's bowels and bones, so that nothing seemed more cruel and horrid, even to those who before had been our enemies. All persons bewailed, not so much the calamitous condition of those on whom those cruelties were practised, as the opprobium cast on themselves and mankind in general." No wonder such barbarities should wring tears from the hardest marble, for Eusebius continues to record in the same chapter one of the most extraordinary miracles related in his history of the early Church :—

" After these horrible barbarities had been practised for many days together, the following miracle took place. The weather was fair, the atmosphere was clear, and the whole face of heaven most serene and bright ; when on a sudden, from all the columns that supported the public galleries throughout the city, there fell many drops in the form of tears, and the Forum and streets (no moisture having been distilled from the air) were wet and bedewed with water from some unknown source; insomuch that a report was immediately spread amongst all the inhabitants, that the earth, unable to bear the horrid impieties then committed, did, in this inexplicable manner, shed tears, and that the stones and senseless matter wept at what was done, in order to reprove the savage and brutal propensities of man. I make no doubt," continues Eusebius, " but that this will be looked on as a fabulous and ridiculous story by future generations; but they did not account it such who had the certainty thereof confirmed to them by the authority of the times in which it happened."*

This was a strange phenomenon; but no matter how it may be accounted for, the very interpretation put on it by the pagans themselves must ever remain to attest the moral triumph achieved by the Christians over the minds and sympathies of their persecutors.

It would be impossible to make even an approximate calculation of the numbers that were massacred during this persecution. For ten long years the storm blew over the Empire, and whilst the blood of thousands flowed in a continuous stream from the public scaffolds, a much greater number perished in the deserts, or in the unhealthy caves of the earth. From an ancient catalogue published by Papebrochius, it appears that in one place, during the lapse of thirty days, fifteen thousand were put to death. Eusebius calls them " an innumerable company throughout every province." In Thebais alone, he himself beheld, during a succession of years, ten, twenty, thirty, and even sixty in a day put to death. " At

* De Mart. Palest., cap. ix.

another time, a hundred men, with very little children and women, were killed in one day, being condemned to various sorts of punishments; in so much that the executioner's sword became blunt, and being unfit for use, was broken, and the executioners themselves being tired, succeeded one another by turns. At which time also," he continues, " we beheld a most admirable ardour of mind, and a truly divine strength and alacrity, in those who believed in Christ, for no sooner was sentence pronounced against the first, than others ran hastily from some other direction to make loud profession of their faith before the judge's tribunal." (Book viii., chap. ix.)

He also relates of a city in Phrygia of which the governor, the magistrates, and all the citizens were Christians, how they all declared with evangelical firmness their determination to die rather than sacrifice. Fire was set to the entire city, and soldiers were drawn around as in a siege, that no one should escape. Thus the whole population, men, women, and children, were destroyed, and went together to eternal crowns of glory. Baronius also makes mention (A.D. 301, No. 47) of a whole congregation who were burnt in their church on a Christmas morning.

Perhaps nothing will give us a better idea of the widespread virulence of the persecution than the impression made on the minds of the Emperors that they had completely destroyed Christianity. So utterly impossible did it appear to them that the Christian Church could any longer subsist that, in the security and unhesitating anticipation of the event, pompous inscriptions were set up in various places to commemorate, amongst other exploits of the Emperors, that they had destroyed the super-

stition of Christ.   The following are two specimens of
the lying inscriptions:—

> "DIOCLETIANUS IOVIUS ET MAXIMIANUS
> HERCULEUS CÆS. AUG.
> AMPLIFICATO PER. ORIENTEM ET
> OCCIDENTEM IMP. ROM.
> ET
> NOMINE CHRISTIANORUM
> DELETO, QUI REMP. EVER-
> TEBANT." *

Again :—

> "DIOCLETIANUS CÆS.
> AUG. GALERIO IN ORIENTE ADOPT.
> SUPERSTITIONE CHRIST.
> UBIQUE DELETA ET CULTU
> DEORUM PROPAGATO." †

We smile when we look at these inscriptions, and then
at the Catholic Church as she is at present, with her two
hundred millions of subjects.   The whole population of
the Roman Empire did not number as many as she can
count in her pale to day.   A few months after these slabs
were attached to the walls of the palace, a Christian sat
on the very throne of the Emperor himself.   Whilst the
sculptor was carving the inscription on what he considered
the tombstone of the annihilated sect, Constantine was
marshalling his troops beyond the Alps, and had perhaps
already read the terrible sign in the heavens that told
him he was destined by the Great Eternal to liberate His
Church and destroy for ever the power of the pagan ; yea,
when those marble slabs were brought from the workshop

---

* " Diocletian Jupiter and Maximianus Hercules, Cæsars, having
extended the Roman Empire through the East and West, and destroyed the name of the Christians, who were ruining the state."

† "Diocletian, Cæsar Augustus, and Galerius adopted in the East,
having everywhere swept away the superstition of Christ, and pro-
pagated the worshp of the gods."

and reflected for the first time the sun of heaven from their polished surfaces, the reigning successor of St Peter was making new divisions of his parishes in Rome, increasing them to the number of twenty-five, in order to meet the religious exigencies of his people, who were multiplying under the sword ! *

How strange to reflect that monuments were once erected to commemorate the downfall of Christianity ! It was at that very time on the eve of its triumph, whilst the dynasty that endeavoured to crush it was in the throes of dissolution. Those very monuments are preserved as curiosities in the museum of the Christian successor of the Cæsars : their reign of terror passed away to give place to the milder sway of the power they thought no more, and now their golden houses, their triumphal arches, and colossal amphitheatres, are but ruins beside the churches that cover the relics of the martyrs whom they slew. Little did Diocletian or Galerius think, when they read with complacency the monuments that commemorated their wonderful doings, that the time would come, when a Christian traveller, from an unknown island in the Southern Ocean (New Zealand), would read the same slabs in the morning in the Vatican Museum, and in the evening sit on a broken arch of the Coliseum to sketch the ruins of the golden palace !

Yet these interesting inscriptions tell a terrible tale of the fierceness of the persecution. Every vestige of the Church was swept from the face of the earth. It was

---

* " Hic (Marcellus Papa) fecit cæmeterium Via Salaria et vigenti quinque titulos in urbe constituit quasi dioceses propter baptismum et pœnitentium multorum qui convertebantur ex paganis et sepulturas martyrum."—*Ex Lib. Pont. in Vit. Morul.* ; and Baronius, Anno 309, No. 4.

pulled down indeed from the high places, and banished from the circles of the rich, but it flourished in the cabins of the poor, who were too despicable to be molested by the haughty pagan. It lived in the Catacombs, whose dark gloomy passages terrified the most zealous of the persecutors ; and whilst the Emperors and their agents saw no longer any traces of the Church on earth, the Christians were gathered in thousands deep in the bowels of the earth, and celebrated the sacred mysteries in basilicas ornamented with all the beauties of art, and chanted the praises of God before marble altars decorated with gold and blazing with light. It could not be otherwise. Almighty God did not intend that his Church should be destroyed. He permitted the visitation in His own all-wise providence ; but had He not kept His hand stretched over it, they would have watched in vain who were set to guard the city. " Nisi Dominus custodieret civitatem, frustra vigilat qui custodit eam." (Ps. cxxvi.)

But Christianity had triumphed and achieved its own emancipation even before the cross was assumed as the signal of victory by Constantine. Proof sufficient had already been afforded that the Church stood in need of no earthly patronage, and could stand without the smiles, or even the toleration, of the world's rulers. Its most powerful and deadly enemies were made in the end to bite the dust in deep humiliation, and proclaim to the world by public edicts that they failed to destroy the Church. The edicts of emancipation, issued by the impious Galerius on his death-bed, seemed to be destined by Almighty God as a solemn finale to all the edicts and efforts of three centuries to crush and annihilate His Church. They were proclamations to the whole world and to all generations that, in despite of the Empire, with all its terrors and its might, it could not only subsist, but flourish and triumph ; that, in a word, its history, its perennity and supernatural mission were epitomised by its great Founder Himself when He said : " THE GATES OF HELL SHALL NOT PREVAIL AGAINST IT."

We will translate a paragraph of the last edict issued by the tyrant Galerius, as an interesting and touching contrast with the inscriptions that declared that Christianity was a thing of the past.

" Whereby all men may know, that they who desire to follow this sect and religion are allowed by this, our gracious indulgence, to apply themselves to that religion which they have usually followed, in such a manner as is acceptable and pleasing to every one of them. Moreover we do permit them to rebuild their chapels.

" That if any houses or estates which formerly belonged to and were in possession of the Christians, and are by the edicts of our parents (Diocletian and Maximian) devolved to the right of the exchequer, or are seized upon by any city, or sold, or have been granted and bestowed upon any one as a token of imperial favour, we have decreed that they be restored to the ancient tenure and possession of the Christians." (Eusebius, book viii., chap. xvi.)

We could not conclude our brief review of this terrible persecution of the Church with a more fitting paragraph than that which declared the triumph of our faith ; but, as the last scene of a tragedy is the most appalling, we have, in the terrible judgments of God on the persecutors, a fit ending to our tale of horrors, and we claim the indulgence of the reader for another moment, whilst we give one from the many proofs of the veracity of the in spired words : " No one has raised his hand against God and prospered."

From the moment that Diocletian had published his first edict, his soul became like the hell the demons ever carry about with them.   Excessive fear and desperation made him insupportable to himself, and to every one who had the misfortune to be near him.   He came to Rome and was hooted by the people, and quitted it by a precipitous flight in the middle of winter, within a few days of the great games which were to be inaugurated in honour of the ninth year of his consulship.   On his journey to Ravenna he contracted a lingering disease, that gave him excruciating pain.   His mind was so completely weakened that he became an imbecile, and at times a perfect lunatic. But the climax of his sorrows was his humiliation.   He was forced by the tyrant Galerius to resign in disgrace the title of Emperor.   He was brought to a large field, about three miles outside the city of Nicomedia, and placed on a magnificent throne, clothed with the purple, and then, before the entire army, and before all the people of the city, he was obliged to divest himself of all the insignia of power, and transfer them to the tyrant, who sat on another throne near him.   The old Emperor cried like a child ; at times gnashing his teeth with impotent rage, and hurling blasphemies against the gods he once served so faithfully.   He was hooted from the field that was the scene of his degradation, and fled, almost alone, to Salona, in Dalmatia, the scene of his ignoble birth, and died there in obscurity, raving mad.[*]

" The other who was next to him in honour," says Eusebius, speaking of Maximian, " put an end to his own life by hanging himself, agreeably to a certain diabolical

---

[*] See " De Morte Persecutorum," cap. xvii.

prediction which promised him that fate on account of his many and most audacious villanies."

But as Galerius was the chief instigator of the persecution, upon him the judgment fell the heaviest. Lactantius* has left a description of the horrors by which he was eaten alive, so hideous as not to bear translation. Suffice it to say, he died the death of Herod, the first persecutor of Jesus Christ. "These diseases," says Eusebius, " did spread incurably, and eat their way into his inmost bowels, from which were generated an unspeakable multitude of worms, and a most noisome stench proceeded therefrom ; for before his disease, the whole mass of flesh upon his body (by reason of the abundance of the food he devoured) was grown to immense fatness, which, being then putrified, became an intolerable and most horrid spectacle to those that approached him. Wherefore, some of the physicians, being unable to endure the exceeding noisomeness of the smell that came from him, were killed. Others of them, when they could administer no remedy (the whole fabric of his body being swelled, and past all hopes of a recovery), by his orders were cruelly slain." (Book viii.) Lactantius says the stench of his rotten carcass was so terrible as to affect, not only the palace, but the whole city. He was kept in this state for a whole year, until a horrible death rid the world of one of the greatest monsters it had ever seen. It was in the midst of those tortures that he issued the edict in favour of the Christians, imploring that, in return for this boon, they would supplicate their God for his recovery. He died on the 15th of May, A.D. 311, just two weeks after he signed the recantation of his blasphemous warfare against the true God.

* As above, chap. xxxii.

CHAPTER XX.

ACTS OF ST. VITUS AND COMPANIONS.

1.

AT the time that Valerian was president, under Diocletian and Maximian, Emperors, the persecution raged against the Christians in the province of Sicily. There was there, at that time, a holy boy named Vitus, who performed many miracles, and day and night implored the mercy of God, who was pleased to give him this reply—

"I will give you, O Vitus, the mercy you seek."

His father, named Hylas, was an illustrious but impious man. When he tried in vain to induce his son to sacrifice to the gods, he ordered him to be beaten with whips, and summoning his tutor Modestus, gave him the following command—

"See that this boy no longer speaks the words we have heard."

An angel of the Lord appeared to the little boy, and comforting him, said—

"I have been given to you as a guardian; I will protect you up to the day of your death, and whatsoever you shall ask of the Lord will be given to you."

But it came to the ears of Valerian the governor, that the blessed Vitus, the son of the most noble Hylas, worshipped and adored the Lord God Jesus Christ. Then the president called the father of this saintly boy, and said to him : " What is it I hear of thy son ? He worships the God of the Christians ? If you wish him to be safe you must endeavour to make him remove this folly."

2. Having heard this from the president, Hylas then called his son, and said : " Most sweet son, listen to the advice of your father, and give up the folly of your worship. How you have been brought to adore a dead man, I cannot tell. If the Prince come to hear it, he will turn on you with all the fury of his power; he will be your ruin and my grief."

The blessed Vitus replied : " Father, didst thou but know this God whom thou callest a dead man, thou too wouldst adore him. He is the Lamb of God, who takes away the sins of the world."

" But, Vitus," said the father, " I know that Christ, whom you call God, was flogged by the Jews, and crucified by Pilate."

" He was ; but this is a great and wonderful mystery,' replied the youth.

3. Hylas was a pagan and could not understand all the child said, yet, with the natural affection of a parent, he feared more the consequences involved in the profession of Christianity, than the slight offered to the gods of the Empire. Whilst he was reflecting how he would induce his son to give up his faith, Almighty God was working wonders through Vitus. The sick through his prayers were cured, the blind received their sight, and the devils whom he cast out were forced to publicly declare the

merits of the saintly youth.   The governor Valerian
heard of what was passing, and ordered Vitus to be
brought before him.   When he came, Valerian said :
"Why do you not sacrifice to the immortal gods ?   Do
you not know that our princes have ordered that any one
found worshipping the man called Christ should be put
to death ?"

But Vitus, filled with the Holy Ghost, and showing no
signs of fear—a thing unusual in that tender age—made
the sign of the cross, and said : "I shall never consent to
worship demons, or stones, or pieces of wood ; I will only
serve the living God, who will always protect me."

Then his father commenced to weep, and cried out in
the court : "Oh ! come and weep with me, for my only
son is going to perish."

But Vitus addressed him, saying : "I shall not, if I can
enter into eternal life."

Valerian then said : "As thou art of noble birth, and
I have heretofore enjoyed the friendship of thy father,
I shall not execute the whole sentence against thee as a
sacrilegious wretch ; but as thou art an obstinate boy, I
must have thee corrected ; lictors, give him a few strokes
with your rods."

4. After they had beaten him some time, the president
said : "Do you consent now ?"

The boy replied : "I told you before, I will only worship Jesus Christ, the true God."

Then the president ordered the lictors to take out the
heavier rods, and beat him severely, but the moment they
approached him the second time, their arms were withered
(Et brachia eorum arefacta sunt).   Valerian's arm suffered in like manner, and he cried out with a loud voice :

Alas ! I have lost my arm, and feel great pain. Hylas, it is not a son you have, but a devil of a magician."

" I am not a magician," said Vitus, " but the servant of the Lord, through whom I can do all things."

" Then cure me," said Valerian, " and I will not call thee a magician."

The Blessed Vitus, raising his eyes towards heaven, said : " O Lord Jesus Christ, Son of the omnipotent and true God, for the sake of those who stand around, I beseech Thee to cure the president's arm, in order that they may believe in Thee." And immediately his arm was cured.*

5. Then Valerian handed the boy to his father, and told him to take him home, and do his best to make him sacrifice. Hylas did so, and endeavoured to change his son by kindness and blandishments : he clothed him in most beautiful garments, and by continual feasting and lewd dances tried to lead him astray, but the holy youth closed his eyes and ears against all seduction, and prayed to God for strength.

6. Then it came to pass that his father led him into a beautiful room, which was instantly filled with a heavenly light, and there appeared a number of angels singing round the holy youth. All the family and domestics gathered near the door. The light was so strong that no one could look at it, and Hylas was struck blind.† When the music had ceased, and the brilliant light disappeared, they found he had lost his sight; he groaned in great pain, and all the maids and attendants were in tears.

* Et statim manum ejus sanum reddidit.—*Acts.*

† Pater ipse splendore reverberante in oculos ejus cæcatus est.— *Acts.*

They laid him on a couch, and surrounded him, weeping and mourning. Valerian, who was his friend, was sent for, and when he came, he inquired what was the matter, and they told him that Hylas had been struck blind. The governor made them bring him to the altar of Jupiter, and there Hylas promised to sacrifice innumerable victims of fatted oxen with gilt horns, if he should be restored to his sight. He promised, too, to dedicate virgins to the goddess Vesta, but his eyes remained closed, and he suffered intense pain.

7. They then led him to his son, and begged on bended knees that he would cure him. Vitus asked him if he would give up the worship of demons, and believe in the true God. Hylas answered in the affirmative, but the holy youth, seeing his thoughts, said : " I understand your reply ; your heart is hardened ; but for the sake of those present, although you are not worthy of it, I will cure you." The blessed Vitus prayed, the scales fell from his father's eyes, and he saw.

Then the father said in a rage: " I thank my gods for having cured me, and not your God." From that moment he thought to kill his son.

8. The angel of the Lord appeared to Modestus, the tutor of the blessed Vitus, a religious and holy man, and told him to take the boy to the sea-shore ; he would find a ship waiting, and proceed instantly where he would point out.

But he said : " I know not the way. Whither shall I go ?"

The angel replied : " I will show you."

The blessed Vitus was then about seven years of age (**Erat** autem B. Vitus circiter annorum septem).

The angel led them to the sea-shore, where the Lord had prepared a small ship, and assuming the appearance of a pilot, the angel said : " Where are you hurrying to, good people ? "

Vitus answered : " Wherever the Lord takes us, we will follow promptly and cheerfully."

Then the angel said : " Where is your passage money ? "

To which Vitus replied : " He whom we serve will pay you."

They got into the ship, and the angel took the helm, and they came to a place called Electorius, and as soon as they landed the angel disappeared. But they went into the country and reached the river Siler, and rested under a tree. The Lord performed many miracles through the blessed Vitus. Food was given them by a celestial eagle. And a multitude of people gathered round him on account of the fame of his miracles. The devils cried out through many : " What hast thou to do with us ? thou hast come before the time to destroy us." Vitus spent his time in teaching the people, and baptized a great number. His constant prayer was : " I have believed, therefore have I spoken ; but I have been humbled exceedingly." (Ps. cxv.) And : " As the hart panteth after the fountains of waters, so my soul panteth after Thee, O God." (Ps. xlii.)

9. In the meantime, the son of Diocletian* the Emperor was tormented by an impure spirit, and the devil cried out by his mouth, saying : " Unless Vitus the Lucanian come here, I will not leave thee."

The Emperor said : " And where can I find this man ? "

* An adopted son—or favourite of the Palace—Diocletian had no natural offspring.

The demon replied : " He is in the Tanagritan territory, near the river Siler."

Then Diocletian sent armed soldiers, that they might quickly bring the youth designated by the demon.

When they arrived at the place, they found the champion of Christ praying to the Lord ; and the leader of the soldiers said : " Are you Vitus ? "

He answered : " I am."

Then he said : " The Emperor needs you."

To which Vitus said : " I am such a worthless little being ; how can he want me ? "

They answered : " His son is tormented by a devil, and so asked to have you brought to him."

Blessed Vitus said : " Let us go, then in the name of the Lord."

When he came to Rome, his arrival was announced to the Emperor, who ordered him immediately to be brought before him.   The countenance of blessed Vitus was extremely handsome, and shining like fire ; his eyes were like the rays of the sun, for they were filled with the grace of God.   Then Diocletian said : " Are you Vitus ? "

But he was silent.

Then Cæsar commenced to interrogate Modestus, but he, being old and of a simple nature, did not know how to give a suitable reply ; and the Emperor ridiculed him.

Wherefore blessed Vitus said : " Why do you question the old man as if he were still young ?   Ought you not rather to respect his grey hairs ? "

Then Diocletian, enraged, said : " How have you such presumption that you dare speak so angrily in the face of our authority ? "

Vitus replied : " We are not angry, who have received

the spirit of simplicity, through the bounty of Christ. We should rather imitate the meekness of the dove. Our Master, who taught us, is of His own nature good : He is great indeed in power, but modest in simplicity. Wherefore, those who wish to be His disciples must be meek and humble of heart, and not passionate or bois-terous."

10. Then the demon, by the mouth of the tortured son of Diocletian, cried out horribly, saying : " O Vitus ! why do you cruelly torture me before the time ? "

To which Vitus replied nothing ; but the Emperor said : " Vitus, can you cure my son ? "

The blessed Vitus replied : " Health, indeed, it is possi-ble for him to regain, which I cannot give him ; but by me Christ, whose servant I am, can, if He wishes, liberate him most easily from this impious enemy." And after Diocletian had besought him, he approached the possessed, and laying his hands on his head, said : " Impure spirit ! depart from this creature of God, in the name of the Lord Jesus Christ." And immediately the devil left him, and killed a great many infidels.*

Then Diocletian, seeing his son cured, and many of the infidels who were mocking at St. Vitus killed, and en-raptured with the beauty of the boy, advised him blandly and kindly, saying : " Dearest Vitus, if you will only con-sent to sacrifice to our gods, I will give you the best part of my kingdom ; I will load you with immense riches of gold and silver, and precious garments, and every kind of costly furniture, and I will esteem you as my dearest and most intimate friend."

* Et statim recessit ab eo dæmon et occidit plurimos infidelium.— *Acts.*

Vitus replied : " I have no need of thy kingdom, nor of thy garments, nor of thy riches ; I have my Lord God, who will clothe me with the stole of immortality, which no darkness can obscure, if I persevere in serving Him faithfully."

Diocletian then said : " Do not act in this way, Vitus, but think rather of thy life, and sacrifice to the gods, lest thou perish by divers torments."

To which Vitus replied : " I esteem inestimably those torments with which you threaten me ; by them I can gain the palm which the Lord has deigned to promise to His elect."

11. Then Diocletian ordered his ministers to cast the blessed Vitus, together with Modestus, into a most vile prison ; and when they were cast into prison, he ordered each of them to be loaded with eighty pounds of iron, and the prison to be sealed with his own ring, so that no one could enter to give them even a drop of water But when they were shut up, immediately a great light lit up the prison, so that the terrified guards looked on with wonder.   The blessed Vitus cried out with a loud voice, saying : " Thou hast inclined to our aid, O Lord ; hasten and free us from this punishment, as Thou didst free the three children in the burning furnace, and Susanna from the iniquity of false witnesses."

At these words of the saint, an earthquake shook the prison, a wonderful light radiated through it, and a delicious odour was spread through the enclosure. Our blessed Lord appeared to them, saying : " Arise, Vitus ; be comforted and strong ; behold, I am with you all days."

And then the vision left them.   The iron that bound and weighed them down was melted like wax ; there were the voices of a multitude of angels, singing with them in the prison, and saying : "Blessed be the Lord God of Israel, for He hath visited and wrought the redemption of His people."

The gaolers, hearing those things, were almost paralysed with fear, and ran to the Emperor's palace, crying out in a loud voice : " O most pious Emperor, help us ; the whole city is perishing, and the people are destroyed."

Hearing these sounds, the Emperor was in consternation, and said to the gaolers : "What is this great misfortune you so unreasonably publish ?"

They answered : "Vitus, whom you ordered us to bind in prison, has been surrounded by a dazzling light ; an ineffable odour fills the cell ; and there is a Man with them (Vitus and Modestus) whose countenance no man dare look on ; He spoke with them, and a multitude of young men dressed in white sang aloud most joyful praises."

12. Then Diocletian, filled with anger, ordered the amphitheatre to be prepared, saying : " I will deliver them to the wild beasts, and I will see if their Christ can deliver them out of my hands."

And when they had entered the amphitheatre, blessed Vitus warned his aged tutor not to be afraid, saying : " Be brave, father, and fear not the sword of the devil, for now our crown is coming."

There was at this exhibition more than five thousand men, without counting women and children, of whom there was a countless number.

When they stood before Diocletian, he said : " Vitus, where do you see yourself ?"

But Vitus, raising his eyes to heaven, replied nothing,

Diocletian, repeating the question, said. "Where do you see yourself, Vitus?"

Vitus then replied : "I see myself in the amphitheatre ; however, do what you are going to do."

"Think of your life," said Diocletian, "and sacrifice to the great gods."

Vitus said : "Never may it be well with thee, Satan, thou rapacious wolf, thou deceiver of souls! How great is thy audacity to persuade me to do these things, after seeing so many wonders! But I possess Christ, to whom up to this time I have sacrificed every thought of my soul, and to whom I now sacrifice all that remains of me."

13. Then unable to contain himself with rage, the Emperor ordered his ministers to prepare the cauldron with lead and pitch. The lictors did as they were ordered, and the blessed champion of Christ was put into it. Whilst they were putting him in, the Emperor said : "Now I will see if thy God can free thee from my hands."

But Vitus was making the sign of the life-giving cross while they were casting him into the oven. The furnace glowed like the sea ; and immediately an angel appeared, who extinguished the heat, whilst blessed Vitus stood in the middle singing a hymn to the Lord, saying : "Thou who hast freed the children of Israel from the land of Egypt, and from a tyrannical yoke and an iron furnace, through Thy servant Moses, give us mercy, on account of the glory of Thy holy name."

And calling on the Emperor, he said aloud : "I thank thee, Diocletian, and thy ministers, for preparing such a pleasant bath and towels for me."

The whole people burst into exclamations, saying :

" Such wonders we have never seen ! Verily the God of this infant is true and great ! " *

Vitus came out of the oven without a stain on his body, but his flesh shone like the snow. Returning thanks to God he said : " Thou hast proved me, O Lord, like gold ; Thou hast tried me with fire, and no iniquity has been found in me." Chiding the Emperor, he boldly said : " Blush, thou devil, with Satan thy father, seeing what wonders the Lord works in His servants."

14. The Emperor, bursting more and more with rage, ordered a lion to be brought in, whose roaring even the men could scarcely bear. When he was let loose, the Emperor said : " Do you think your magical arts will prevail this time ? "

" Stupid and foolish man ! " cried out Vitus, " Do you not see that Christ the Lord is with me ? At His words the angels will deliver me from every pain and from thy hands."

And when the lion came towards him he made over him the sign of the cross, and he fell at his feet, and licked them (plantas ejus lingebat). Then the blessed Vitus said to Diocletian : " Behold, impious man, the very animals give honour to God, and you do not recognise your Creator ; even if you now believe in Him, I will promise you salvation."

Diocletian said : " Thou mayest believe in Him and all thy kind."

Vitus, smiling said : " Thou hast said well ; for I and all that are like me, that are born of God by faith, in whom I have been regenerated, desire a perpetual crown in heaven."

* Tanquam mirabilia nunquam vidimus; vere enim verus et magnus est Deus infantis hujus !

In that hour about a thousand persons believed in Christ. Diocletian said : "Seeing your doings, many of the people are beginning to believe in those arts by which you overcome fire and the wild beasts."

Vitus replied : " Fire and beasts are not ruled by arts ; but because they are creatures they give honour to their Creator, my Lord Jesus Christ. But you should be the more confounded ; because, although a rational creature, you are worse than insensible things and irrational brutes."

15. Then Diocletian ordered his attendants to have Vitus, and Modestus his tutor, and Crescentia his nurse, who, on account of his preaching, believed in Christ, extended on the rack. Then Vitus said : " Ridiculous and cowardly you show yourself to be when you command a woman to be tortured."

But the saints of God were stretched on the rack. so that their bones were dislocated and their bowels appeared. In this torment the blessed Vitus cried out : " O Lord God, save us in Thy name, and in Thy power deliver us ! "

Immediately there was a great earthquake and terrible lightnings ; the temples of the idols fell, and a great many people were killed. The Emperor also fled away terrified ; and striking his forehead with his hand, cried out in a loud voice : " Woe is me ! I have been shamefully conquered by a mere child ! " *

An angel descended from heaven and lifted their bodies from the rack, and immediately they found themselves transported once more near to the river Siler, and reposing under a tree. Vitus invoked the Lord once more, and

---

* Væ mihi, quia a tantillo infantulo turpiter superatus sum !—

said : " O Lord Jesus Christ, Son of the living God, complete the desire of those who wish to glorify Thy name by sufferings of martyrdom ! preserve them, O Lord by Thy grace from the dangers of this world, and bring them to the glory of Thy magnificence." And when he had finished his prayer, there came a voice from heaven which said to him : "Vitus, thy petition has been granted." And immediately their holy spirits left their sacred bodies in the appearance of snow-white doves, and accompanied by angels singing in joy, they flew towards the distant heavens.

16. For three days a celestial eagle guarded their remains. On the third day, Florentia, a noble lady, was driving by in her chariot on the banks of the river, when suddenly the horse became restive and caused her to fall in the centre of the stream. She was commencing to sink when St. Vitus appeared to her walking on the water. Florentia cried out, with a loud voice : " Save me if you be an angel of God ! "

To which the blessed Vitus replied : " I am Vitus, sent by the Lord, who is the Author and Preserver of human life, to save thee, in order that thou mayest bury our bodies ; and whatsoever thou askest, in the name of the Saviour, by our prayers thou wilt obtain."

Florentia, being saved from the torrent, collected the bodies of the saints, and embalmed them with spices, and buried them in the same place in which they died, called Morianus.

St. Vitus, together with Modestus and Crescentia, suf-fered on the 17th Kalends of July, our Lord Jesus Christ reigning : to whom is all honour, glory, power, and majesty, through all ages. Amen.

CHAPTER XXI.

META SUDANS.

NEAR the Coliseum, a stone's throw from the Arch of Constantine, there stands a dilapidated ruin, which has given origin to some discussion amongst antiquarians. Its large circular base and ruined conical fragment of masonry with tube for water, leave little doubt that it was at one time a fountain. As the lovers of antiquity are privileged to make any amount of absurd conjectures, this ruin has passed in their imagination to castles and towers of grandeur far surpassing its past or present pretensions. But time has played with the works of man, and turning gigantic buildings upside down, has left their massive remnants as puzzles for the solution of generations who tread on the dust of fallen nations. Notwithstanding the variety of opinions as to its real destination, antiquarians are pretty fairly agreed on the name it bears, as the *Meta Sudans.**

---

*Metam Sudantem ante arcum Constantini et Amphitheatrum constituunt fontem eorum qui ludos frequentabant extinguendæ siti percommodum eminente Jovis simulacro quam in numines expressam habemus. Extat hodieque semirutu absquesi mulacro et fonte juxta Coliseum vulgo dictum uti eam Romanorum ruinarum icones repræsentant.—*Donatus, lib. 3, Romæ Veteris.*

When the gladiator had struggled for life with the king of the forest, or felled a more formidable opponent in a fellow-prisoner, he was permitted the luxury of a bath, to revive his exhausted frame in this fountain of cool and crystal water. Its ruddy and crimson dye soon told the share it took in the bloody games of the Amphitheatre, for hither the panting victor hastened to cleanse his own wounds, or remove the stains of his victim's blood. Some will have it flowed with oil, but we have no further evidence for this beyond the custom mentioned by some ancient writers, that the gladiators rubbed their skins with oil before entering the arena. This strange nondescript ruin has, however, besides its name, another circumstance of hallowed reminiscence handed down to us in the records of sacred history. It was at one time the shrine of a martyr's relics ; it is mentioned in connection with the martyr Restitutus, a noble Roman youth, who forms the subject of this sketch.

The readers who have been to the Eternal City will find in these touching records, allusions to places well-known in rambles through the Forum. They carry us in thought to the scene of the greatest events of the past, through monuments whose name and history have been partly spared in the whirlwind of ruin and desolation that has swept over this city of magnificence.

Few of the monuments of the Forum have a certain history. It is painful to the student of archæology to find the discrepancy between authors about each column, each fragment of wall—each foundation cleared from the *débris* of past centuries. More than once the lesson of human vanity has been given to us, together with an out-rage to our feelings in our musings over the old Forum

No sooner had we roused our thoughts to a pitch of veneration, suitable for the study of the mighty temple of Jupiter that shone with burnished gold, or the majestic temple of Concord, that shook under the eloquence of the immortal Cicero, when some other writer or some more recent discovery broke in on our reverie, and bid us transfer our adoration to some other broken fragment of masonry or solitary column that adorns this wilderness of ruin.   The great Cardinal Wiseman has jocosely given us his experience of the antiquarian discrepancies that hang around the old Forum ; his words have more truth to day than when he penned them perhaps forty years ago.

" The revolutions that used to take place in the old Forum," he writes in his Essays and Reviews, " are nothing compared to those that are now daily witnessed in it.   In ancient times the senators or tribunes might change sides ; but certainly not the temples ; one candidate might jostle another out of his place, but one large building could hardly be so unneighbourly to its fellow of brick and mortar ; one faction might drive the other back and even out of the sacred precincts ; but it would have been unusual, we fancy, for one portico to send another with all its columns, rank and file, a-packing from the station it occupied for some centuries : some patriot might put to open shame a turbulent demagogue, but we imagine the ancients never saw the front of one building outface another till this one turned its back upon its rival.   Yet all such wonderful evolutions have we beheld among the buildings of the Roman Forum—not unaptly compared by the late Sir W. Gell, to a country dance, in which temples change sides, monuments, cross-hands, and columns lead down the middle. We cannot imagine a more dangerous ex

posure of parental authority to contempt, than would
occur should any gentleman who had visited Rome only
twenty years ago, rummage out his journal and the notes
he made after the most approved guide books of the day,
and proceed in person to show his boys the lions of ancient
Rome. Why the young sparks (we speak from experience) would laugh at the old gentleman's beard upon
hearing his antiquated antiquarianism. He naturally
takes them to the Church of Araceli on the Capitol, and
tells them with great feeling that this is the site of Jupiter
Capitolinus, and tries to work up their minds to a suitable
pitch of enthusiasm. But the rogues have found out in
their guide books that since their papa was last in Rome
the said temple has quietly walked across the area on the
top of the hill, and placed itself on its other extremity,
where, by a lucky coincidence, the Archæological Institute
has established itself. He descends into the Forum and
points out three columns of beautiful form composing
an angle of a portico at the foot of the Capitol. These,
everybody has known from time immemorial as part of
the Temple of Jupiter Tonans. But there everybody has
been wrong ; for now they are considered as part of the
temple of Saturn. Eight other columns stand beside
these, which twenty years ago you would have taken any
wager belonged to the Temple of Concord, celebrated as
the theatre of Cicero's indignant eloquence. But alas,
within the last twenty years, the edifice has passed
through many transmutations, having been changed first
by Nibby into the Temple of Fortune, then by Fea into
that of Juno Moneta, later by Piale into that of Vespasian, since by Canina into that of Saturn, and lastly by
Bunsen back again to that of Vespasian, which for the

present it remains.   The hero of a Christmas pantomime
could not have endured more changes."

Yet the Capitol, the triumphal arch of Severus, the
Coliseum and *Meta Sudans* are like fixed stars amid this
everchanging mass of ruins.   Seventeen hundred years
ago they bore the same names as they do now, although
one of the great old Romans raised from the dust in which
he has slept for centuries would scarely recognise, in the
remnants that stand, the majestic structures that were
familiar to his eyes in the days of their magnificence.
Near these monuments many a brave Christian found his
crown.   Amongst them was the martyr who is connected
in history with the Meta Sudans.

"We have found this man powerful and eloquent in
speech, teaching the people that the worship of our gods
is vain, saying they have but an imaginary existence ; he
belongs to some strange sect they call Christian."

Thus spoke some rude soldiers as they presented to the
Prefect of the city a young noble citizen, with his hands
bound behind his back.

"Who are you or whence do you come?" asked the
Prefect, Hermogenes, with a menacing frown.

"I am a Roman citizen of noble birth ; if you wish
my carnal name, I am called Restitutus, but in the profession of my faith I am a Christian."

"Have you not heard the orders of the Prince?"

"What have they commanded?" asked Restitutus
mildly.

"That all who will not sacrifice to the omnipotent gods
should be punished by various and terrible torments,"
said the Prefect, becoming excited, and watching the
noble youth impatiently, in the hopes he had already terrified him into submission.

"I know the commands of *my* Emperor," boldly replied the Christian, "whoever will deny *Him* will perish in eternal torments."

"Cease to speak thus," cried the President, "but come hither and sacrifice to the revered deities, that are the guardians of the Empire, and you will be a friend of Cæsar; otherwise, you shall feel the weight of our indignation, and shall be tortured with fire."

"I am prepared," Restitutus mildly but bravely replied, "to offer myself in sacrifice to my Lord Jesus Christ."

With this conversation the Acts introduce the brief but touching history of one of those noble youths cut down like beautiful flowers in the terrible storm that blew over the garden of the Church—flowers that still give fragrance in the sanctity of their names, and the hallowed memories with which they are shrouded in the pages of sacred history. Like many other of the victims of those cruel days, we have no interesting particulars of his youth. Doubtless the constancy and the miracles that invariably sanctioned the teachings of the martyrs had struck and converted the generous heart of our young hero; he may have seen the animals play around the servants of Christ in the Amphitheatre; he was present, perhaps, when the silent prayer of some youth like himself threw the idol from its pedestal, and dashed it to the earth in a thousand pieces; or, perhaps, was one of the many who gathered through curiosity around the *accursed stone,* but for whom the last dying prayer of some martyr going to his crown, opened the clouds of heaven, and drew down the grace and gift of faith. He was a nobleman of wealth and position, who abandoned the treacherous path of worldly honours

to follow in the humble path of the followers of the cru
cified God. Brave, the youth that would rush through
the devouring flames of a conflagration to save a victim;
that would plunge into the stormy sea to save a drowning fellow-creature; brave, the youth who yearns for the
front of the battle, and rushes fearlessly into the thickest
of the fight; but braver far the young man who renounces
the fascination of wealth, the smiles of fortune, and the
gilded picture that fancy paints for the fervid youthful
imagination. Such was the conduct of Restitutus.

The intrepid reply of the martyr roused the tyranny of
the Prefect, and he ordered his mouth to be beaten with
stones; but he did not feel any pain, God by a miracle
had deadened the sense of feeling.

"What do you expect to gain by this obstinacy?"
asked the President.

"For the love and fear of my Lord Jesus Christ, I
have despised the Court (militiam intra palatium), and
now I wish only to serve in an everlasting warfare a
celestial King."

"But," rejoined the President, "in consideration of
your youth and beauty, approach and sacrifice to the gods,
that you may receive the reward of great dignity and
power."

Restitutus replied : " In serving the true God of Heaven
I have not lost nor demeaned my dignity ; the dig-
nities, the honours of earth, fade like the things of earth
—as are gone the flowers of summer and the snows of
winter, so have passed the glory and worldly dignity of
our ancestors—but that profession which takes its nobility from an eternal source is like it in its eternal dura
tion."

Truly the martyr spoke with a sublime appreciation of the eternal character of the Christian's warfare. The Prefect who made him suffer for his faith has long since passed into oblivion, notwithstanding the wealth and power that shone around him in the giddy hour of his reign. He is not now known except in the infamy of his cruelty, which is recorded by sacred writers in handing to posterity and eternal fame the noble youth who had despised even the splendours of the Pagan Court, and wisely chosen the eternal dignity of the Christian warfare.

He is stript of his clothes. The biting lash twines in serpentine coils around his symmetrical limbs; each stroke is registered in livid and blue marks on the tender flesh. Yet the agony of pain indicated by the suffering flesh was removed from the spirit of the martyr; by a miracle of God he felt no pain. Braver than ever, and with an eloquence that will be designated as the supernatural gift promised to the martyrs, the youthful Restitutus reproached his judge for his cruelty and hard-heartedness.

" Wretched enemy of God," he said fervidly, " see what our Lord does for those who love him ; where are thy threats and thy horrible torments ? Ought you not to abandon your impious sect and worship Him who alone is great, and frees his servants from the tortures of their persecutors ; how much better to recognize Him as God, instead of the powerless gods of wood and stone that you so foolishly adore ; idols, that can neither help themselves nor you."

Strong, fearless reproof like this was a great crime in the martyrs of Christianity. The Christian prepared

to meet death—beyond which no other evil was terrible
—was eloquent and fearless before the tribunal of the
pagans. Restitutus is again beaten, but this time with
whips with small balls of lead attached to the thongs
Again God preserved him—again the Prefect foamed—
again the martyr fearlessly pronounced the awful sentence
of retribution written in the book of life, against the hardened Prefect.

The prison scene **was** the most remarkable in this
tragedy of real life.   God permitted his servant to
perform a   miracle of an extraordinary character,
in which we scarcely know whether we are more struck
by the power imparted by God to Restitutus, or the
hardness and blindness of those who reaped the advantage of the miracle.   It reveals the terrible fact that even
in the days of the martyrs, there were blind, hardened
hearts who would not believe—not even if they saw the
dead raised to life ; they were many then—their number
is legion now.

When Restitutus was cast into prison he found the
gloomy dungeon filled with the wretched outcasts of Roman society, the murderer, the robber, the seditious, the
victims of intemperance and passion, whose souls were
red in the deep stain of crime, and breathing blasphemy
rather than prayer. Yet for such the loving, forgiving
heart of Jesus yearns, and his martyrs come like the
cheerful sunlight that shines equally on the good and
bad to console those self-degraded victims of crime.   No
sooner is the noble youth cast in amongst them when
they gather around him and beseech him to set them free
as other Christians had done in the same and other prisons in the city.   Restitutus did not hesitate.   He threw

himself on his knees and prayed aloud to God. The foundations of the prison were shaken, a beautiful light burst through the rocky walls, and a delicious odour was diffused throughout the sombre filthy prison. At the same moment the heavy iron door grated on its hinges, and was rolled back by some invisible hand.

"See," said Restitutus, "what God will do for those who love him; if any of you, fellow prisoners, wish to save your souls, stay here with me; if the love of life and liberty are thy desire—then flee. The Lord has burst thy chains and unbarred thy prison door." Without waiting to thank, and regardless of the fate of their benefactor, they struggled through the narrow entrance to hasten to daylight and liberty, nor did they stop their flight till the dawn of the next day.*

The next morning the gaolers came to the prisons; they found the doors wide open; their inmates fled—all save the Christian youth who was kneeling like a seraph in an aureola of light, his hands folded on his breast and in an ecstasy of prayer, unconscious of the arrival and intrusion of the astonished guards. Even they dared not enter, but whilst some remained to look in with increasing wonder on the angelic youth, others hastened to inform the Prefect of the strange event. Even he is struck with terror, but in his worldly wisdom he dare not show a weakness before the messengers; feigning courage he ordered the martyr to be brought before him again ; when Restitutus once chained was led before him, he commenced in a prepared speech—

---

* Exeuntes vero omnes simul e carcere abierunt unusquisque in fugam tota nocte, etc.—*Arts, May* 29, *Bollandists.*

" How long shall thy magic arts triumph ; how long will you continue to blaspheme our gods and defy our torments in immunity from pain ? How come you to burst the very chains and free from their merited doom the robbers and cut-throats of our public prisons? Do the principles of thy creed enjoin such a doubtful mo-rality ? "

" Do not attribute to magic," replied Restitutus, ' the works of the right hand of God. He who came from Heaven to save sinners, who ate with them, was counted amongst them, and crucified with them, knows how to break their bonds when occasion offers for his greater glory."

" Sacrifice ! " shouted the Prefect, interrupting the holy youth.

" To what sort of gods do you command me to sa-crifice ? To those perhaps made by the artisan from wood, bronze and stone, images without life or sense, but which indeed represent devils that shall suffer to-gether with the worshippers in eternal fire."

" It is an insult to the gods and to myself to permit this man to insult us any longer. Take him, lictors, to the temple of Jupiter on the Capitol, and if he still refuse to sacrifice, let him be beheaded there as a warning to this foolish sect."

What the temple of Jerusalem was to the carnal Jews, what the great St. Peter's is to modern Christians, such was the great shrine of the chief of the gods on the Capi-tol of ancient Rome. " Arx omnium nationum " in the eyes of Cicero, and for 1000 years the great centre around which rallied all that was grand or absurd in the Ritual of Paganism. This temple was commenced by Tarquinius Priscus'; it was increased and adorned by various rulers in after ages. In the history of the eternal city it marks three important epochs in which it was burnt to the ground by fire. It was finally built with surpassing magnificence by Titus, and he finished it by gilding its roof with 12,000 talents of gold—a fabulous expenditure when calculated with the value of gold of the present day. It was afterwards twice struck by lightning at the prayers of the Christian Martyrs, and again nearly consumed by fire—fire sent from heaven to check the abomination of its impious sacrifices.

It was in consideration of his nobility Restitutus was ordered to the Capitol. The Roman criminal law, especially the clauses providing for the execution of criminals called Christians, required the sentence to be carried out at one of the milestones outside the city gates. Hence we so frequently find in the Acts of the Martyrs that they were beheaded at the second, seventh, and sixteenth milestone on the Appian, Latin, or Salarian Ways.

"The soldiers vainly endeavouring to get him to sacrifice," say the Acts, " led him out of the temple into the square of the Capitol and there decapitated him ; they cast his body near the triumphal arch of Severus that the dogs might devour it ; but Justa, a holy matron, came at night with some servants and stole the body, wrapt it in precious cloths and odoriferous balm, brought it to her house alongside the Meta Sudans, whence she brought it in her own chariot to her vineyard at the sixteenth milestone, where she had it honourably buried." Acts, 29th May. Bollandists.

CHAPTER XXII.

THE LAST MARTYR.

MAXENTIUS has been drowned in the Tiber, and Constantine has marched in triumph to the capital. With a loud voice and by inscriptions he made known to all men the standard of salvation; he erected an immense cross on the highest part of the Capitol, and placed under it this inscription : " By this salutary sign, the genuine type of fortitude, I have liberated and freed your city from the slavish yoke of a tyrant, restoring the Senate and people of Rome to their pristine splendour and dignity." It is the cross that is triumphant on the Capitol. Behold, the greatest miracle in the records of history ! Rome had seen many wonders in her twenty-six centuries of existence, but the scene on the highest of her seven hills, on the morning after the battle of the Saxa Rubra, was the strangest, whilst at the same time the most important in the history of her varied career. That which was the most abject, the most despised, and the most persecuted thing in the world, becomes in a moment the emblem of triumph, the true type of fortitude, the instrument of liberation and redemption to a stricken and trampled people ! This was a miracle incomparably greater than the vision of the cross given to Constantine. It involved a revolution of dynasties, and a change in the hearts of men, that could only come from the right hand of God. Even in the limited perceptions of human reasoning, we could not imagine another miracle more calculated to convince the pagan world of the divinity of the crucified God, whom it endeavoured to despise. After centuries of persecution, after every opposition that human power or human malice could bring against His Church, that Church is now triumphant in the emblem of its immortality, in the cross on its Capitol.

Some of the most inveterate pagans could scarcely believe their senses; they moved away muttering blasphemies against the God whom they still hated, but whose power they were forced to acknowledge ; the Christians gathered nearer and nearer to the beloved symbol of their hopes ; they kissed it and bedewed it with many tears ; they sang around it, in loud and cheerful tones, the praises of the royal prophet who had foretold its triumph. Far away in the distance and down the slopes of the Capitol, retiring bands of Christians were heard singing : " Who is like to Thee, O Lord, among the gods ? Thou hast been glorified in the saints, admirable in glories, doing wonders."

But, perhaps, this is an ill-timed congratulation for a triumph that is to last but an hour. The Coliseum is not yet converted. We have not yet finished its scenes of horror, and Christian blood must flow again in its arena. The title of our present chapter recalls scenes of bloodshed and persecution as violent as any we have recorded. Nevertheless the triumph of Constantine was lasting, complete, and universal. He was but an instrument in the

hands of God to effect the perfect establishment of **his**
Church.   His miraculous escape from the court of Galerius, his generosity, his prudence and nobility of mind,
and, above all, his victorious march from Gaul, destroying
with a handful of men the overwhelming forces of the
Empire, were all means adopted by God, to place the
Church in the centre of the world, on a basis that would
never again be. shaken by any storm, to commence her
visible and external mission amongst men, and to bring
to her bosom all the nations of the earth.   Immediately
after the triumph of Constantine, she raised her head
with independence ; she shook off the appearance of
weakness which shrouded her infancy, and showed the
world that her existence and her mission were no longer
doubtful, trembling, or destructible.   In this sense, the
triumph of Constantine is more glorious, more perfect,
and more manifest to-day than sixteen centuries ago,
when Catholicity was declared to be the religion of Rome.
Although there were martyrs after the time of Constantine, and the persecution of Julian revived for an hour
the tyranny of paganism, yet these were but the charac-
teristics of the Church's union with her crucified Master ;
they were strokes of correction from the hands of a Father;
they were not signs of weakness, but proofs of life and
strength.   She had never again to flee from amongst
men ; her Catacombs are abandoned to the sleeping dead
who await resurrection, and the Coliseum will never
again be the battlefield of her faith.   Yet there was
another martyrdom in the Coliseum.   The streams of
blood that flowed from the veins of perhaps a thousand
martyrs of the faith had not filled up the measure of its
iniquity ; there seemed to be still wanting some blood of

another character ; and the last flow of the ruddy stream which was to complete the dreadful holocaust of human beings sacrificed in this mighty amphitheatre was to be the blood of a martyr of charity. Let us come to this last and touching scene, recorded of the martyrs of the Coliseum.

One of the first acts of Constantine was to condemn by public edict those scenes of bloodshed, which were so uncongenial to the spirit of Christianity. This was an important event, not only in the history of the Coliseum, but in the history of Rome. The people loved these spectacles with a blind fanaticism. It had frequently happened, in the past history of the city, that infuriated mobs, breathing violence and fury, and threatening to deluge the streets with patrician blood, were calmed by the games of the Circus and Coliseum. The popularity of each new Emperor depended in a great measure on the character of the games with which he entertained his subjects. In the midst of war, famine and public grief, they would pour in reckless crowds to the intoxication of the amphitheatre and the circus ; the more blood to be shed, the greater the enthusiasm of the people ; the more impious and cruel the games, the greater was supposed to be the piety to the gods ! Hence the closing of the Coliseum was a desperate step, which at other times would have caused a rebellion that would have cost the Emperor his throne. Although all the power of Constantine was brought to bear on the fulfilment of the edict, it was not until nearly a hundred years after his death that the last gladiatorial show took place in the Coliseum.

Christianity was slowly, but surely, sweeping away every vestige of paganism from the city. The elevation of the female sex and the expulsion of slavery were leviathan undertakings that engrossed all her energies for nearly two centuries.   Honorius renewed the prohibitory law of Constantine, but to no purpose.   The games were no longer maintained by the public purse, but there were found senators and nobles rich enough to rival the imperial entertainments of other days.   The Coliseum had no longer its martyrs, but still it had its victims.   At length the gentle influence of Christianity triumphed ; the unceasing prayers of the Christians had pierced the clouds of heaven ; even this most cherished institution of idolatry and infamy must yield to the regenerating spirit of the Church, and the Coliseum closed its long career of horror and bloodshed by a tragedy as terrible as any we have yet recorded, but redounding more to the glory and honour of that faith which conquered Rome.   A poor monk named Telemachus, who had passed his life as a solitary in the deserts of the East, was inspired by God with a holy zeal to put an end to the profanities of the public spectacles.   He succeeded, but it cost him his life.

Far away in the depths of the Lybian deserts, he had heard the Coliseum of Rome was still reeking with the blood of human victims.   Perhaps a description of its horrors was given to him by some fugitive penitent, who had learned the emptiness and dangers of the world, and had fled to solitude to prepare for eternity.   He conceived the idea of making a generous effort to destroy this brutal passion ; he felt that something should be done, even though he should have to leave his desert and shed his own blood in the undertaking.   Long and fervently did he recommend the thought to God.   In unbroken nights of prayer and fearful austerities, in many tears and deep humility, he prayed for some token of the divine will. What could he do, he thought, a poor ignorant hermit, slow of speech, bare-footed, and clothed in coarse sack-cloth? Kings and Popes and martyrs had failed to era-dicate the evil, yet would he succeed? Fearing some lelusion of Satan, he paused and doubted, but grace urged him on; an interior voice said to him: "I can do all things in Him who comforts me." He penetrated deeper into the trackless wilds of the desert to consult an old and experienced anchoret, who was a disciple of the great Paul, the first to sanctify those homeless regions. The aged monk told him to go, for God had accepted his sacrifice.

At length he seizes his staff, and, with many tears, bids farewell to his beloved cell, his rude cross, and the little stream whose constant murmurs joined him in the praises of God. The desert was a home of delights, but the world before him was dark and gloomy. No soldier ever moved with braver step to the battlefield than Telema-chus to his combat with the proud passions of men. He moves on through crowded cities, through cultivated plains and wild mountain passes—he seeks no roof but the open canopy of heaven; the stone in the desert has been the only pillow he has used for years past. After a journey of weeks and months, and perhaps years, at length wearied, footsore, but delighted, he arrived under the walls of the Eternal City. The brilliant sun of heaven was reflected from the glittering domes of the imperial metropolis of the world. The eyes of the poor monk were dazzled with temples covered with silver and gold, and interminable vistas of marble columns around palaces and theatres which were raised on every side with a magnificence and splendour such as fancy would paint for the cities in the land of dreams. He enters the city, and moves through its crowded streets unconscious of the universal gaze of the people, who are attracted by his extraordinary dress. Some laugh, others insult him, all despise the poor monk, whom angels are leading to a sublime destiny.

As far as we can learn, it was on the morning of the 1st of January, A.D. 404, that Telemachus entered Rome. The games usually celebrated during the Kalends of January were inaugurated at the expense of a rich senator; and although far inferior in magnificence, they exceeded in brutality the spectacles of the golden age. Telemachus moved with the crowd towards the amphitheatre. When he mounted the Capitol, with its fifty temples still smoking with the sacrifices of abomination, he shuddered, for he knew the demons had still possession of that part of the city. What were the emotions of his heart when another moment brought the mighty amphitheatre full into his view? It rose in the valley beneath the Capitol with stupendous majesty, towering over the temples and arches that lined the Forum—immense, like the Pyramids he had seen in his passage through Egypt, more beautiful than anything that had yet met his gaze in that city of wonders, and raised in the air higher than the surrounding hills, with a solidity that would seem to defy decay or the ravages of time. He descended the Way of Triumph, unconscious that he himself was walking to a triumph—one of the greatest the world ever saw. He passed under the arches where noble martyrs had been often dragged to be exposed to the wild beasts; and a cold feeling of horror passed over him as he looked for the first time at the blood-stained

arena, whose horrors had haunted his dreams, whose conversion was the unceasing petition of his prayer. It
was early in the day, and the games had not yet commenced; the people were pouring into the benches; he
took a seat, and heedless of the buzz of a thousand voices
around him, in a few moments became wrapt in communion with God, as if he were praying on the banks of his
little stream in the desert.

Wrapt in prayer, with his hands folded on his breast,
he seemed to the Romans like a vision from the other
world. His dress and strange appearance, the halo of
sanctity which was suffused around the true servant of
God, and which never can be concealed, made the gathering crowd gaze on him with mingled sentiments of contempt, surprise and reverence. Who or what is he?
was asked by each wondering stranger as he suddenly
stopped short to gaze on the extraordinary apparition
that sat motionless on one of the benches. Some thought
he was a poor fool, and was not to be minded; others
said he was some truant slave from the East; others,
again, that perhaps he was a messenger from the oracles,
for those important persons were generally clothed fan-
tastically, and wrapt in mystery and gloom. But another
moment will show them that he indeed is a messenger
from the oracles of Eternal Wisdom, to teach the world
the great truths uttered in the revelations of the gospel.

The games have commenced. Like Alipius, he is
roused from his reverie by the inhuman shout that hails
the first batch of combatants. Four naked, stout, and
fierce-looking men have bounded into the arena; they
feign cheerful looks, and each one is certain of being
victorious. They march around the arena according to

the old custom of the games, that the people may select their favourites to bet on them and anticipate their victory. As they pass around, some take their last farewell by a long steady gaze and a kiss of the hand to some friend in the upper benches. In spite of their efforts to smile bravely on death, their countenances bear the pallid stamp of desperation, and nature betrays her fear of dissolution; it was a blind fury that made them hasten to the combat, not what the Romans call bravery. Now they are measuring swords and are matched by the prefect of the games; they pass a few moments in playful fencing with wooden swords; then come the glittering steel blades, burnished and brightened for the deadly struggle; they seize them, and in another moment the game of bloodshed has commenced. But see! the monk has risen; he flies through the benches; he leaps over the iron rail of the podium, and with a giant hand seizes the combatants and whirls them round him.

No pen could describe the scene that followed. The people were like a lion deprived of his prey by an inferior animal. Never did the old walls of the amphitheatre ring with a louder or wilder scream of frenzy; at the very moment their excitement was becoming intense, they were thwarted by this daring stranger, and their indignation was roused to fury. We should give but a faint idea of the feelings of the mob when Telemachus appeared in the arena to stop the gladiators, if we imagined a capuchin monk, clothed in the sackcloth and cord of St. Francis, rushing on the stage of the Alhambra in London to reprove the indecent levities of its ballets. The gladiators were thunderstruck, and stood in terror as if in the presence of a supernatural being. The holy monk endea voured to address the people, but they hissed, and hooted, and screamed with fiendish rage; and at length, as if unable to control themselves any longer, they tore up the seats and benches, and in a few minutes the air became filled with a shower of broken fragments of seats and pavements hurled from every side of the amphitheatre on the head of Telemachus. He knelt, and stretching his arms towards heaven, offered his life for the conversion of this great theatre of infamy. The martyr of charity fell, and covered in his fall one of the darkest stains on the arena of the amphitheatre. Where the venerable Ignatius and a host of others suffered, the body of this glorious martyr of charity fell beneath the heavy fragments of marble seats and ornaments hurled down upon him from every bench of the amphitheatre, then crowded with the demons who rejoiced in the degradation of the human race. Terrible as was the judgment wreaked on this poor unarmed monk for daring to thwart them in their cruel sports, yet that monk succeeded; the gladiators he separated never met again. His sacrifice was accepted in heaven, the Coliseum was converted. The Emperor Honorius immediately prohibited all spectacles in the Coliseum, and sanctioned the law with the severest penalties. There was one more desperate effort made a few years afterwards to resuscitate the murders of the amphitheatre—but the blood of Telemachus was triumphant—the inhuman sport of the gladiatorial spectacle was henceforward a stain of the past. In the noble self-sacrifice of one man, Christianity expiated the crimes of three hundred years, and raised the moral and rational character of the human species over the brutal passions that degraded it.

The excitement of the people increased, and spread like a fire through every bench. Some fled in terror and sent alarming rumours through the city; the people flocked in additional thousands to the amphitheatre, and increased the noise and confusion. The prefect ordered the trumpets to be sounded, and sent for the gladiators to resume the combats, but in vain; a decree was written in heaven which no human power could change. At length the military were ordered to disperse the crowd, and the sports of the day were declared to be terminated.

We cannot but admire the zeal of Telemachus. We love to hang over this last tragedy of the Coliseum as one of the sublimest and most interesting of the early Church. One shudders indeed at the awful fate of the poor monk, but his pain was momentary. His sacrifice was the highest degree of virtue that man can exercise towards his fellow-man; and now his crown is bright and eternal. His charity was that fire which consumes everything. It assumed a heroism of self-denial that is beyond nature; and gave him that shining mark by which men were to know he was the follower of the Saviour who loved so much.

It must have appeared strange to the Romans that the death of one man could have produced such an unexpected result. The wonder increased when they heard that the murdered man was poor, a stranger, and a hated Christian. Human life was of so little value in those days, that poor slaves were often put to death by tyrant masters and mistresses for some accidental injury offered to a pet dog or cat. In the Coliseum especially, where it was not unusual to see a hundred gladiators fall in one day, death may be said to have been the most common spectacle witnessed in its arena. Yet the death of this poor monk not only separated the gladiators in their murderous attack on each other, and caused the crowd of cruel spectators to be dispersed into the streets, but it wrung from the supreme power of the Empire a definite and inviolable prohibition of this inhuman sport. So triumphant, so perfect was the success of the mission of Telemachus, that, not only in the Coliseum, but in all the amphitheatres throughout the Empire, the sword of the gladiator was broken in pieces, and the degrading profession of being a skilful murderer was for ever annihilated. This is but one of the many facts recorded in history which show how the Catholic Church regenerated the world. The agents of Divine Providence have been little and despicable, but their works have been miraculous and eternal in their influence on the destinies of men.

CHAPTER XXIII.

TELEMACHUS STILL TRIUMPHANT.

1.

FIVE years after the tragedy we have described in the last chapter, the Coliseum witnessed another scene equally strange and thrilling. Not that there were any more martyrs to shed their blood in its sanctified arena, but every page in the history of this great ruin is a scene of horror. The powers of darkness made a desperate effort to restore the reign of terror in the Coliseum. For a moment they seemed to succeed; the blinded populace shouted with joy, and the slave was armed again with the sword of the gladiator. But He who accepted the sacrifice of Telemachus knew well how to thwart the designs of the impious, and, at the time in which it pleased Him, He scattered them like chaff before the wind. It was not without a dreadful struggle that the Romans gave up the fascinating bloodshed of their amphitheatre, and their last effort to restore its terrible spectacle was surrounded with horror and confusion that gives a thrilling finale to our chapter of blood. We give a scene from one of the most tremendous judgments of God in the history of man—the commencement of His greatest mercy !

The hour of retaliation had at length dawned on Rome —that hour long set apart in the decrees of Providence for a fearful vindication of this unconverted city. The Goths and barbarian tribes from the north-east of the Empire were led on by Alaric to its plunder. These rough, uncouth tribes had been treasuring up in their traditions every defeat and every injustice they had suffered from the Roman arms. Long had their chiefs, like the prophets of old, uttered their prophetic woes against this proud queen of the universe. Revenge was their god, and the plunder of Rome was the elysium of their delights. When the hour came they were let loose by Almighty God, and five or six hundred thousand of the most brutal soldiers poured down towards the ill-fated city, and before the Romans knew their danger, Alaric had made his way through the beautiful plains of Italy, and the wreck of cities and smoking ruins were the traces of his victorious march.

The Romans were indulging in every excess, and thought of nothing but the amusements of the Circus and the Coliseum. Their apathy and blindness to the terrible ruin which threatened them was the first sign of the fate that decreed their fall. The haughty Senate and patricians pretended to smile at the audacity of a barbarian king coming to attack their city. They looked at their arches of triumph, the trophies of victory beyond number that met their gaze on every side, the temples of so many gods, and of heroes and emperors deified for their deeds in arms ; and with complacent pride they scorned the idea of their becoming a prey to a barbarian. How should she tremble, amid so many pledges of dominion, whose walls, cemented with the gore of so many captive victims, were sufficiently guarded by the terrors of the Roman name, and by the dreadful shades of so many conquerors ? But their arrogance was soon humbled by misfortune. Whilst they were yet reclining in their tricliniums, the bands of Alaric, impatient for the moment of assault, came bursting through the marble halls and pleasure-grounds of her suburban villas, and rushed and thundered onwards over every opposition, until they broke like a deluge of blood and confusion against her gates.

By a skilful disposition of his troops, Alaric encompassed the walls, commanded the twelve principal gates, intercepted all communication with the adjoining country, and diligently guarded the navigation of the Tiber, upon which Rome depended for the sustenance of her innumerable population. The doomed city gradually experienced the distress of scarcity, and at length the horrid calamities of famine. The hour of revenge had commenced its horrors on the ill-fated city. The people began to die in hundreds through hunger, and as the public sepulchres were outside the walls, and in the possession of the enemy, the stench that arose from so many putrid and unburied carcasses infected the air, and the miseries of famine were soon aggravated by those of pestilence.

It was in this extremity that a deputation was sent from the Senate to the Gothic camp to sue for terms. When the members of the deputation were introduced to the tent of Alaric, they maintained a haughty bearing, to make it appear they were equally prepared for war or peace. They said, if the king of the Goths refused to sign a fair and honourable capitulation, he might sound his trumpets, and prepare to give battle to an innumerable people inured to arms, and animated by despair. "The thicker the grass, the easier it is mowed," was the reply with which the barbarian mocked them, to the great amusement of his officers, who burst into loud and insulting laughter at this stroke of rustic wit. He then dictated the terms on which alone they might expect to have the city spared :—The surrender into his hands of *all* the gold and silver within the walls of Rome, whether it belonged to the state or to individuals ; *all* the rich and precious movables, and all the barbarians detained as slaves.

"If such, O king," said one of the ambassadors, "are the things you must have from us, may we ask what it is you intend to leave us ?"

"Your lives," replied the haughty conqueror.

There being no longer any human hope, it was resolved by the Romans to resort once more to the aid of the immortal gods. It was alleged by some that the city of Narni had been recently saved from the Goths by certain mystic rites and sacrifices of the Etruscans, who were then in Rome ; and these same execrable practices, consisting in dark incantations by the gore of murdered captives, were solemnly performed by public edict from the Capitol. It was in vain that the Christian senators exclaimed against this horrible impiety; their voices were drowned in enthusiastic exclamations for the restoration of pagan rites, and in execrations and blasphemies of Christ. It is related by Sozomen, that the most reflecting of the Romans looked upon the calamities of the city as a just judgment on its incorrigible attachment to idolatry. But the lightnings of Jupiter were not hurled on the tents of the Goths; the horrors of famine and pestilence increased, and the humbled Senate was forced to send another embassy to the enemy, to even beg for mercy. A temporary respite was purchased by the doomed city; but she is weighed in the balance, and destined to fall. Alaric retired for the winter to the fair and fruitful regions of Tuscany, enriched by the wealth of the capital and reinforced by forty thousand slaves, who broke their chains, and joined the barbarian camp, in the hope of one day revenging the cruelties practised on them during their servitude. They had that revenge a few months afterwards; it was stern and terrible.

The conditions of capitulation were not kept, and Alaric came with a portion of his troops to terrify them into compliance with their promise, or in reality to sack the city, for which he thirsted, in spite of all these compromises and delays. On the occasion of his second investment of the city, the pagan Attalus was made Emperor at the dictation of Alaric. This man was raised to the purple for the sole purpose of being degraded, and that the imperial dignity itself might be disgraced and exposed to derision. A few weeks afterwards, the purple was ignominiously torn from his back, and himself and his courtiers made slaves to the barbarian king. Nevertheless, during his brief career he did all he could to introduce the horrid superstitions of paganism. The smoke of impure sacrifices once more rose up from the city. The cruel sports of the Circus and the Coliseum were commenced again in honour of the immortal gods. The scene that passed in the Coliseum on this occasion is one amongst the strange reminiscences of this venerable pile. It is to introduce it to the reader that we have related the historical facts of the preceding pages.

From the death of the monk Telemachus, the Coliseum had been silent. The gladiatorial profession was proscribed and through the horrors of the famine every animal in the city was slain. Yet the new Emperor must celebrate his accession to the crown by the games of the Circus and Coliseum. The people still clung with blind fanaticism to the institutions of the past ; they believed the gods delighted in scenes of bloodshed more than themselves, and to appease the imaginary tyrants that were supposed to sway the destinies of the Empire, the dried-up arena must flow again with the purple stream of human blood. Hence, some thousands of dying slaves were pushed into the arena to fight with each other for their lives. The plague and famine were raging around, and people were dropping dead in the streets ; nevertheless, the benches of the Coliseum were filled with famishing myriads, who came to gaze in wild frenzy on the horrible spectacle.

When Attalus and his pagan officers appeared in the royal tribune, he was not saluted with salvoes or vows for a long and protracted reign, but with the hideous clamour of the people demanding to have a price put on the bodies of the slaves who were about to be slain. But Almighty God did not permit the impiety to succeed. The wretched slaves would have allowed themselves to be slain like sheep, but they were so prostrate through hunger and sickness that they were not able to raise their arms against each other ; they would have willingly submitted to their fate, for death would have been a welcome release from their miseries. They called on the lictors to come and dispatch them ; they raised their hands towards their masters to kill them or give them food. The scene was one of the most terrible of all the

horrors witnessed in this temple of the furies.   A starving mob poured into its marble benches to enjoy the cruel
sport of a gladiatorial butchery, and then to feast on the
flesh of its victims.   The air was rent with blasphemies
against every god, from Jupiter to Diocletian.   The
demons who revel in the miseries of mankind were present in countless legions, and consequently louder, and
more terrible than every other sound, were the blasphemies against the sacred name of Christ.   The slaves wept
and moaned and screamed, and the mob howled louder
and louder for food.   The mock Emperor fled in terror ;
the crowds were dispersed without the feast of human
blood ; and in fear and confusion, amidst the shouts of
pain and despair, mingled with the most horrible blasphemies ever uttered by man, the Roman populace took
their adieu of their beloved gladiatorial shows.

2.

But the horrors of this terrible day were but the commencement of a darker night of woe.   The impieties of
the brief reign of Attalus hastened the calamities that
were hanging over the ill-fated city.   Almost at the same
moment when the pagan faction of the Roman people
were endeavouring to re-establish the bloody scenes of
the Coliseum, Alaric announced to his barbarians, who
were wintering in the north, that they would march on
the morrow for the long wished-for sack of Rome.   The
news was received with shouts of joy ; the Dacian gladiator is not to die unavenged, for Alaric had said before
Byron :—

"Arise, ye Goths, and glut your ire.

The first scene in the awful drama of the degradation of Rome was the mockery of its king. The barbarian chief ordered Attalus to meet him on his march. The proud representative of the Cæsars had no alternative but prompt obedience. Attalus came up to the Gothic host on a plain near Rimini, and not far from the spot where the first of the Cæsars crossed the Rubicon to commence the great dynasty which Attalus was to close. Here he was ignominiously stript of purple and diadem before an immense concourse of Romans and barbarians, and the would-be Emperor of the world was told he might enjoy life as a slave in the service of the Gothic chief. When these indignities were completed, the order to resume the march was received with savage exultation, mingled with peals of laughter at the mock majesty and sudden down-fall of the Roman Emperor. Alaric and his armed bands are now in the hands of Heaven for a terrible vindication of the insulted majesty of that God whose sacred name in humanity was at that very hour blasphemed within the walls of Rome. On his march, when passing a narrow defile in the Apennines, a holy hermit threw himself before him to intercede for the doomed city.

"Servant of Heaven," cried Alaric, "seek not to turn me from my mission. It is not from choice I lead my army against that devoted place ; but some invisible power that will not suffer me to halt for a single day urges me on by violence, continually crying out to me without ceasing : ' Forward ! march upon that city—upon Rome, and make it desolate ! ' "

At the hour of midnight, the Salarian gate was silently opened, and the Romans were suddenly awakened by the tremendous sound of the Gothic trumpet. Thus was the mystical Babylon, like its prophetic type, the city of Belshazzar, surprised in the midst of its security. The Romans had such confidence in their lofty rock-built walls, that like the Babylonians when the Persians surrounded their city, they indulged in their accustomed revels, and then retired to their beds without even the slightest shadow of apprehension. Procopius says the senators were fast asleep when the Goths were entering the gates.

"The cruelties exercised on this occasion," says the Italian annalist, "cannot be related without shedding tears. The city, constructed as it were of the spoils, and overflowing with the tribute of so many nations, was now at the mercy of the infuriated barbarians. They were lighted on their way by flaming palaces and temples, from the villa of Sallust—a perfect sanctuary and garden of Epicurus—on to the Suburra, the Forum, the Capitol, and, above all, to the golden house of Nero. They were guided in their pursuit of plunder and blood by the forty thousand fugitives, who laboured, during that night of horrors, with more assiduity than ever they had shown under their taskmasters' stripes, to requite the offices they had received at Roman hands, and to wash out in patrician gore the hateful vestiges of their chains. The unutterable, barbarities which Rome had so often perpetrated during the sieges and massacres and burnings of a thousand years, were now retaliated vigorously on herself. Her nobles were subjected to tortures the most cruel and ignominious, to wring from them their hidden treasures ; the plebeians were mowed down in such multitudes that the survivors did not suffice to bury the dead. The Forum, the Circus, and the Coliseum, the Capitol, the streets, the theatres, the baths and temples, ran with blood. The palace halls and chambers were scenes of the most brutal debauchery, immorality and murder. The seven-hilled city was in flames ; the trophies and monuments in which the lords of the earth most prided themselves were the chief objects of Gothic rage ; and Orosius relates that it was said by eye-witnesses of these terrors, that the trophies, temples, and other public edifices, that defied by their solidity the brands of the barbarians, were struck with thunderbolts from heaven.

But the Almighty, whilst punishing with so terrible a chastisement the obstinate remains of paganism in Rome, caused His mercy to shine forth at the same time with His justice. He preserved the Christians by a miraculous interposition of His providence. He inspired the barbarians with a respect and reverence for the unoffending members of His Church, so that in the midst of all the horrors and confusion of the sack of the city, they were led by the barbarians themselves to places of security. The Coliseum was a witness to this miracle. It happened thus :—

It was proclaimed by the king of the Goths that he warred not against St. Peter. He ordered the churches and places consecrated to Christian purposes to be respected ; appointed the two great Basilicas of the Apostles as inviolable sanctuaries of refuge ; and so strictly was this order observed, that the soldiers not only halted in their career of slaughter on arriving at these hallowed precincts, but many of them conducted thither such as moved them to pity, that, under the protection of the Apostles they might be saved from the rage of those who might not be found equally compassionate. As the bar-

barians were rushing in every direction through the city
in quest of plunder, it happened that a holy virgin, who
had grown old in the divine service to which she had
consecrated her whole life, was discovered in her convent
by a Gothic chief, who demanded all the gold and silver
in her possession. She replied with Christian composure,
that the treasures in her keeping were immense ; but
while the Goth stood in admiration and astonishment,
gazing at the splendid hoard of massive gold and silver
vessels which she revealed, the virgin of Christ observed :
" Before you are the sacred vessels used in the divine
mysteries at the altar of St. Peter the Apostle ; presume
to touch them if you be so minded ; but mark ! the consequences of your sacrilege shall be on your own head ;
as for me, too feeble to defend them, I shall not vainly
attempt resistance."

Struck with reverence and religious awe, and not a
little moved by the holy enthusiasm of the nun, the chief,
without attempting to lay his hand upon the sacred treasure, sent word of what had happened to King Alaric.
An instant and peremptory order was returned to have
all the vessels promptly conveyed to the Basilica of the
Apostle, and to guard and protect the nun and all the
other Christians who should chance to join in the procession. The convent was situated on the Cœlian Hill
(probably near the Lateran), so that the entire city was
to be traversed in order to reach St. Peter's. It was then
that an astounding spectacle presented itself to the eyes
of all. Through the greatest thoroughfares of the city,
and amidst all the horrors of that night, a solemn train is
seen advancing, with the same order and measured step
as if it moved not through scenes of slaughter, violence

and conflagration, but through hallowed aisles on some joyous festival. A martial retinue of the Goths marches as a guard of honour, to adorn the procession with their glittering arms, and to defend their devout companions who bear the sacred vessels of massive gold and silver aloft on their heads. The voices of the barbarians are united with those of the Romans to swell the hymns of Christian praise ; and these sounds are heard like the trumpet of salvation, re-echoing far and wide through the destruction of the city. The Christians start in their hiding-places as they recognise the celestial canticles, and crowd from every direction to follow the vessels of St. Peter. Multitudes of the pagans themselves, joining loudly in the hymn of Christ, take part in the procession, and thus escape under the shadow of the sacred name, that they may live to assail it with greater violence than ever.

We mentioned that the Coliseum was a witness to this wonderful procession. It passed under its very arches, and the mighty womb of its interior echoed for the first time perhaps the Christian song of praise. Some hundreds of frightened and despairing wretches had taken shelter in its long corridors and dark arches ; they knew it was impervious to the fire-brands of the enemy, and no human arm could shake its massive travertine. There were some Christians amongst them ; and no sooner did they hear the well-known tones of the Psalms of David, than they rushed from their hiding-places in wonder, to join the bands of the children of Israel, led by a supernatural interposition from the woes that were increasing around them. Joined by the fugitives from every side, the pageant seemed interminable ; and in proportion as it is lengthened by new accessions, the barbarians vie with each other for the privilege of marching as guards on either side, armed with their battle-axes and naked swords.

Thus it was that Heaven displayed its power to conduct the objects of its solicitude, through the very midst of despair and death, to a harbour of safety. The city was as it were sifted of the Christians that still remained in it, by means of this procession. In the very crisis of ruin they were separated and saved from the common havoc by the intervention of angels. But the most astounding feature of the miracle was the sudden transition of the Goths from fury to mildness. They abandoned the pursuit of plunder, and wielded their reeking weapons to protect the lives and treasures of their vanquished enemies.

CHAPTER XXIV.

THE COLISEUM IN THE MIDDLE AGES.

"ALTHOUGH the dynasty of Romulus and Augustus had closed," says the author of "Rome as she Was and as she Became," "the genius of paganism had not yet expired. Surviving the enormous empire it had so long animated with unearthly vigour, and invested with majesty so terrible, this direful spirit sat brooding yet among the ruins of the seven hills. Its retrospects were not those of repentance, but of desperation ; its antichristian feeling was, if possible, more malignant than in the days when a Nero or a Julian officiated as its pon·tiffs. Its only solace was to lay the odium of all the calamities of the world at the door of Christianity, to mutter curses against it, and to defend with might and main every surviving vestige of superstition."

The spirit of paganism still lingered within the walls of the amphitheatre. It had no longer its martyrs and gladiators, but yet there was many a noble victim to its cruel and bloody sport. The combats of men with beasts were not forbidden by law, and were continued for nearly another hundred years. This species of amusement was sanctioned by Honorius and Theodosius, who both re·gulated the law concerning the hunting of wild beasts, in order that certain countries might be reserves, in which the imperial ministers alone could hunt to procure wild beasts for the games of the Circus and the Coliseum.

No sooner had the Goths passed away, loaded with the spoils of the city, than the Romans, who had escaped the horrors of the siege, and had secreted themselves in the hills of Alba Longa, on the mountains of Tibur, returned to the city.

"It is not to mourn over tombs," says the author just quoted, "or to supplicate around altars, but to hasten to their beloved Circus, that the fugitives pour back like the tide to a strand deformed with wrecks. There they vociferate that all they require are spectacles, and daily rations as of old, to indemnify them for the visits of the Goths. The crowds that had so lately fled before the swords of the barbarians were soon recalled by the hopes of plenty and pleasure. The queen of the seven hills replaced her crown of laurel, and haughtily readjusted it as if it had only been slightly ruffled by the storms of war."

Cassiodorus, who flourished in the first twenty years of the sixth century, as secretary to King Theodoric, tells us, in the fifth book of his Varieties, that these games with the beasts, which he calls detestable, not only existed in his time, but there was a kind of necessity for maintaining them, to gratify the depraved tastes of the people. The days of their greatness are passed, and that indomitable spirit, that was only fanned into irresistible fury by a slight defeat, is crumbled to dust like the trophies of its past victories. The Goths have quietly moved away with their spoils, and no sword is raised to avenge the insult; no veteran bands are rallied under the victorious eagle to chase the barbarians to their mountain homes, or to avenge the ruin they had wrought on the imperial city. There was a time when Rome alone would have annihilated for ever the very name of the barbarian race that should dare to cross the distant frontier of the empire. But that day is gone ; the martial spirit of the people has fled, and the hour of judgment has come ; the greatest glory and skill in arms that is now applauded by this fallen people, is the triumph of the bestiaries in the arena of the Coliseum.

The last reference we find made to these games is in the Chronicle of Senator. He relates that, about the year 519 of Christ, when Cilica Generus was elected consul, he celebrated his nomination by great games in the amphitheatre. He caused an immense quantity of wild beasts to be brought with great expense from Africa, and they were all slain in a few days in that arena, not yet surfeited with the blood of perhaps millions of victims. After this Rome passed through two centuries of misfortune and woe ; the wails of grief and anguish from the starving and dying multitudes were not broken for a moment by the wild shout from the Circus or the Coliseum. Under the repeated sieges of the Goths, and the last terrible devastation under Attila, the city became a ruin around the gigantic amphitheatre, which seemed to raise its indestructible walls higher and more majestically over the ruins of fallen palaces and temples that strewed the plain around it.

At the commencement of the seventh century, when the sunshine of peace in the new dynasty of the papacy commenced to dawn on the ill-fated city, the Coliseum, although abandoned, stood alone, amid a wilderness of desolation, "a noble monument of ruinous perfection."

Rich and luxuriant was the grass that grew in its abandoned arena; the seeds of flowers and weeds that floated on the gentle zephyrs were arrested in their flight by the mountains of masonry, and soon its bleak walls were decorated with a thousand blossoms. The wild winter wind howled through its long dark vomitories with ghostly echoes, and the still more solemn scream of the bird of solitude rang loud and shrill from its eyry amid the crumbling supports of the mighty velarium. Those walls, that so often shook with the thunders of a hundred thousand voices, were shrouded with the silence of death; no human sound broke the dreadful stillness, save the cautious step of some truant schoolboy hiding in its corridors; or the exclamations of delight from some wondering antiquary pausing to admire its marvels of science and art; or, perhaps, the gentle murmur of prayer breathed by the kneeling pilgrim in the blood-stained battlefield of the Church's martyrs. Amongst the pilgrims to this sacred spot were bishops and cardinals, and the great Pope Gregory, in whose hands the clay of the arena turned into blood. Here, too, came in the same century the Patriarch of the western monks, under the cowl he had adopted as the helmet of the spiritual legions who were to fight under the papal king against the powers of darkness. It was one of Benedict's disciples that broke the silence of history in those centuries, when he visited this greatest monument of the past, in his pilgrimage to the eternal city. A stronger or more beautiful panegyric of the great amphitheatre could scarcely be penned, than the sublime prophecy uttered by Venerable Bede towards the end of the seventh century—

> " While stands the Coliseum, Rome shall stand ;
> When falls the Coliseum, Rome shall fall ;
> And when Rome falls, the world."

Some doubt is expressed by modern historians as to the precise time when the immense fabric commenced to crumble to decay.   Many suppose it must have suffered, like most of the great buildings of the city, during the Gothic reign of terror and ruin ; but from the expression of contemporary writers, Marangoni and other antiquaries are of opinion, that it remained in a perfect state up to the end of the eleventh century.   The immensity and massive denseness of its travertine walls seem to have defied all efforts to level it , even in its present ruinous state, whilst only two-thirds of the original structure exist, it would take a thousand men several months to make it even a heap of rubbish.   The Goths, who found easier prey in the minor buildings of the city, left this splendid monument to moulder under the slow but certain ruin of time.   But the political commotions of the latter part of the eleventh century drew around the amphitheatre another terrible wave of devastation and ruin, in which its massive and imperishable walls were shaken and disfigured.   This happened in the Pontificate of St. Gregory VII., about the year of our Lord 1084.

Gregory. who was known in his earlier career as the deacon Hildebrand, was a poor austere monk, raised by Almighty God to the chair of Peter, in order that, by his sanctity and prudence, he might stem the progress of sinful abuses which were creeping into the very sanctuary of the Church. At the time of his election, the whole German Empire groaned under the tyranny and curse of a bad and immoral king. A greater contrast could not be conceived, than the dissolute morals of Henry IV., and the blameless life of the austere monk whom he was permitted to confirm as the successor of St. Peter. The terrible strife between virtue and vice, which characterises the reign of Gregory VII., was foreshadowed in the letter which the newly elected Pope sent to this impious king, to persuade him to prevent his nomination ; " for," said he, " if I be declared Pope, I shall have to punish you for your crimes." His election was confirmed, for Heaven had decreed it. After long endurance, and vainly waiting in the patience of his hope for the conver- sion of Henry, he at length excommunicated him, and deprived him of his throne. The impious German sus- tained the cause of Gilbert the Anti-pope, and marched on Rome. He encamped in the Vatican fields; but a sudden and unexpected attack, by a handful of the Pope's soldiers, completely surprised and disconcerted his army ; a plague broke out amongst his troops, and he was obliged to retreat to the north.

He came a second time, with a larger force, and greater hatred against the successor of St. Peter. He besieged the city once more. He set fire to St. Peter's, but the Roman people, under the immediate presence of Gregory himself, extinguished the flames before they had injured the Basilica. At length, after a siege of two years, by bribery, the Lateran gate was opened to the German, and Gregory took refuge in the Castle of St. Angelo. For a month they surrounded the colossal tomb of Adrian, and tried in vain to seize the Pope, or even to pass the bridge, to take possession of St. Peter's. Relief came to the imprisoned Pontiff, in the person of Robert de Guiscard, a Norman captain, but a feudal chief, of the Papal dominions. He was a hard, unfeeling conqueror, whose cruelties had already been condemned by the very Pontiff he came to save. Henry fled at his approach ; but his partisans and a great number of the Roman people dared to resist Guiscard ; but they paid dearly for it. The haughty conqueror did not hesitate a moment ; he burnt the city, and cut his way with the sword till he reached the Castle of St. Angelo, and freed its papal prisoner.

On this occasion, it was the friends of order, and not its enemies, that endeavoured to sweep from the face of the earth every vestige that still remained of pagan Rome. The whole city, from St. John's Lateran up to the Capitol, was laid in ruins. Some of the most remarkable monuments of antiquity, which had escaped to a great extent the fury of the Goths, and which still were the pride and glory of the city, fell under the iron hand of the enraged Guiscard. When he had gained the Capitol, over a field of smoking ruins, the people saw his desperate resolution to destroy the city. They gave up the Pope ; Guiscard took him away to a quiet retreat in Salerno, where the great and holy Gregory sank under his many trials.

It would be difficult to say how much of the Coliseum was ruined on this occasion. Marangoni, whom we believe to be the most critical in his research, says : " Not only all that could be destroyed by fire within its rockbuilt walls, but its beautiful and artistic porticoes were

ruined in the unsparing revenge of this friendly **Goth.**
The seats in the interior were nearly all marble, but **still**
there were wooden benches in the upper tiers, besides
supports and ornaments, scattered through the immense
fabric.   That portion which looks towards the Cœlian
hill, and the arch of Constantine bore in a particular
manner the brunt of this storm, and it was from the fallen
masses that lay here in crumbling heaps, that the material
of several of the palaces of modern Rome was afterwards
taken, as from an immense quarry of brick and travertine.   Many of the Popes and Cardinals have been
accused, by superficial writers, of being the first spoilers **of**
this beautiful edifice ; indignant antiquaries despise **the**
names of Paul the Second and the Cardinals Riario **and**
Farnese, as having ruthlessly plundered this majestic
monument of the past, to raise palaces of luxuriant splendour amid the despicable and irregular homes of **the**
mediæval city.   The truth is, that these men, who **were**
animated by laudable motives to enrich and embellish
the city, were only guilty of removing indiscriminate
heaps of rubbish which lay for centuries around the **old**
walls of the amphitheatre, as the sad traces of the **re-**
venge of Guiscard."   But more of this question **further**
on.

Soon after the demise of Gregory VII., the Coliseum
was turned into a fortress.   The political disturbances
and parricidal rebellions of the children of the Church
had reached the summit of their fury, and it is not at **all**
improbable, that some of the immediate successors **of**
Gregory took refuge from the fury of the storm within
the walls of the Coliseum.   The Pontiffs who reigned in
those troubled times had to encounter greater perils than

their predecessors, when they celebrated the holy mysteries in the dark caves of the earth. Rival factions had divided the city between them ; the tombs and theatres of the old Empire became the castles and fortresses of the new aspirants to power. The Orsini had taken possession of the Castle of St. Angelo ; the Colonnas were masters of the Mausoleum of Augustus ; and the Frangepani, the most powerful of all, fortified the Coliseum. Surely the untravelled reader will wonder how the tombs of the dead became strongholds of war. Do we really mean that the mouldering monuments of the forgotten dead are filled with thousands of armed men, and become impregnable fortresses ?

Such was the stupendous magnificence of the mausoleums of Imperial Rome, that even now, after the storms and wars of two thousand years, their mighty ruins are still the pride of the city. The imperishable walls of the tomb of Adrian form to-day the only castle and fortress in the possession of the legitimate successor to the throne of the Cæsars, Pius IX.

Muratori relates that, when Innocent II. ascended the throne, he took refuge under the protection of the Frangepani family in their palace and fortress of the Coliseum, being forced from the Lateran palace by the Anti-pope Gilbert, the same who raised his impious arm against the sainted Gregory VII. (" Ad tutas domos Frangepanumde Laterano descendit, et apud Sanctam Mariam novam et Cartularium atque Coliseum," &c.) In the history of Fr. Tolomeo, Bishop of Torcello, a contemporary, we find the same corroborated in these words : " Se recollegit in domibus Frangepanensium quæ erant infra Coliseum ; quia dicta munitio fuit tota eorum " (He secured himself in

the abodes of the Frangepani, which were within the Coliseum, for that fortress was entirely theirs). Passing
over uninteresting details of the amphitheatre as a fortress,
changing proprietors according to the fortunes of war, we
will bring our readers to a strange scene that happened
within its walls in the year 1332.

Nearly six centuries have passed since the Coliseum
rang with the deafening shout of a fascinated crowd of
spectators. Many and strange the vicissitudes it has
passed through since its last bloody entertainment.
Through every century from its foundation, its history
was entwined with the sorrows of the Roman people.
Although it no longer echoed the plaintive sigh of the
dying gladiator, yet many a wail of grief broke the solitude of its deserted seats. Its walls were smoked by
fire, were shaken and destroyed in some places by the
lightning of heaven, and disfigured in others by the im-
plements of war. The wreck and ruin of every element
of destruction that humbles man in the proudest of his
works, had shorn the mighty amphitheatre of its magnificent details, leaving its rocky skeleton as a monument
of genius and art, triumphant over savage and brutal
force. Its reminiscences are gathering deeper interest
as centuries roll on, and the ever-changing vicissitudes of
time give its history a varied page. Strange and interesting is the scene that is now before us. Its dilapidated
tiers are once more filled with thousands of people, the
arena is again tinged with blood, and the deafening
chorus of an excited crowd is echoed through the ruins of
the fallen city. It would seem that the spirits of the old
Romans were permitted to leave the gloomy realms of
Pluto, to revel for an hour in the great theatre that was

for many centuries the scene of their pleasure and their infamy. This extraordinary reunion in the Coliseum took place under the following circumstances :—

During the abodes of the Popes at Avignon in the year 1305, Clement V., endeavouring to quell the internal dissensions that robbed Rome of its peace, sent three Cardinal Legates into Italy, and gave them power to act in his name for the peace of the people. It was during this administration that the Coliseum was transferred to the Senate. Muratori, who mentions the circumstance, does not give the date of this transfer, but merely intimates that it was during the years 1328 and 1340. Just at this period a profound peace reigned in the city. The impious King Luis of Baniera had retreated to the north, and his Anti-pope, Nicholas II., was booted and even stoned out of the city by the repentant Romans. A few years of sunshine and calm, so unusual in those centuries of political storms, gave the people an opportunity of indulging in some of the pastimes of peace. The senators wished to show their joy and gratitude for the munificent gift of the Coliseum, and determined to open the amphitheatre once more with some great spectacle for the people. A grand bull-fight—a species of cruel amusement which had become very popular in the southern countries of Europe at this time—was proposed to commemorate this great event.

All the nobles of Italy were invited to take part in this entertainment, and for weeks and months previous preparations were made for the reunion. The Coliseum became the workshop of a thousand artisans ; the sound of the mallet and the hammer has taken the place of the clanging of arms and trumpets, and the ribald songs of soldiers.   Temporary benches were erected on the massive framework of brick and travertine, and the débris that had choked the passages and disfigured the arena were completely removed.   All the preparations being finished, the day for the great entertainment was fixed for the 3rd of September, 1332.

It was indeed a strange sight to see the Romans hastening enthusiastically to the long-forgotten pagan amusements of their city.   All business was suspended, and thousands of gay sight-seers poured in from the neighbouring towns and villages.   Early after daybreak the crowd commenced to gather round the old amphitheatre.   The noble ladies of the city came in three parties—all in full dress, and led by three beautiful and wealthy princes, unanimously elected by the different groups.   We can agreeably fancy ourselves standing in the old arena, and see the ever-increasing tide of gay colours and gayer faces pouring into the benches.   We have often stood in imagination in the same spot, whilst recording in these pages the scenes of the first centuries.   Now we miss, indeed, the strong giant frame of the ancient Romans, and the dazzling gold and jewelled dais of the Emperor's seat; there is no gorgeous velarium to stay the rays of the scorching sun, and disperse them in soft mellow tints; the podium is no longer glittering with the wealth of the Empire; the senators are few, and the graceful toga has disappeared; no vestal virgins or lying augurs lend contrast to the colours by the peculiarities of their dress, and impart a religious solemnity by their presence to the amusements of impiety.   The banners of the noble families float over the arena, and represent the ruling powers of the fallen Empire, for in these days every nobleman was a king in his own fortress. Yet the people are peaceable and orderly, the ear is not offended by horrible blasphemies against the true God, no obscenities and shameful immoralities beguile the time of the waiting crowd ; the demon of paganism no longer sat on the imperial throne. This was the first, but will not be the last, Christian gathering within the walls of the Coliseum.

Those who were to engage in the combat against the bulls were all, without exception, the sons of noblemen. We find amongst them names of families still flourishing amongst the aristocracy of Italy. The young men were dressed in the richest colours, and each bore a motto on his forehead ; this was generally some short sentence expressing virtue and courage, and culled from remarkable events in the past history of the city. We will give from Muratori a few of the most interesting and beautiful. They were called out by lot, and the first to appear in the arena, amid the deafening greetings of the crowd, was Galeotto Malatesta, of Rimini. He was dressed entirely in green, carried in his hand a naked sword of ancient shape, and on a cap of iron he had these words " I alone am like Horace ! " Then came Cicco della Valle, dressed half black, and half white, and from a scimitar-like sword there hung a purple ribbon with these words in gold " I am Eneas for Lavinia ! " Mezzo Astalli was clothed entirely in black, because he was in mourning for his wife, and his motto was " Thus disconsolate do I live ! " Young Cafferello was dressed in a lion's skin, and had for motto " Who is stronger than I ? "

The son of Messer Lodovico della Palenta, from Ravenna, clothed in red and gold, bore on his forehead " If I die covered with blood, sweet death ! " Savello di

Anagni, all yellow, with motto "Let every one beware of the folly of love." Cecco Conti had a beautiful dress of the colour of silver, and these words "Thus is faith white." Pietro Cappocci, dressed in the colour of the carnation flower, had these words round his neck "I am the slave of the Roman Lucretia;" meaning that he was the slave of chastity, personified in the chaste Lucretia of ancient Rome.

There were three of the Colonna family, who were the most powerful in Rome at this time, being in possession of the Capitol; they were dressed in white and green, and their mottoes were tinged with pride on account of their power. The eldest had "If I fall, ye who look on me will also fall," intimating that they were the honour and support of the city; the second had "So much the greater so much the stronger;" and the third "Sorrowful but powerful."

Thus about fifty noblemen, young, healthy, and beautiful, bounded into the arena, all exquisitely dressed; the sun sparkled from burnished swords and jewelled buckles, the colours of the rainbow mingled together in every variety of contrast, giving brilliancy to the scene. But this amusement had a tragic end, perfectly in keeping with the blood-stained history of the Coliseum. Many of the young men dressed so gaily are but a few moments from a terrible death and eternity; before the sun set on that day of cruel sport, many a wail of sorrow rent the warm air. The scene reminds us of a pleasure party caught in the rapids of Niagara. Amidst dancing and music and the blinding joys of intemperance, they recklessly turn the boat's head to the rapids, hoping to rescue themselves before the terrible fall, but too late; the oars are power-

less ; the helm disobeys ; one moment, and they are whirl-
ing over the seething mass and hurled into the abyss. In
the wild folly of youthful vanity those noble young men
built castles of valour, and easy conquests over the infuriated bulls ; they relied too much on their agility, the
sharpness of their swords, and the strength of their arms.
During the day's amusement, eighteen of the flower of
the Italian nobility were slain and nine wounded.

As may be imagined, bull-fighting met with no further
encouragement in the eternal city. For a few hours of
brutal amusement, noble houses were deprived of their
support, and heirs and families were cast into mourning
and gloom ; that day became a sad anniversary in the
calendar of many a mother, wife or betrothed one. The
games were to last several days, but the fatal consequences
of the first sufficiently cooled the public ardour ; instead of pouring again delighted crowds to the Coliseum,
as the old Romans were wont to do, they went in mourning and sorrow to the Church of St. John Lateran, to
assist at the obsequies of the fallen young men. Their
mangled bodies were laid in the same tomb in the nave
of the Basilica, where they have been now sleeping for five
centuries, uncared for and unknown ; pilgrims from every
land under the sun tread thoughtlessly on the mosaic
pavement that covers their forgotten tomb ; they wake
not for the loud peals of the organ and choir that ring
through the majestic aisles of this maternal Basilica ; they
await the music of the trumpets of the last day.

CHAPTER XXV.

OTHER REMARKABLE EVENTS.

TWO centuries of silence have rolled over the Coli seum since the fatal events narrated in the last chapter. Sixteen hundred years had now left the traces of their passage on its crumbling walls. It was, however, comparatively perfect when man came to the assistance of time to destroy the noble ruin. For half a century, all the power of the lever, the crane, and the buffalo, were employed to drag its immense boulders of travertine from their rocky bed. We have said silence hung over the mighty ruin, but we mean the silence of history, and the absence of countless crowds yelling with frantic joy; yet there was the clear-ringing sound of the stone-cutter's hammer; there was the creaking of the ponderous cranes, lifting huge masses of stone, and the well-known cry of the buffalo-driver calling his beasts by name, and forcing them by the steel goad to drag away the rifled marble travertine of the last and greatest monument of ancient Rome. Not only the masses which were loosened and had fallen to decay, but an immense quantity of the intact building was quarried away to embellish the city, that has arisen on the very *débris* of the mighty Rome of the past.

Some historians have endeavoured to brand the authors of this spoliation with the guilt of sacrilege; and Gibbon, speaking of the Coliseum, says : " Of whose ruin, the nephews of Paul III. have been the guilty agents, and every traveller who views the Farnese Palace, may curse the sacrilege and luxury of these upstart princes." Perhaps if those who helped to ruin the Coliseum had not been princes of the Church, the criticism might have been less severe. It must also be remembered that the Farnese Palace was erected from the designs of Sangallo, under the immediate direction of Michael Angelo, and is uni versally admitted to be one of the finest palaces in Rome, perhaps in the world. Whilst its magnificence and artistic perfection give rise to expressions of wonder and delight, enough of the Coliseum remains to tell its own tale of splendour and immensity. Not only the Farnese, but the Cancelleria, St. Mark's, and the fronts of several churches in the city, were supplied with material from the amphitheatre ; and the gigantic proportions of this splendid ruin may be gathered from the fact, that modern Rome owes the magnificence and solidity of its architecture to that spoliation, which is scarcely missed from the immense pile itself. The material remaining after the plunder of the amphitheatre, has been estimated at a value of five millions of crowns (£1,000,000).

It is certain, however, that all antiquaries, and the lovers of ancient architecture in particular, must condemn the ruthless plunder and spoliation which left the majestic ruin in its present state. Whatever excuse may be allowed for the Pauls and their nephews (as Gibbon sarcastically calls them), for the removal of even the loose and separated materials, nothing can be urged in justification of their immediate successors, who quarried the travertine from the intact building itself. It is uncer· tain at what precise period the Roman Government put a stop to this demolition ; most probably the ruin was taken under the paternal protection of the Popes, during the reign of the sainted Pius V., in 1565 ; certainly, from this time, it was held in the highest veneration by both government and people, and although in after times it served the public weal as a hospital or a manufactory, it was no longer plundered by luxurious princes.

Under Sixtus V. (A.D. 1585), the Coliseum underwent another change. No city was ever more indebted to its sovereign than was Rome to this great Pope. Whilst churches and convents and bridges sprang up on every side, the crumbling ruins of the ancient city were sup- ported and protected by walls of modern masonry. The prostrate obelisks were raised on suitable pedestals in the public squares, and works of art were dug from the earth to ornament and increase the attraction of the museums, which, under his care, were becoming the richest in the world. This energetic Pontiff conceived the idea, that every ruin of the ancient city should be an ornament or a service to Christian Rome. The Coliseum was a favourite monument ; it received a double share of atten· tion. For some time he thought how it could be made to serve his poor people, preserving it, at the same time, even in its ruinous state, as a noble memento of the past. He at length conceived the idea of converting it into a woollen manufactory, in order to give employment and a home to the poor. The fertile genius of Fontana soon designed this castle of papal munificence ; thousands of poor artisans were employed ; some portions of the ruin verging towards the arena were removed as impeding the plan ; workshops and comfortable apartments were to rise, magic-like, over the podium of the old amphitheatre, and the dried-up aqueducts were repaired and cleaned out to bring fresh springs from the Campagna, to supply the fountains that were to play in the arena. The sum of twenty-five thousand crowns (£5000) had already been spent on the works, when death took away the enterprising Pontiff. The stupendous scheme sank with him to the grave ; the works were abandoned, and a few brick walls remained to tell of the enterprise and philanthropy of Sixtus V. The celebrated Mabillon has said : "Vixisset Sixtus V. et Amphitheatrum, stupendum illud opus integratum nunc haberemus" (Had Sixtus V. lived, we should now have the amphitheatre, that stupendous work, entire).

Clement XI. (in 1700) finding it had become a place of refuge for thieves and assassins, closed up the entrances to the lower arches, and established in the interior a saltpetre manufactory. This, which also failed like the works of Sixtus, was the last attempt to secularise the ruins of the Coliseum.

Whilst the vicissitudes of spoliation in one reign, and of preservation in another, were passing over the great building that had survived both friends and foes, there was always a deep feeling of respect and veneration, in the heart of the people, for the spot which had been sanctified by the blood of so many martyrs. Through every century there were holy souls who loved to pass hours in prayer in its consecrated arena. And long before it was entirely handed over to the service of the cross, it had witnessed some of the most solemn and sacred func-

tions of the Church. Although we have no positive docu
ments to prove the fact, we have no doubt that for many
years during the middle ages, the holy sacrifice was
celebrated in its safe and commodious arches. After the
devastation of the Goths, and the centuries of internal
wars that rolled over the ill-fated city, the churches had
fallen to decay, and many of them were dangerous and
unsafe for use. Is it to be wondered at, under these
circumstances, that the Coliseum should be used as a vast
temple in which the clean oblation of the altar should be
offered to the Most High? Many smaller churches
sprang up around it. Cencius Camerarius mentions a
few which have long since disappeared. There was the
'*Holy Saviour of the Roto of the Coliseum,*" the "Holy
Saviour *De Insula et Coliseo,*" and the "*Forty Martyrs of
the Coliseum.*"*

There is a vague tradition of an ancient monastery
having been perched in the corridors of the second tier.
Some poor religious sisters had fled to the solitude of its
desolate arches, like doves who build their nests in the
abandoned eyry of vultures. The sweet and measured
music of their sacred canticles echoed harmoniously
through the mighty ruin, and formed a strange contrast
with the fiendish shouts of other days.

Here also took place a species of sacred performance
very popular with our ancestors. These were the mystery
plays of the middle ages ; and the life-like representation
of the Passion on Good Friday was particularly remarkable. On a large and open stage, stretched towards the
Cœlian Hill, the whole scene of the Passion and death of

---

* I have not found the Acts of these martyrs.—AUTHOR.

our blessed Lord was represented; every person mentioned
in the Sacred Scripture was faithfully portrayed. Thousands poured in to see these representations ; they continued with the permission and sanction of the spiritual
authorities of the city until the reign of Paul III. Truly
the representation of the sufferings of Christ never had a
more suitable theatre than this Calvary of His disciples.

Bacci, in his Life of St. Philip Neri, relates of this great
father that he had from his childhood a great devotion to
the martyrs. Hence he passed whole nights in prayer in
the Catacombs of St. Sebastian. He often repaired to
the Coliseum, to honour the martyrs who suffered in its
arena. On one occasion, when wrapt in prayer in the
arena, the demon appeared to him in an immodest shape,
and endeavoured to distract and tempt him ; but the
saint had recourse to God, and the evil spirit was obliged
to leave him to finish his devotions in peace.

An extraordinary circumstance is related of one of the
disciples of St. Ignatius in the life of that father, by
Maffei (Book iii., chap. ix.). Almighty God was pleased
to try the infant institution just founded by St. Ignatius ;
this, however, was the surest sign of His favour and
benediction. It happened that the house of the professed fathers was reduced to such distress that they had
barely the necessaries of life. John Cruccio, who was a
colleague of the saint and procurator of the house, was
a humble soul of exalted virtue, and with the permission
of the venerable founder, he went to St. John's Lateran
to pray to Almighty God for relief for the Order. On
returning home he passed through the Coliseum. He
was met in the arena by a stranger, who handed him a
purse with a hundred crowns (£20), and immediately

disappeared.   The astonished procurator hastened to
tell St. Ignatius of the unexpected gift ; the saint did not
seem the least surprised, but, kneeling down, thanked
God who had deigned to hear their prayers.   It is said
of this same St. Ignatius that he had great devotion to
the martyrs of the Coliseum.

In the life of St. Camillus de Lellis, a contemporary
of St. Philip Neri, and founder of the Order of Regular
Clerics for ministering to the Sick, we find another
extraordinary favour granted at the Coliseum.   When
Camillus was a young man studying for the priesthood,
he went one morning with a number of other youths to
the Church of St. John Lateran to receive the tonsure
from the hands of the Cardinal Vicar.   It was found,
however, there was some mistake in his dimissorial
letters, as he belonged to the diocese of Chieti ; he was,
consequently, with much shame and disappointment
separated from his companions.   The holy youth bore
the cross nobly, and cheerfully accepted the mortification
as coming from the hand of God to try his patience.
His submission did not pass without its reward.   On
his way home, when he came to the Coliseum, something
told him he would get over his difficulty in a few hours.
At the same moment he met Father Francis Profeta, his
companion and friend, who told him not to be in the
least disappointed at what had happened, for all would
be right before sunset.   This was an inspiration given
him by God in behalf of the holy youth.   On reaching
the hospital of St. James of the Incurables, where he
lived, he found a priest from his own diocese waiting for
him.   The good father was much afflicted at the disappointment of Camillus, and immediately went with

another priest to the notary of the Cardinal, and testified on oath to the authenticity of the exeat of Camillus. He was sent for at once, and admitted into the ecclesiastical state, which filled him with a joy he had never felt before.

In the year 1703, the Coliseum suffered severely from an earthquake. This event is memorable in the annals of the city, as well as in the history of the amphitheatre. Two or three heavy shocks had already been felt during the latter part of the month of January, and the people were in consternation. On the 2nd of February, Clement XI. held a papal chapel in the Sixtine, in honour of the purification of the Blessed Virgin Mary. At the end of the mass, two very heavy shocks of earthquake were again felt; they were much severer than any of the former. All the prelates in the Sixtine were terrified ; the roof cracked as if about to fall on the Pope and Cardinals ; the holy father knelt down, and every one present joined in a silent and trembling prayer for the preservation of the city. The bell tower of St. Augustine's and the obelisk in the piazza Navona were seen to lean forward as if about to fall, and many old houses in the neighbourhood fell to the ground. When the rumbling noise had ceased, and the vibration, which seemed to be the effect of the shock, had died away, the Pope with all the Cardinals repaired to the tomb of the Apostles, to thank God for their delivery. On the Scala Regia he was met by one of the Penitentiaries of the Basilica, who endeavoured to dissuade him from going into the church, for they had seen the mighty dome itself rocking to and fro, and threatening every moment to come down in a mass on their heads. Nevertheless, the courageous Pontiff entered the Basilica, and remained more than an hour in prayer at the tomb of St. Peter.

On the following morning (Feb. 3), about three o'clock, the last and most terrible shock was felt. A sound like thunder rolled through the city; three arches of the Coliseum fell to the ground; every house was seriously shaken, and many people were flung forward on the earth through the vehemence of the shock.

In the midst of the confusion, some wicked men circulated the report, that it was revealed to the Pope that the city was to be destroyed, and that the people should leave it at once. Their object was robbery and plunder. The report gained ground, and a terrible scene ensued. Men and women and children rushed in crowds to the gates, carrying what valuables they could in their arms; mothers, with tender infants at the breast, and feeble old men on the shoulders of stalwart youths, and boys and girls half dressed, ran after their terrified parents, seeking refuge in the fields outside the city. Exclamations of terror and fright were heard on every side, as if the day of judgment had come. Whilst the poor people were trembling in the open Campagna, during the whole of that cold February night, expecting every moment to see their homes in flames or swallowed up in the earth, thieves were pillaging their houses, and making away with every valuable they could lay hold of. In the morning, the Pope sent his guards through every place of refuge, and ordered the people to return, for the report was false, and he assured them there was no longer any fear for the safety of the city.

When calm was restored, the holy Pope celebrated a mass of thanksgiving in the Church of Santa Maria in

Trastevere, and walked bareheaded in a procession to the Basilica of St. Peter. He then proclaimed that, for a hundred years, the vigil of the Feast of the Purification should be kept a strict fast. This fast was renewed in 1803, by Pius VII., and is still kept with devotion in Rome, in memory of this great event.

About eleven years after the event we have recorded, the Coliseum was rapidly becoming the resort of thieves and vagabonds, who concealed themselves by night under the dark and sombre passages of its arches. The venerable Angelo Paulo, of the Carmelite Order, had just erected a hospital in the adjoining street of St. Clement, and was a frequent eye-witness to the profanation of the venerable ruin. Fired with a holy zeal for the honour of the martyrs, he procured the authorisation of Clement XI., in 1714, and by public subscription, in which the Roman people liberally joined, he removed the débris of the fallen arches, closed up the open passages, and even secured the principal entrances by wooden gates, which were locked at night to prevent the free access of animals and evil-designing men. No traces of these gates remain at present.

Our next notice of the amphitheatre is in the reign of the great Pope Benedict XIV., A.D. 1740.

A few years sufficed to sweep away the barriers that impeded for a while the destruction of the ruin. The venerable Angelo Paulo had gone to his reward, and the Coliseum became worse than ever—the home of infamy and vice. The evil went on increasing, but silently and unknown to the authorities. At length, crime became its own informer—a terrible tragedy revealed the *after-dark* scenes of the Coliseum.

A holy man, named Francis Parigino, wishing to lead a solitary life, repaired to the silent corridors of the amphitheatre, assuming with the permission of the authorities, the guardianship of the little chapel that was dedicated to our Mother of Sorrows on the second tier. He had not been long in his retreat when, in the dead of the night, his solitude was broken by the sound of human voices in the arches beneath. The noise increased, and he heard every word that was uttered. His horror may be imagined when he heard a hoarse, rough voice distinctly say : "I'll murder you if you don't do as I tell you." Then the scream of a female rung loud and shrill through the silent ruin. Recommending himself to God, he rushed bravely to give assistance to stay the hand of a murderer. But when he reached the spot whence the sound proceeded, all was as still as death ; and with his heart beating hard in his breast, he groped his way through the dark and sombre arches. It was in the depth of winter, and not even a straggling moonbeam broke through the darkness. He paused to catch even the sound of the breathing of a human being, but the wind was strong, and sighed mournfully through the haunted ruin. At length, trembling and terrified, he heard a noise near him. Before he had time to speak or stir, a strong rough hand seized him by the throat, and the blow of a knife brought him to the ground.

When morning dawned, the poor hermit came to his senses. He found himself lying in a pool of blood which flowed from seven wounds of a stiletto. The first had taken away consciousness, and he had not felt the **pain** of the others. His first act was to raise his heart towards heaven to thank God that he was so far preserved. There was no friendly hand near to help him to his little chapel, for he wished to offer his wounds to his dear mother whose image he venerated so much. After much struggling and pain, falling several times through weakness, he reached his beloved capella. He poured forth all his soul in prayer ; he asked but for grace to do the will of God. Whilst kneeling as well as he could before the altar of the Madonna, he suddenly felt a change come over him ; the pain left his wounds ; he thought some delicious ointment was poured on them ; he was cured. For hours his tears of joy, surprise, and gratitude fell on the tiled floor of the little church. With a heart bursting with that interior joy and peace that surpasseth all understanding, he could only exclaim : "O, my good mother! my good mother ! "

It is the property of Almighty God to draw good from evil. The rumour of the attempted murder and the miraculous cure spread abroad, and numbers came through devotion or curiosity to see the hermit and his Madonna. One day Benedict XIV. came to the Coliseum to venerate its martyrs, for whom he had a great devotion. He sent for the poor hermit, and heard from his own lips all that had happened. The zealous Pontiff was inspired with a holy zeal to save the venerable pile from further profanation. He ordered the governor of the ity to issue an edict, threatening the galleys and exile to persons found loitering about these hiding-places after nightfall. Great repairs were undertaken at his own expense ; the chapel was renewed ; the Stations of the Cross already erected were reconstructed on a larger and grander scale, and an impulse was given to the devotion and reverence towards this remarkable ruin that has not

died away to this day. It was on this occasion that the
confraternity of *The Lovers of Jesus and Mary on Calvary*
was instituted. They go in procession from their little
church in the Forum to the Coliseum every Friday afternoon ; a sermon is preached by a Franciscan monk on
the Passion, and then in wet, or heat, or cold, the pious
members go through the beautiful devotions of the Way
of the Cross. The great St. Leonard of Port Maurice
was the preacher who opened these devotions ; and the
fire of his eloquence and love seems to animate the humble monks who follow in his footsteps, for there is scarcely
any devotion so sincere, or so loved by the Roman people,
as the Stations of the Cross in the Coliseum on Friday
evenings. Pious souls gather from every portion of the
city to join them ; and their recollection and piety, their
penance in the sackcloth of the confraternities, and kneel
ing bareheaded on the sandy arena, strike with reverence
and awe the giddy strangers who have come to scoff and
ridicule. Their thoughts are suddenly taken from scenes
of gladiators, and shouts against the Christians and the
cross, to see that cross borne in triumph on the same spot
by the Christians themselves. Could any return more
pleasing be given to our blessed Lord, for the insults He
received in the Coliseum, than the humble devotion of
those pious souls around His saving cross ? Alas ! such
is not the case now. The Goths from Piedmont have
entered by the Salarian gate and they wage war against
the Pope, the feelings of the people, and the cross of
our blessed Lord. The Coliseum will bear for centuries
to come the traces of the desecration it suffered in the
nineteenth century, from the government of Victor
Emanuel. The cross has been pulled down from the

arena—the stations levelled to the ground, and the soil uselessly and maliciously disturbed. The spoilers are aware that the ground-work of the interior was opened in the commencement of the eighteenth century by Fea, and others, and had to be filled in again from the noxious effects of its stagnant waters. This interference with this hallowed ruin marked at its time the reign of French desecration—the downfall of its dynasty, and the shameful exile of its ruler. We know not what the future may bring, but in the ever recurring cycle of human vicissitudes the unmeaning profanation of this venerable ruin may mark, in the history of ages to come, the short-lived reign of Piedmontese usurpation. About the year 1775, another remarkable hermit took possession of the little chapel on the second story. He was a Frenchman, who gave up all worldly possessions to follow our blessed Lord in evangelical poverty. This holy man spent many sleepless nights in prayer in the Coliseum. Often the Divine Spirit flooded his soul with joys unknown to the sleeping world around ; to him there was neither darkness nor silence in the lonely ruin ; the splendour of the angels who kept him company was more brilliant than the dazzling brightness of the meridian sun ; the music of the heavenly choirs, so often heard by him in his ecstasies, floated in celestial harmony through the cold bleak arches of this abandoned monument of the past which served him for a home. When this poor hermit of the Coliseum had breathed his pure soul into the hands of God, a thousand voices proclaimed through the city that a saint was dead. Public opinion had him immediately enrolled on the calendar of sanctity, and miracles without number proved that this judgment was

ratified in heaven. A few years later he was proclaimed
" Blessed " by the infallible voice of the Holy See ; and
one of the last, though not the least, remarkable names
that swell the lengthy catalogue of Rome's spiritual heroes
was Benedict Joseph Labre, the hermit of the Coliseum.

The first half of the nineteenth century, so stormy and
eventful in the nations around, rolled a silent wave over
the Coliseum. With the exception of timely repairs
instituted by the four last Popes, and the ever-increasing
devotion and reverence of the people, we have nothing
to record. The immense buttresses erected by Pius VII.,
on the side facing St. John's Lateran, form a splendid
specimen of modern masonry. In the last arches of th
outer wall in this quarter, there is a peculiar phenomenon
of art, worthy the attention of the stranger. The key
stone of one of the arches has fallen completely into the
supporting brick wall of modern work. All around, the
mighty travertine blocks are rent with gaping fissures ;
the whole ruin seems ready to totter and fall to a thousand pieces at the first gust of wind ; yet this is the safest
portion of the ruin.

The immortal Pius IX., in the midst of all his troubles,
has not forgotten the venerable ruin that bears, through
so many centuries, the marks of paternal care from the
Holy See. Under the able superintendence of Canina,
many of the interior arches which threatened to fall have
been secured, and seem to defy the ravages of time for
centuries yet to come.

In the dark hour of trouble that passed over Rome in
1848, the Coliseum had its share of the profanation and
impiety that drove the Pope from his throne. An apostate priest usurped the pulpit of the Franciscan Friars ;

instead of a moving address on the love and sorrows of the Crucified, a fanatical mob was regaled by a tissue of blasphemies against everything sacred in time and eternity. Led on by the fallen Gavazzi, the ungrateful Roman populace made the old Coliseum ring with that dreadful shout that so often shook its foundations when filled by their pagan ancestors, " Down with the Pope "— "Death to all tyrants." These, and similar expressions used on this occasion, were but another form of those blasphemies which so much delighted the evil spirits in the first centuries ; they had the same object in view, the ruin of souls and the annihilation of Christianity ! But that power which is centred in Pius IX., and triumphed of old in a thousand battles with the powers of darkness, in the very same arena of the Coliseum, laughed at its enemies in their folly ; yea, laughed at them, too, in their terrible transit to eternal doom !

CHAPTER XXVI.

THE CONCLUSION.

IT is with regret we find ourselves at the last chapter of this little book. We feel as if we were about to part with an old friend. The occasional hours we have spent over the records of this great ruin, the history of which we have but sketched in these pages, will in after years afford the most cheerful reminiscences, and matter for the deepest meditation. A few weeks more, and thousands of miles will separate us ; the briny ocean will roll its unceasing tide between us and that great monument, in whose arena we have stood in rapture and delight, but memory will often again bring us back in spirit to these old walls. For some there is poetry, eloquence and philosophy in the ivy-clad ruins of the past ; although nothing more may be known of them, than that they are the crumbling walls of a castle, an abbey, or a church, still they have their attraction ; fancy flings around them all the charms of art, and clothes them with the beauty of romance. The active mind sums up tales of human vicissitudes ; battles, and murders, and deeds of daring and crime, are flung around them ; and thus, creative fancy invests with poetical magnificence the humblest monument of the past. But the old amphitheatre is a ruin that needs not the aid of fancy to increase it in size or importance. Its immensity and magnificence, as it stands even now, after the shock and destruction of centuries, form a picture grander and more perfect than any castle ever built by imagination on the clouds around the setting sun. No fancy, no poetry could invent a more marvellous history. The greatest wonders found in the records of the past; scenes of love, of bravery, of crime and cruelty, form a romance of terrible reality, that shrouds the Coliseum with an interest and a veneration that no other ruin in the world can command.

Roman in its origin, Oriental in its size, Grecian in its architecture, Jewish in the labourers who built it, cosmopolitan in its spectacles of men and beasts from every clime, and Christian in the blood that sanctified it during three centuries, it was the theatre of the most bloody and cruel pleasures, and the temple of the most heroic virtue. In the lapse of ages, it adapted itself to the exigencies of each era. At one time a fortress, now a convent, then a hospital; an arena and circus for a bull-fight and a tournament; a quarry supplying material for the most sumptuous edifices; a manufactory; a robbers' den; and in the end, a sanctuary and a shrine to which pilgrims resort from the furthest ends of the earth. Thus, in a few words, we sum up its extraordinary and interesting history. After centuries of infamy and cruelty, it is now the hallowed temple wherein is preached the law of self-denial and expiation. The regeneration of Rome is beautifully portrayed in the destinies of its greatest pagan monuments. The pantheon, once the centre of all the aberrations of idolatry, is now the temple of all the Christian virtues. The temple of Jupiter

on the Capitol, the culminating point of Rome's dominion over the world, is now replaced by the Church of
Ara Cœli—the church of the Crib—the abasement of the
Man-God—the contempt of all the grandeurs of the world.
The palace of the Cæsars, which was the emporium of all
the riches of the world, is reduced to a few ivy-clad walls,
which protect a convent of voluntary poverty, raised
amid the very débris of the Golden House ; and the
Coliseum, the theatre of the furies and the passions, becomes a monument sheltered under the wings of religion,
and dedicated to the cross, to the self-denial and humiliation taught us in the Dolorous Way of Calvary.

It remains now that we see the Coliseum by moonlight.
The effect is truly charming. The French have beautifully called the moon the sun of ruins. Her rich mellow
rays give all old walls a fantastic existence ; but there is
no monument of antiquity in which the effects of reflected
light are so beautiful as in this ruin. The Romans pre-
fer the time in which the moon is rising between Frascati
and Monte Porzio, so that they may see the whole splendour of its silvery light poured down on the most perfect
part of the immense fabric. The broken arches and
isolated fragments, under the magic influence of moonlight, assume the appearance of castles, of temples, and
triumphal arches, rising on each other to the heavens in
fairy splendour. Mighty walls seem riven in twain, and
appear to bend over their centre of gravity, like the leaning towers of Pisa and Bologna, suspended in the air, and
threatening every moment to fall with a tremendous
crash. Here a broken and a fallen column assumes the
appearance of a dying gladiator or a martyred Christian ;
there a cornice, half buried in the ruins, reminds you of

a lioness gathering herself up for a spring on a tiger or a bear ; and here again a heap of earth, lit up by some scattered rays that steal through the fissures in the great wall, seems like a gigantic elephant about to perform extraordinary manœuvres at the command of his keepers ; the plants and flowers that deck every portion of the ruin, and move to and fro in the gentle breeze, remind you of the moving masses that once filled these desolate benches.

But we have been inadvertently intruding on the domain of the poets. The Coliseum by moonlight is a theme sacred to the Muses. Cold and insipid is the prose of the historian, compared with the sublime verses of Byron and Monckton Milnes. We will give an extract from each of those writers. Let the beauty and power of their gifted pens lend the magnificence of a transformation scene to this last page of our chapter of tragedies : let the joy and elevation of feeling found in reading those sublime and eloquent verses of the immortal dead, make the reader forget the shortcomings of the pen that now closes its labours of love.

I do remember me, that in my youth,
When I was wandering upon such a night,
I stood within the Coliseum's wall,
'Midst the chief relics of almighty Rome ;
The trees that grew along the broken arches
Waved dark in the blue midnight, and the star
Shone through the rents of ruin ; from afar
The watch-dog bayed beyond the Tiber ; and
More near, from out the Cæsars' palace, came
The owl's long cry, and interruptedly,
Of distant sentinels, the fitful song

Begun and died on the gentle wind.
Some cypresses beyond the time-worn beach
Appeared to skirt the horizon, yet they stood
Within a bowshot. Where the Cæsars dwelt,
And dwell the tuneless birds of night, amidst
A grove which springs through levelled battlements,
And twines its roots with the imperial hearths,
Ivy usurps the laurel's place of growth ;
But the gladiator's bloody circus stands,
A noble wreck in ruinous perfection !
While Cæsars' chambers and the Augustan halls
Grovel on earth in indistinct decay ;
And thou didst shine, thou rolling moon, upon
All this, and cast a wide and tender light,
Which softened down the hoar austerity
Of rugged desolation, and filled up,
As 'twere anew, the gaps of centuries,
Leaving that beautiful which still was so,
And making that which was not, till the place
Became religion, and the heart ran o'er
With silent worship of the great of old ;
The dead but sceptered sovereigns who still rule
Our spirits from their urns."

—Manfred.

———————

I stood one night, one rich Italian night,
When the moon's lamp was prodigal with light,
Within that circus whose enormous range,
Though rent and shattered by a life of change,
Still stretches forth its undiminished span,
Telling the weakness and the strength of man.
In that vague hour which magnifies the great,
When desolation seems most desolate,
I thought not of the rushing crowds of yore,
Who filled with din the vasty corridor !
Those hunters of fierce pleasure are swept by,
And host on host has trampled where they lie.
But where is he that stood so strong and bold,
In his thick armour of enduring gold—

Whose massive form, irradiant as the sun,
Baptised the work his glory beamed upon
With his own name, Colossal?—From the day
Has that sublime illusion slunk away,
Leaving a blank, weed-matted pedestal
Of his high place, the sole memorial?
And is this the miracle of imperial power,
The chosen of his tutelage, hour by hour.
Following his doom, and Rome alive? Awake,
Weak mother! orphaned as thou art, to take
From fate this sordid boon of lengthened life,
Of most unnatural life, which is not life
As thou wert used to live. Oh! rather stand
By thy green waste, as on the palm-flecked sand,
Old Tadmor, hiding not its death;—a tomb.
Haunted by sounds of life is none the less a tomb.
Then from that picture of that wreck-strewn ground,
Which the arch held in frame-work, slowly round
I turned my eyes and fixed them, where was seen
A long spare shadow, stretched across the green,
The shadow of the crucifix—that stood
A simple shape, of rude, uncarved wood,
Raising erect and firm its lowly head
Amid that pomp of ruin,—amid the dead
A sign of silent life;—the mystery
Of Rome's immortal being was then made clear to me.

THE END.

If you have enjoyed this book, consider making your next selection from among the following . . .

St. Philomena—The Wonder-Worker. *O'Sullivan* 6.00
The Facts About Luther. *Msgr. Patrick O'Hare* 13.50
Little Catechism of the Curé of Ars. *St. John Vianney* 5.50
The Curé of Ars—Patron Saint of Parish Priests. *Fr. B. O'Brien* 4.50
Saint Teresa of Ávila. *William Thomas Walsh* 18.00
Isabella of Spain: The Last Crusader. *William Thomas Walsh* 20.00
Characters of the Inquisition. *William Thomas Walsh* 12.50
Blood-Drenched Altars—Cath. Comment. on Hist. Mexico. *Kelley* 18.00
The Four Last Things—Death, Judgment, Hell, Heaven. *Fr. von Cochem* 5.00
Confession of a Roman Catholic. *Paul Whitcomb* 1.25
The Catholic Church Has the Answer. *Paul Whitcomb* 1.25
The Sinner's Guide. *Ven. Louis of Granada* 12.00
True Devotion to Mary. *St. Louis De Montfort* 7.00
Life of St. Anthony Mary Claret. *Fanchón Royer* 12.50
Autobiography of St. Anthony Mary Claret 12.00
I Wait for You. *Sr. Josefa Menendez* .... .75
Words of Love. *Menendez, Betrone, Mary of the Trinity* 5.00
Little Lives of the Great Saints. *John O'Kane Murray* 16.50
Prayer—The Key to Salvation. *Fr. Michael Müller* 7.00
Sermons on Prayer. *St. Francis de Sales* 3.50
Sermons on Our Lady. *St. Francis de Sales* 9.00
Passion of Jesus and Its Hidden Meaning. *Fr. Groenings, S.J.* 12.50
The Victories of the Martyrs. *St. Alphonsus Liguori* 8.50
Canons and Decrees of the Council of Trent. *Transl. Schroeder* 12.50
Sermons of St. Alphonsus Liguori for Every Sunday 16.50
A Catechism of Modernism. *Fr. J. B. Lemius* 4.00
Alexandrina—The Agony and the Glory. *Johnston* 4.00
Blessed Margaret of Castello. *Fr. William Bonniwell* 6.00
The Ways of Mental Prayer. *Dom Vitalis Lehodey* 11.00
Fr. Paul of Moll. *van Speybrouck* 9.00
St. Francis of Paola. *Simi and Segreti* 7.00
Communion Under Both Kinds. *Michael Davies* 1.50
Abortion: Yes or No? *Dr. John L. Grady, M.D.* 1.50
The Story of the Church. *Johnson, Hannan, Dominica* 16.50
Religious Liberty. *Michael Davies* 1.50
Hell Quizzes. *Radio Replies Press* 1.00
Indulgence Quizzes. *Radio Replies Press* 1.00
Purgatory Quizzes. *Radio Replies Press* 1.00
Virgin and Statue Worship Quizzes. *Radio Replies Press* 1.00
The Holy Eucharist. *St. Alphonsus* 8.50
Meditation Prayer on Mary Immaculate. *Padre Pio* 1.25
Little Book of the Work of Infinite Love. *de la Touche* 2.00
Textual Concordance of The Holy Scriptures. *Williams* 35.00
Douay-Rheims Bible. *Leatherbound* 35.00
The Way of Divine Love. *Sister Josefa Menendez* 17.50
The Way of Divine Love. (pocket, unabr.). *Menendez* 8.50
Mystical City of God—Abridged. *Ven. Mary of Agreda* 18.50

Prices guaranteed through December 31, 1995.

Miraculous Images of Our Lady. *Cruz* 20.00
Raised from the Dead. *Fr. Hebert* 15.00
Love and Service of God, Infinite Love. *Mother Louise Margaret*. 10.00
Life and Work of Mother Louise Margaret. *Fr. O'Connell* 10.00
Autobiography of St. Margaret Mary 4.00
Thoughts and Sayings of St. Margaret Mary 3.00
The Voice of the Saints. *Comp. by Francis Johnston* 5.00
The 12 Steps to Holiness and Salvation. *St. Alphonsus* 7.00
The Rosary and the Crisis of Faith. *Cirrincione & Nelson* 1.25
Sin and Its Consequences. *Cardinal Manning* 5.00
Fourfold Sovereignty of God. *Cardinal Manning* 5.00
Dialogue of St. Catherine of Siena. *Transl. Algar Thorold* 9.00
Catholic Answer to Jehovah's Witnesses. *D'Angelo* 8.00
Twelve Promises of the Sacred Heart. (100 cards) 5.00
St. Aloysius Gonzaga. *Fr. Meschler* 10.00
The Love of Mary. *D. Roberto* 7.00
Begone Satan. *Fr. Vogl* 2.00
The Prophets and Our Times. *Fr. R. G. Culleton* 11.00
St. Therese, The Little Flower. *John Beevers* 4.50
St. Joseph of Copertino. *Fr. Angelo Pastrovicchi* 4.50
Mary, The Second Eve. *Cardinal Newman* 2.50
Devotion to Infant Jesus of Prague. *Booklet* .... .75
Reign of Christ the King in Public & Private Life. *Davies* 1.25
The Wonder of Guadalupe. *Francis Johnston* 6.00
Apologetics. *Msgr. Paul Glenn* 9.00
Baltimore Catechism No. 1 .... 3.00
Baltimore Catechism No. 2 .... 4.00
Baltimore Catechism No. 3 .... 7.00
An Explanation of the Baltimore Catechism. *Fr. Kinkead* 13.00
Bethlehem. *Fr. Faber* 16.50
Bible History. *Schuster* 10.00
Blessed Eucharist. *Fr. Mueller* 9.00
Catholic Catechism. *Fr. Faerber* 5.00
The Devil. *Fr. Delaporte* 5.00
Dogmatic Theology for the Laity. *Fr. Premm* 18.00
Evidence of Satan in the Modern World. *Cristiani* 8.50
Fifteen Promises of Mary. (100 cards) 5.00
Life of Anne Catherine Emmerich. 2 vols. *Schmoger* 37.50
Life of the Blessed Virgin Mary. *Emmerich* 15.00
Manual of Practical Devotion to St. Joseph. *Patrignani* 13.50
Prayer to St. Michael. (100 leaflets) 5.00
Prayerbook of Favorite Litanies. *Fr. Hebert* 9.00
Preparation for Death. (Abridged). *St. Alphonsus* 7.00
Purgatory Explained. *Schouppe* 13.50
Purgatory Explained. (pocket, unabr.). *Schouppe* 7.50
Fundamentals of Catholic Dogma. *Ludwig Ott* 20.00
Spiritual Conferences. *Tauler* 12.00
Trustful Surrender to Divine Providence. *Bl. Claude* 4.00
Wife, Mother and Mystic. *Bessieres* 7.00
The Agony of Jesus. *Padre Pio* 1.50

Is It a Saint's Name? *Fr. William Dunne* 1.50
St. Pius V—His Life, Times, Miracles. *Anderson* 4.00
Who Is Teresa Neumann? *Fr. Charles Carty* 2.00
Martyrs of the Coliseum. *Fr. O'Reilly* 16.50
Way of the Cross. *St. Alphonsus Liguori* 75
Way of the Cross. *Franciscan version* 75
How Christ Said the First Mass. *Fr. Meagher* 16.50
Too Busy for God? Think Again! *D'Angelo* 4.00
St. Bernadette Soubirous. *Trochu* 16.50
Passion and Death of Jesus Christ. *Liguori* 8.50
Treatise on the Love of God. 2 Vols. *St. Francis de Sales* 16.50
Confession Quizzes. *Radio Replies Press* 1.00
St. Philip Neri. *Fr. V. J. Matthews* 4.50
St. Louise de Marillac. *Sr. Vincent Regnault* 4.50
The Old World and America. *Rev. Philip Furlong* 16.50
Prophecy for Today. *Edward Connor* 4.50
The Book of Infinite Love. *Mother de la Touche* 4.50
Chats with Converts. *Fr. M. D. Forrest* 9.00
The Church Teaches. *Church Documents* 15.00
Conversation with Christ. *Peter T. Rohrbach* 8.00
Purgatory and Heaven. *J. P. Arendzen* 3.50
Liberalism Is a Sin. *Sarda y Salvany* 6.00
Spiritual Legacy of Sr. Mary of the Trinity. *van den Broek* 9.00
The Creator and the Creature. *Fr. Frederick Faber* 13.50
Radio Replies. 3 Vols. *Frs. Rumble and Carty* 36.00
Convert's Catechism of Catholic Doctrine. *Fr. Geiermann* 3.00
Incarnation, Birth, Infancy of Jesus Christ. *St. Alphonsus* 8.50
Light and Peace. *Fr. R. P. Quadrupani* 5.00
Dogmatic Canons & Decrees of Trent, Vat. I. *Documents* 8.00
The Evolution Hoax Exposed. *A. N. Field* 6.00
The Primitive Church. *Fr. D. I. Lanslots* 8.50
Ven. Jacinta Marto of Fatima. *Cirrincione* 1.50
The Priest, the Man of God. *St. Joseph Cafasso* 12.00
Blessed Sacrament. *Fr. Frederick Faber* 16.50
Christ Denied. *Fr. Paul Wickens* 2.00
New Regulations on Indulgences. *Fr. Winfrid Herbst* 2.50
A Tour of the Summa. *Msgr. Paul Glenn* 18.00
Spiritual Conferences. *Fr. Frederick Faber* 13.50
Latin Grammar. *Scanlon and Scanlon* 13.50
A Brief Life of Christ. *Fr. Rumble* 2.00
Marriage Quizzes. *Radio Replies Press* 1.00
True Church Quizzes. *Radio Replies Press* 1.00
St. Lydwine of Schiedam. *J. K. Huysmans* 7.00
Mary, Mother of the Church. *Church Documents* 3.00
The Sacred Heart and the Priesthood. *de la Touche* 7.00
Revelations of St. Bridget. *St. Bridget of Sweden* 2.50
Magnificent Prayers. *St. Bridget of Sweden* 1.50
The Happiness of Heaven. *Fr. J. Boudreau* 7.00
St. Catherine Labouré of the Miraculous Medal. *Dirvin* 12.50
The Glories of Mary. (pocket, unabr.). *St. Alphonsus Liguori* 9.00

Brief Catechism for Adults. *Cogan* 9.00
The Cath. Religion—Illus./Expl. for Child, Adult, Convert. *Burbach*. 9.00
Eucharistic Miracles. *Joan Carroll Cruz* 13.00
The Incorruptibles. *Joan Carroll Cruz* 12.00
Pope St. Pius X. *F. A. Forbes* 6.00
St. Alphonsus Liguori. *Frs. Miller and Aubin* 15.00
Self-Abandonment to Divine Providence. *Fr. de Caussade, S.J.* ... 16.50
The Song of Songs—A Mystical Exposition. *Fr. Arintero, O.P.* ... 18.00
Prophecy for Today. *Edward Connor* 4.50
Saint Michael and the Angels. *Approved Sources* 5.50
Dolorous Passion of Our Lord. *Anne C. Emmerich* 15.00
Modern Saints—Their Lives & Faces. *Ann Ball* 18.00
Our Lady of Fatima's Peace Plan from Heaven. *Booklet* .... .75
Divine Favors Granted to St. Joseph. *Père Binet* 4.00
St. Joseph Cafasso—Priest of the Gallows. *St. John Bosco* 3.00
Catechism of the Council of Trent. *McHugh/Callan* 20.00
The Foot of the Cross. *Fr. Faber* 15.00
The Rosary in Action. *John Johnson* 8.00
Padre Pio—The Stigmatist. *Fr. Charles Carty* 13.50
Why Squander Illness? *Frs. Rumble & Carty* 2.00
The Sacred Heart and the Priesthood. *de la Touche* 7.00
Fatima—The Great Sign. *Francis Johnston* 7.00
Heliotropium—Conformity of Human Will to Divine. *Drexelius* ... 11.00
Charity for the Suffering Souls. *Fr. John Nageleisen* 15.00
Devotion to the Sacred Heart of Jesus. *Verheylezoon* 13.00
Who Is Padre Pio? *Radio Replies Press* 1.50
Child's Bible History. *Knecht* 4.00
The Stigmata and Modern Science. *Fr. Charles Carty* 1.25
The Life of Christ. 4 Vols. H.B. *Anne C. Emmerich* 55.00
St. Anthony—The Wonder Worker of Padua. *Stoddard* 4.00
The Precious Blood. *Fr. Faber* 11.00
The Holy Shroud & Four Visions. *Fr. O'Connell* 2.00
Clean Love in Courtship. *Fr. Lawrence Lovasik* 2.50
The Prophecies of St. Malachy. *Peter Bander* 5.00
St. Martin de Porres. *Giuliana Cavallini* 11.00
The Secret of the Rosary. *St. Louis De Montfort* 3.00
The History of Antichrist. *Rev. P. Huchede* 3.00
The Douay-Rheims New Testament. *Paperbound* 13.00
St. Catherine of Siena. *Alice Curtayne* 12.00
Where We Got the Bible. *Fr. Henry Graham* 5.00
Hidden Treasure—Holy Mass. *St. Leonard* 4.00
Imitation of the Sacred Heart of Jesus. *Fr. Arnoudt* 13.50
The Life & Glories of St. Joseph. *Edward Thompson* 13.50
Père Lamy. *Biver* 10.00
Humility of Heart. *Fr. Cajetan da Bergamo* 7.00
The Curé D'Ars. *Abbé Francis Trochu* 20.00
Love, Peace and Joy. (St. Gertrude). *Prévot* 5.00
The Three Ways of the Spiritual Life. *Garrigou-Lagrange, O.P.* ... 4.00

At your Bookdealer or direct from the Publisher.

Prices guaranteed through December 31, 1995.

NOTES

NOTES

NOTES

NOTES

NOTES

NOTES

NOTES